WHO CAN HOLD THE SEA

 Bantam Books / New York

WHO CAN HOLD THE SEA

The U.S. Navy in the Cold War, 1945–1960

JAMES D. HORNFISCHER

Copyright © 2022 by The Estate of James D. Hornfischer

All rights reserved.

Published in the United States by Bantam Books,
an imprint of Random House,
a division of Penguin Random House LLC, New York.

BANTAM BOOKS and the HOUSE colophon are registered trademarks
of Penguin Random House LLC.

Image credits are located on page 425.

LIBRARY OF CONGRESS CATALOGING-IN-PUBLICATION DATA

Names: Hornfischer, James D., author.
Title: Who can hold the sea: the U.S. Navy in the Cold War, 1945–1960 /
James D. Hornfischer.
Other titles: U.S. Navy in the Cold War, 1945–1960
Identifiers: LCCN 2021043097 (print) | LCCN 2021043098 (ebook) |
ISBN 9780399178641 (hardcover) | ISBN 9780399178658 (ebook)
Subjects: LCSH: United States. Navy—History—20th century. |
Sea-power—United States—History—20th century. | United States—
History, Naval—20th century. | World politics—1945-1989. | Cold War.
Classification: LCC VA58.4 .H67 2022 (print) | LCC VA58.4 (ebook) |
DDC 359.00973—dc23
LC record available at lccn.loc.gov/2021043097
LC ebook record available at lccn.loc.gov/2021043098

Printed in the United States of America on acid-free paper

randomhousebooks.com

2 4 6 8 9 7 5 3 1

First Edition

Maps © James M. Fenelon

Book design by Virginia Norey

*To all the U.S. men and women who have served in uniform
for a better Afghanistan since September 11, 2001.
Your valor matters.*

Whosoever can hold the sea has command of everything.
—Themistocles,
Athenian navalist (524–460 B.C.)

Contents

Arleigh Burke, superstar, vs. the B-36, the "billion-dollar blunder" / Navy morale plunges / Oct. 1949: Arthur Radford vs. the Air Force / Adm. Denfeld relieved / Forrest Sherman becomes CNO / China goes red / George Marshall, Communist? / Oct. 25, 1949: on Quemoy, Chiang routs Mao and plans for 1950 / Truman slashes the fleet / Soviets covet a unified Korea, destabilize South Korea

THIS IS A BOOK ABOUT THE NAVY, BUT IT'S ALSO ABOUT FOREIGN
affairs. It's about presidencies, war and peace, America in the world.
Politics and policy, morals and war. About innovation: atomic weapons
and propulsion, computerization and guided missiles.

This is a long book. To paraphrase Ben Franklin, this book twice as
easily could have been three times its length, even though it covers just
about half of its ultimate subject. In this book too, the span of time, the
range of events, the surge of ideas, the flow of money, the spectrum of
characters are many.

Naval history can encompass the full variety of technical programs
in naval aviation, submarine and amphibious warfare, surface ship tactics, intelligence, command, administration, shipbuilding, basing, and
operational stories from the four corners of the world. My ambition has
been to sample all these fascinating morsels while focusing on the main
dish: the worldwide geopolitical rivalry between the U.S. Navy and the
Soviet Union.

Research: thoroughgoing, comprehensive, and hopelessly incomplete. The merest glance at the finding aids of NARA (National Archives and Records Administration) or NHHC (Naval History and
Heritage Command) suggests the depths of data that await a writer
looking into naval history. That history will need to be told by another
on another day.

This book is also about humanity, and the fragility of it. You know
James D. Hornfischer as a passionate author of books of our nation's
war in the Pacific and, with this book, the Cold War. Jim wrote about

the wars fought by our neighbors, brothers and sisters, aunts and uncles, fathers and grandfathers. For the past two years Jim has been fighting his own war. I don't want to dwell on this, nor would Jim want me to, but I believe his readers would want and deserve to know of Jim's courage. In the early days of 2020, just months before the pandemic hit our shores, Jim was diagnosed with an inoperable glioblastoma brain tumor.

Jim wanted to live each day as fully as possible, and I wanted to honor him by following that lead. He didn't keep his diagnosis a secret, but he didn't talk about it much either. Jim fought very bravely for eighteen months, in every area of his life, and was largely pain-free throughout his illness and the cancer's progression. For that I am intensely grateful. Jim passed away peacefully here at home in Austin, Texas, surrounded by family, friends, our springer spaniels Sullivan and Skye, and his books, having converted his library into a first-floor bedroom.

Jim's illness was progressive and there were periods when he could not be as productive as he would have liked, but he continued to write and work every day until he was no longer able.

This book is his last published work, and as his illness progressed, his writing told that story within a story. Please regard this text as a last letter from an old friend, and please understand that your friend was simply not able to wrap up the story with his usual finesse and depth of detail.

Jim believed, as I also do, that others of this generation and future generations will carry on telling the stories of our great nation's history. Share your stories with your children and grandchildren, nieces and nephews, so that they are engaged in our nation's history and our country's continued fight for freedom and democracy. Encourage our next generation, take them to air shows, museums, and libraries, ignite the spark of curiosity in our future historians and writers so that they can continue to tell stories for us all to read.

—*Sharon and Jim Hornfischer,* autumn 2021

WHO CAN HOLD THE SEA

Introduction

THE STORY OF THE U.S. NAVY'S COLD WAR IS NO TIDY WAR story, or even a campaign narrative. Chronicling the twists and turns of the tumultuous early years of the Cold War at sea, looking at the flow of global events of the U.S.-Soviet and capitalist-Communist rivalries through the lens of maritime power, is the mission of this book. Readers acquainted with my earlier books will find this one much broader in scope. I offer it knowing that it's prone to fall short here and there. Those interested in submarines will know better books on submarine development. Korean War buffs will find the definitive history and fuller microhistories elsewhere. Enthusiasts of naval aviation will have read more complete histories of aircraft carriers. Aficionados of strategy and its cousins, doctrine and tactics, will sate themselves on more specialized accounts. So what *does* this book propose to do, and what was my reason for writing it?

This is a work of synthesis, an interweaving of politics and war, of operations and presidential and command decision, of culture and politics, time and place, threat and perceptions of threat, the exigencies of survival and the consequences of victory and defeat. The Navy is its focus because the geopolitics of the U.S. has been driven by maritime realities more than by any other single force.

Naval operations since the age of sail have been global in scope. Today the fleet is the first thought of U.S. presidents confronted with an international emergency. Whenever a crisis flashes, the first question asked is, "Where are the aircraft carriers?" But the Navy's role encompasses more than naval aviation. Since World War II, surface ships and submarines have all been tools for projecting American power and presence, influencing events worldwide.

Though landsmen speak of the world's seven seas, there is in fact only one global ocean. So the experts at the National Oceanic and Atmospheric Administration declare. The modern U.S. Navy has never needed this reminder, certainly not in the nuclear age. Its contest for command of the world's maritime commons against the only planetary rival it has ever faced—the Soviet Union—illustrates the singularity of the ocean as both an avenue of influence and an actual or potential field of battle.

It has often been said that America has never been invaded by a foreign power thanks to its blessings of geography. But oceans are defensive barriers only to the extent that a nation's fleet can master them. Just as surely through history, oceans have been avenues of conquest. The message was clear during the American Revolution and remains equally so today. U.S. fleets, usually operating far from home, have undertaken the defense of America since the U.S. Navy's establishment on October 13, 1775.

The story of the Cold War at sea is the story of the contest to secure the freedom of the world. During this time, the U.S. Navy carried, for the first time, a transoceanic mandate evidenced by its permanent deployment from forward overseas stations. In some areas of the world, U.S. fleets were based exclusively at sea, free entirely from dependence upon land. The state of affairs would have been alien and unimaginable to the navy of America's founding, when naval officers and their men served only during time of conflict, returning to their farms and estates during peacetime. The aim of this book is to develop the story of this global institution as a protector of the national interest. It is a story of geopolitics in theory and practice. Beyond the intrigue of the U.S.-Soviet rivalry are stories of confrontation between fleets, bare-knuckled human strife over strategic concepts and war policy, and technological revolution and disruption, all of it the stuff of a sprawling, worldwide drama.

This book continues the story concluded in the last of my four books on World War II, *The Fleet at Flood Tide,* which covered the conclusion and aftermath of World War II in the Pacific. But the story actually reaches all the way back to the American Revolution. Just as the ideas of Sir Julian Corbett begat Nelson at Trafalgar, and the ideas of Alfred Thayer Mahan begat Admiral William F. Halsey off Tokyo, the cumulative learning curve of the centuries led to a Cold War contest of even greater complexity, in which naval officers and those interested in national and maritime affairs ought to be mindful of the major events of the past.

1

FLEET AT A CROSSROADS

WHEN ADMIRAL WILLIAM F. HALSEY, JR., ARRIVED IN NEW YORK City early in the morning on Friday, December 14, 1945, snow blanketed nearly the entirety of the Empire State. An overnight storm had forced the cancellation of most flights into La Guardia Field, so he traveled up from Washington by rail. He took a waiting limousine from Penn Station to the Waldorf-Astoria Hotel, refreshed himself with a nap, then donned his whites and took the limo to the airport in Queens. A motorcade was awaiting the conqueror of the Pacific. A Navy band greeted him with a flourish. Two battalions of sailors presented arms as the cannoneers of an honor guard fired a seventeen-gun salute, two short of what the newly minted five-star admiral deserved. Holding his greatcoat tight against the wind, Halsey joined New York Mayor Fiorello H. La Guardia in an open car.

Halsey was less than two months home from Japan. After the boozy celebration in Yokohama that had marked his relief from occupation duty and fleet command, he had flown home to Pearl Harbor, then begun a homeward transit that ended with the festal passage of his flagship, the battleship *South Dakota,* along with thirteen other vessels, under the Golden Gate Bridge on October 15.

A worldwide homecoming was under way. Demobilization was the word of the day. The drawdown was swift and its effects stunning. Just ninety days after Tokyo's surrender, with its mission switched from crushing Japan to saving her, the U.S. military was giving away its strength at a rate of 1.5 million men a month. As Admiral Chester W. Nimitz, the Pacific commander in chief, wrote to Secretary of the Navy James V. Forrestal, after four years of war, peace was an abnormal state. "The vast machine that had gained victory had to be ground to a stop, and flow of material had to be checked, then reversed. The problems of demobilization and return to a peacetime basis were in some respects more difficult than those of continuing the war." On the day Halsey arrived in New York, nine harbors on the East and West coasts were scheduled to receive seventy-nine ships bearing more than sixty-two thousand war veterans. From Calcutta and Marseille, from Bermuda, Antwerp, and Manila, the maritime carriage that had delivered America's armies worldwide brought them home again, just in time to celebrate Christmas—"the first in six years not mocked by universal war," Nimitz noted. The newspapers published the itineraries, listing returning ships and units. In New York, the arrival of the passenger liner *Queen Mary,* bringing home 11,409 combat veterans from Southampton, England, that same day would have been the story had Halsey not taken the headlines.

As the leading public face of the Navy, he was the one officer who could be counted upon to command a crowd. His peers during the war—Raymond Spruance, Marc Mitscher, Nimitz himself—were by comparison distant from the public, disinclined to speak of their work, secretive and necessarily so, they said. The Navy employed a small handful of public relations officers to buffer its leaders from the inquiries of the press. But with controversy now raging between the Army and Navy over their postwar roles, missions, and appropriations, the brain trust of the sea services realized that the game of public affairs might be a contest for their survival. This more than any surplus of ticker tape on Wall Street accounted for Halsey's presence in an open limo on a bitter winter's morning.

The car accelerated into the bustle of Queens, then pushed south on Thirty-fourth Avenue across the Meeker Avenue Bridge toward Brooklyn. The energy of the crowds sustained through Greenpoint and all the way to the ramp of the Manhattan Bridge. Crossing the East

River, Halsey could look down over the waterfront headquarters of the New York Port of Embarkation, from which half of the wartime armies fielded by the United States had shipped overseas. The Brooklyn Navy Yard, employing at its wartime peak more than 71,000 workers, had constructed just eighteen months earlier the battleship *Missouri,* following in the wake of the *Iowa* and *North Carolina,* out Lower New York Bay and into action. The last of the *Essex*-class carriers, the USS *Oriskany,* was launched here sixty days before Halsey arrived. Her sister ship *Reprisal* languished incomplete, awaiting use in ordnance tests and scrapping.

The U.S. Navy ended World War II with nearly 1,200 combatant ships, 41,000 planes, and 3.4 million personnel. It had 758,000 civilians on its worldwide payroll, more than half of them at the government-owned naval shipyards at Bremerton, Boston, Charleston, Mare Island, New York, Norfolk, Pearl Harbor, Philadelphia, Portsmouth, San Francisco, and San Pedro, and naval aviation centers such as Pensacola, Florida, Whidbey Island, Washington, and Corpus Christi, Texas. The Navy's infrastructure of yards, bases, and shore facilities was the product of about $12 billion in wartime investment that drove a sixteenfold increase in its prewar size. Navy expenditures on plant facilities were 25 percent larger than the plant accounts of General Motors, U.S. Steel, and AT&T combined. The Bureau of Ships alone had an investment account nearly as big as U.S. Steel. Though new ships were still coming—the Brooklyn yard had put the aircraft carrier *Franklin D. Roosevelt,* the third of the big new *Midway*-class flattops, into commission in October—the Navy that had bestridden the world in the winter of 1945 was coming home to shrink and diminish, discharging its strength back into the nation.

In Philadelphia, experimental techniques of ship preservation were ready for mass application in a $40 million effort that would put 1,896 ships into an inactive reserve by September 1, 1946. The light cruiser USS *Brooklyn* was the first combatant to undergo "mothballing." The metaphor from the coat closet understated the intricacies of preserving such a large vessel in a state that would make possible her return to service within thirty days of an activation order. Yard workers removed all perishable and combustible stores, including food, batteries, fuel, and explosives. Metal surfaces susceptible to corrosion, such as motors, pumps, and engines, were sprayed with a waxy rust retardant. Sensitive equipment that could not be removed for dehumidified storage received an additional airtight casing, woven with five layers from a spray gun and sealed with a coat of aluminum paint. Inside, dehumidifiers connected to ventilation ducts and fire mains allowed the ship to inhale dry air and exhale humidity. Where airflow did not reach, desiccants and other drying agents did the job passively. After the six-month process was finished, a complement of just five officers and fifty-nine men aboard could maintain a cruiser like the *Brooklyn* during her long sleep in the "zipper fleet."

The rapid pace of the demobilization concerned President Harry S. Truman. A believer in a "prepared soldier-citizenry," he was working that December on a bill to enact universal military training. The new law would require every male between the ages of eighteen and twenty to report for a year of indoctrination followed by six years in the reserves. With such a base of manpower available to redeploy hundreds of mothballed ships, a wartime fleet could be more quickly surged in case of war. "We can with fairness no longer look to the veterans of this war for any future military service," the president would write.

Meanwhile, the imperative to cut costs fell upon the Pentagon like a weather front. At the urging of Truman and with the full support of the War Department, the Senate was considering a bill to unify the Navy and War departments, along with a new department designating the Air Force as a single administrative entity. S. 2044 would put the tripartite Pentagon under the leadership of a single Secretary of Common Defense and deprive the secretaries of war and the Navy of their long-standing membership in the president's cabinet. The push for change had begun the day before Germany surrendered, on May 7, 1945, when the Army's top civilian administrator, Secretary of War Henry L. Stimson, wrote Secretary Forrestal to argue that the two departments should be unified. With one powerful secretary supervising the entire defense establishment, Stimson said, there would come a windfall of savings. "The principle is settled. . . . The problem is merely to achieve the most effective possible execution of an established policy. . . . I think it will be our duty to report that belief to the Congress in the earnest hope that your department can come along then, or later, with a concurring view."

Stimson's insistent voice was that of a man secure in his relationship with the White House. Having engineered the 1930 London Naval Treaty that had limited the size of interwar fleets, the Army boss was now promising to outdo himself, impairing the position of his rival service by unilateral decree. But Forrestal thought the service heads, Congress, and the Joint Chiefs of Staff should take the time to absorb more carefully the lessons of the Second World War, which at the time had yet to be won. That was where the matter lay until August, when the twin flashes of atomic light destroyed Japan as a war-making power.

Truman never stopped thinking about the implications of the new weapon. It promised to change everything. The chiefs of the U.S. Army, who relished the atomic bomb's transformative power, were using the revolution in atomic weapons to make some startling pronouncements. The leaders of the strategic air forces in particular wasted no time advancing their sweeping claim to primacy based on their exclusive capacity to deliver atomic weapons across the oceans. The bombs ended one war and started another. In the offices of Congress and in the angled corridors of the Pentagon, the longest-running civil war in American life flared anew: the quest of generals and admirals to bring the other service to heel.

In November, General Dwight D. Eisenhower had stunned the Navy leadership by telling the Senate Military Affairs Committee that a merger would have saved the country 25 percent of the $265 billion it had cost to fight the war. The Navy's budget writers considered this a lurid fantasy. "I will wager that even he had no idea of the figures with which he was playing," wrote the assistant secretary of the Navy, H. Struve Hensel, to *The New York Times,* which itself called Ike's number a "flash guess." Cost savings was one angle the Army played in support of "defense unification." Another claim was equally striking: that naval forces had become superfluous in winning wars. At a meeting of a Senate special committee on atomic energy in December, a senator who had been impressed by Army presentations said to a Navy official, "Atomic energy has driven ships off the surface of the sea. I don't see how a ship can resist the atomic bomb."

Halsey had come to New York to make the Navy's case—the first act in what would become an all-hands barnstorming tour by the leading lights of the sea services. Though Halsey was unsurprised to find politicians trafficking in specious generality, he was dismayed that experienced warriors were joining them, including Jimmy Doolittle, the Army aviation hero who had staged the bold 1942 air raid on Tokyo that would forever bear his name.

He had told a Senate committee that the aircraft carrier, the most important ship in the fleet, had two notable attributes: "One attribute is that it can move about. The other attribute is that it can be sunk. . . . It is going into obsolescence." To Halsey, this argument was mendacious.

In rebuttal, he had explained to the senators how he had led carriers to Okinawa, standing by for three months in support while under nearly constant aerial suicide attack, then steamed within eighty miles of Tokyo to strike Japan's homeland. Operating in this manner four thousand miles from Pearl Harbor, he had lost not a single flattop, he said. Doolittle's dismissal of the carrier puzzled Halsey, for like Halsey, the general had always seemed to promote the common cause of the services in war.

While Halsey's fleet roamed the Western Pacific, the Army's B-29 Superfortresses razed Japan's largest cities with conventional explosives and incendiaries, burning out more than sixty metropolitan areas through the frightful and destructive summer of 1945. But none of these advances would have been possible without the use of island bases seized and held by the Navy. And thanks to the Navy's command of the seas, the continental United States was never attacked in return. The commanding general of the Army Air Forces, Henry A. "Hap" Arnold, finally lost his bet, wagered in 1942, that an enemy bomb would fall on Washington, D.C., during the war. Yet the bomb droppers persisted in being bomb throwers. To Halsey it was apparent that it was all an orchestrated political attack.

As the motorcade turned onto the FDR Drive, a cold gust carried away Halsey's dress cap and dropped it in a puddle of slush. A Victory ship in the East River cut loose with a long siren blast as the admiral waved to the crowds on South Street. Shouts descended from office buildings in the financial district's "canyon of heroes" as his limo rolled past curbside double ranks of mounted police. Ticker tape and colored paper filled the air. Halsey and Mayor La Guardia arrived at City Hall in Lower Manhattan to find the park across the street occupied by fifteen hundred sailors, Coast Guardsmen, and a Marine Corps honor guard, who remained frozen at attention as the dignitaries stepped to the granite curb. Halsey's wife, Frances Grandy Halsey, and their daughter, Margaret Spruance,* joined them in the chambers of the City Council, where Mayor La Guardia conferred upon Halsey New York City's Medal of Honor, making him the fourth World War II commander so honored, after Nimitz, Eisenhower, and General Jonathan Wainwright. The mayor proclaimed that "the deep-rooted affection we have for the Navy, the men who command it, and the men who serve in the Navy, is so deep in men's hearts that no politicians in Washington can take it away." They would continue to try.

It frothed Halsey's Irish to see colleagues turned opportunists, using exotic propaganda to erode the Navy's long-cherished autonomy. Though he was reluctant to oppose his commander in chief, he had been candid in his testimony to the Senate Military Affairs Committee the previous week. Envisioning someone like General Arnold in charge of the whole Pentagon, the admiral turned acerbic. "I, for one, am unwilling to have the chief of the Army Air Forces pass on the question of whether or not the Navy should have funds for building and maintaining a balanced fleet. One might just as well ask a committee composed of a Protestant, a Catholic, and a Jew to save our national souls by recommending a national church and creed."

The editorial writers of the *San Francisco Chronicle* considered the Army's "pell-mell, hell-for-leather campaign" as "somewhat too purposeful . . . too glib, too pat. The time for slam-bang action is behind

* Preston Lea Spruance, who married Halsey's daughter, was a distant cousin of Admiral Raymond Spruance, Halsey's close friend and fellow fleet commander in the Pacific War.

us for the moment." Having served as a naval attaché in Germany for
two years, Halsey had observed how a single military department, the
Wehrmacht, became a cartel that grew to dominate the civilian government. The failings of Hitler's "Prussians," and of Premier Tojo, too,
stood as cautionary tales about the folly of letting an all-powerful army
dominate war policy and strategy.

After World War II, each service could claim primacy in its realm of
combat operations. Only the Air Force could skirt a contested hemisphere and flatten a metropolis in a flash. Only the Navy could carry
out an offensive over the oceans and sustain it with a mobile logistics
train and airpower from out of the blue. Although the strategic air
forces had exploited their unique ability well, even in the Pacific, it had
been Navy technical know-how and innovation that made it possible to
weaponize atomic fission in the first place. The chief weapon maker at
Los Alamos, the man who had flown to Hiroshima and armed the uranium bomb in flight, was a Navy captain. As long as the world's land-
masses were separated—or connected—by a single body of water, fleets
would be their master. So the joust between land and sea warriors had
gone, all the way back to the Phoenicians and the Carthaginians, when
a sailor was merely a soldier who was brave enough to board a trireme
and range beyond sight of the coast.

After lunch at City Hall, Halsey's motorcade rolled north up Fifth
Avenue to Fifty-seventh Street, hanging a right to the Waldorf-Astoria,
where the celebrity admiral retired to take his rest. That evening, before an influential audience in the hotel ballroom, Halsey pressed the
Navy's case, arguing from principles long ago articulated by sea-power
advocates such as Alfred Thayer Mahan and Sir Julian Corbett, whose
ideas about the great strategic utility of mobile, flexible naval strength
had been borne out in six years of worldwide ocean warfare nearly a
generation after the last of them had passed on.

"It was axiomatic that the tide of war changed with the ebb and flow
of sea power," Halsey said. He knew that Japan's failure to follow up
the Pearl Harbor attack and land decisive blows against the American
fleet had resulted from the dominance of Japan's army over its navy in
strategy. When Allied forces turned the tide, they did so on the back of

naval power, from the Pacific Fleet's ambush of the Japanese carriers at Midway to the seaborne offensive at Guadalcanal two months later, and then carrying Marine divisions through the Central Pacific. As surely now in peace as then in war, the ocean stood as a barrier and a battle-field, water to be surmounted or controlled by forces on the water. "Nothing has happened since V-J Day," Halsey said, "to shorten the eight thousand miles of water between us and the enemy."

Halsey as a spokesman was not given to finesse. His calling card through the war had been brashness and bluster. He could be counted upon to articulate colorfully and memorably the public's resentment and anger toward the Japanese. He was aggressive, sometimes to a fault, and inspired his subordinates with his forcefully articulated mes-sage of unity, determination, and well-organized mass violence inflicted upon an enemy that deserved it. "Kill Japs, kill Japs, kill more Japs" was one of his messages. His reward for this talent for theatrics was to be adored by the public.

Sea power, as he saw it, was about more than the ability of one's own ships to destroy their opposite numbers on the sea. Halsey subscribed to the view of his boss, Nimitz, who would shortly explain, in a speech to the National Geographic Society, how a country's naval power derived from the life and work of every citizen. It was national power in the broadest sense. "Sea power has its roots deep in the core of our country. They draw nourishment from the farms and ranches that feed our men. They derive from our mines, our logging camps, our mills and factories. There is scarcely a village in the geographical center of the continent which does not contribute in some way to America's sea power." The dynamic was easily seen in Navy towns like New York, Norfolk, San Diego, and Bremerton, but it inhered in the work of farmers in Iowa, too, of scientists in labs from Berkeley to Woods Hole, of hydraulic press operators squeezing hot steel ingots in Allentown, of managers drawing up shipbuilding contracts in Washington, and in the union halls of the yard workers whose labor fulfilled them. Mahan, too, had argued that sea power was linked holistically to national life. As Nimitz would put it, "Modern war is total. No nation can wage suc-cessful war which fails to utilize its industrial capacity to the fullest extent. It is not enough to have a great industrial plant. That plant must be mobilized, supplied and made an integral part of the war machine."

As the controversy between the services escalated in the middle of 1945, Secretary Forrestal commissioned a close personal friend and former Wall Street colleague, Ferdinand Eberstadt, to study the problem of how to administer the potentials of this "war machine." During the war, Eberstadt had worked with Forrestal in coordinating America's industrial mobilization for the worldwide struggle. A gifted administrator, he was now asked to evaluate the issue of defense unification. Eberstadt delivered his report to the Navy secretary in September. He concluded that the answer was better coordination, but not merger. His prescription was a system of coordinating Pentagon agencies rather than a monolithic executive hand, a system that would preserve the dynamic competition of separate military departments through the establishment of three coequal services under a single secretary. As well, Eberstadt recommended a top-level decision-making brain trust, the National Security Council, which was charged with advising the president. He also proposed the creation of a National Security Resources Board to manage the flow of matériel to meet the needs of the military, and a Central Intelligence Agency to produce and analyze national intelligence, consolidating the reporting that had been coming in diversely from the War Department's intelligence division, the Office of Naval Intelligence, and the State Department. Truman finally turned away from the abortive efforts of a divided Joint Chiefs of Staff to broker an agreement that would shape the nation's war-making apparatus. He left it to the Senate Military Affairs Committee to handle debate and finalize legislation.

Eberstadt's plan stood above the hubbub of testimony that filled the Senate committee chamber through the end of 1945. Testifying in October, Forrestal urged "the creation of a mechanism within Government which will guarantee that this Nation shall be able to act as a unit in terms of its diplomacy, its military policy, its uses of scientific knowledge, and finally, of course, in its moral and political leadership in the world—a leadership that shall rest on moral force first and on physical force so long as we shall need it."

This was a large, intellectual vision of the mission and purpose of a security state. The challenge was to close gaps not just between Army and Navy, but between foreign policy and military policy, national strategic planning and logistics, and the problems of mobilization faced by the Pentagon and civilian agencies. Bucking the will of Major General Leslie R. Groves, who supported a top-down Pentagon run by "military statesmen," Eberstadt's scheme relied upon civilian leadership, crystallizing Forrestal's belief that talented individuals who did not wear uniforms, drawn from all across corporate, academic, and philanthropic life, should lead the nation's effort to gather and assert its power in the world. Standing impressively apart from the War Department's stridency and projected through the prism of Forrestal's energy and vigor, Eberstadt's plan impressed the Senate committee as the prudent way forward. After the debate was settled, President Truman tapped James Forrestal to lead the centralized new department that would become known in a few years as the Department of Defense.

Born in Matteawan, Dutchess County, New York, in 1892, Forrestal had come to public service after making good in private life. Abandoning an early career in local newspaper journalism in favor of an Ivy League education—Princeton by way of Dartmouth—he ran out of funds to complete his degree and went to work on Wall Street, at the investment bank of Dillon, Read & Co. He served four years as a naval aviator in World War I, then returned to making his fortune. By the age of forty-six, in 1938, he was the top bond salesman at the firm, and finally named its president. As war consumed Europe in the summer of 1940, President Roosevelt appointed Forrestal undersecretary of the Navy, which involved him closely in the complicated project of expanding naval and military forces, in close collaboration with the two service secretaries, Frank Knox and Henry Stimson. Elevated to Navy secretary after Knox's sudden death in office in April 1944, Forrestal presided over the surge of the fleet to its world-beating size. Carried along by his abundant energy level and work ethic, he observed the conquest of Iwo Jima from a landing craft, remarking famously as the colors flew over Mount Suribachi, "Raising that flag means a Marine Corps for the next five hundred years."

There was dynamism in his short, compact physical bearing, his brisk gait, ready wit, and spark of intellectual interest in a wide variety of subjects. When victory came, Forrestal drew upon his gifts of persuasion to convince Truman to accept Japan's opposition to the U.S. demand of unconditional surrender. By leaving Hirohito on the throne—respecting Tokyo's request that the United States not "prejudice the prerogatives" of the emperor—Truman made a concession to the pride of the defeated. Amid the ensuing controversy, it was Forrestal who convinced the president that even with this concession in place, the surrender could still be characterized as unconditional so long as the defeated regent was made openly subordinate to the Allied supreme commander, General Douglas MacArthur.

He was a practitioner of pure power politics but knew that the moral authority of America was its greatest strength. He was a boxer in the style of the New York Athletic Club, streetwise in the sense of the suburban-dwelling bond trader—a master of liar's poker—coiffed with an Ivy League education whose veneer he polished all the more vigorously because the degree was incomplete. He was willing to fight not only for Nimitz's vision of sea power as deriving from every activity in American productive life, but for a vision of America's role in the world as both leader and organizer in a fractious world arena. If that world was to become a community, it would be possible, Forrestal thought, only with U.S. leadership, the victorious democracy investing its credibility and standing in the world to promote self-determination and freedom wherever it showed aspiration.

Some people found him humorless, so devoted as he was to his grave and serious work. "Forrestal seemed to be testing himself against some formidable, impossible standard of persistence and stamina," his biographers wrote, "pressing against ordinary physical and intellectual limits, implicitly insisting that the challenge never be relaxed."

"It seems to me that the position in which we find ourselves today is not unlike that of Britain after the Napoleonic wars," Forrestal testified that January to the Senate Foreign Relations Committee. "Britain, having spent twenty years and much of her resources in defeating the attempt of Napoleon to conquer Europe, was anxious to withdraw from that continent. She found great difficulty in doing so, however, without exposing Europe and eventually herself to a recurrence of the very threat of which she had just disposed." Like Britain in 1939, the United States was an insular nation facing the rise of a continental dictatorship with imperial ambitions. The president of the Naval War College, Admiral Raymond Spruance, made the point with his customary sobriety and clarity to the Senate Naval Affairs Committee in the summer of 1946, deriving from that geopolitical fact the conclusion that the Navy had to be the nation's first line of defense.

The Army/Navy dispute might have seemed trifling relative to the challenges Truman faced in managing the postwar military drawdown while preparing to confront an assertive Soviet Union in the far corners of the world. But the problem filled Forrestal's days as a matter of both principle and prudence. For all the obvious distinctions that were woven through the identities of the two services as separate combat arms, the public debate over unification seldom got beyond talking points and emotion. "Unification has a pleasant sound, like mother love," said Halsey's former chief of staff and future chief of naval operations (CNO), Vice Admiral Robert B. Carney. "Although nobody knows what it is precisely, it's something we ought to do and anybody who resisted it was a churl." Forrestal saw intellectual laxity in the Army's case, which glossed over the services' meaningful and mutually reinforcing differences. He considered the Army and Navy identities as complementary assets. Their competition produced original thinking and enterprise—and breakthroughs that never would have seen the light of day had one side been able to bulldoze the other.

Distinct traditions and cultures were at the heart of the services' identities, habits of thought, and operational modes. As Rear Admiral Luis de Florez, the assistant chief of the Navy's Office of Research and Inventions, put it to the Senate Military Affairs Committee in December, "The Navy is essentially an engineering organization." At its heart was technical activity and research. It commanded the world's "largest aggregation of horsepower," he said. Moreover, mobility and flexibility were the Navy way. Ships could operate either alone or as part of a fleet hundreds of vessels strong, as a mission might require.

By contrast, the Army was a mass-manpower organization, he said. Its strength was counted in rosters of personnel twenty thousand strong. "Its mechanization is incidental to its operation and not comparable to the naval establishment, which employs relatively few men per unit of horsepower and firepower," de Florez said. When it had to move, the Army walked nearly as often as it rode. And unlike soldiers, sailors did not fight individually. They were effective only by use of the ships and aircraft that they manned. This led to divergent philosophies and doctrines and produced differences in attitudes toward innovation and procurement. Tanks and motorized artillery were tools. Warships were collective identities, like very small colleges or very large fraternities. As a "type organization," the Army organized its forces by their function, and preferred that sea forces likewise remain together under a seagoing command and air forces under an air command. The Army thought all pilots should belong to a single air force, believing that pilots of any service could do equally well whatever it was that naval aviators did.

The Navy, on the other hand, coveted its freedom to use whatever tools it might need to carry out its missions. This made it a "task organization," de Florez said. Its leaders were not satisfied to organize by dividing and separately administering their diverse equipment by its type. Admirals believed passionately that aircraft had to be part of their mix. Given the unique difficulties of flying them from ships, a specialized aviation cadre was needed within the fleet.

These arguments could seem abstruse, but they mattered when the shooting started. Without the Navy's own dive-bombing squadrons, specially designed for use aboard carriers and trained and integrated within a task force, there would have been no victory in the Battle of Midway. "There appears to be no sound basis for one department of the government to dictate to another as to the tools which it may be permitted to use to accomplish its mission," a Navy Department paper argued. The Army saw the Navy way as duplicative and wasteful. And yet any efficiencies that Great Britain might have found when it unified its entire tactical air command were lost in the disasters that were enabled by stifling the growth of carrier aviation in the Royal Navy, whose inferior planes gave it no way to intervene effectively as Norway, France, Crete, and Singapore fell to the Axis. Despite London's great record of innovation in other areas—radar notable among them—the Fleet Air Arm lagged U.S. naval aviation by perhaps fifteen years when the war began.

Given the bold claims coming from the U.S. Army's strategic aviation corps after the war, the issue of proper roles and missions developed as a three-sided debate. General Hap Arnold and his tribe, advocating an independent Air Force, were a pox on the houses of the Army and Navy alike, for some of them argued that the atomic bomb had made armies obsolete, too. Most admirals were happy to leave each service to cultivate its particular strength. Few of them objected to the idea that the Army should have its own tactical air force specializing in the support of ground forces, as it was consistent with the task-oriented Navy principle that "in a well-functioning team, the line knows what the backfield is doing." But if it were deprived of the ability to fly its own planes from its own ships, the Navy would lose mission effectiveness. For aviation admirals such as Forrest Sherman and Arthur W. Radford, whom Forrestal had tapped to make the Navy's case in detail before Congress, such a sacrifice was a nonstarter. Given that the Navy secretary was about to install naval aviators in top vacant posts—with John Towers replacing Raymond Spruance as commander in chief, Pacific, DeWitt C. Ramsey becoming vice chief of naval operations, and esteemed World War II carrier task force commander Marc Mitscher to resume command of carriers at Norfolk—naval aviation's place in Forrestal's department seemed more secure.

They were partisans when they had to be but were often ineffective as infighters. Admiral Carney lamented how poorly he and his peers performed at Pentagon conference tables "in the manipulation of the agenda and the rules of order and the general staff work, at which the Army was superb." The Navy's most effective advocates, Forrestal and Eberhardt, were civilians. But they seemed to be carrying the day in the Senate. The sale had yet to be closed, and the admiralty's biggest names were always willing to be heard in the national debate. In Halsey's estimation, it was time to fight fire with fire.

That night in December, he paid his freight. "The merger medicos have made a hasty diagnosis—have offered a pink-pill remedy," he told his audience at the Waldorf-Astoria.

> Merging two complex organizations will not produce efficiency nor economy. Merger would add nothing to unified field command—we can achieve that end far better through the coordinated planning on the Joint Chiefs of Staff.
>
> No. Merger is not necessary. It is not desirable. It is plainly dangerous. It would destroy the initiative of individual services. It would hamstring their right to advance. It would deprive them of representation before Congress and the people. It would substitute military for civilian control. It might lead to military dictatorship.

At a time when the rival services were full of confident claims about their missions in the age of the atomic bomb, the new weapon was in fact a wildcard for both. The Navy's shipbuilders had been keen on the idea of testing its effects upon ships since the middle of the war. In 1944, planners at the Manhattan Engineer District at Los Alamos had discussed testing the new weapon against Truk, a Japanese base in the Caroline Islands, bypassed in the westward Pacific offensive. Shortly after the surrender, Senator Brien McMahon of Connecticut, who had called the bomb "the most important thing in history since the birth of Jesus Christ," argued again for its use against the emperor's fleet. The naval architect who served as chief of the Navy's Bureau of Ships, Rear Admiral Edward L. Cochrane, agreed there was a need for "broadscale experiments with the atomic bomb to clear up its major influence on naval warfare." On October 1, 1945, he and his colleague at the Bureau of Ordnance, Rear Admiral George F. Hussey, had proposed to the chief of naval operations, Admiral Ernest J. King, a program of tests in which atomic bombs would be detonated against different types of ships. And so, just prior to his relief as CNO by Chester Nimitz, at the beginning of the unification debate in early December, King picked up that proposal and presented it to the Joint Chiefs of Staff. It called for the detonation of three plutonium weapons of the Fat Man type. The first would burst in the air, the second and third underwater.

The experts in Los Alamos considered the tests a dangerous idea. Having met with his technical staff at the end of November, Major General Thomas F. Farrell, the lab's deputy commander, wrote to his boss, General Groves, that the underwater explosion in particular "would contain so many major hazards that it should be ruled out at this time." Farrell envisioned radioactive seawater traveling on ocean currents into commercial shipping lanes, entering vessels through their seawater pumps, leaching through steel hulls, and spreading to populated areas. The local dangers were considerable enough to warrant extreme caution. The water in the lagoon would be "a witch's brew," wrote the leader of a technical group, Henry W. Newson, probably with "enough plutonium near the surface to poison the combined armed forces of the United States at their highest wartime strength." Newson warned that boarding the ships would remain dangerous indefinitely because of irradiated particles trapped in melted paint. He suggested that if the test had to be carried out, animals should be placed on the ships to measure the effects of radiation on a crew. Other technicians at Los Alamos believed such a test should be unnecessary, as most anything anyone wanted to know about the effects of the bomb could be predicted by computation based on theoretical physics. But with the day surely coming when atomic weapons could be used against American forces, the Joint Chiefs of Staff felt a duty to gather data from actual field tests. Once again, navies were on trial against the onslaught of modernity.

A generation earlier, in 1921, the War Department anchored some antiquated warships off the Virginia Capes to face attack from land-based planes under command of the country's leading aviation evangelist, Brigadier General Billy Mitchell. Now again the doctrines of a future war—and the roles and missions of the various military branches in it—would turn on the recorded effects of revolutionary weapons against hardened steel. The world's first atomic explosion had taken place in July 1945, a test in the New Mexico desert. The second and third blasts were the war shots over Japan. The fourth, fifth, and sixth would measure just what the revolution portended for the fleet.

The man who would be in charge of the Cold War's first test of atomic weapons against warships was Rear Admiral William H. P. Blandy. The fifty-six-year-old ordnance specialist, a native of New York, was valedictorian of the Naval Academy class of 1913, and while he had served ably as an amphibious task force commander in the Pacific during World War II, he was an obscure technocrat when Admiral King appointed him to the new post of Deputy Chief of Naval Operations for Special Weapons in December 1945. In early January, a subcommittee of the Joint Staff Planners headed by Major General Curtis E. LeMay asked Blandy to draw up, in collaboration with scientists from Los Alamos, a scheme to expose warships and a variety of test cargoes to atomic blasts at Bikini Atoll in the Central Pacific. The Joint Chiefs of Staff approved the plan with no major changes, and after President Truman followed suit on January 10, Blandy set to work, as head of a new Army-Navy organization known as Joint Task Force One, answerable to the Joint Chiefs. The first atomic naval test would take place on May 15. As Blandy and his deputy, Rear Admiral William S. "Deak" Parsons, the weapons design expert who had flown in the *Enola Gay* to Hiroshima and armed the Little Boy uranium bomb in flight, got busy, a sense of "slam-bang action" returned to the Navy Department's daily life.

At a press event on January 12, Nimitz introduced the Navy's post-war leadership to the Washington press corps. Blandy was "the star of the conference, from the standpoint of current public interest," wrote *The New York Times*. Blandy—his friends called him Spike—referred to the Office of Special Weapons as the Navy's Buck Rogers Division. The decision to enlist the Hollywood space-opera hero, adapted from the pages of *Amazing Stories* to become a leading toy ray gun franchise as well, was canny, for Blandy's office had cognizance of all Navy work on advanced systems, including the atomic bomb. His project at Bikini would offer evidence on any number of important questions. The one that resonated most strongly in Forrestal's office was this: In a world whose face was seventh-tenths water, should the sea service become a casualty of the victory it had helped deliver, just because of the advent of this new bomb?

Admiral Halsey, for one, was not worried. As he told the New York State Bar Association in January, "Ships should not be particularly profitable targets for atomic bombing. . . . Their ability to move makes them almost impossible targets for super rockets. In short, they are hard to hit."

As Spike Blandy, Deak Parsons, and their partners in Joint Task Force One and at Los Alamos went to work, top secret science prepared for its debut as public spectacle. The results of Operation Crossroads would enlighten the whole watching world.

2

Memo from Moscow

America's number two diplomat in the Soviet Union in early 1946 was a Princeton-educated Wisconsinite named George Frost Kennan. Having signed on with the new United States Foreign Service in 1925, the forty-two-year-old chargé d'affaires at the U.S. embassy in Moscow was already a man of the world. Taking overseas posts in Geneva, Hamburg, and Berlin, he had landed in 1931 in Riga, Latvia, where he followed Soviet economic affairs. In the spring of 1934, a few months after Franklin Roosevelt opened diplomatic relations with the Soviet Union, Kennan joined Ambassador William C. Bullitt, Jr., at the new U.S. embassy near Red Square.

It was a heady assignment for the son of hardscrabble Scots-Irish settlers of eighteenth-century Connecticut and Massachusetts. His mother passed away before he could form a living memory of her. He was never close to his father or stepmother, although he adored his older sisters. At the age of eight, he was sent to Germany to stay with his stepmother in order to learn German. He attended a military preparatory school in Wisconsin and arrived at Princeton in the fall of 1921. A strong introvert, Kennan had a hard time navigating life in the Ivy League, with the result that his college experience was a trying, lonely affair.

Soon after the State Department sent him to Moscow, what became known as the Great Purge began. As Stalin's onslaught of show trials targeted the old hands of the Soviet military, including some of its most experienced generals, Kennan was swiftly schooled in the perverse brutality and terror of Kremlin political intrigues. After four and a half years, he departed for other assignments and served well and ably. Then, in 1944, the ambassador to the Soviet Union, W. Averell Harriman, requested his services, and he returned to the Soviet capital.

Kennan's gimlet eye was equal to that of any other Soviet watcher in the State Department. He believed that memories in America were short. People had forgotten or perhaps never even known of Stalin's murderous Great Purges, the pact between Moscow and Berlin that destroyed Poland, or the betrayals of promises the Soviet Union had made to the Allies. Idealists, Kennan thought, had invested too much hope in the incipient United Nations organization, believing the Soviet Union could be coaxed into productive membership. Pro-Stalin propaganda received a considerable boost from the efforts of *New York Times* Moscow bureau chief Walter Duranty, the "anti-Kennan" who defended Stalin consistently, publishing several denials that Stalin had engineered the mass starvation of farmers in Ukraine. THERE IS NO FAMINE OR ACTUAL STARVATION NOR IS THERE LIKELY TO BE, read one of his 1931 headlines pertaining to the calculated humanitarian crisis. For such "useful idiocy"* Duranty won a Pulitzer Prize in 1932.

In February 1945, at the Black Sea resort city of Yalta, on Crimea's coast, President Franklin Roosevelt and British prime minister Winston Churchill had met with Stalin to discuss the shape of the postwar world. The points of agreement were far reaching, from the terms of surrender to offer Germany, to stipulations for membership in the United Nations, to the guarantee that the Soviet Union would join the war against Japan. There was agreement as well that the people of Eastern Europe would have the right to "create democratic institutions of their own choice," with free elections to be held as soon as possible. Churchill had been famously, courageously skeptical regarding the trustworthiness of Adolf Hitler at a time when his superiors were eager

---

* The term "useful idiots," often attributed to Lenin although there is no evidence he ever actually used it, referred to Soviet-friendly progressives in the West who could be counted upon to defend the Communist Party's position without seeing its malignancy or its cynicism.

to trust him. "Poor Neville Chamberlain believed he could trust Hitler," Churchill said. "He was wrong. But I don't think I am wrong about Stalin." The test, as Churchill saw it, would involve the restoration of the government of Poland.

The rehabilitation of the shattered nation within its own borders, its western territories now to be shifted into Germany as a quid pro quo for the Russian annexation of its mostly Catholic eastern territories, held a special place in the heart of anyone with a bent toward justice. After the war, Durbrow, as the deputy head of State's Eastern European division, had been directly involved in the Polish matter, helping to negotiate the details of the bargain struck at the Tehran Conference in 1943. He had arranged for the exile government in London to order its most important underground leaders within Poland to come out of hiding. Durbrow coaxed from the Polish leadership the names of fifteen of these men, former anti-Soviet resistance commanders all, and had them surface from underground and present themselves to the Soviets.

The Soviet watchers in the State Department never got over how they had made possible the slaughter that followed. The grim details were not revealed until May, when Stalin's foreign minister, Vyacheslav Molotov, met with U.S. officials in San Francisco during the forty-six-nation conference that established the Charter of the United Nations. Having signed off on the creation of the international body under the directorship of a Soviet-sympathizing former State Department official, Alger Hiss, the foreign minister might have had reason to celebrate. But Molotov was in foul spirits. He had taken the full brunt of Harry S. Truman's Missouri candor when he met him at the White House. Soviet breaches of the Yalta agreement had infuriated the president. In San Francisco, Molotov had his revenge. He informed the U.S. delegation laconically that the Polish leaders had all been traitors. According to Durbrow, Molotov said, "I wasn't sure, but I've double-checked it. They all turned out to be pro-Nazi, anti-Soviet. They've all been executed."

Durbrow was aghast. "I gave them those names," he said. "That's the kind of an ally we had."

Now, a year later, the root antagonism that would drive the Cold War for two generations was revealed in bright living color as the Communist Party of the Soviet Union prepared its slate of Stalin loyalists for membership in the Supreme Soviet. In the run-up to the elections that were to take place on February 10, 1946, Soviet officials barnstormed from Leningrad to the Urals on behalf of their ticket.

Watching closely at the Moscow embassy, George Kennan reported to Washington two days before the vote, referring in telegramese to the "CRESCENDO OF SOVIET INTERNAL PROPAGANDA EFFORT OF UNPARALLELED DIMENSIONS WHICH HAS OCCUPIED AN ARMY OF OVER TEN MILLION PEOPLE, PARTY MEMBERS, AND OTHERS FOR OVER TWO MONTHS." The chargé d'affaires, a connoisseur of the Soviet state's machinations, called the rigged nomination process the "REAL SECRET OF SOVIET ELECTORAL SYSTEM. . . . THE PARTY CANNOT LOSE."

If the unbroken streak of Communist candidates winning unanimous nomination had elements of a miracle, Kennan noted to his colleagues in Washington, "SINCE PREVAILING LOCAL PHILOSOPHY RULES OUT HAND OF DIVINE PROVIDENCE AS ORIGIN OF SUCH SINGULAR UNIFORMITY OF INSPIRATION, IT MUST BE ATTRIBUTED TO A MORE EARTHLY AND FAMILIAR AGENCY."

The agency to which George Kennan referred was no mere bureau of operatives. It was the cult of personality and permanent executive authority of a man born in Gori, Georgia, on December 17, 1878, with the name Iosif Dzhugashvili. The world came to know him by the pseudonym under which he had published an essay on Marxism at the age of thirty-five: Stalin. A day before the election, he gave the speech that many Soviet watchers said began the Cold War.

Addressing voters at Moscow's Bolshoi Theater on February 9, Stalin held forth on his favorite themes. He pointed to victory over Nazi Germany in World War II as proof of the efficacy of Communism and the legitimacy of the Soviet Communist Party. He blamed "the capitalist world" for the century's major wars. The recent global conflict had been "a great school which examined and tested all the forces of the people," Stalin said.

It ruthlessly tore down all the veils and coverings that concealed the actual features of states, governments, and parties, and brought them onto the stage without masks and without make-up, with all their defects and merits. The war was something in the nature of an examination of our Soviet system, of our state, of our government and of our Communist Party, and it summed up their work and said, as it were: Here they are, your people and organizations, their life and work. Scrutinize them carefully and treat them according to their deserts. The war proved that the Soviet social system is a genuinely people's system, which grew up from the ranks of the people and enjoys their powerful support; that the Soviet social system is [a] fully viable and stable form of organization of society.

More than that. The issue now is not whether the Soviet social system is viable or not, because after the object lessons of the war no skeptic now dares to express doubt concerning the viability of the Soviet social system. Now the issue is that the Soviet social system has proved to be more viable and stable than the non-Soviet social system, that the Soviet social system is a better form of organization of society than any non-Soviet social system.

In that familiar onslaught of words, George Kennan saw desperate insecurity—and a declaration of war. He considered the speech notable for the weakness it conveyed, and weakness was always more dangerous than strength. Stalin's riff of defensiveness and self-justification was followed by a recap of the feats of military industry that had beaten Hitler—thirty thousand tanks, forty thousand airplanes, two million automatic rifles. Each number produced loud applause in the streets.

Audiences overseas were equally impressed. The speech caused a stir at the State Department. According to the chief of the Division of West European Affairs, H. Freeman Matthews, "Stalin's speech of February 9 constitutes the most important and authoritative guide to postwar Soviet policy." Opinion at State's headquarters in D.C.'s Foggy

Bottom neighborhood had long been split. Foreign service officers with the most direct experience with the Kremlin—"Russia hands" such as Durbrow and Kennan—held little hope that accommodation and quid pro quo could succeed in bringing the Soviet Union into an international "community." Ambassador Averell Harriman, on the other hand, believed that providing economic assistance to the former ally was not only called for on its face, but could help the United States avoid economic decline at home, driven by the sharp falloff in heavy industrial production.

But America had been down this road, the skeptics pointed out. With Nazi armies closing on Stalingrad, the United States had given more than $9 billion in arms to the Soviets under the Lend-Lease program, shipping heavy war matériel to Stalin's northern ports, through the Persian Gulf, and across Iran. Beginning in the early days of the German invasion and continuing for a month after Berlin surrendered, the shipments finally totaled 7,000 tanks, 52,000 jeeps, 363,000 trucks, 9,700 fighter aircraft, 3,800 light bombers, and 300 submarine chasers and torpedo boats. Matthews deemed Stalin's forgetfulness outrageous. "It should be given great weight," he wrote, "in any plans which may be under consideration for extending credits or other forms of economic assistance to the Soviet Union." But Stalin's foreign audiences seldom considered the internal pressures besetting the Soviet dictator. The human and material costs of the war in Russia had been paid by people who enjoyed none of the privileges that belonged to the powerful. Difficult questions were unavoidable—the German invaders had made it all the way *to the Volga*? But asking such questions was dangerous. So was the act of writing satire and poetry. As these could be particularly effective threats to the dictator's stature, the Communist Party Central Committee dealt harshly with satirists and poets. The Gulag swelled as millions were arrested, imprisoned, and exiled to Russia's Arctic wastelands for the crime of asking questions. In the gulags they joined those imprisoned for pilfering bread to feed their starving children.

James Forrestal, however, viewed the February 9 speech as "a major pronouncement of a most ominous kind"—and a blueprint for external action. When he met with Supreme Court justice William O. Douglas on February 17 to convey Truman's hope that Douglas would accept a cabinet position, Forrestal asked the jurist for his thoughts on Stalin's speech. Douglas called it "The declaration of World War Three." Forrestal saw it this way: After years of Western efforts to bargain with Stalin, to treat him as an ally, to enlist him in common causes with favors given for favors in return, to restrict discussion of disagreements between a Washington and Moscow to private channels, here was a strong indicator that the dictator was unwinnable, that he had little interest in the kind of good-faith cooperation envisioned by the organizers of the United Nations.

The Navy secretary had been arguing for months with his counterpart at State, James Byrnes, about the role Russia should have in the occupation of Japan. Byrnes thought the Russians should have one. Forrestal disagreed. He had seen "the locust-like effects of their occupation wherever they may be." In the northern sector of Korea, Soviet forces had hauled away the generating machinery from the hydroelectric plants on the banks of the Yalu River, facilities that had provided 30 percent of the power used in the American zone south of the 38th parallel. Collecting State Department dispatches, Forrestal documented "an unrelieved picture of Soviet high-handedness, unilateral action, and aggressive pressure." And yet voices at Foggy Bottom still urged continued displays of good faith, hoping for that unicorn to appear, the reasonable quid pro quo. Could Moscow be trusted to administer Korea, a rehabilitating nation on the brink of mass starvation?

Now the Soviet premier had declared to his voters and the entire world that there could be no peaceful coexistence between the economic systems of communism and capitalism. He had declared a new greatpower competition against not only capitalism, but against the "fascism and reaction" that was present in "bourgeois democracies and elsewhere." His snub to the victorious alliance was striking. "He didn't mention Lend-Lease or his allies or the United Nations or anything— all the things in FDR's grand design went pffft. . . . Shot down right there officially by Uncle Joe," Durbrow would say. The Red Army's triumph, Stalin said, would be quickly consolidated in preparation for this new struggle. He announced a Five-Year Plan that provided for a tripling of the Soviet Union's output of iron, steel, and coal, and near doubling of oil production. The purpose of this industrial surge, he said, was to stand ready to confront "the capitalist encirclement." With the Communist Party taking more than 99 percent of the 101.4 million votes cast, on voter turnout of 99.7 percent, he was free, as ever, to claim a mandate to do whatever he wished.

Confronted with this, the State Department wanted to hear from its top Russia hand. Durbrow asked around: "Have we heard from George?" Kennan had already received a request for his "interpretive analysis" of the preelection speeches by Soviet officials in the week before the vote. He had duly reported on the oratory of Molotov and others. When the word came back to Durbrow that the radio teletypewriter at the Moscow embassy had been silent, a little nudge was drafted and sent under Secretary Byrnes's signature. "We know you're busy. Hoping you find time to give us your analysis of Uncle Joe's speech."

Kennan was more than just busy. As the Moscow embassy's number two, he had been running the office since the departure to Washington of Ambassador Harriman in January 1946. He was worn down and sick, suffering from fever, stuffed sinuses, and a toothache, topped with side effects of the sulfa drugs he had taken as a remedy. Prompted by Washington, where Stalin's speech had had "something of the effect of a shot on Fort Sumter," as the historian John Lewis Gaddis would write, Kennan raised himself and put hand to pen.

Given that Stalin's audience had been domestic, his remarks given amid an ostensibly competitive legislative election, it was not obvious that the speech was meant as an official expression of foreign policy. But since the Soviet Union had no executive official but Stalin, whose power was unchecked and whose word was the one, only, last, and highest voice of the state, Kennan regarded the speech as consequential. The dictator's words were delivered at a fraught moment as Harry Truman concerned himself with Soviet designs in the Far East and was pressing Byrnes to be more forthright in his own reporting to Washington. The diplomat composed his reply accordingly.

Running a bit north of five thousand words, his telegram was far longer than any the Moscow embassy had ever sent via the teletype.

Kennan used the novelty for dramatic impact. "I apologize in advance for this burdening of telegraphic channel," he wrote, "but questions involved are of such urgent importance, particularly in view of recent events, that our answers to them, if they deserve attention at all, seem to me to deserve it at once." What became known as the Long Telegram hit Foggy Bottom's teleprinter on February 22, 1946.

It was widely considered a masterpiece of geopolitical analysis, so keenly insightful and elegantly written that Kennan must have started it well before the applause had died down in Red Square. Indeed, some part of him had been working on it since 1934, when he first began observing up close the phenomenon of the Communist Party and its machinations. The telegram analyzed Moscow's geopolitical thinking and ideological conceits; connected it to Russian national psychology; distilled years of its propaganda messaging; forecast the methods by which the Kremlin would pursue its goals; and recommended a strategic approach for the United States to follow in coming years.

The Soviet Union's hostility to the West could no longer be wished away, Kennan wrote. It was implacable. Moscow saw itself trapped within a "capitalist encirclement," facing a perpetual threat that made peaceful coexistence impossible. Central to Stalin's worldview was this vision of unending binary world struggle. The Soviet dictator had been explaining it for years to all who would listen. In 1927, Kennan noted, Stalin had said to a delegation of American workers that there were "two centers of world significance," one capitalist and one socialist. "The battle between these two centers for command of [the] world economy will decide [the] fate of capitalism and of communism in [the] entire world." The recent predations of Germany and Japan stood for "capitalist" ambitions in Stalin's telling. But with both enemies beaten, Moscow needed a fresh incarnation of the threat. Where the United States sought to corral the world's nations into a system of international cooperation and restore Germany and Japan to a productive if demilitarized sovereignty, it hoped it could bring along the Soviet Union into common cause. Where the State Department saw the mutual benefit of brokering conflict to prevent future wars, all Moscow saw was cynicism

and aggression. Where Russia reeled from the loss of upward of twenty
million war dead and aimed to restore geographic buffers that would
prevent another invasion, Washington saw aggression and empire
building. At a moment of worldwide exhaustion, Stalin announced the
existence of an irrepressible, permanent global conflict. Kennan did not
miss the message. Like Justice Douglas, he saw it as the beginning of a
new world war.

Stalin had the political reflexes of a perpetually fear-bound despot.
With the blood of the war still all over the ground, he needed the Soviet
people to see the Communist apparatus as legitimate. When he boasted
of the Red Army's victory, it was not just to celebrate; it was to secure
his hold on power. Kennan saw a deep psychological syndrome at work.
Moscow's "neurotic view of world affairs," as he called it, was partly in
the tradition of an "instinctive Russian sense of insecurity." As well, he
explained, the Kremlin leaders "invariably sensed that their rule was
relatively archaic in form, fragile and artificial in its psychological foundation." They feared what might happen if their people were ever exposed to the lifeways of the advanced West. So gravely did Moscow
regard the danger of such "foreign penetration" that it resolved to hide
from its people the true facts of the world and conceal the reality of its
own national affairs.

Kennan noted that Communist Party dogma suited Russian national
psychology. The tenets of Marx and Lenin were not new, he observed.
They had "smoldered ineffectively for half a century in Western Europe" before they "caught hold and blazed for the first time in Russia."
The austere, abstract, and intellectualized system of political ideology
saw all areas of life arising from economic constructs and the social
strata that was built upon them. Marxism denied individual rights in
favor of a subsuming systemic credo that advanced the needs of the
many as defined by the state. Kennan wrote, "Only in this land which
had never known a friendly neighbor or indeed any tolerant equilibrium of separate powers, either internal or international, could a doctrine thrive which viewed economic conflicts of society as insoluble by
peaceful means." In this dogma the Kremlin

found justification . . . for the dictatorship without which they did not know how to rule, for cruelties they did not dare not to inflict, for sacrifices they felt bound to demand.

In the name of Marxism they sacrificed every single ethical value in their methods and tactics. Today they cannot dispense with it. It is [the] fig leaf of their moral and intellectual respectability. Without it they would stand before history, at best, as only the last of that long succession of cruel and wasteful Russian rulers who have relentlessly forced [the] country on to ever new heights of military power in order to guarantee [the] external security of their internally weak regimes.

Soviet leaders, Kennan argued, thereby lived in a state of "self hypnotism" that required them to maintain their woeful ignorance of the outside world. This was what he called the "unsolved mystery":

Who, if anyone, in this great land actually receives accurate and unbiased information about [the] outside world. In [the] atmosphere of oriental secretiveness and conspiracy which pervades this Government, possibilities for distorting or poisoning sources and currents of information are infinite. The very disrespect of Russians for objective truth—indeed, their disbelief in its existence—leads them to view all stated facts as instruments for furtherance of one ulterior purpose or another. There is good reason to suspect that this Government is actually a conspiracy within a conspiracy; and I for one am reluctant to believe that Stalin himself receives anything like an objective picture of [the] outside world. Here there is ample scope for the type of subtle intrigue at which Russians are past masters. Inability of foreign governments to place their case squarely before Russian policy makers—extent to which they are delivered up in their relations with Russia to good graces of obscure and unknown advisers whom they never see and cannot influence—this to my mind is the most disquieting feature of diplomacy in Moscow, and one which Western states-

men would do well to keep in mind if they would understand
the nature of difficulties encountered here.

Kennan's forewarning of "subtle intrigue" dilated into a review of
Soviet ideological forays abroad, influence operations that were carried
out "on an unofficial or subterranean plane" and thus deniable when
exposed. In Eastern Europe most notably, Stalin was practicing the
kind of insinuative penetration operations of which Kennan warned.
Kennan explained that Stalin believed that "the capitalist world is not
all bad." As the Soviet leader saw it, there were "certain wholly enlightened and positive elements" within the otherwise corrupt Western
bourgeoisie. These included overtly Communist factions, and also "certain other elements (now described for tactical reasons as progressive or
democratic) whose reactions, aspirations, and activities happen to be
'objectively' favorable to interests of USSR. These last must be encouraged and utilized for Soviet purposes," Kennan explained. In fact, the
Roosevelt administration had been well penetrated. The Soviets' covert
effort to undermine the U.S. government and establish a secret network in its power centers would continue as if the war had never ended.

The subversive campaign to undermine Western ideas, values, and
psychology would be carried out worldwide through a "far-flung apparatus" of sympathetic elements. Some of this would be done by way
of a "central core" of those belonging to Communist parties. Though
these people would keep the appearance of "acting in unrelated public
capacities, they are in reality working closely together as an underground operating directorate of world communism" under Moscow's
direction, Kennan said. Supporting them unwittingly, Kennan warned,
would be a domestic element of "partisans of certain political tenden-
cies within their respective countries, genuinely innocent of conspirato-
rial connection with foreign states." Labor groups, youth and women's
organizations, racial and religious societies, social and cultural organizations, and book publishing companies would be targets of Soviet penetration, not just in the United States but everywhere, Kennan wrote.

If this analysis would expose Kennan to the criticism that he was
himself a bit paranoid, his rebuttal was rooted in his direct experience

with Russia's mastery of the tools of the paranoid art. He had witnessed how the Communist Party of the Soviet Union, fearing penetration by foreigners, had committed itself to waging destabilizing underground offensives of its own against its rivals. The ravaging of Poland, north-ern Korea, and Manchuria, in war and in peace, conducted in covert ways that avoided notice by the exhausted Western publics, were his cases in point.

Yet in spite of the darkness at work in Moscow, Kennan concluded that the United States should approach its rival calmly and "with good heart." The Communist Party was losing its ability to inspire the Soviet people emotionally, he sensed. Its propaganda was "basically negative and destructive." America's first challenge, then, was soberly to recog-nize the nature of the phenomenon. "We must study it with [the] same courage, detachment, objectivity, and [the] same determination not to be emotionally provoked or unseated by it, with which [the] doctor studies [the] unruly and unreasonable individual." Public education was paramount. Properly done, it could defuse the hysteria of anti-Soviet attitudes. Only an actual decline in the integrity of American institutions could open that risk. "World communism is like [the] ma-lignant parasite which feeds only on diseased tissue," George Kennan wrote. "This is [the] point at which domestic and foreign policies meet. Every courageous and incisive measure to solve internal problems of our own society, to improve self-confidence, discipline, morale and community spirit of our own people, is a diplomatic victory over Mos-cow worth a thousand diplomatic notes and joint communiqués." On that foundation, he argued, the United States should put forward a positive vision of the kind of world it would like to shape. Promises of freedom had to find balance with the assurance of security. In making this prescription, Kennan was declaring that America was already in a global competition with the Soviet Union.

3

TOWARD CONTAINMENT

KENNAN WOULD MARVEL THAT HIS TELEGRAM HAD SUCH AN IM-
pact, defining as it did the nature of the Soviet Union and its goals in
the world. Official Washington seemed ready to hear it. "If none of my
previous literary efforts had seemed to evoke even the faintest tinkle
from the bell at which they were aimed," he would later write, "this
one, to my astonishment, struck it squarely and set it vibrating with
a resonance that was not to die down for many months." Still, he
was understating its effect. The Long Telegram described the Soviet
Union's ambitions, pathology, and modus in a way that was indelible.
Kennan's descriptive flair, his talent for laying his hands on the subtle
textures of Moscow's *modus belli* and announcing its nature, would in-
form the aggressive anticommunism of the Truman administration as
no other source.

Although not the words used by George Kennan, "containment"
and "anticommunism" became the bywords of Harry Truman. Executive Order 9835, issued in March 1947, required loyalty checks from
government employees and barred most Communist Party members
from the public payroll. Truman didn't need the help of any Republi-
cans like Senator Joseph McCarthy to deal with the subversives in his
backyard. What his movement needed was intellectual heat. The most
Russia-savvy of American diplomats, Kennan articulated the nature of
a geopolitical threat in tones that were at once measured and discerning

and yet galvanizing too. Kennan called a weary nation to a new purpose. In his essay he left no doubt who America's rival was. He was also
explicit about the greatest risk of confronting it: "that we shall allow
ourselves to become like those with whom we are coping."

Among those particularly impressed with Kennan's writing was the
U.S. naval attaché in Moscow, Vice Admiral Leslie Clark Stevens, for
whom James Forrestal's own son, Michael V. Forrestal, worked. Stevens wrote to Admiral Nimitz's office, recommending that the entire
Navy Department read Kennan's telegram. Americans did not grasp
the "utter ruthlessness and complete unscrupulousness of [the] Soviet
ruling clique. Its breath must be literally felt on the back of neck before
really appreciated," he wrote. Secretary Forrestal needed no persuasion. He was sold on first reading. Kennan's ideas closely tracked his
own.

In George Kennan, James Forrestal found a rare thing: a foreign
service officer with a strong sense that diplomacy and strategy were
closely interrelated, who saw the link between hard and soft power,
who was immune to the naïveté about Joseph Stalin's will to power that
had settled over Foggy Bottom at the staff level. If most generals and
admirals were technocrats, disinclined to think historically or politically, diplomats often neglected the steel realities of national power and
the dividends of its maintenance. The Navy secretary read Kennan as a
kindred voice. Here was a diplomat who could define and meet a threat,
one who was willing to stand his ground on principle and wield arguments in intellectual combat when necessary.

With a contest under way for the confidence of Europe, President
Truman sought a more robust approach to dealing with the Soviet
Union. Irritated with Secretary Byrnes for "beginning to think of himself as an Assistant President in full charge for foreign policy," as the
president would write, Truman had instructed the secretary of state on
January 5 to be more accountable to the White House. He also articulated, for the benefit of his accommodation-minded chief diplomat, his
own view of the Soviet threat. "Unless Russia is faced with an iron fist
and strong language another war is in the making. Only one language
do they understand—'how many divisions have you?' . . . I'm tired of

babying the Soviets." Truman made the case for his own primacy in U.S. foreign affairs. He would stand with Forrestal in recognizing the fleet as the most useful tool in his kit, even as he pared its strength, flesh from bone.

ON FEBRUARY 25, Vice Admiral Forrest Sherman observed that the Navy was due to render honors to Turkey's deceased ambassador to the United States, Mehmet Munir Ertegun, by returning his remains to his home country. Typically a cruiser performed such a task. Would it not make more of a statement to use a larger battleship? And if a battleship, why not the storied ship that his wife, Bess, had christened, the mighty *Missouri*?

Forrestal had wanted for months to show a stronger Mediterranean presence in the face of Soviet provocations in Europe. The Kremlin was applying pressure in Turkey, Italy, Greece, the Adriatic states, and North Africa from Tangier to the Suez Canal, determined, it seemed, to gain political leverage that would permit Moscow to access the strategic naval corridor of the Middle Sea. Turkey's control of the Dardanelles, a choke point that restricted the Soviet fleet from venturing into the Aegean Sea and the eastern Med, was a constant irritant to Stalin. His refusal to yield control of another strategic nexus, the oil-rich region of northwestern Iran, as required by the agreement struck in Tehran in 1943, disturbed the Allied capitals. As Britain carried out its own promised evacuation on March 2, Secretary of State Byrnes insisted to Molotov that the Soviets keep their pledge, adding that the United States could not remain indifferent. The response from the Kremlin was unspoken but thunderous: Soviet armored columns moved toward the border with Turkey and Iraq.

Forrestal felt it was time for the United States to reprise the spirit of Thomas Jefferson's young republic, which had sent naval forces to confront piracy by North Africa's Berber states. On February 28 he asked Secretary of State Byrnes whether he supported Sherman's idea of sending the battleship *Missouri* with a task force to the Med. Though Byrnes had often disagreed with Forrestal in the matter of assessing risk, he said that he liked the idea of deploying at least the *Missouri*. A message needed to be sent.

Any doubt that the Atlantic powers meant to send a joint message to Moscow disappeared on March 5, when Prime Minister Winston Churchill appeared in Fulton, Missouri. The speech he delivered became famous as a warning about Soviet designs in the world beyond its boundaries. Referring to the "Iron Curtain" that the Kremlin was drawing around Eastern Europe, he called for Britain and America to stand as allies against Soviet Communism. Churchill had not lost his touch for the timely flourish of rhetoric. He crystallized what many people were feeling in their bones, displayed a buoyant spirit of conviction, and, as George Kennan had before him, motivated James Forrestal to seek out Churchill to establish a meeting of minds. Though Truman would take criticism for letting a foreign head of state hold forth so strongly during a visit, he welcomed the robust anticommunism for which the British prime minister stood.

On the tenth, the Navy secretary lunched with Truman's chief of staff, Fleet Admiral William Leahy, and the former U.S. ambassador to the Soviet Union, William Bullitt, Jr. Having once held out great hope for U.S.-Soviet relations, Bullitt was troubled by Russia's conduct and hoped the White House would take a strong stand. Afterward, Forrestal saw Churchill for more than an hour. "He was very gloomy about coming to any accommodation with Russia unless and until it became clear to the Russians that they would be met with force if they continued the expansion," Forrestal would write, referring to Moscow's pressure on Greece, Turkey, and Italy. "He agreed with my analysis not only that we are dealing with Russia as a national entity but with the expanding power of Russia under Peter the Great plus the additional missionary force of a religion."

At the U.S. embassy in Moscow, George Kennan argued the futility of appealing to Stalin's better angels. He was sure those cherubs had fallen. Kennan wrote to his colleagues in Washington, "Some of us here tried to conceive [of] the measures our country would have to take if it really wished to pursue, at all costs, the goal of disarming Soviet suspicions. We have come to the conclusion that nothing short of complete

disarmament, delivery of our air and naval forces to Russia, and resign-
ing of the powers of government to American communists would even
dent this problem: and even then we believe—and this is not facetious—
that Moscow would smell a trap and would continue to harbor the most
baleful misgivings."

Those words could just as well have come from the Navy secretary.
Forrestal and Byrnes thought it might be time to give Stalin reason to
think again. Though the Truman White House had yet to declare policy that could give coherence to such a naval deployment, the president
expected the fleet to insert itself into the vacuum. It was the only service
branch that could do so with a sense of heavy and sustained capital
presence. Forrestal wanted to force the Kremlin to audit the risks of its
behavior. A show of resolve in the Med might make the Soviets reconsider the potential costs of their covert project to destabilize war-
weakened Europe.

IN EARLY MARCH, by James Forrestal's initiative, the U.S. Navy established the new Eighth Fleet at Norfolk. Admiral Jonas H. Ingram, the
commander in chief of the Atlantic Fleet, gave it the bulk of his aircraft
carrier strength and placed it under command of the best and saltiest
flag officer for the job, Marc Mitscher. Though it was meant to resemble the type of naval task force that had won the Pacific War, Mitscher
would have a long way to go before it could stand even as a shadow of
the old Task Force 58. Some powerful new ships, however, gave him a
creditable foundation upon which to build.

On hand at Norfolk were two of the three new *Midway*-class aircraft
carriers, the USS *Midway* and *Franklin D. Roosevelt*. With a length of
968 feet and a displacement of 55,000 tons fully loaded, the new flattops
were more than half again as large as those of the *Essex* class of World
War II. With armored flight decks and triple-partitioned hangars, they
were engineered to avoid the nightmare that had haunted U.S. carriers
during the war: contagious fires below. Though their upsized dimensions made them unable to transit the Panama Canal, they could carry
half again the *Essex*'s capacity of ninety aircraft.

In Norfolk, they were joined by the *Essex*-class carriers *Leyte* and *Philippine Sea,* four escort carriers, the battleships *Missouri* and *Wisconsin,* eight cruisers, fifty-four destroyers, twenty destroyer escorts, and fifty-one submarines. For the time being, though, expectations would have to be checked. Mitscher faced a hard climb to bring the striking force to the level of proficiency that just six months earlier had seemed its birthright. What his ships lacked was the one thing that turned any warship into a weapon: a full complement of sailors properly trained for the job.

When Mitscher reported to Norfolk to fly his new four-star flag on the *Franklin D. Roosevelt,* he found a shortage of experienced pilots, aircrew, and aviation-rated sailors. The Eighth Fleet chief of staff, Commodore Arleigh Burke, called it a "sad situation." The drawdown that had sapped the Navy of most of the Atlantic Fleet suffered an additional handicap because commanders in the Pacific had been hoarding senior people and filling ships returning stateside with short-timers, who were susceptible to leaving the service. Burke said, "People were flocking to be discharged and we were putting ships out of commission, and before the ships could get out of commission there was nobody left in the ships to decommission them, let alone mothball them." Training schools were left short of instructors. To staff the most essential schools with the barest skeleton crews, Burke put some ships out of commission in order to make their best petty officers available for reassignment. Ingram promised to do everything possible to round up more experienced men. "There wasn't a single ship of the Atlantic Fleet that was capable of any kind of a combat operation," Burke said with only a touch of latter-day exaggeration. Though Forrestal liked the idea of sending a squadron with the *Missouri* to the Mediterranean, Byrnes thought it would be too much to send two carriers to join them. For Nimitz, the fleetwide personnel shortage would make it hard to justify such a large deployment. The carriers, especially, had to relearn some basics.

As Mitscher was assembling his team at Norfolk, the carrier USS *Midway* was returning from Arctic Ocean waters. An exercise there d tested the ability of carriers to operate in extreme cold. Rear Admiral John H. Cassady, advised by officers from the Canadian navy, took his ships into low-pressure areas where conditions of ice, snow, and cold were amplified by foul weather. On March 13, fifty-five-knot winds put the *Midway*'s escorting destroyers into capsize-threatening rolls whenever they had to turn broadside to the swells in order to avoid ice floes. "Men working in exposed spots learned that the old timers' stories of icy Arctic winds were not idle tales," a participating officer wrote. The first lesson of Operation Frostbite was important: that carriers could operate well in the far North Atlantic, even north of the Labrador Sea. In polar latitudes, the temperature of the ocean, warmed by the Gulf Stream, moderated the bitter cold that prevails on nearby shores. When land bases were blanketed by extreme cold, relatively warmer sea temperatures, averaging around 27 degrees Fahrenheit, kept the ice from hardening to the point where it stopped aircraft from flying. Cassady found that carrier planes could fly where land-based planes could not. Joint Chiefs of Staff war plans would be written on the assumption that U.S. airpower would control the airspace over the Arctic. Yet looking "down" upon the globe from the northern polar axis, it was easy to see that America's prospective enemy was well positioned to dominate the kingdom of ice. In a time when proficiency had declined, the Arctic exercise was a boost for the Navy's confidence. It expanded the map, promoted new thinking about where and how the fleet could operate. It was lost on no one that unexplored parts of the world were becoming strategically important.

ON MARCH 22, the *Missouri* departed Norfolk without escort, bound for Turkey. After a nine-day solo transit of the Atlantic, she arrived at Gibraltar, where she became the flagship of Admiral Henry K. Hewitt, commander of the U.S. Twelfth Fleet. Based in London, the once-powerful command had run the 1944 Normandy landings. Ever afterward, it had lacked a reason for being. Joined by the cruiser USS *Providence* and the destroyer *Power,* the *Missouri* transited the Dardanelles and the Sea of Marmara, finally dropping anchor at Istanbul on the Bosporus, right on the doorstep of Joseph Stalin's Black Sea squadron.

Predictably attracting so much public interest and press attention, the *Missouri*'s mission was rated a rousing success. On the eve of the battleship's arrival, a Turkish columnist wrote that his countrymen regarded "the most colossal American warship as the symbol of an idealism which aspires to realize tomorrow's peace." Thereafter, she called at Piraeus, Greece, joined by a Turkish and two Greek destroyers. Greek citizens crowded the rocky bluff overlooking Phaleron Bay, waving handkerchiefs as the *Missouri* issued a main battery salute. With the vessel close enough for onlookers to hear the announcements from her loudspeakers, the ship was, as an Athens newspaper claimed, like a "sedative" to a "warlike neurosis" arising from Soviet maneuvers in the region. With Moscow aiding the rebellion by Greek Communists (who were largely managed by Tito in neighboring Yugoslavia), the effect of the American presence was powerful. Another editorialist wrote, "Around us here and over the Balkans hovers the great Russian shadow. So America comes here, too, to tell us: 'Hold tight, and you may be sure we are with you.'" An indication that the Kremlin had received the message came when Foreign Minister Molotov complained of the continuing U.S.-British alliance and the reach of American bases around the world.

The idea that the United States was imposing a global Pax Americana was rhetoric for Communists everywhere in 1946. The notion was laughable to Harry Truman. Speaking to reporters at the White House on April 17, the president pointed out that in the "frenzied demobilization" since war's end, almost seven million men had received discharges from the Army alone. He would call it "the most remarkable demobilization in the history of the world—or disintegration, if you want to call it that." Of all the victors in war of the past several centuries, Truman thought it noteworthy that none had thrown to the ground the fruits of victory as fast as America had. It was not the American way to maintain a large military in peacetime. Though Truman lamented that the United States was "stripping itself of the strength necessary to support its moral leadership" at the United Nations, his insistence upon thrift all but assured that the military would continue to shrink. The president required about $6 billion a year to go to servicing the national debt. Of what was left, no more than one-third could be allocated to national defense. The Pentagon was left to pinch its pennies.

The president professed the federal budget to be "one of my more serious hobbies." And Forrestal saw the president's insistence upon thrift in that same light: the work of an amateur, and simplistic, akin to home economics. Truman's pay-as-you-go manner of financing national defense was "a parochial view, with which (it must be said) most Americans in the late spring of 1946 would have agreed," Forrestal noted. "First you paid your debts; then you decided how much you could afford for the vast business of government."

The Navy felt the squeeze. Though a service magazine would call Forrestal's proposed 1947 appropriation "the largest peacetime Navy budget in U.S. history," the amount that the president finally requested from Congress, $3.8 billion, deserved no such superlative. It was a reduction of more than 80 percent from naval expenditures in 1946. Of all the Navy's bureaus and departments, the Marine Corps could claim victory for suffering the smallest cut: Its $353 million was just 75 percent less than its 1946 allocation. Following the war years, when $184 billion had been spent to produce 1,250 major combatant ships, 90,000 armored vehicles, 300,000 aircraft, and more than 500,000 artillery pieces, the future was austere. In 1946, the active-duty fleet had 319 major combatants, with 176 assigned to the Pacific and 143 in the Atlantic. The three *Midway*-class aircraft carriers were the most capable of the thirteen flattops on active service. The *Franklin D. Roosevelt, Midway,* and two *Essex*-class ships were part of the Atlantic Fleet. The *Coral Sea* was the pride of the Pacific Fleet's nine-carrier force. The four *Iowa*-class battleships were evenly split between the two fleets. The Pacific Fleet had twenty cruisers, the Atlantic eight. Though a ready reserve fleet was maintained on each coast for use in training—three fast carriers in the Atlantic and two in the Pacific, all six battleships of the *North Carolina* and *South Dakota* classes, evenly divided, and a total of eighteen cruisers and forty destroyers—the active forces were threadbare, and not just in hulls. Manpower had been cut perilously close to the half-million-man level that Nimitz and Forrestal considered the minimum.

With worldwide responsibilities after the war, the Navy needed to maintain fifty-three bases. Pearl Harbor and the islands of Guam and Saipan anchored the fleet's forward presence in the Pacific, with secondary bases at Okinawa in the Ryukyus, in the Philippines, and at the Port of Balboa on the Panama Canal. In the Atlantic and Caribbean, the center of gravity was Roosevelt Roads in Puerto Rico, with important secondary bases and stations at San Juan; Guantanamo Bay, Cuba; Trinidad; Bermuda; Coco Solo in Panama; Argentia, Newfoundland; and St. Thomas, Virgin Islands.

As he set about restoring competency of the combat fleet to protect such a widespread domain, Admiral Mitscher invited the president to come to Norfolk. He was keen for him to see the Atlantic carrier striking force in its postwar operational debut. Involving both the *Midway* and the *Franklin D. Roosevelt* running with reduced crew complements, the exercise would cultivate a state of readiness that had been all but lost in nine short months.

Truman arrived at Atlantic Fleet headquarters on April 22 with his chief of staff, Fleet Admiral William D. Leahy, among his entourage of two dozen. Helping the president to appreciate the U.S. Navy had been a pet project of Chester Nimitz during his whole tenure as CNO. Whenever Truman visited his "Little White House" in Old Town, Key West, which had once served as an officers' quarters on the submarine base there and was now a seasonal home for the president, Nimitz invited him to ride along on submarines and ships. When Truman was piped aboard the *Franklin D. Roosevelt* to join Forrestal, Leahy, Nimitz, and Mitscher on the carrier's navigation deck, the effect was precisely what Mitscher wanted. As word spread of the VIP gathering, all hands in the task force realized an opportunity was at hand. As soon as the elements of the striking force made rendezvous about a hundred miles southeast of the Virginia Capes, the show began.

Truman watched raptly as the task force carried out demonstrations of the tradecraft of naval air combat, from air gunnery to communications to radar-enabled direction of fighter planes. Somewhere over the horizon, the *Midway* was preparing to launch a mock air attack on the large circular formation centered by the flagship. Arleigh Burke didn't think the president noticed how raggedly executed it all was. Burke and the Eighth Fleet operations officer, Charles D. Griffin, occasionally had to step in and micromanage things, as when a destroyer captain didn't know how to shift his station in the screen on order from Mitscher.

When the pilots from the *Midway* arrived overhead and the Helldivers began their runs, Burke suspected the Air Force might take advantage of the occasion. Several air bases were within range of the exercise and the heirs of Jimmy Doolittle were always ready to inflict trouble. Burke directed the radar operators to watch for bogies at high altitude.

"While the president was in the flag plot looking at all the scopes and seeing how this fleet was controlled, we picked up a few blips out to the west at high altitude," Burke recalled. "So they told Admiral Mitscher and he told the president that we thought there might be some bogies on the screen. We knocked off our exercises and orbited our air groups higher, putting them in position for attacks against these bogies. Sure enough, it was the Air Force, coming out to bomb the fleet."

Everyone was delighted that the commander in chief was on hand to see what ensued: a beautifully executed Navy ambush. Twenty miles out, F4U Corsairs pounced out of the clouds. The combat air patrol caught the intruders and made it a rout. "We clobbered the hell out of them, on an exercise basis," Burke said. "The president chuckled all the time. He thought it was a hell of a good thing for the Air Force to do, and for us, too. It would have been a hell of a setback if we'd been caught not prepared for that sort of monkey business. He was very happy."

When Burke and Griffin finally turned in after two days on their feet, stealing naps on the steel deck during pauses in the action, they were exhausted. Much of what they had seen fell short of their exacting standard. The U.S. carrier task force was but a shadow of what had ruled the seas less than a year ago. They had been redesignated as "task fleets," which seemed to lack the majesty of the unmodified noun. In the Pacific, the Third and Fifth fleets were gone. The First Task Fleet, powerful in name only, was an administrative organization on the West Coast. Its main operating forces sailed under the flag of the Seventh Task Fleet, whose forebear, the Seventh Fleet, had been created in 1943 to support General MacArthur's army. The Second Task Fleet in Norfolk gave training and administrative support to the Sixth Task Fleet in the Mediterranean, facing the primary axis of Soviet naval ambitions.

Tight budgets kept plans from flourishing afloat. With little money to operate, commanders had few opportunities to go to sea and train. "They simply didn't know how to handle a group of ships," Admiral Dennison lamented. Captains turned in formation at their peril. The pilots were no less green. Just one in four had flown in combat before.

The idea of operating fast carriers out of the East Coast was a novelty in every way. For four years, the trade of naval air warfare had been practiced only in the Pacific. In the Atlantic, the Navy's effort had concentrated on escorting convoys to Europe and defending against submarines, with the occasional excitement of a German battleship to chase. As Mitscher and Burke sought to revive the best of their days, it was possible, in that bank of fog between wakefulness and sleep, to feel that they were in another ocean altogether, running with the fast carriers again, masters of their universe.

Exercises continued for six more weeks as Mitscher sharpened his crews in the Caribbean. Off Culebra, near Puerto Rico, a mock amphibious landing was staged. Going over the beaches at Medio Mundo, the First Special Marine Brigade under Brigadier General David R. Nimmer rediscovered their own birthright of the world war, embarking onto landing craft, forming up at the line of departure, and assaulting a defended shore. They rehearsed how to take an airfield while keeping contact with flanking units, holding radio contact with fire support ships while Corsairs buzzed the treetops. By the middle of May the majority of Nimmer's men, fresh from boot camp at Parris Island, were dusty veterans of Puerto Rico's coral-sand roads.

Further out at sea, the *Midway,* deemed crippled, faced simulated attack by the cruisers *Macon, Dayton,* and *Little Rock* while her destroyer screen made smoke and struck back with torpedoes. When it was over, the participating ships had punch lists of repairs a hundred items long. Yet exuberance prevailed. "They were surprisingly good, the air squadrons particularly," Mitscher would say. He thought the men had earned some liberty. Some free time at Guantanamo Bay was their cherished reward. The festive mood carried with them all the way back to New York for Fleet Week.

The procession of the task force consumed all of May 27. The *Missouri,* back from the Med, led the column into the harbor against a driving rain, eventually mooring at the Hudson River pier at West Seventy-second Street. The *Franklin D. Roosevelt* brought up the rear, mooring at Pier 90 at West Fiftieth Street.

The sense of purpose and presence was a boost to morale at a time when the news was full of strife between former friends. At the Paris Peace Conference, the pressing question was how the Allied powers should govern Germany in peace. As debate over the governance of the partitioned nation and the details of its denazification continued, Foreign Minister Molotov leveled accusations of a U.S.-British conspiracy. With France maintaining a studied neutrality—Charles De Gaulle's coalition government was possible only by robust participation of the Communist Party—Molotov charged that the leading Allied powers were waging "an offensive against the Soviet Union" and complained about U.S. naval and air bases "in all parts of the globe." As Washington was coming to understand, Moscow's vision of siege, and sense of opportunity too, reached outward in all directions from its colossal Eurasian expanse.

That summer, on Admiral Jonas Ingram's watch as the commander in chief of the Atlantic Fleet, U.S. carrier airpower took root on the East Coast for the first time. The ability to deploy carriers worldwide gave rise to the question: What rival nation, and whose blue-water fleet, might it need to fight? In spite of their interest in submarines, the Soviets had nothing resembling a major surface task force. What were U.S. carriers to do against the icebound land colossus of which George Kennan had so darkly warned? In the short term, the question did not need an answer. After the war, Washington did not view the Atlantic primarily as a naval battlefront. The journalist Walter Lippmann spoke for prevailing official opinion in the West when he wrote, in the midst of World War II, "The Atlantic basin is not the frontier between Europe and the Americas. It is the inland sea of a community of nations allied with one another by geography, history, and vital necessity." It was an open question whether the Soviets could be coaxed to join that community.

The commander in chief of Soviet naval forces in 1946, Admiral of the Fleet Nikolay G. Kuznetsov, presided over a force of 241 submarines, 3 uncompleted 64,000-ton battleships, 7 heavy cruisers, 2 light cruisers, and 60 destroyers and other ocean escorts. Devoid of aircraft carriers and lacking a tradition in naval aviation, the Soviet navy had little capacity for projecting power in the modern mode.

WHEN THEY SPOKE on June 6, Forrestal and Byrnes agreed that the *Missouri*'s visit to Istanbul had been a great success. The Navy secretary mentioned his idea of "sending casual cruisers unannounced" to the Mediterranean, "not a fleet or task force, but in small units . . . so that we may establish the custom of the American flag being flown in those waters." Their regular presence would be a tonic to local nerves. Wherever the opportunity presented itself, Forrestal shared his sense of alarm about Soviet ambitions. Nimitz suggested that the two service secretaries attend the next meeting of the Joint Chiefs of Staff, where Secretary of War Robert Patterson would be present for a discussion of the Soviet threat in Europe.

At that meeting, held on June 10, the Army analyzed the danger of the Soviet buildup of ground forces facing the north German plain. "It was ominous," Forrestal recorded. Neither Britain nor the United States had the forces to repel it, "nor was there much else, in Turkey, France, or Spain on which to rely." Forrestal knew from history that America was not alone in having enjoyed a long period of military dominance. A few days later, Forrestal heard Sumner Welles express a dim view about a world out of balance. But such things were never permanent. Forrestal had warned the Senate in January of "conditions which ensured the failure of an apparently impervious formula. In our own cases security of the nation has to be viewed not merely in the light

of our military power, but in the light of restoration of balance throughout the world."

Balance was very much on Forrestal's mind when he flew to San
Francisco on June 24 to begin a world tour to assess the state of his fortress. From Treasure Island, he flew to Bikini Atoll in the Central Pacific. His first order of business there was to witness the show that Joint
Task Force One was about to put on for the world.

4

The Big Jolt: Operation Crossroads

IN THE SPRING OF 1946, BY ORDER OF GENERAL CURTIS LeMAY, Paul W. Tibbets reported to Army Air Forces headquarters at Bolling Field in Washington, D.C., to discuss the setup of Operation Crossroads, the world's first test of atomic bombs against warships. As the first man to use such a weapon in combat, Colonel Tibbets was considered an important source of counsel. He might well have been the best available pilot to fly the B-29 that would drop on Bikini, too, but with a great many aviators angling for the honor of following in the great Billy Mitchell's footsteps by destroying a fleet, it was decided to stage a competition.

Later that year, outside Albuquerque, ambitious rivals took turns taking a B-29 to thirty thousand feet over a test range, releasing dummy weapons, and executing the blast-evasive diving turn that Tibbets had perfected during the war. It should have been no surprise that he and his bombardier, Thomas Ferebee, scored the smallest average error, 237 feet. The surprise came when the job was handed to another crew. Tibbets was incensed. He smelled politics. As Halsey could have told him, it was everywhere.

In Washington, the frenzied political season had delayed the legislative agenda to the point that the fourteen Congressmen named to serve on a presidential commission to observe the test could not make it to

Bikini by the appointed date in May. The Joint Chiefs of Staff accommodated them by postponing it six weeks. Meanwhile, the Army continued with its bombastic rhetoric. Speaking before the Aviation Writers Association in March, Hap Arnold's successor as commanding general of the U.S. Army Air Forces, General Carl A. Spaatz, asked, "Why should we have a navy at all? . . . There are no enemies for it to fight, except apparently the Army Air Force. In this day and age, to talk of fighting the next war on the oceans is a ridiculous assumption. The only reason for us to have a navy is just because someone else has a navy and we certainly don't need to waste money on that." To launch an atomic-armed B-29 from the sea, Spaatz mused, would require an aircraft carrier with a flight deck six thousand feet long.

But the questions posed by the atomic bomb went beyond the methods of their delivery. The question of what nations should be allowed to have them was on the table as well. Secretary of War Stimson and others, including the head of the U.S. delegation to the UN Atomic Energy Commission, Bernard Baruch, believed the secret of the bomb should be shared with the Allied nations. Stimson thought America had a duty to promote atomic research for peaceful application. He supported a plan floated by Baruch, known as the Acheson-Lilienthal Plan, which provided for the UN-supervised cessation of atomic weapons development and the destruction of all stockpiles. The secretary of the treasury, Fred M. Vinson, and Attorney General Tom C. Clark thought America should maintain its exclusive ownership of the secret, hold it close, leverage it, and accelerate research. Stimson countered, "We do not have a secret to give away—the secret will give away itself." Joseph E. Davies, who had served as U.S. ambassador to the Soviet Union in the years before Hitler invaded, told a newspaper that Russia "in self-defense, has every moral right to seek atomic-bomb secrets through military espionage if excluded from such information by her former fighting allies." In denying the bomb to Stalin, Davies said, the West was "sowing the seeds of war." Harnessing its peaceful potential in a consortium of nations would make possible its control, Stimson said. James Forrestal considered the bomb "the property of the American people" and believed the national effort in atomic research, like defense policy more broadly, should sit under civilian control. And so the divergent partisan politics of atomic weaponry took root.

But it was one thing for Washington to place such trust in the United Kingdom and Canada. Could the other nominal Allied power, the Soviet Union, operate in good faith within an international order? The Soviet representative on the UN Security Council, Andrei Gromyko, said that Moscow would go along, but insisted upon self-monitoring without supranational authority or inspections. The Soviets, who had stolen most of the secrets of the bomb via its agents within the U.S. program, coveted the freedom to build their own bomb. The design flaw of the UN Security Council was manifested at the start: All sides rejected the others' proposals.

As preparations continued to carry out Operation Crossroads, Forrestal urged UN observers not to see the test as a "gesture of war aggression or a threat." As a live-fire exercise of unprecedented scale, it needed a benign public rationale. News reports were scaring the public, adding energy if not rigor to the case against it. Urgent requests to cancel the exercise began arriving daily in Admiral Blandy's "fan mail" soon after his appointment as Joint Task Force commander was announced. His correspondents envisioned diverse dire consequences: blast-induced earthquakes and tidal waves, new mountains pushing up from below the sea, oceans turning to gas. One letter writer feared the atomic concussion could blow out the bottom of the sea and let all of the water run down the hole. Another believed it would destroy gravity itself. Admiral Blandy was enlisted to deny each of these things, including the accusation, leveled by a critic, that he was "an atomic playboy, exploding these bombs to satisfy his personal whim." Still, a major London insurance carrier, advised by its actuaries as to this new spectrum of risk, decided that their life policies would no longer cover death by atomic explosion.

A numerous and passionate citizenry wrote Blandy objecting to the plan, adopted from Newson's suggestion, to place animals on the target ships. "Nothing that the German doctors did in the Belsen Concentration Camp was any worse than this," wrote a woman from Hartford,

Connecticut. To such complaints Blandy's office issued a form response: "The medical advisors of the Army and Navy were very insistent that if they are to assume the responsibility for the future defense, welfare and treatment of personnel of the Armed Services, they must know more precisely just what biological effects may be encountered in such attacks." To this a correspondent replied, "Would not fresh blood from the slaughterhouse suffice—or criminals from prisons, volunteers, with the promise they will be granted a pardon?"

As the planners of Joint Task Force One procured pigs, goats, and rats to stand as passengers on the target fleet, they were determined to keep bystanders out of the way. In February, the U.S. naval officer who served as military governor of the Marshall Islands ordered the evacuation of Bikini Atoll's 167 residents so that the experiment could be performed "for the good of mankind." On March 7, they were moved to another island, Rongerik. Bikini's small church was disassembled and taken there too along with several dozen prefabricated thatched-roof huts, and cisterns for twenty-three thousand gallons of fresh water to hold the residents until rainy season. With its native community gone, Bikini was idyllic, shining pure and white against the dazzling stasis of the Central Pacific. The atoll had been spared the fury and tumult that had washed over its neighbors in the Marshalls during the war. The struggle against Imperial Japan had turned Kwajalein and Eniwetok into battlefields, then into gathering places for warriors and heavy cargoes, and then showcases of efficient transport and the marshaling and projection of military power. But Bikini, located about two hundred miles northwest of Kwajalein, had been uninteresting to strategists. None of the twenty-three coral divots that formed it could hold an airfield, and the lagoon enclosed by their arc was too small to shelter fleets. Bikini remained a grace note of white against the sea rolling blue, thronged by sea birds and fish. Late in the spring of 1946, the invasion of modernity began.

Unlike the first atomic test, conducted in New Mexico in July 1945 in extreme secrecy and with meager instrumentation, Operation Crossroads would be a meticulously recorded experiment—Armageddon in a field laboratory. The advance echelon of Joint Task Force One included explosives technicians, who without fanfare began demolishing coral reefs to expand the lagoon to hold the seventy-three-ship target fleet. Scientists of the Los Alamos Laboratory's Measurement Group arrived on May 5, housed in the laboratory ship *Cumberland Sound.* They oversaw the installation of metal towers on the beach, festooned with cameras and sensors to measure airborne blast, shock waves in the water, and seismography. Calibrated poles, sunk into the lagoon floor within view of the cameras, would enable measurement of wave heights. Hydrophones mounted on buoys would read and retransmit water pressure readings. Plans were drawn up to deploy drone boats to take water samples. B-17 Flying Fortresses operated by remote control would drop air-blast gauges and test the air for radiation. A Navy oceanography group would study the bomb's effects on the biology, geology, and fisheries of the lagoon. Teams from the Naval Research Laboratory and the Army Signal Corps would measure the reflection of radar waves and other electronic phenomena in the intensely ionized atmosphere. Geiger counters placed on the target ships would relay their readings by telemetry.

So voluminous was the technical preparation that it was a bit of an anticlimax when the sacrificial fleet itself began to arrive. At the end of May, from Pearl Harbor, obsolete and scheduled for disposal, came the battleships *Arkansas, Nevada, New York,* and *Pennsylvania,* the aircraft carriers *Independence* and *Saratoga,* the heavy cruisers *Pensacola* and *Salt Lake City,* a dozen destroyers, eight submarines, and assorted amphibious vessels and auxiliaries. Three Axis warships were among the guinea pigs: Japan's battleship *Nagato* and light cruiser *Sakawa* and the German heavy cruiser *Prinz Eugen.* The latter had been taken into U.S. service at Bremerhaven, Germany, in January. With her crew of 574 German sailors, long of hair and wearing brown dungarees, and under eight U.S. Navy officers and eighty American enlisted men, she had steamed across the Atlantic to Boston, then to Philadelphia, where two of her eight-inch guns were extracted from her forward turret and study was made of her nickel-steel armor plate and her installation of hull-mounted hydrophones—listening devices that enabled her to detect enemy ships at long range. When orders came to leave for the Pacific, the German crew was discharged and she set sail for Panama.

As technicians continued making ready the array of test sensors, the Army checked the handiwork of its quartermasters in Hawaii, who had installed on the decks of the ships the equivalent of a whole supply depot. Drums of oil and bales of trousers; cartons of combat boots, cotton drawers, and leather gloves; boxes of pork loin and smoked hams. All were stacked on pallets and lashed to the deck with steel cable. Because the effect of radiation on hydrocarbons and synthetic products was of special interest, the ships embarked drums containing different grades of gasoline, DDT, and more dangerous chemicals.

Secretly dispatched from the Edgewood Arsenal in Maryland and set up on the decks of the *Nevada* and the *Independence* were fifteen boxes of artillery shells loaded with mustard gas, nitrogen mustard, phosgene, cyanogen chloride, and tabun, a nerve agent. Most of June was consumed with meticulous preparations to set up the target fleet array, installing their payloads and sensors, and checking and rechecking the systems by which the bombs would be set off and their effects registered and recorded. The night before the test, at Kwajalein Island, about two hundred miles to the southeast of Bikini, the seaplane tender *Albemarle* disgorged a parcel to the pier to which she was tied. It was a twenty-kiloton atomic bomb.

On the morning of July 1, the day of the airborne blast, the amphibious command ship *Appalachian* arrived in Bikini lagoon and dropped anchor about twenty miles east of the target fleet, embarking members of the international press. Nearby were two other VIP-carrying ships—the *Blue Ridge,* with the military observer party, and the *Panamint,* accommodating officials from the United Nations Atomic Energy Commission, and journalists, invited with President Truman's approval to witness "Test Able."

Excitement spilled through the ships lying at anchor. A UN delegate from China was pleased to see the *Nagato,* for she had participated in the bombardment of Shanghai and other cities. "We are glad to see all vestiges of Japan's naval power wiped out by this terrific weapon," he

said. Though military effects were downplayed by the Truman administration as the purpose of the test, most observers had no illusions that
it would reveal much about the potential for peaceful uses of atomic
energy. A Soviet official who was said to be in charge of the uranium
supply of the Soviet Union's nuclear initiative, Dr. Semion P. Aleksandrov, showed an interest in the Sherman tank secured to the flight deck
of the *Saratoga*. "It will be interesting to see what happens to it. Such
knowledge is needed in the event of a third world war."

Before sunrise, a pair of B-29 Superfortresses took flight from Kwajalein and set course north for Bikini. The press observation aircraft,
nicknamed "the Voice," was equipped to relay news stories by radio. It
took off first so it would be in position to report on any disaster that
might befall the bomb-carrying plane on takeoff. From his swivel seat
in the bomber's fire-control station, news correspondent Frank Bar-
tholomew peered through the bubble window with field glasses as the
other B-29, *Dave's Dream,* flown by Major Woodrow P. Swancutt, lifted
off under watch of a fire brigade. In the bomb bay was a twenty-three-
kiloton fission weapon that a wag had labeled "Gilda," the title of a new
film featuring the superstar Rita Hayworth, whose pin-up likeness was
pasted to the ballistic case.

On schedule, the non-target ships—destroyers on patrol, repair
ships, transports used as quarters, and ships outfitted with instruments
of measurement and control—withdrew to safe areas outside the lagoon. Then the order went out for the setup crews to leave the seventy-
three ships in the target array. The last two men off the battleship *New
York* were Brooklyn representative John J. Rooney and the ship's former skipper, Lowe H. Bibby. The captain raised the red-and-yellow-
striped pennant of an abandoned ship, then took a piece of chalk,
climbed atop a turret, and wrote in neat block letters OLD SAILORS NEVER
DIE. Eyes glistening, he said to Rooney, "That sign will still be there this
time tomorrow," then stepped down the gangway, leaving Rooney to be
the last man off. Rooney said to a reporter that the ships "that had been
so alive suddenly seemed dead, peopled only by ghosts."

In the center of the array was the battleship *Nevada*. Painted bright
red and marked with a flashing strobe light for ease in spotting, she was

the aiming point for Swancutt's bombardier, Major Harold H. Wood, whose bomb would detonate at an altitude of fifteen hundred feet. The ships were positioned so as to receive gradated severities of damage, and to allow the majority of ships to survive so that their instruments could be harvested for data.

Flying in tight circles over the task force, the Voice intercepted the radio chatter between the command ship *Blue Ridge* and *Dave's Dream*. Admiral Blandy authorized Major Wood to drop "Gilda" any time after his first test run over the *Nevada*. After the second pass, he felt conditions were right. At 8:25 A.M. he activated the electronic tone indicating that release of the bomb was imminent. The radio chatter abruptly stopped as the radio transmitter in *Dave's Dream* issued its shrill whine. Observers had been warned not to look and they turned away. Wearing blackout goggles that allowed them to stare comfortably at the sun, they could scarcely see the silhouette of their neighbor at the rail, to which some held fast to brace against the expected concussion.

Filtered by goggles, the explosion appeared first as a purplish-white flash, a pinpoint that washed out all vision with about the same intensity as the sun. A great ring of steam grew rapidly in a fast-expanding circle. This was produced by the pressure front, which was itself visible as a shadow racing over the water's surface, ruffling the waves. When it reached the beach, the trees shook once and hard, like dish mops in a giant hand. A steward's mate standing at the starboard rail of the *Appalachian* muttered, "Hosanna, Lord, I'm still alive." But journalists observing on the *Panamint* were considerably underwhelmed. Led to expect cosmic fireworks, they now felt sour, cheated. They thought they had a front row seat to a stellar show, but from twenty miles away there was no impressive sound, heat, or shock. From sea level, the expanding ring of steam washed out the most striking visual effects. About ninety seconds along came a low rumble, like a distant thunderclap. Professor Aleksandrov shrugged, pointed at the rising cloud, and said, "Not so much. Large noise in newspapers. Small noise in reality." The Russian scientist borrowed a portable typewriter and began tapping a report to the Soviet government. None of the shipboard observers saw the rainbows they had been promised. "It was admired like a fairly unusual sunset," the Associated Press reported. "Within half an hour most observers were stretched out on deck chairs with bewildered expressions on their faces."

The effects were seen most impressively from the air. Aircraft were better equipped to approach and observe the fireball after the blast wave rushed by. After the expanding ring of condensation had dissipated, there it stood, rising skyward and spreading, coruscating through white-pink-white and sherbet-orange, the mushroom head turning out, and surging through the middle as the edges collapsed around. It took more than an hour for the cloud to dissipate in the stratosphere.

In the afternoon, Blandy permitted the observation flotilla to enter the lagoon for a closer look at the target ships. From twenty miles away, using a field glass, an observer could see the tops of the tallest masts. After an hour and a half of steaming, the superstructures of all the major target ships came within view. The pinnacle of the *Nagato*'s foremast tower caught the eye. A black plume rose from the *Saratoga,* but as she came within view, thirty aircraft were still parked on her flight deck amid the thickening gouts of smoke.

The aircraft carrier's former commanding officer, Captain Stanhope Ring, studied the *Saratoga* through a long glass, cringing as if wounded. As the *Panamint* carried him closer, he breathed more easily. The fires seemed to have diminished. "It could be controlled easily if men were still aboard. At least she's still afloat," Ring said.

Still afloat. This was the astounding result of the airborne blast, known as Test Able. Just five ships were sunk outright, the largest of them the cruiser *Sakawa,* 8,000 tons, which didn't go down till the next day. The destroyer *Lamson* capsized and needed several hours to sink. Many expected the *Nevada* to be a loss, sitting at the hypocenter, where blast pressures would be estimated at one hundred pounds per square inch. All that was visibly wrong with the battleship was a wrecked Kingfisher floatplane on her after catapult, a destroyed utility crane, and several sizable dishes in her main deck.

The *Saratoga,* twenty-three hundred yards from the explosion, was hit from almost directly astern. Nearly all of the test items on the flight deck were destroyed. Metal containers burst, glass containers melted. But a field safe, scorched on the outside, kept its documents safe.

Moored a hundred yards astern the *Nevada,* the submarine *Skate* capsized briefly but stood promptly aright, buoyancy preserved by her stout pressure hull. The fires on the *Saratoga* were produced by the ignition of her exposed pallets of Army supplies. The cruiser *Pensacola* had her funnels and upper works battered and bent forward but was otherwise intact. On the *Prinz Eugen,* shadows of her turret were cast upon her light gray superstructure, indicating the bearing of the flash. The more heavily armored ships, the *Arkansas, Nagato, New York,* and *Pennsylvania,* had only superficial scars, bent plating in their superstructure and upper works. Just six hundred yards from the hypocenter—much closer than expected—the battleship *Arkansas* was hit from the starboard quarter, from about four o'clock. The flash ignited the pallets of quartermaster stores, which burned intensely enough to leave charred outlines on the deck. Worst off, a wholesale floating ruin, was the aircraft carrier *Independence*. With her high freeboard and silhouette, she presented a near-vertical face to the blast and showed poorly for it. The shock wave caved in her port quarter, carried away her island superstructure, and swept the flight deck of all test items, including the containers of chemical weapons and eight aircraft. When gasoline in the hangar deck ignited, secondary explosions tore through her. But even she remained afloat.

Though Blandy announced from his flagship, "The bomb was dropped with very good accuracy. I must say here that I am very well pleased. . . . It could not have been better," something had gone wrong. Indeed, *Dave's Dream* had dropped the bomb eighteen hundred feet off target. Taking an unplanned direct hit was the USS *Gilliam*. The landing ship tank (LST) contained sensors that were not supposed to be destroyed. Other ships were too far from the blast for their instruments to perform their function.

At Kwajalein, Curtis LeMay went ballistic. "What the hell happened?" he demanded of Paul Tibbets, whose consolation was to serve as a technical adviser to the aerial task force. Tibbets told him that incorrect ballistic data had been dialed into the bombsight in *Dave's*

Dream. "The reporters didn't ask embarrassing questions, and the air force managed to leave them with the impression that the whole thing was a success," Tibbets wrote. When he talked to Carl Spaatz, the general shook his head and said, "We'll hear about this for the rest of our lives." For the bombshell Rita Hayworth, this premiere had been a rare flop.

THE ATOMIC CLOUD was just a few hours gone when boats began motoring around the lagoon, crews playing streams of water across the targets in an effort to decontaminate them. As soon as they were considered "Geiger sweet," radioactivity levels within tolerances, Admiral Blandy's deputy, Deak Parsons, sent technical survey teams aboard the damaged ships. Overhead, remote-controlled fighter aircraft, F6F Hellcat drones launched from the carrier *Shangri-La,* flew through the ionized air with photographic plates taped to their control sticks to read radiation levels. Fifty-four hours after the explosion, inspection teams began boarding the target ships. Blandy said he expected to have an idea of the bomb's efficiency in a day or two, though better results would take as much as a month.

Airborne radiation levels proved to be minimal. But on the ships themselves, it was another matter. As Congressman Rooney had said, the vacant ships felt dead, like the lairs of ghosts. Were they still the same? Something had undoubtedly overcome them. The survey crews would soon see this on their Geiger counters, which popped and crackled as the small boats closed in.

Though the largest of the target ships seemed to take the physical battering well enough, the question of human survivability was darker. The best measure of it was the "biological test material" installed on board. Two hundred pigs, two hundred goats, and four thousand white rats had been distributed among the ships, in corrals and metal boxes placed atop gun mounts, signal platforms, wherever crews stood at stations. Some of the pigs wore standard Navy antiflash suits and were smeared with antiflash lotion. Some of the goats were shaved to expose bare skin. "The medics generally feel they could do much more good in the interests of science if the animals are wounded than if they are killed," said the head of the Navy medical section, Captain R. H. Draeger. He wanted "radiation-sick animals, not radiation-dead ones." He got them. On the forecastle deck of the *Pennsylvania,* which was sixteen hundred feet from the hypocenter and struck from astern, a billy goat and a nanny goat "seemed lonesome but otherwise unharmed unless by slow-acting radiation." They were taken to a specially equipped transport for study.

The Bureau of Ships was optimistic about the results, for the target ships had withstood the pressure loads imposed by the aerial blast. No ship was atomized. None disintegrated or glowed with radioactivity. Much of this had to do with the inaccuracy of the bomb. "The net result of this was that much of the data that was expected to be collected was lost because the important ships were in the middle of the array," said Captain Frederick Ashworth, one of Blandy's deputies. Any given ship's actual distance from ground zero was unknowable because of uncertainty about the degree of error. However, good relative measurements were recorded by beer cans placed around the decks of the target ships—their movement revealed the flow of the shock wave—and by a device known as a Penney harp. The brainchild of Los Alamos physicist William Penney, this was an array of metal pipes of differing lengths welded to a base plate. The degree to which each pipe was bent indicated the strength of the overpressure. "The earliest indication of the yield of the bomb came shortly after the test shot by collecting Penney's harps and observing the various deflections of the pipes," Ashworth said.

But it was Captain Draeger's findings, as well as the radiation measurements taken by Deak Parsons's technical team, that suggested the truest extent of the damage caused by the bomb. It was the penetrating electromagnetic radiation from the blast, more than blast or heat damage, that put the Bikini fleet out of action. Study of the animals revealed that "the initial flash of principal lethal radiations, which are gamma rays and neutrons, would have killed almost all personnel normally stationed aboard the ships centered around the air burst and many others at greater distances. . . . The effects of radiation exposure would not

have incapacitated all victims immediately, even some of the most severely affected might have remained at their stations several hours.
Thus it is possible that initial efforts at damage control might have kept
ships operating, but it is clear that vessels within a mile of an atomic
bomb air burst would eventually become inoperative due to crew casualties."

Even with the benefit of gross tactical error, with the bomb detonating a third of a mile off target, confounding sensors and leaving most of
the target ships afloat, the bomb had done something unexpected.
Though ships had defied it, they had been made combat-ineffective all
the same. Even still, it would be three weeks before Operation Crossroads showed the world the true face of Armageddon.

WHILE THEY PREPARED to stage the underwater blast, known as Test
Baker, Blandy, Parsons, and the Joint Task Force One brain trust explored the state of the target fleet while the Navy and Army chiefs back
home refined their arguments about the meaning of the bomb for their
services. The extent of radiological danger seldom appeared in the press
reports, in part because the data was held close by the technical team,
and in part because of the pyrotechnics of Test Able were underwhelm-
ing to observers. No such ennui would follow the detonation of planet
Earth's fifth atomic explosion.

Around midnight on July 23, puttering out to a landing craft situated in the middle of Bikini's lagoon, came the final executioner of the
target fleet. A thirty-three-year-old physicist and wartime veteran of
the Manhattan Project, Dr. Marshall G. Holloway was the director of
the Los Alamos field unit assigned to Crossroads, known as B Division.
With a team of technicians, under armed guard, Holloway boarded the
LSM-60, which had been modified with a special well through which a
watertight casing holding the plutonium implosion weapon would be
lowered. He checked the casing that held the Fat Man–type bomb, the
derrick that would lower it through the well, the tall radio mast that
would receive the detonation signal, and the radio circuitry that would
activate the timed detonator. Holloway and company spent the night

with the bomb, then left the vessel at six A.M., making the fifteen-mile ferry run across the lagoon to the *Cumberland Sound,* flagship of the Los Alamos Group, where Holloway took a seat at a control panel full of pushbuttons. Pressed in sequence, they started an atomic clock that began the fifty-second countdown to Test Baker.

Observing in a B-29 seven thousand feet above the lagoon, the correspondent Don Whitehead wrote, "This may be a preview of things to come—a pushbutton war with atomic weapons set off by radio impulses from a control board miles away. . . . There is a sense of unreality about this whole fabulous world of science where man unleashes forces equal to twenty-thousand tons of TNT merely by touching finger to button." Los Alamos's Manhattan District scientists nicknamed the Baker bomb Helen. "Helen of Troy, the face that launched a thousand ships," they explained. "Helen of Bikini, the bomb that sank a thousand ships—we hope." Detonating ninety feet below the surface of the lagoon, Helen displayed her power and it was fantastic. The device churned up a storm of vapor that formed a sphere that obscured most of the target array as it expanded with the pressure wave. On the *Panamint,* observers had no need to wear polarized goggles this time, as the water in the lagoon absorbed the initial flash. They watched through binoculars as the condensate evaporated, unveiling a towering cauliflower head of seawater and mud. Almost half a mile wide, it stood atop a base surge that pushed outward with a wave several hundred feet high. Against the wall of water surging outward from the hypocenter, not even a battleship stood a chance. The foaming ram hit the *Arkansas* first.

Battleships were typically majestic in death. Not the *Arkansas*. Situated two hundred fifty yards from lagoon zero, her 562-foot length registered as a dark mote in photographs, oriented to the vertical, dwarfed by the water that enveloped her and tossed her onto her side to swamp and sink immediately. The wall of water, traveling several hundred yards before it hit other capital ships, lost some of its wallop, and they did not sink right away. But the shocks delivered to their hulls from below and the surge of seawater that washed over their decks left them decidedly out of trim. As the cauliflower head peaked at about a mile high, it began to collapse, producing a second, more chaotic base surge that doused them once again in radiation-rich steam and spray, leaving lethal toxins in everything it touched.

When the mist cleared and ships were still visible, a cheer went up among the press observers in the observation B-29. But the celebration gave insufficient due to the damage wrought by the bomb. Four hundred yards from the blast, the carrier *Saratoga,* her flight deck swept clean and island carried away, was fractured below the waterline and seeping. Listing sharply, she went down by the stern about an hour later. The *Nagato* suffered flooding that would take her down in five days. Some wondered whether Bikini itself would be swamped by a radioactive tsunami, but the waves reaching shore were on the order of about seven feet.

The explosion bombarded the lagoon with unstable free neutrons, which rendered sodium, iodine, and other elements in the water highly radioactive—producing in the lagoon the radioactive equivalent of many hundred tons of radium, whose effects upon humans could be lethal after a few hours. The biggest of the survivors, including the *New York* and *Nevada,* were physically present but haunted by these ghosts. After the remote-controlled boats had collected their water samples and destroyers rushed them to Kwajalein for analysis, it was found that radiation levels were high enough to keep inspection parties at bay for four days, and even then only at their peril. All the pigs on all the ships were dead within a month.

5

THE NEUTRON BURN

WHEN BLANDY'S FLAGSHIP, THE USS MOUNT MCKINLEY, DE-parted Bikini's inner anchorage on August 2, radioactivity was found in her plumbing. "The green slime on the ship's side at the waterline has been gathering radioactivity enough to make itself felt in the crew's quarters," wrote Colonel A. W. Betts of the Army Corps of Engineers, who was on board, "so that the fleet is forced out into less active water for a while. A few days out here should lower our activity sufficiently to permit us to reenter the inner anchorage.... With the exception of crews doing the decontamination, most of us are now merely sitting on our hands waiting for the ships to cool down to where they can be boarded."

Four days later, on the first anniversary of the atomic attack on Hiroshima, Betts wrote to this same correspondent, Brigadier General K. D. Nichols, Farrell's successor as Manhattan District deputy commander: "Our advance into the target area has been so slow that I can see a long delay before any real information is to be gained from a study of the target ships. The last tolerance time limit I heard quoted for the *New York* and the *Pensacola* below decks was from five minutes to half an hour, and this they would permit only to essential workers in a salvage party.... Experience so far seems to indicate that the process of decontamination of very hot vessels is going to be a very long drawn out affair. Those vessels that have been washed several times show that

after the first treatment, which usually cuts the activity about fifty percent, very little progress is made with subsequent washings. They do
not get real results until they can get the ship cool enough to put a crew
aboard that can really scrub things down well.... They are working
hard at keeping the *Pensacola* pumped out to try to correct a list of almost ten degrees that was developing. The chief difficulty is that of
getting salvage personnel aboard. It is still a hot ship." Hot indeed. It
did not require extensive testing to conclude, as the Joint Chiefs of Staff
Evaluation Board did in less than a week in a highly classified report,
that the ships had been made "radioactive stoves, and would have
burned all living things aboard with invisible and painless but deadly
radiation."

On August 7, Colonel Stafford L. Warren, who was the Manhattan
District's chief medical officer and directed radiological safety protocols
for the Crossroads tests, reviewed the risks presented by gamma, beta,
and alpha radiation and recommended that the Bikini target survey
project be terminated. While pondering Warren's request, Blandy
pushed back on the idea advanced by the Los Alamos group that the
tests had proved the vulnerability of fleets. General Groves wrote on
August 7 that Test Able "definitely established that any capital ship can
be destroyed by an atomic bomb by means of an air burst properly
placed." Blandy wrote, "Such an oversimplified question could have
been answered in the affirmative a year ago without a test. The real
questions were much more complex and related to the radii at which
various kinds and degrees of damage would be suffered by various
types of ships in order to determine required changes in design and in
spacing of ships in port and at sea." Certainly the Army's failure to hit
a red-painted, strobe-lit target at anchor opened the possibility that
Blandy was right. The Bureau of Ships calculated that the "danger radius" of a twenty-kiloton airburst was about nine hundred yards, where
air pressure was 20 psi. But the lessons of the ensuing weeks were not
lost on him.

Admiral Blandy agreed to slow down the survey in order to improve
safety, but declined to end shipboard work altogether. "He insists on
continuing a program of decontamination no matter how long it may

take," Betts complained to Nichols on August 9. Noting that the clas-
sification reviewers who handled the work product of Joint Task Force
One had stamped his correspondence SECRET, Betts concluded that "the
Navy considers this contamination business the toughest part of Test
Baker. They had no idea it would be such a problem and they are break-
ing their necks out there to find some solution."

The danger, as Dr. Warren saw it, was that as gamma radiation exposure fell to safe levels, below one roentgen* per day, survey parties
would come under pressure to put in longer hours, thus increasing the
risk of secondary contamination of the hands, feet, and clothing with
alpha-emitting dust and debris. Alpha radiation, which does not penetrate human skin as gamma radiation does, was harmful if inhaled or
ingested. Wooden decks were sponges for toxic fallout that could not be
easily cleaned. As shipboard ventilation systems were heavily infested
with dust-carrying alpha particles, Warren wrote, it was inadvisable to
operate them. Movement of air created an inhalation hazard "the exact
magnitude of which is not known but which may be serious," Warren
wrote. "Unfortunately this hazard persists long after gamma radiation
does." Compounding the problem was the fact that plutonium, which
formed the fissionable core of the two bombs, was not detectable using
Geiger counters. When the captain's cabin in the *Prinz Eugen* was
found to contain traces of the highly radioactive element, it was clear to
Blandy that the potential for danger was everywhere. Once he began
writing articles for *Life* magazine in 1947, Stafford Warren would dismay some of his peers in the Manhattan District with his antiatomic
activism. But his misgivings were sincerely held. "I never want to go
through the experience of the last three weeks of August again," he
would say.

When Warren urged Blandy to cancel Test Charlie, the deepwater
detonation that was to have been the third phase of Crossroads, the
admiral was in a tough position. He had just decided to recommend to
Admiral Nimitz, the chief of naval operations, that the majority of the

* The term "roentgen" (after the German physicist Wilhelm Röntgen, discoverer of
X-rays) dates to 1928, having originated in the medical field as a measure of ionization
in air caused by gamma rays and X-rays.

surviving target ships at Bikini be taken out of commission because they were unsafe to board, but that decontamination work continue on the *Pennsylvania, New York, Nevada, Prinz Eugen, Salt Lake City,* and five submarines so that they could be used in the third test. But on August 10, Warren showed Blandy the evidence that changed his mind. It was an X-ray image of a fish, an autoradiograph. A pattern of radioactive alpha particles had projected a perfect outline of the creature, suggesting that plutonium had been absorbed all through it, to its scales. Blandy looked at this and said, "Then we call it all to a halt." He recommended to the Joint Chiefs that all decontamination efforts cease, and they did. Test Charlie was soon thereafter canceled as well, owing to the difficulty of anchoring these irradiated ships in deep water. The radioactive mess had become impossible to manage.

THE SOVIET WITNESSES to Operation Crossroads were unsettled and disturbed by what they had seen. Paul S. Galtsoff, a marine biologist who worked for the U.S. Department of the Interior, had built a rapport with one of the two official Soviet observers at Bikini during their time together in the Pacific. A native White Russian who had emigrated as an adult after the 1917 revolution, Dr. Galtsoff was fluent in Russian and had found Simon P. Aleksandrov a garrulous companion. On the afternoon of July 26, shortly after Test Baker, Galtsoff noted that Aleksandrov was absent from a meeting on the *Panamint* to which observers had been invited to discuss the second explosion. Later that day, he found the Russian and asked him to explain his absence. "He said the only thing he could think about," Galtsoff wrote, "was Mr. Bullitt's book." The former U.S. ambassador to the Soviet Union was an outspoken anticommunist. Aleksandrov was incensed to see Bullitt's new anti-Soviet tract, *The Great Globe Itself,* reviewed in the pages of the ship's newsletter, and doubly so when his letter of complaint to the captain of the *Panamint* was not published.

Summoning such a degree of "threat and vituperation" that it kept Galtsoff awake several nights, Aleksandrov shouted that Operation Crossroads had been nothing more than a scripted show meant to frighten the Soviets. Test Able, he said, had been "a flop" that would cost America dearly in diplomacy and good will. The United States, he said, would be forced to save face by conceding control of Trieste, the valuable Italian port city on the Adriatic, to its occupying Yugoslav Communists, who were clients of Moscow. Test Baker had been "an equally bad mistake," he said. It did not scare the Soviets and would cost the Americans a peace treaty with Russia over Europe and Japan. Aleksandrov observed darkly, "America is vulnerable in many places. Her cities like Buffalo, Pittsburgh, and Denver may easily be bombed. We have wonderful planes and a few other things which will be a surprise to you Americans."

The salvo of complaints and boasts continued: U.S. espionage in Europe is "very clumsy and childlike, while that of the Soviets is refined and scientific"; America had stolen most of its uranium supply from the Belgian Congo and Germany, and had tried to snatch a German atomic physicist from the Soviet zone of occupation; the United States was trying to establish "a Nazi regime" in China and interfering with Soviet interests there. He said the Soviet Union, by right of its size and importance, should control the Mediterranean and have free passage to the Atlantic. Aleksandrov said that the visits the scientific observer party had made to Guam before the Bikini test had been in poor taste, as Guam and other Pacific bases existed for the sole purpose of attacking the Soviet Union. When Galtsoff tried to deflect him, bringing up a collegial presentation on the 1944 battle for Guam that had been given to the group by a U.S. Marine officer, this seemed to trigger Aleksandrov, too. He replied, "Send them, these good fighters of yours, to northern Korea and we will lick them and crush them to powder. I wish you would send them so we could show you!"

Galtsoff did not sleep well that night or the next. He made notes of the conversation in his diary and complained to the captain of the *Panamint*. He wondered about this Professor Aleksandrov. Was he really a scientist? Galtsoff, one of the world's leading experts on shellfisheries, wasn't sure. Semion Aleksandrov's accent was that of a peasant. "He was about what one would expect a high-grade foreman to be," Galtsoff would write. When the Soviet mentioned that his duties entailed delivering uranium ore to concentrating plants, and that he had regular contact with Lavrentiy Beria, Stalin's head of internal security, and Vyacheslav Molotov, the minister of foreign affairs, Galtsoff concluded Aleksandrov was a member of the NKVD, the secret police service that had carried out Stalin's campaign of assassinations and purges in the late thirties and was believed to be supervising construction of Soviet atomic plants. The only other Russian on the *Panamint* was a man named Mikhail Meshcheriakov. He, too, claimed to be a doctor. But hearing his "vague and childish" discussion of nuclear physics, Galtsoff figured him, too, for a spy.

A few days later, in Honolulu, during a cocktail party held for the Operation Crossroads foreign observers, the Russian-born wife of an American naval officer struck up a conversation with Meshcheriakov. He became "almost violent," Galtsoff reported, in expressing his surprise that the U.S. government did not treat Japanese living in Hawaii as Moscow treated its own ethnic minorities. With half a million Tartars sent to labor in Siberia's mines, he said, the Black Sea area was completely free of their disloyal like. He said the same had been done with the Mongolians who lived on the Caspian Sea. Two and a half million of them, accused of collaborating with the Nazis during the war, had been shipped to the frozen regions, and the name of their republic, Kalmykia, was stricken from all maps. He told the poor woman that America's refusal to use such methods was a sign of its abject weakness. She did not take this well.

The unwitting plunge by these American civilians into the paranoiac subtleties and sudden explosions of U.S.-Soviet relations during the early Cold War echoed tremors that were intensifying in Washington at the time. The day after, the Joint Chiefs of Staff delivered a startling verdict to Harry Truman on the worldwide ambitions of the Kremlin. Having been asked by the president's special counsel, Clark M. Clifford, to advise the White House on Soviet policies that touched on U.S. national security interests, the Joint Chiefs returned with an endorsement of a subcommittee report that raised a worldwide alarm. On the abundant evidence of the buildup of its war potential, to the continued occupation of oil-rich northwestern Iran, the murderous purges of dissent and installation of puppet regimes within its neighboring countries in Eastern Europe, its continued occupation of Manchuria and systematic pillaging of industrial machinery there, its efforts to sabotage peace settlements in China and Western Europe, and its subversive meddling in U.S. politics with violent propaganda and encouragement of labor strikes, there was but one ringing conclusion. These facts required "a full realization that the Soviet Union and the United States, with their respective allies, were locked in a deadly conflict, below the level of a 'shooting war' but a war nevertheless. World domination was the Soviet objective." It was a maximalist case.

James Forrestal could have written it himself, had the need arisen. It had not. The Navy secretary had already made headway sponsoring George Kennan's message. Having made it required reading for thousands of naval officers, he personally distributed it to the rest of the cabinet, congressmen and senators, businessmen and journalists. Amplified by Forrestal's evangelism, the Long Telegram grew as a taproot beneath the official U.S. policy toward the Soviet Union. That policy would become known as "containment."

WHEN OPERATION CROSSROADS was over, all hands from the Joint Task Force, along with the representatives from twelve countries, began the long transit back to the U.S. West Coast. News had broken in the interval that Harry Truman had put the seal on a major piece of legislation concerning the U.S. atomic program. On August 1, 1946, the president signed into law the Atomic Energy Act, sponsored by Senator McMahon of Connecticut. Set to take effect the first of the new year, it kept the U.S. atomic program under American jurisdiction and seemed to shrink the hopes of internationalists who wanted to see the UN given control of all atomic weapons. The Atomic Energy Commission, to be established in the coming months, would own all U.S. atomic plants, license all atomic research, and produce all atomic weapons. A key provision of the act placed the AEC under civilian control, with no military members. Though Truman said the new body would cooperate with the Manhattan District, and with the Army and the Navy, it fell to

AEC chairman David E. Lilienthal and his five-man board to manage "responsibilities as great as any men have ever assumed in peacetime," the president would say. Their first responsibility, for the time, was to ensure the American monopoly on the bomb.

The Soviets were most assuredly provoked. On August 12, after the traveling retinue from Bikini had returned to San Francisco, a newsman asked Dr. Aleksandrov at a press conference, "Why did you go to Bikini? Were you a personal representative of Mr. Stalin?" This launched him into a public statement, translated by Galtsoff, that made news around the world. "The Soviet government is planning sometime to have a demonstration of the atomic bomb. I was sent to Bikini to see how it was carried out." Aleksandrov said his government was farther along than most people think. When the program was ready for a test, he said, the Soviet government would invite foreign observers to Siberia in the same proportion as the United States had just done. He ignored follow-up questions about the status of Soviet fission experiments. After Galtsoff confirmed to reporters that Aleksandrov had said to him privately that the Soviets had the bomb, Aleksandrov changed his story, claiming he had said only that "*if* Russia had such a bomb, she would conduct such a test." Galtsoff was startled by the Russian's audacity. He was not alone. Thereafter, for the rest of the time Aleksandrov was in the United States, all the way back to New York, he was in the company of an agent from the Soviet consulate in San Francisco. She refused to give her name and Aleksandrov refused to introduce her.

When Galtsoff realized that he and the one other American with whom Aleksandrov had engaged happened to be employees of the U.S. government, he began to suspect that the Russian might have been using him. It would be just the way of the NKVD to traffic in manipulation, suggestion, and bluff. Perhaps the Soviets meant to use the press event as some sort of psychological operation. Was Aleksandrov trying to use Galtsoff to somehow send a message to Washington? Some phenomena were too complex for a mere ocean scientist to know.

★ ★ ★

AFTER JOINT TASK Force One departed Bikini, the Navy continued carrying out its own diving surveys of the target fleet. This went on through the end of August under cognizance of its Bureau of Ships. Divers examining the hull of the *New York* found the radiation levels at the bottom of the lagoon too high to permit them to remain long near the floating wreck. On the nineteenth, they shifted their efforts to the *Arkansas,* lying upside down on the bottom at twenty-nine fathoms. The parts of the battlewagon that weren't buried under mud were covered in silt eight to ten inches deep. As an underwater probe measured radioactivity close to the ship exceeding 8.0 roentgens per hour, with the probe running off the scale at times, dives were limited to fifteen minutes. Through poor visibility, the divers determined that she had taken a Herculean blow. Her keel was buckled and corrugated though intact, hull plates washboarded around her structural members, and her hull deeply indented aft of turret two.

Admiral Cochrane at the Bureau of Ships believed that "the atomic projectile is not an economical weapon in a military sense for use against naval vessels at sea" owing to its high cost relative to its likelihood of destroying mobile and dispersed targets afloat, and that the tests showed that current ship designs were "sound and adequate and that future developments should be evolutionary rather than revolutionary." The Navy confirmed in September that construction on two nearly finished new combatants, the last of the *Iowa*-class battleships, the *Kentucky,* and the large cruiser *Hawaii,* would be delayed pending design changes required by Cochrane's people after studying the results of Operation Crossroads. There were hatches and doors to strengthen, flimsy topside works to draw away, machinery to mount so as to tolerate atomic-age shock. But realists found no comfort in incrementalism. The integrity of structures was the least of the reverberations of Bikini. In the atomic age, a true revolution was at hand.

Radiation, Cochrane conceded, was "the most significant and threatening single feature of an atomic weapon attack." And in the psychological power derived from the human species' revulsion to it, the bomb acquired a transcendent and horrible potential. It lent radiant color to the debate in Washington about the roles and missions of the services.

What use was there in a concentration of ships when a single bomb could cripple them all at a stroke? All the litigants could find something in the Bikini tests to advance their case.

After Forrestal had unpacked from his trip around the world, having gained what his diary called "a quick view of its huge, intricate and ominous problems," he sent regrets for a reception that evening and kept his appointment calendar for the next day blank. He was overcome by the sense of pressure from Moscow, acute, latent, and menacing. The American ally, Nationalist China, convulsed with civil war. Truman's special envoy, General George C. Marshall, was in the midst of a futile gambit to negotiate an end to the fighting and bring the insurgent Communists into a unified government led by Chiang Kai-shek's U.S.-friendly government, while a small force of U.S. Marines guarded critical railway lines against sabotage. Korea was frozen in a schism at the 38th parallel. As Stalin eyed control of Manchuria, he absorbed Eastern Europe like a gangster moving into a new territory. His intelligence agents infiltrated to monitor and intervene in the activities of political parties. He moved Red Army regiments to the Soviet border with Turkey, aiming to pressure or even control the strategic waterway of the Dardanelles. Forrestal saw everywhere Soviet advances that cost America some of its standing. "We should be watchful of our sinking prestige on half a dozen threatened fronts," his diary records. "But the country in mid-1946 was not in the mood for either realism or exertion."

Forrestal spent his day of rest reading a book on the English constitution. He was duly impressed by the bomb. While the Navy would urgently explore ways to take nuclear weapons to sea, neither Forrestal, Nimitz, nor anyone else in their department suffered from the illusion that the Navy could now retreat to the fortress of its harbors and shower fission weapons upon its enemies. Tight budgets notwithstanding, the fleet needed to be in the world.

On July 26, Forrestal reported to the cabinet on the success of the Bikini test. That summer, in Paris, talks were under way among the Allied powers to decide how occupied Germany should be governed and Europe could be stabilized. At the grand hotel Le Meurice in the 1st arrondissement, Secretary of State Byrnes confronted his Soviet counterparts as they gamed the agreements that had been struck at Yalta and Tehran during the war. Bargaining with Communists, Byrnes found, was a game of bluster, deceit, and grand larceny. George Marshall, who was in China at the time, deep in his negotiations to end the civil war, was learning this too. Good faith and pursuit of common interests were handicaps in a parley with the cynical. The more deeply felt the idealism, the deeper the disadvantage at which one operated. The head of the U.S. military delegation to the Paris talks, Vice Admiral Richard L. Conolly, had spent his professional life suspicious of the Soviets. He regarded the talks as "a snare and a delusion all the way through." The high-level dispatches that Conolly had seen pass Secretary Byrnes's desk "show conclusively that they never were an ally of ours," Conolly said. "They were always demanding, but never made any concessions in return." Though Conolly considered Byrnes a "good fighter," the admiral thought he "was pretty well hog-tied before the damn thing started," owing to the secretary's necessary loyalty to previous bargains and understandings at Tehran and Yalta. His counterparts had no such compunctions. Having shown their cards in Manchuria, where they were uprooting and hauling away all the capital infrastructure they could lay their hands on, the Soviets now insisted on taking a larger proportion of the surrendered Italian fleet than had been agreed. Rome's submarine force was of particular interest to them.

Conolly might have wondered why. Among his Russian counterparts was a "good, square-headed lieutenant general," a naval officer who knew nothing about naval matters, and some "Merchant Marine types" who struck him more as lawyers or commissars than as men of the sea. Conolly saw them as "a bunch of actors" whose performance in diplomacy "confirmed to me my suspicions of fifteen years' standing about the Russians."

Having come to Paris straight from the Pentagon, Conolly had been influenced by Secretary Forrestal's suspicion of Soviet intentions. Forrestal "saw a long way ahead of even Mr. Truman," the admiral thought, "and he was ahead of Mr. Byrnes at that time in his criticism and doubt and suspicion of the policy and intentions of the Soviet Union. There's no question about it." Forrestal, who was a Democrat, an idealist, and a patrician long loyal to FDR, had a Texas Ranger's sense of right and wrong. He was no pushover for the internationalist wishful thinking that often prevailed at the United Nations.

Under Byrnes, the State Department's consuls struck Conolly as "wishy-washy and weak kneed, always wanting to compromise. You don't get good relations with the USSR that way. . . . You'll compromise yourself into the poorhouse in nothing flat. We used to call it buying the horse all over. You'd compromise one day, and they'd come back with increased demands the next day; you'd compromise on that, and pretty soon . . . all you have to do is cut things in half enough times and you end up with a pretty slim slice." It would be James Forrestal who moved the State Department into alignment with the Pentagon in seeing the Soviets as a threat.

In Paris, Conolly embraced the role of "salesman" for a policy that Forrestal, Nimitz, and Vice Admiral Forrest Sherman, Nimitz's deputy CNO for plans and policy, were increasingly insistent upon: a more robust forward military posture in the Mediterranean. They had a willing partner in Senator Arthur Vandenberg, chair of the Senate Foreign Relations Committee. The Michigander was effective in building Republican support for Truman's emerging policy of containment, soon to be known as the Truman Doctrine. He helped see to it that the UN Charter did not prohibit its subscribing nations from making their own regional security agreements. This carve-out would ultimately enable the creation of the North Atlantic Treaty Organization (NATO). Conolly urged Vandenberg to keep military forces in Europe and warned against the perils of reverting to prewar isolationism.

Forrestal considered America's approach to dealing with geopolitical crises as haphazard and improvisational. His support for a unified Pentagon arose from his wish to integrate the ends and means in national security policy. Ideas and arms, pronouncement and follow-through. The Navy needed, he thought, more than any other single thing, to assert itself where the conflict arose.

An opportunity was at hand in the Middle Sea to ensure that Soviet power moved only with American permission. The fulcrum of leverage was the Dardanelles, the thirty-eight-mile strait connecting the Sea of Marmara and the Aegean Sea. It was a choke point that restricted the flow of Soviet power into the Med and the world. But having sent the battleship *Missouri* to make a one-time impression on the Kremlin, the White House had no standing force in the Mediterranean to check Soviet temptations. The U.S. naval presence in the Med was downright threadbare, in fact, a mere remnant of what had been left over after North Africa was seized in 1942. Nimitz, Sherman, and other Navy higher-ups wanted a constant presence in the Mediterranean. Though the Soviets might dominate the Eurasian continent with their armies, without access to the Mediterranean their power would be contained like a ship in a bottle.

Admiral Sir John Cunningham, the British First Sea Lord, professed to support the idea of a permanent U.S. fleet in the Med. However, the problem of command relationships endured. The sensible and effective administration of diverse national naval forces, some of them given to Supreme Allied Commander, Europe, would remain contentious. With or without a formal agreement, Cunningham said, the United States would be free to use British bases at Gibraltar or Malta. Soon to withdraw from Greece, Britain would leave a void that one or the other superpower would inevitably fill.

When Vice Admiral Bernhard H. Bieri first arrived in Naples to start his tour in command of U.S. Naval Forces Mediterranean in June 1946, the assets at his disposal consisted of a cruiser, a destroyer, and "a lot of skeleton naval bases that were left over from the war," Bieri said. While plans were afoot to expand the American presence, his first task was addition by subtraction; he would close out the remnants of the 1945 Mediterranean war effort. In Naples, three hundred U.S. personnel occupied a wartime shore establishment of commandeered houses and modest officers' and enlisted quarters around the city. Algiers, Rome, and Palermo had similar wartime legacies. Nimitz directed Bieri to roll it all up, sell off whatever didn't need burning, and bring the long-timers home. Bieri requested and received another squadron of destroyers, a destroyer tender, and a new light cruiser, the *Fargo,* to help him do the job. His major task was to remove a squadron of PT boats from the Sicilian capital.

Though Washington forbade U.S. ships to call at Egypt—American uniforms resembled those of the hated British and were likely to provoke trouble—and Spain and Albania were off-limits too, the Mediterranean naval forces were a frontier in the matter of both operations and foreign protocol. Bieri had no direction from the Pentagon governing how he should operate his fleet, nor guidance from the State Department defining his political posture with respect to other nations. When Forrestal met with the chief of naval intelligence, Rear Admiral Thomas B. Inglis, on July 20, this deficit was a major issue. Inglis saw the State Department as "inclined to hold aloof from military people and to be unaware of the very great influence that the Navy particularly can exercise in Europe," Forrestal recorded. "Its prestige was high, the record of its accomplishments in the Pacific widely known, and its personnel disciplined and of good conduct."

The government of Josip Broz Tito in Yugoslavia was threatening Trieste at the time. When the Communist dictator's aircraft strafed a U.S. Army transport near the embattled city late in the month, Forrestal complained that State "loves to run the ball until it gets too hot to carry. Then, without calling signals, it is swiftly passed to the military, who are expected to make a touchdown." Bieri found himself left to his own devices. When the Italian naval commander at Naples, Rear Admiral Carlo Balsamo, was invited to meet with Bieri at Naples, the American admiral was surprised to learn that his guest's reception by a salute-firing honor guard was an unprecedented courtesy. The British had never accorded him such respect. Thereafter, Bieri never had trouble with the Italians.

The Royal Navy was cooperative in allowing port visits to Malta and Gibraltar, but did make clear that U.S. ships should not visit Palestine, a royal mandate that was turning against the Crown. With an insurrection developing in Yugoslavia, Bieri urged Admiral Sherman to ask State to develop policy guidance for his command. As it happened, Sherman was shortly on his way to the Med, part of a naval liaison

group headed by Admiral Mitscher, who had been named to replace
Jonas Ingram as commander in chief of the joint U.S. Atlantic Command (CINCLANT). Mitscher and his chief of staff, Commodore Arleigh Burke, with Sherman and his assistant, Captain George Anderson,
flew by DC-4 to London. At Twelfth Fleet headquarters there, Admiral Hewitt received the group heartily, then led them to meet with the
top brass of the Royal Navy.

Seated at the head of the long green table at the British Admiralty,
Admiral Sir John Cunningham, the First Sea Lord, proposed to the
Americans that a joint Mediterranean task force be established under
British command out of Malta. The Royal Navy wanted help from the
Americans, Cunningham said, and proposed to use the extant British
communications and intelligence system to support the new squadron.

After Cunningham made his case, Mitscher sat stoic and silent. The
silence endured to the point of awkwardness, moving Cunningham to
ask, "Admiral, you do agree with us, don't you?"

Mitscher said simply, "No." He said nothing more.

A further long silence ensued. "Everybody but Admiral Mitscher
was embarrassed," Burke later noted. Then Cunningham spoke again:
"The British have a solution for situations like this. Let us now have
tea."

Through the ice-breaking hiatus, Mitscher offered no elaboration on
his monosyllabicity. It was only when the group reconvened, and when
the British pressed again for an explanation, that Mitscher finally
added, "The nation that furnishes the forces furnishes the command."

His health was on the verge of failing, but nothing suggests that poor
health accounted for Mitscher's terseness in London. To the old air admiral, the question was a simple one. He had seen Admiral Ernest
King stonewall the British when they tried to move into the Pacific in
1945. (The British Pacific Fleet was eventually allowed to operate as a
task force within the U.S. Fifth Fleet.) Sherman would have preferred
a fuller, more collegial discussion about an Allied fleet in the Med, but
Arleigh Burke, who attended the meeting at Mitscher's insistence,
thought that direct, straight, and sober was the best way to talk to the
British. Mitscher might as well have said to the First Sea Lord, "Sir,

Britain has lost hold of Palestine. The Jews and Arabs are at war, and your garrison is in the middle, under siege. How can England promise to run this fractious sea?" Mitscher's mulish intractability sent the same message, and the way was open to establish the U.S. Sixth Fleet in the Med, ending its status as a British lake, dating back to the Royal Navy's seizure of Gibraltar from Spain nearly 250 years earlier.

From London, Mitscher, Sherman, Burke, and Anderson flew to northern Europe, touring Brussels, Frankfurt, and Berlin. Then they flew to Rome. After being received by the pope at his lakeside summer residence at Castel Gandolfo, southeast of the Italian capital, they went on to Naples to call on Admiral Bieri and the head of the Italian navy. Taking in the state of Europe's war-battered cities and seaports, Anderson said to Sherman, "Admiral, it would be worth $50 billion to prevent this from happening again. We've got to get Europe rehabilitated as fast as we can." Sherman agreed. Anderson pointed to that exchange as the moment when the Navy, in the dynamic persona of Admiral Sherman, soon to ascend to chief of naval operations, got behind the Marshall Plan and the Truman Doctrine. But the senior member of the delegation was not well. On the plane to Malta, Admiral Mitscher collapsed. Diagnosed with a failing appendix, he was operated on by the British and was left to recover while the U.S. fleet began a series of goodwill ports of call.

On August 16, the *Franklin D. Roosevelt* and a task group under Rear Admiral John H. Cassady reached Lisbon, and thereafter began the goodwill tour. As the fleet made port visits from Gibraltar to Cyprus, festive appearances did not mask the strategic seriousness of the operation. The call at the Greek port of Piraeus on September 5 constituted what some would consider the first overt American move in the Cold War. After the air group from the *Franklin D. Roosevelt* flew more than 120 sorties over Athens, skywriting *F-D-R* among the clouds, Cassady said that the "air show" had been carried out by request of the Royalist government. Fresh off a landslide victory, it had just returned to power from exile. Visiting Greece less than two weeks later came virtually every Royal Navy vessel in the central and eastern Med. Led by a group based at Malta, with the cruisers *Ajax* and *Liverpool,* they were on what the Admiralty called a "summer cruise." It was an impressive demonstration of Western support for a friendly government confronting covert Soviet pressure and violent internal Communist insurrection. "You have no idea how much it contributes to the general politeness and pleasantness of diplomacy when you have a little quiet armed force in the background," George Kennan told an audience at the National War College in 1946, adding that such a mobile military presence was "probably the most important single instrumentality in the conduct of U.S. foreign policy."

Mitscher, after recovering from his surgery, returned to Norfolk in the cruiser *Little Rock* on September 10. He was not well enough to attend the change of command ceremony in New York, so Arleigh Burke did the honors, relieving Ingram's number two as chief of staff. This left Burke nominally to serve as CINCLANT until he could hand the post over to Mitscher when he returned to the office. But the pace of work was fast, and Burke noted that "it was quite obvious the Admiral was not up to snuff."

Three weeks later, the job grew in magnitude when Secretary of the Navy James Forrestal announced that to protect its interests and support its policies in the area, the United States would keep naval forces permanently in the eastern Atlantic and Med. The *New York Herald Tribune* praised the decision as the first to "formally link naval operations with American foreign policy." The Atlantic Fleet headquarters at Norfolk became the East Coast nerve center that exercised overall command of, and provided the support of, the new forward area. The four-star commander in chief of the Atlantic Fleet served concurrently as the commander in chief of the joint U.S. Atlantic Command (CINCLANT). Like CINCPAC, its powerful counterpart at Pearl Harbor in Hawaii, the Norfolk billet had cognizance over most of a hemisphere. Now, like the Pacific Command, CINCLANT had the surface combat forces to exercise that power.

The high stakes of the new commitment to the Mediterranean, in concert with the urgent diplomacy of the Paris Peace Accords, made Harry Truman exceedingly sensitive to the fact that for most of the past year, the White House had not been speaking with a single voice on the foreign policy that undergirded its military policy. Truman's secretary of commerce, Henry A. Wallace, had been a particularly sharp thorn in his side.

Wallace, who had been Franklin Roosevelt's wartime vice president, was strongly at odds with Truman's warnings about Soviet ambitions in the world. In March 1946, Wallace had told the Senate Armed Services Committee that the president was encouraging a "deliberately created crisis" in order to rally support for universal military training. Then, in September, he made an infamous speech at Madison Square Garden in New York, where he announced, "We are reckoning with a force which cannot be handled successfully by a 'get tough with Russia' policy. 'Getting tough' never bought anything real and lasting, whether for schoolyard bullies or businessmen or world powers. The tougher we get, the tougher the Russians will get."

It struck Truman as amazing that the high office holder who had helped FDR manage a ruthless alliance of convenience with Stalin in order to defeat Hitler by the toughest of means could now continue to express real sympathy for the Soviet dictator, whose murder toll exceeded even that of the Nazi leader.

"Far too often," Wallace said, "hatred and fear, intolerance and deceit have had the upper hand over love and confidence, trust and joy. Far too often, the law of nations has been the law of the jungle; and the constructive spiritual forces of the Lord have bowed to the destructive force of Satan."

Truman did not care at all for Wallace's pious invocation of Old Scratch to characterize U.S. policy. Nor did Attorney General Tom Clark, who had ordered J. Edgar Hoover's FBI to open a counterintelligence investigation of Wallace's ties to the Soviet Union. Hoover, having long suspected Wallace of harboring allegiance to the Kremlin and undermining American interests, kept the former vice president under surveillance and regularly reported to Truman on the FBI project.

There was damage control to be done overseas. *The New York Times,* citing "Washington observers," had reported that Wallace's criticisms "had shaken United States unity in foreign affairs." "The effect upon the small and friendly nations has been particularly disastrous," a piece by Harold Callender revealed. It complicated the position of Secretary of State Byrnes at the Paris Peace Conference. Truman finally decided he had no choice but to demand Wallace's resignation. "The United States must stand as a unit in its relations with the rest of the world," he said in a September 21 statement. Wallace agreed to step down. Reporting Wallace's removal on page one that day, C. L. Sulzberger's story led, "The international position of the United States was greatly reinvigorated today."

But the energies of the Atlantic Command's top man and its most experienced carrier task force commander were fading. As 1946 turned cold, Marc Mitscher was noticeably a shadow of himself. "He didn't care much about the fleet," said Arleigh Burke. "He was obviously tired." A short hospitalization for bronchitis in January revealed that he had had a heart attack.

Mitscher's mood soured. One morning he called for Burke to tell his chief of staff, "I want you to burn all my papers." He gestured to several file cabinets that he wanted disposed of. Burke did not follow through. A few days later, when Mitscher inquired, Burke flat out refused. "There's a lot of history in there, a lot of things nobody has, and they ought to be preserved," he said.

"All right, I'll burn them myself," Mitscher said. Burke saw history in the balance. Mitscher did too. "There's stuff in there that's detrimental to people. There are statements that I've written without knowing the full story which are critical of people and which I now wish I hadn't written and that aren't actually even true. There are other things in there that are carelessly worded and people can misinterpret it any way that they want, and they will. I don't want to leave anything." He knew he was dying. He had his way, and with the strike of a match he ensured that his personal records went with him.

In Mitscher's last days, "He didn't want to see anybody," Burke said. "He didn't want to see his wife, Frances, and he didn't want to see me. He didn't want anybody to look at him because he was fading." He passed away on February 3, just sixty years old. "When he died I put out a dispatch that the admiral had slipped his cable," Burke said, "the old thing of slipping your moorings."

* * *

VICE ADMIRAL RICHARD Conolly was still working for Secretary
Byrnes at the Paris Peace Conference when he got the news that Nimitz, as chief of naval operations, had named him to succeed Hewitt as
commander of the London-based U.S. Twelfth Fleet. Conolly considered his diplomatic tasks in Paris "splendid preparation" for running
the new naval command in the Med.

Eventually to be known as U.S. Naval Forces Europe, Eastern Atlantic and Mediterranean, or CINCNELM, it would emerge as one
of the Navy's three most prestigious theater commands alongside
CINCLANT and CINCPAC. That prestige would be the by-product
of the strategic geography of the Mediterranean, whose control had always been essential to the defense of Europe. As Middle Eastern oil
grew in geopolitical value, the Middle Sea, as a vital link in the line of
communication from the Atlantic to the Suez, grew in standing in the
eyes of war planners. Seldom mentioned in press accounts of the day
was the fact that U.S. naval forces there were a potential atomic offensive threat to the southern flank of any Soviet invasion of the West. It
was no accident that Conolly, as an adherent of the Forrestal/Kennan
view of the Kremlin, was put in charge of the Mediterranean navy, a
forward-area offensive force.

A series of war-planning studies prepared by the Joint Chiefs of Staff
code-named Pincher looked to the Allied navies to support the defense
of southern Europe in the event of a Soviet attack, and to hold open the
sea lines of communication from the approaches of Gibraltar to the
Suez Canal. The Soviet threat, the Pincher studies reasoned, was political in nature but was given intimidating weight by the ability of the
Red Army to overrun Europe. Moscow's continued occupation of certain Iranian oil fields reflected its strategic aim, U.S. war planners
thought. The Soviet Union, "although desiring to avoid a major conflict for the next several years, will commit an act or series of aggressions vitally affecting the security of the British Empire or the United
States or both, leading to war between the United States/Britain and
the USSR." The Joint Chiefs urged a united diplomatic front against
Moscow. Meanwhile, the military forces in being—meaning largely the

Navy—would be relied upon to hold the line. This accounted for the presence of the bulk of U.S. carrier forces in the Atlantic. Forrest Sherman recommended avoiding Arctic operations and instead pushing the carriers into the eastern Med, where the mission of naval aviation would be to keep Turkey from being overrun using conventional, not nuclear, weapons—an acid test for the fleet's capacity to handle two principal operating challenges: projecting power ashore and waging antisubmarine warfare.

Not since the Navy had accepted the defense of Australia and the Philippines as a core mission prior to World War II had its mandate expanded so dramatically and on the basis of so few capital assets. On October 17, Nimitz had set the "normal strength" of the Mediterranean naval force at one division of cruisers (totaling four), one squadron of destroyers (ten), and "sustaining auxiliary vessels as necessary."

6

UNALTERABLE COUNTERFORCE

IN HIS WORKING SESSIONS IN PARIS, ADMIRAL RICHARD CONOLLY had witnessed Soviet paranoia and the cynicism from close aboard. Though his new London headquarters would be at 20 Grosvenor Square in London's West End, he lived in a country estate known as Romany. He did most of his work there, using a telephone that connected to his headquarters through a switchboard at the British Admiralty. In England as in the Mediterranean, the effects of the war remained profound. Conolly found that the British, having faced down the Luftwaffe before they staged Western Europe's liberation, were of mixed opinion regarding the prospect of war with the Soviet Union. As Conolly put it, some felt, "If we are going to have it, for God's sake, let's have it now and get it over with." Others, fearful and still mourning their dead, worried that the impulsive Americans, if provoked, might start a fight that would draw them in.

It was unclear how war might be a useful response to Moscow's campaign of political subversion. Soviet agents were agitating among labor groups everywhere. In France and Italy, the Communist Party was an active part of the governing caucuses. According to Arleigh Burke, the French navy chief of staff, Vice Admiral André-Georges Lemonnier, "was trying to establish a navy that was loyal to France" and not international Communism. The resistance forces that had helped save France from the Nazis enjoyed a natural surge in political popularity;

many of the groups were expressly Communist. Moscow exploited these sympathies to extend its political control. Lemonnier and his subordinates, notably Rear Admiral (Contre-Amiral) Pierre Barjot, who commanded French naval forces in Morocco, had their hands full removing Communists from the ranks of naval leadership and were committed to supporting the U.S. naval presence in the Med.

From intelligence sources available to Secretary of State Byrnes, Conolly had learned of the covert measures the Soviets were employing to control Czechoslovakia. Stalin had been strongly displeased when the Czechs accepted an invitation to join the Paris talks. Its foreign minister, Jan Masaryk, had carried on like the rest of Prague's leaders—"practically under the thumb of the USSR," Conolly said. Though Masaryk had voted the Communist Party line at the conference, appealing vaguely for peace and talking in generalities, Conolly saw that "he was out of sympathy with what he was agreeing to, but tied to the chariot wheel of the USSR even then," when the Czech diplomat still had his life and his country its independence.

ON JANUARY 6, 1947, in his State of the Union address to Congress, Harry Truman justified the unification of the military services on grounds that it would enhance national security at a time of budget cutbacks. By the middle of that year, the Army would be reduced to 1,070,000 officers and men, half of them deployed abroad in occupation duty. The rolls of the Navy, including the Marine Corps, would stand at 571,000 by fiscal year 1948, close to the minimum set by Admiral Nimitz. Further reductions being "impracticable," Truman said it would be up to Congress to determine whether the military could maintain even these low levels after expiration on March 31 of the Selective Training and Service Act of 1940, the first U.S. law that imposed peacetime conscription.

And yet even with these reduced resources, the military was about to receive a sweeping new mission. "We have a higher duty and a greater responsibility than the attainment of our own national security," the president said. "Our goal is collective security for all mankind."

The idea that the United States should tend to the security needs of the entire human race was enough to give any military administrator fits. Certainly it served to make the squabbles that were consuming the Pentagon seem parochial. On January 16, in a joint letter to President Truman, Secretary of the Navy James Forrestal and Secretary of War Robert P. Patterson, who had succeeded Henry Stimson in September 1945, reported that they had resolved their differences on the question of defense unification, in the spirit of a proposal given to them by the president the previous June. The Navy's lead negotiator, Rear Admiral Forrest Sherman, and his Army Air Forces counterpart, Major General Lauris Norstad, had worked out the compromise with Forrestal that preserved naval aviation and an independent Marine Corps but cost the Navy secretary his position in the cabinet and gave land-based antisubmarine and reconnaissance aviation missions to Air Force pilots. It preserved the Navy's role in the most important ways, substantially in line with the ideas of Forrestal and his Wall Street friend Ferdinand Eberstadt. Though the stakes of the dispute as seen by the Navy had never much impressed the White House, Forrestal proclaimed a great victory to all ships and stations: "The integrity of the Navy Department and the Naval Establishment including the Marine Corps and Naval Aviation, and the continuation of their traditional functions in peace and war, has been preserved to the end that Navy may best discharge its great responsibilities to the nation." But the question of the Navy's purpose in the world had been posed anew by the events at Bikini.

In January 1947, less than two weeks into his job as the new superintendent of the Naval Academy, Rear Admiral James L. Holloway, Jr., was presented with a proposal by Army Chief of Staff Dwight D. Eisenhower to essentially merge the Naval Academy with the United States Military Academy at West Point. Eisenhower believed the curricula of West Point and Annapolis should be as close to identical as possible and proposed a full-scale exchange program in which West Point cadets and Annapolis midshipmen would each spend their third year at the other service academy. Holloway's bluntly phrased rejection drove a furious Eisenhower to complain to Chief of Naval Operations

Chester W. Nimitz that Holloway had assaulted his proposition as "the ultimate in ridiculousness."

ON FEBRUARY 21, without forewarning, the British embassy in Washington informed the State Department that the United Kingdom, owing to the strain of fulfilling its overseas commitments, was stopping all forms of aid to Greece and Turkey. The news registered like a tremor. Truman and Marshall convened at once. "The urgency of the situation was emphasized by dispatches from our representatives in Athens and Moscow," Truman wrote. U.S. Marine Major General Oliver P. Smith recorded his belief that "only the presence of British troops had so far saved Greece from being swallowed into the Soviet orbit." A special committee of the State, War, and Navy departments concluded, Truman continued, that "Greece needed aid, and needed it quickly and in substantial amounts. The alternative was the loss of Greece and the extension of the iron curtain across the eastern Mediterranean. If Greece was lost, Turkey would become an untenable outpost in a sea of Communism." Even the Brits acknowledged as they withdrew that both countries were vulnerable to becoming Soviet clients. They hoped explicitly that the United States would fill the void, for such a development would mean the end of British influence in the Mediterranean. Truman did that and more.

On March 12, the president appeared at the Capitol, where he asked Congress to lend a hand. The fortunes of the two besieged democracies were linked, he said, and that region was increasingly of strategic interest. In 1947, the Pentagon estimated its oil requirements, in case of a major war, at double the level of World War II, when consumption exceeded 1.3 million barrels per day. With civilian industry rapidly changing over from burning coal to burning oil, Forrestal calculated that the domestic oil supply would fall short of the needs imposed by a major war by at least two million barrels a day. His concern that a regional war over Israel would disrupt U.S. supplies was behind his opposition to the Balfour Declaration establishing the state of Israel.

Forrestal had been forced to become an expert in oil production soon after the war, when Truman seized much of America's refining and pipeline capacity in response to a national labor strike, placing it under Navy control. The cancellation of war contracts and the swelling ranks of available labor meant that the days of the forty-eight-hour work-week were over. A return to a forty-hour workweek led unions to demand a 30 percent pay increase to keep take-home pay level. The oil companies agreed to a 15 percent increase, and the unions began a work stoppage.

By executive order, Truman directed the Navy Department to seize one-third of the refinery capacity of the United States. Forrestal was given the power to operate the oil facilities of the United States as an owner, hiring employees and entering into contracts, with the FBI enforcing his authority.

The saying credited to Napoleon, "An army marches on its stomach," had been overturned by the hunger of machines. Petroleum, as the principal motive source for armies, air forces, and fleets, was devoured during World War II in a volume sixteenfold that of food. Forrestal knew that America had been fortunate in war years to be able to draw upon large domestic oil reserves. But with average production in the United States having fallen to about five million barrels a day in 1947, any spike in demand produced by a war emergency would require output to grow by at least 40 percent, Forrestal thought. Such an expansion being infeasible, reliance on foreign oil would ensue. The rising U.S. demand for crude, and the development of sources of supply in the Middle East, made that region a proper national security concern of the United States.

As the value of the Middle East began to appreciate in Washington's strategic calculus, Forrestal regarded with increasing alarm the Soviet provocations in the region, such as its continuing occupation of northwestern Iran, which were almost concurrent with Mao Tse-tung's Christmas 1947 report to the Chinese Communist Party Central Committee that it emulate the nine-nation Communist International recently set up among nine nations in Belgrade, by establishing a similar organization "to coordinate the liberation movements of the billion people of the Far East." Fears of that type of coordinated expansion intensified the Truman administration's call for a human-rights-based foreign policy. In the words of the Truman Doctrine, it became "the policy of the United States to support free peoples who are resisting attempted subjugation by armed minorities or by outside pressures."

Of several men who helped Truman shape and drive this articulation, which animated U.S. national security policy for the ensuing forty-two years, none was more influential than James Forrestal. George Kennan had merely elaborated upon Forrestal's own thinking, containment having already taken root in the Truman administration.

But the Navy secretary knew what to do with the keen analysis Kennan had offered him. He arranged to have Kennan lead the State Department's internal national security think tank, the Policy Planning Staff, created that spring by the new secretary of state, George Marshall, after his return from China, where he had spent more than a year as a special envoy of Truman's trying in vain to broker an end to China's civil war.

Kennan's conversations with Forrestal about Moscow's ambitions compelled him to write, for Forrestal's personal edification, a six-thousand-word paper titled "Psychological Background of Soviet Foreign Policy." In it, Kennan made the case that the aspirations of Marxism as embodied in the Soviet state would have been familiar to Edward Gibbon, the scholar of Rome, who had written, "From enthusiasm to imposture the step is perilous and slippery; the demon of Socrates affords a memorable instance of how a wise man may deceive himself, how a good man may deceive others, how the conscience may slumber in a mixed and middle state between self-illusion and voluntary fraud." Kennan wrote that "it was with this set of conceptions that the members of the Bolshevik Party entered into power."

Kennan asked Forrestal if he would object to the paper's publication. The eventual essay, "The Sources of Soviet Conduct," appeared in the July 1947 issue of the journal *Foreign Affairs,* published under the pseudonym "X." Kennan urged Washington to formulate "a policy of firm containment to confront the Russians with unalterable counter-force at every point where they show signs of encroaching upon the interests of a peaceful and stable world." The policy that should be put into effect was "the adroit and vigilant application of counterforce at a series of constantly shifting geographical and political points, corresponding to the shifts and maneuvers of Soviet policy, but which cannot be charmed or talked out of existence." Though Kennan would try to distance himself from it in later years, there was no mistaking the military implications of such a global command. Kennan's notion of containment as requiring application of counterforce gave direction to foreign policy makers in the Truman administration, and now the influential magazine brought his thinking to a wider public.

Kennan's authorship of "the X article" was immediately apparent to those who knew his muscular prose style. Among those who were neither enlightened nor amused was George Marshall. Though the new secretary of state liked the idea of his department taking the lead in articulating strategy, he was disturbed to find it published in detail for all to read. He called in Kennan, who explained how the article had come to be written, and let his raised eyebrows do the talking.

Kennan saw a clarifying moral urgency in Moscow's challenge to the West. "The issue of Soviet-American relations," he wrote, "is in essence a test of the overall worth of the United States as a nation among nations. . . . The thoughtful observer of Russian-American relations will find no cause for complaint in the Kremlin's challenge to American society. He will rather experience a certain gratitude to a Providence which, by providing the American people with this implacable challenge, has made their entire security as a nation dependent on their pulling themselves together and accepting the responsibilities of moral and political leadership that history plainly intended them to bear."

George Kennan emerged as the leader of a cadre of Soviet specialists in the State Department who were determined to push back against Moscow's covert aggressions in the world. The group, which included Loy Henderson, director of the Office of Near East and African Affairs (which encompassed Greece and Turkey), Charles Bohlen, the special adviser to the secretary of state, and Elbridge Durbrow of the Eastern European Division, would be at odds with a predominant culture within State that had been outwardly sympathetic to the Soviet Union since the late thirties. But the group had a champion in James Forrestal. With his round-the-clock energy and persuasive passion, Forrestal built a fervently anticommunist coalition within the Navy and State departments. More than anyone else, he shifted official opinion in Washington toward active opposition to Soviet efforts to destabilize democratic governments and their free economies.

Clark Clifford, counsel to the president, did not believe that Congress, in drafting the 1947 Defense reorganization, intended to authorize the Central Intelligence Agency (CIA) to run covert actions. George Kennan, the head of policy planning at State, proposed to create a secret bureau within his department to run them. In war, the new bureau would report to Defense. In peace, it would be operated by State, which would nominate its director. It would have its offices, however, in the CIA—presumably so that State could disavow it. Though Director of Central Intelligence Admiral Roscoe H. Hillenkoetter did not believe his agency should run covert operations as well as intelligence collection, the National Security Council (NSC) finally approved Kennan's proposal to give teeth to the CIA in conducting "black ops." The director of the new dirty tricks arm was Frank Wisner, a dashing Wall Street lawyer who was an old friend of Kennan's. Kennan himself, of course, was responsible for the U.S. effort to operate covertly in kind. "I think we have to face the facts that Russian successes have been gained in many areas by irregular and underground methods," he would write to Forrestal. "I do not think the American people whatever approve of the policies, which rely fundamentally on similar methods for their effectiveness. I do feel, however, that there are cases where it might be essential to our security to fight fire with fire." Covert operations would continue under the auspices of the State Department even after the formation of the Central Intelligence Agency in 1947.

But Kennan performed his most visible and important work as head of the Policy Planning Staff. He produced a paper urging an expansive program of American economic aid to Western Europe. The European Recovery Program, eventually carried out by Secretary of State George C. Marshall, would bear the secretary's moniker, the Marshall Plan.

Forrestal had discussed it as an element of U.S. postwar security as early as January 1946, when he explained to the Senate Foreign Relations Committee that the aim of helping Europe "is not to forge an iron ring around any nation or to set up an aggressive military threat to any other nation. Our purpose and object is totally and exclusively to prevent another war by the creation of the political and economic and social equilibrium which is requisite to the maintenance of peace." Soviet designs in Europe and around the world, to the extent that they upended the equilibrium, required an active response.

Kennan's paper, amplified by Truman's March 12 speech, weighed on Congress as it considered the package of military and economic aid to Greece and Turkey that the White House had proposed. The proposed amount of $400 million was not considered a huge sum of money, given that it matched what New Yorkers collectively spent on consumer goods on a typical day. Opinion in the capital, shaped by Forrestal, urged a sustained, active approach. For the United States, the stakes in Greece and Turkey were far larger than the stability of the two countries themselves. He did not use the phrase "domino effect," but that's exactly what was on his mind as he contemplated the disruptions in Athens and Ankara. "America could not, and should not, let these free countries stand unaided," Truman would write. "To do so would carry the clearest implications in the Middle East and in Italy, Germany, and France." He found himself in powerful agreement with his new secretary of state, George C. Marshall, that "there was no time to lose in finding a method for the revival of Europe." But Truman's promise to support besieged democracies around the world was read to apply at all times and everywhere.

On June 6, speaking at the Harvard University commencement, Marshall articulated the broad strokes of the Western European Recovery Program. Though he had failed to bring stability to China, torn by a decade-long civil war, conditions in Western Europe seemed to make large-scale rebuilding projects possible. There was exhaustion, yes, but it was a victorious one. To reconstitute the political and social forces that gave its citizens both national identities and a relative sense of security, America would have to underwrite the economies of Europe. A recovery project there might succeed where Marshall's project in China had failed. Western Europeans tended to share a civic and political vision.

Though historians would measure the scope of the Marshall Plan in dollars, it would have had, like any idealist's project, little chance of success without support of arms. Given that the Navy was the only one of the three service branches that had the mobility, power, and quality of presence to carry out Truman's commitment to resist Soviet subversions and carrying out Kennan's idea of applying "counterforce at a series of constantly shifting geographical and political points," the Truman Doctrine would rely upon the fleet even as the administration squeezed it of the funding that permitted it to operate worldwide.

The Navy could perform this role lawfully and openly from the neutral territory of the sea. The Truman Doctrine, in other words, implied a naval doctrine. And the naval doctrine belonged to James V. Forrestal.

IN JUNE 1947, in Cambridge, Massachusetts, the Joint Chiefs of Staff Evaluation Board held its final meeting on the subject of Operation Crossroads. It was clear that the test had literally been a shot heard round the world. A secret side project of Joint Task Force One made this quite literally the case. Inspired by reports that the 1883 eruption of the Krakatoa volcano in the Dutch East Indies had been heard continents away without aid of special equipment, the Army Signal Corps built listening stations in Germany, Manila, San Francisco, Oahu, Alaska, and New Jersey, each hoping to detect the blasts on a photographic oscilloscope sound recorder monitoring sensitive low-frequency microphones set up at the corners of a two-mile square. Though the results of the test known as "EX-62: Long-Range Acoustic Observation of the Atomic Bomb Explosion" were held strictly secret, the Evaluation Board's conclusions would reverberate through the government and animate atomic policy for sixty years.

The Evaluation Board, which included two civilians and six flag officers, chaired by the president of Massachusetts Institute of Technology, Dr. Karl T. Compton, released its observations and major conclusions. The first of them seemed to encompass the largest revelation of Operation Crossroads, which colored them all: "If used in numbers, atomic bombs not only can nullify any nation's military effort, but can demolish its social and economic structures and prevent their reestablishment for long periods of time. With such weapons, especially if employed in conjunction with other weapons of mass destruction, for example, pathogenic bacteria, it is quite possible to depopulate vast areas of the earth's surface, leaving only vestigial remnants of man's material works."

But the board did not derive from this dystopian vision a mandate to banish atomic weapons. Quite the opposite. Its findings were a conflicted admixture of brute military realism peppering up the internationalist's postwar dream, and in this sense they echoed Truman himself. Although the board conceded that "only the outlawing of all war and the setting up of an adequate International control of weapons of mass destruction can lift this threat from the peoples of the world," it concluded that, owing to the lack of "absolute guarantees of abiding peace, the United States has no alternative but to continue the manufacture and stockpiling of weapons of nuclear fission and to carry on continuous research and development for their improvement and improvement in the means of their delivery," by means of "the coordinated development of atomic weapons and weapon carriers and their integration into a series of devices, each with a tactical or strategic purpose." Surprise attacks, being probable, as history had shown, required a policy of prevention through strength.

"Any aggressor must be overcome with superior force," the final report concluded. "Inseparable from the development of bombs and bomb carriers should be planning of naval surface and submarine vessels from which atomic bomb carriers may be launched or discharged." The vulnerability of those naval platforms, the board concluded, would be minimal, as mobile targets offered a low return on investment to an attacker. The board's bottom line blended idealism and realism in equal parts. "A peace enforced through fear is a poor substitute for a peace maintained through international cooperation based upon agreement and understanding. But until such a peace is brought about, this nation can hope only that an effective deterrent to global war will be a universal fear of the atomic bomb as the ultimate horror in war." The bomb remade the world by seeming to render it perishable.

On July 26, in the rear cabin of his presidential aircraft, a specially configured Douglas C-4 Skymaster named the *Sacred Cow,* Truman signed the National Security Act of 1947 into law, enacting the intent of Congress "to provide a comprehensive program for the future security of the United States." The least of its provisions redeemed the struggle of the Navy to preserve both naval aviation and the Marine Corps as arms of the fleet. The act codified the existence of FDR's most useful advisory body, the Joint Chiefs of Staff, effectively ending the system of improvisation by which he had made military policy. It provided a legal basis for the Joint Chiefs' very existence, further conferring upon it the responsibility for establishing unified commands in "strategic areas," "subject to the authority and direction of the President and the Secretary of Defense." Unified commands were quickly established in seven such areas—Atlantic, Pacific, Alaska, Northeast, European, Caribbean, and Far East.

The act established as well the U.S. Air Force as a third separate service; created the CIA to direct and coordinate the collection and analysis of national intelligence outside the United States; established the NSC to help the president coordinate national security policy; and it effected "unification" by commissioning two new coordinating agencies, the Munitions Board and the Research and Development Board, to manage defense mobilization and R&D, respectively. Alongside this new integrated National Military Establishment, the Atomic Energy Commission would manage the American atomic program, giving expressly military tasks such as the assembly and storage of atomic bombs to the Armed Forces Special Weapons Project, created by Forrestal and Patterson under the leadership of General Leslie Groves, the military chief of the Manhattan Project.

The new defense establishment and its atomic auxiliary, each led by a civilian, reflected the sweeping mission that defense policy encompassed after World War II. "Unless there is permanent peace—

guaranteeing national security through international control of all means of war—immediate and continuous preparation for the contingencies of atomic warfare is the part of prudence," the Evaluation Board concluded. A novel element in the new thinking was the idea of establishing a national intelligence service, the CIA. "Protection against the catastrophic consequences of an atomic bomb surprise attack will require an intelligence service with a far greater effectiveness than any such agency that this country has ever had in peace or war," the board declared. "Such an agency, charged with the duty of constant, worldwide scrutiny to determine whether atomic weapons (or other weapons of mass destruction) are being manufactured or readied for use, must be the first bulwark of our national defense." As the Manhattan Project and the experiment at Bikini had shown, scientific inquiry was at the heart of a warrior's work. Civilian scientists, long partners of warriors in the matter of atomic war, investigated a broad array of physical phenomena, from the behavior of electrical wave forms to magnetics, optics, sound, and energy. The design of weapons and sensors required more than engineering knowledge. It needed an expert understanding of the underlying physical and natural sciences themselves. After Operation Crossroads, the trend that gave it to Archimedes to help defend Syracuse against Roman invasion and to Michelangelo to fortify the Florentine Republic accelerated to escape velocity. The weaponization of science continued apace.

When Truman signed the National Security Act, nearly a year after the Crossroads test, a full-scale scientific resurvey project was under way at Bikini, under the leadership of the Navy's leading oceanographer, Commander Roger Revelle, who led Joint Task Force One's scientific group and later was named to head the geophysics branch of the Office of Naval Research. His program employed fifty scientists and technicians from leading universities under contract to the Navy. They looked at the diverse scientific phenomena related to the bomb, from the spread of radioactivity in marine life to its effects on the metabolism and growth of reefs.

Drilling produced core samples from layers more than 2.5 million years old, revealing that Bikini sat atop a bed of limestone two thousand feet thick and confirming Charles Darwin's view that atolls were formed by slowly sinking volcanoes festooned with growths of coral.

The beach showed only low levels of radiation, and the crop of coconuts and papaya was abundant. Emerald-clear water around the docks glinted with brightly colored fish. The air was full of flies, spiders, moths, crickets, and butterflies. A Navy cook lured a local dog with a ham bone. "Pluto," black and white and bushy-tailed, "consented to being petted, and appeared healthy and well nourished on a diet of crabs, clams and other forage," the Navy reported. Touching her nose, a sailor remarked, "She may be a hot dog radiologically speaking, but her nose is cold and where I come from that means she's healthy." In spite of all this, a ban on swimming in the lagoon was upheld. Core samples five feet thick, taken from the silted center of the target area, measured radioactive decay at nine thousand beta particles per minute per gram. "Fishermen found that one-fourth of the fish they caught had radiation in their organs, and that distribution of irradiated fish in the lagoon was widespread." While there were "no positive indications of damage to any plants or animals from radioactivity," an increase in brown algae and the death of submerged corals reflected a change in the biological balance. Determining the causes required more investigation.

It *all* required more investigation. The atomic bomb would shape the entire forty-four-year span of the Cold War. Made ever smaller and more easily deployable, with larger and larger payloads, it would place every crook and crevice of the world under threat of ruin. War planners schemed to win atomic exchanges, even as they and every policy maker had no sense of consequences, and prudence demanded keeping the weapon in Pandora's box. Humility, terror, curiosity, eager innovation, and abject paranoia would be the diverse by-products of the bomb.

But it might have been an Army intelligence officer who best expressed the equanimity of the proponents of naval power in the early atomic age: "Sea power is a theory. It is a principle of war. Theories can no more be destroyed by bombs than ghosts can be destroyed by bullets, or than a proposition of Euclid can be destroyed by a battery of field artillery. . . . The atomic bomb, therefore, cannot operate to destroy sea

power." Admirals leading task forces out of harbors knew they were
vulnerable to elimination at a stroke. Just let the enemy try to find and
target them, they would say. In turn, shortly after the issuance of Joint
Task Force One's final report on the Bikini test, the Navy began to explore the use of atomic weapons by the fleet.

7

An Atomic Fleet

ON SEPTEMBER 2, 1947, THE USS *MIDWAY* DEPARTED NORFOLK escorted by four destroyers and set course for Bermuda, their mission shrouded in secrecy. Though a reporter received a tip that something unusual had taken place at the pier—a crane had hoisted aboard a large missile of some kind—his inquiries to the Pentagon met a thick stone wall. Nimitz's headquarters said that nothing could be released for publication with respect to the confidential project known as Operation Sandy. After the carrier had vanished over the horizon, several helicopters flew out to meet her carrying a VIP entourage that included some high Army brass.

Four days along, as the *Midway* pushed through rolling swells in the Atlantic about 250 miles south of Bermuda, her unusual payload, a V-2 rocket of German manufacture, was rolled from the hangar deck to an elevator and lifted up to the flight deck. Having survived trial by ice in the Arctic during Operation Frostbite, the *Midway* was braced for a trial by fire in Operation Sandy, the U.S. Navy's first test of the ability of ships to launch strategic ballistic missiles.

The commander of this small task force, Rear Admiral John J. Ballentine, considered himself an old conservative. He wasn't sure he saw the profit in risking a valuable new carrier in such a dangerous experiment. Budgets were as tight and the state of training little better than when Mitscher had led the Eighth Fleet carrier striking force earlier that year. When Ballentine assumed command of Carrier Division 1 at Norfolk in June, he found that the ships Mitscher had used in that exercise, the *Franklin D. Roosevelt* and *Midway,* could not even go to sea at the same time. In order for one of them to sortie, the other had to loan out two-thirds of its complement and stay behind at Portsmouth with a skeleton crew aboard. Ballentine had seen this before. He remembered how the Navy had "thrown everything away" after World War I. He was serving in the battleship *Arizona* in the summer of 1919 when the Navy secretary announced what Ballentine called "a general discharge at will." Tied to a pier in New York, the *Arizona* saw half her crew disappear into the warrens of the city. The ship was left "completely helpless," he said. The forward turret that he supervised almost at once went from ninety men to fifteen. For the ship to get under way again, the captain sent shore parties into the streets to round up enough new recruits to come directly to the ship. A generation later, the same dynamic was at work.

Stuffed full of liquid combustibles and high explosives, the *Midway* was a risky platform for an experiment like this. The process of mixing the V-2's fuel compound, pure liquid oxygen and diluted ethyl alcohol, and pumping two thousand gallons of it into the missile on the seesawing flight deck, could turn a mishap into a disaster. Captured German footage showed the type of cataclysm that could ensue, and Ballentine feared "a heck of a deck fire" if a swell caused the missile to fall over and an electrical circuit touched off an inferno. Admiral George Hussey of the Bureau of Ordnance wished Norfolk could have chosen a less essential ship for the rocket test. But to aviation advocates, the value of the carrier as a strategic weapon was precisely the point they wanted to make.

The officer in charge of the rocket test was Rear Admiral Daniel V. Gallery, the Navy's vice CNO for guided missiles. Never one to shy away from risk, he considered the *Midway* well equipped to manage the risks with her armored flight deck, advanced firefighting systems, and steady seakeeping qualities. Plus a certain audacity was built into Dan Gallery. During the war, he had won fame for capturing the German submarine *U-505* in the North Atlantic. Towing his prize into

Bermuda, Gallery carried off an unparalleled intelligence coup. It was the Navy's first seizure of an enemy ship at sea since the War of 1812. Now, in his new role, he believed strongly in exploiting advanced German technology. In 1946, a V-1 "buzz bomb" had been test-launched from a U.S. submarine off the California coast. Having studied the Navy's trials of the weapon at the White Sands Proving Ground in New Mexico, he understood that its modest two-hundred-mile range could be extended geometrically by the cruising radius of a carrier. Aboard a ship like the *Midway,* the V-2 could be a transoceanic weapon. Returning to Bermuda, the site of his fame, Dan Gallery would use the German missile to usher in the age of ballistic naval weaponry.

At first light on September 6, the rocket was ready on the forward flight deck, standing tall in the grip of a retractable gantry. About 250 miles southeast of Bermuda, when the tracking radars on the destroyers confirmed that their beams were ready to follow the missile, the countdown entered its final hour. Admiral Ballentine was marveling at the complexity of all the circuits that needed checking when, about a half hour before launch, he received a report that another vessel, a tramp steamer, had been spotted on a course that left her closing unwittingly with the missile's calculated point of impact on the sea. Knowing the stakes of the test, Ballentine responded that he would fire anyway. With five minutes left in the countdown, Admiral Gallery came running up to the task force commander. He was looking "rather wild-eyed," Ballentine thought. Gallery insisted the launch take place immediately. Ballentine assumed it was urgent, and it might well have been for the steamer as it continued to close with the calculated point of impact. Ballentine ordered an immediate launch.

The rocket crews made the missile's initial stage flash to life. When the main stage lit off, the carrier's flight deck disappeared briefly from view, engulfed in smoke. Then out of the swirl, high above, a long white plume marked the V-2's ascent. It was quickly apparent that something was wrong. The path of the missile was curving away at a forty-five-degree angle. Ballentine's first thought was that while the tramp steamer might be safe, other ships might be plying the un-searched seas below the missile's unexpected path. Though the gyro stabilizers labored to right the missile, the horizontal shear prevailed, carrying the missile on a hypotenuse until it exploded at twelve thousand feet. As Vice Admiral Forrest Sherman, Nimitz's deputy CNO for operations, watched through binoculars from the flag bridge, the weapon returned to the sea in pieces, splashing down three miles from the carrier.

The V-2 test was a failure on its face. But accurately firing the missile was not the goal of the demonstration. Its purpose was revealed as crew scrambled to clear the flight deck of the launching apparatus after the rocket was away. The launch, it turned out, was mere prologue to something the Navy was keen to show its colleagues in the Air Force. Within less than sixty minutes of ignition, F4U Corsairs were taking to the skies from the carrier's forward catapults.

Sherman was quick to underscore the versatility of the ship. He told reporters afterward, "We have taken a big rocket out to sea, launched it off a carrier, and we know we can do the same thing over again in quantity. After we got the rocket off, we launched and landed aircraft and proved indisputably that that could be done the same day, and we gained a great deal of very valuable information, some of it highly technical."

Though Gallery himself considered the launch little more than a public relations exercise, Sherman pronounced it transformational. A V-2 weapon at sea, he said, "would add great flexibility to a fleet so that in the future half a dozen rocket ships could bombard while eight or ten carriers employed their aircraft to cover the rocket ships." If the wandering ascent of the missile deserved to inspire no such confidence, a Navy newsreel called Operation Sandy "a preview of what will become a routine naval operation." Gallery considered it "a spectacular stunt that focused a lot of high-level Navy attention on the guided-missiles program, made some of our top people aware of things to come."

After the results of the Bikini test came in, construction of the battleship *Kentucky,* last of the *Iowa* class*,* and the large cruiser *Hawaii* (with a twelve-inch main battery, she was just as well described as a battlecruiser) had been delayed by a redesign effort to reinforce them against atomic blasts. Now the rationale was floated that they might be converted into offensive ballistic-missile ships, carrying U.S.-made V-2 rockets and longer-ranged nuclear-capable cruise missiles. The Navy soon thereafter ordered conversion of the seaplane tender *Norton Sound* as a test bed for new guided missiles and their instruments.

The significance of Operation Sandy was indicated by the pedigree of the VIPs who had helicoptered out to observe. Present on board was not only Admiral Sherman, but three of the Pentagon's top technical leaders: the deputy CNO for air warfare, Vice Admiral Donald B. Duncan; Major General Everett S. Hughes, the Army's chief of ordnance, who oversaw ballistics research at the White Sands and Aberdeen proving grounds; and the president of Purdue University, Frederick Hovde, who chaired the Guided Missiles Committee of the Joint Research and Development Board.

The name of another VIP would have stood out to any Russians who were monitoring Operation Sandy: Spike Blandy, the new commander in chief of the Atlantic Fleet. Though anyone with that job might have been expected to ride along on such a novel exercise, the presence of America's "atomic admiral" at Operation Sandy suggested that the wizard of the Bikini tests was interested in ballistic missiles. The former chief of special weapons had found himself a figure of controversy late the previous year, when he was shown in *The Washington Post* celebrating the Bikini test by festively cutting an iced cake that was shaped to resemble a mushroom cloud. Now he was the face of the Navy in Norfolk, looking out over the Atlantic, managing diverse missions that included supporting naval operations in the Mediterranean, the only one of America's sea lines of communication* that the Pentagon deemed under Soviet threat at the time. Having demonstrated the potential of carrier-launched transoceanic striking power in Operation Sandy, and the effects of atomic weapons in Operation Crossroads, the Navy's highest-ranked atomic ordnanceman was sending a message.

Returning to Norfolk after the V-2 test, Blandy ordered the *Midway*

* "Sea lines of communication" is a term of art that has nothing to do with the sending or receiving of messages per se. It refers to the system of sea routes and transport that any modern navy exists to protect.

to help train a new air group. After thirty days in port, the carrier received orders to lead a task force across the Atlantic. As the *Midway* prepared to get under way, the news broke that Navy Secretary James V. Forrestal had been confirmed as America's first secretary of defense. It seemed an exquisite form of compromise that the defense bureaucracy in the Pentagon was to be led by its most principled critic. (Secretary of War Robert Patterson had been Truman's first choice for the job.)

With Ballentine in command, the carrier would join U.S. naval forces in the Mediterranean for a four-month deployment in the first naval arena of the Cold War. In late 1947, the politics was in place to support keeping a fleet in the forward area, even if the money wasn't.

THE QUESTION THE Navy faced in 1947 was suggested by the nature of the missile exercise just completed: What could the sea services do in a war against a land power as prodigious as the Soviet Union? On the European continent, from the Baltic along the axis of divided Germany and all the way around to the Levant, Soviet armies dwarfed their Western counterparts. The Joint War Plans Committee estimated that the Red Army alone, not counting the armies of its satellites, fielded fifty-one divisions in Germany and Austria and twenty in Hungary and Yugoslavia, backed by a "central reserve" in the USSR totaling 152 divisions, amply supported by tactical aircraft. Against this the United States, Great Britain, and France fielded a total of nine divisions in Germany. In the Soviet frontier neighboring the Near and Middle East, Moscow had fifty additional Red Army divisions standing behind its aggressions against Iran and Turkey. As British forces were first on the ramparts there, the Joint Chiefs believed that conflict between British and Russian forces could threaten a wider war.

The fact that the Soviet Union did not rely upon seaborne imports suggested that the blockade, a major function of any fleet, would have little effect on it. Moscow's approach to naval power reflected this immunity. It had never really troubled itself to build a navy. In 1946 its operating forces were unimpressive, a collection of coastal patrol vessels, minesweepers, and submarines, the best of the latter, captured German specimens. Yet the Kremlin's political ambitions roamed the Mediterranean and the world. In Italy, Greece, Yugoslavia, and Turkey, Moscow sponsored political turmoil that posed a constant threat to the peace.

It was this political threat that the Truman Doctrine was meant to address. The means by which it operated were economic, which is to say, they were political. Thus, in spite of the audacity of the policy's ambition, it was in line with a prescription offered during the war by a perspicacious student of Alfred Thayer Mahan. "For any given nation," William H. Hessler had written in an essay that the U.S. Naval Institute awarded its top prize in 1944, "a geopolitics must be tailor-made, fashioned out of the basic materials of geography. . . . It is a policy, a scheme of national action, stemming from stated national aspirations, conditioned by geographic facts. . . . Geopolitics implies a conscious dovetailing of military policy with national interest and aspiration. Geopolitics fulfills itself when it becomes an imperative to develop specified weapons and forces, to be used in specified directions at specified times, in order that the nation may grow, survive, prosper, or otherwise measure up to a commonly agreed objective." The fulfillment of the Truman Doctrine, then, depended upon a revival of both popular opinion and political will to justify the expenditures to bolster nations that were politically fragile and faced with a concentrated political assault from Moscow.

A new defense buildup was out of the question as the U.S. deactivated its military capability under a hard ceiling of a $14.4 billion annual expenditure. A void of power opened up in Europe. What developed after Germany's collapse was familiar to anyone who had been an adult in 1918 and seen the previous continental war end.

The United Nations Charter, to be signed in 1949, would help to deny the Soviet Union the fruits of economic disruption and political chaos in the West. But given the military imbalance of the immediate postwar period, the United States would have the responsibility for providing the security umbrella that allowed the recovery to succeed. Restoring equilibrium was a job for more than just military hardware.

The balance of power in Europe stood on a bargain between the four Allied victors, the United States, Britain, France, and the Soviet Union. But the sheer size of the Red Army left the West with little leverage. It was only at sea that the West enjoyed superiority over Moscow. It was in this context that Forrestal's cherished vision of a permanent Mediterranean naval force gained momentum. It would no longer do to keep the naval forces based on the U.S. East Coast confined to Boston, New York, Norfolk, and Charleston.

The arrival of the USS *Midway* and her task force at Gibraltar on November 17, 1947, with Rear Admiral John Ballentine in task force command, was a sight for Vice Admiral Bieri's sore eyes: at last, an aircraft carrier for his threadbare Mediterranean command. Bieri's home overlooking the Bay of Naples, Villa Emma, had once belonged to a mistress of Lord Horatio Nelson. From its heights, the need for rebuilding was visible almost everywhere. At the pier, sunken ships still reclined. Ashore, buildings were shattered, communities rent asunder. Prime Minister Alcide De Gasperi was struggling to push through reforms that might slow inflation, which had hit 60 percent. As a condition for receiving $150 million in U.S. aid in January, he had blocked Communists from participating in his coalition government. In the political disturbance that followed, Italy's tradition of murder in the shadows escalated to a terrifying intensity. A May Day speech by the Italian Communist Party secretary in Sicily was interrupted by machine gun fire that killed eleven people. Though a gang leader and a Sicilian separatist were blamed, the Communist-controlled labor movement accused De Gasperi of complicity with the Mafia and the rich and called for a general strike.

With that as the backdrop, the plans of the United States and Britain to withdraw their troops from the country, which had no army of its own, seemed to threaten any hope that Italy could stand as an anchor of anticommunism on Europe's southern flank. With a national election coming in April 1948, and a Communist coup d'état a possibility, just as it was in Greece, the beleaguered Italian government welcomed any signal of support it could get. The arrival of the USS *Midway* task force in November filled the bill for De Gasperi and his Christian Democrats. With the city of Trieste threatened by Yugoslavia's Communist insurgency under Tito, Admiral Conolly thought the Italians needed reassurance that the United States was with them. As CINCNELM, he ordered Admiral Ballentine's *Midway* to steam off to Genoa and send its aircraft to overfly northern Italy, from Trieste to the rural communities of the Po Valley.

In Milan, the Communist uprising had become a full-on insurrection. The chief of police was complaining to a U.S. Army intelligence officer about how egregiously the Americans and British were about to abandon Italy to the Communists when a flight of gull-winged F4U Corsairs rumbled by. "The Army may be leaving," the American told him, "but the Navy is still here." Carrier visits to the Med started a regular rotation beginning in 1947, marking a new day for the U.S. Navy and its worldwide mission in peacetime.

Ballentine found the Mediterranean expansive, fully oceanic in scale. Though the fleets that had been native to it in World War II had paid for their inability to escape its confinement—all the beautiful capital ships of Italy and France had been bottled up, captured, or destroyed—it remained the case that the distance from Gibraltar to Beirut, twenty-three hundred miles, was 15 percent greater than the distance from Gibraltar to Reykjavík, Iceland. Land was usually out of sight from shipboard. And yet carrier pilots found in the Med that havens for emergency landings were almost always within reach. "It's an ideal place to operate an aircraft carrier," Ballentine said. All around were spectacles to inspire a sailor's imagination: Marseille, Corsica, Pompeii, Malta, Athens, Istanbul, Antalya, Morocco, Tangiers, Rome. In the Messina Strait, passing between Sicily and the toe of Italy, shifting currents strong enough to spin destroyers seemed to channel Scylla and Charybdis, the beasts of legend. Transiting it, Ballentine learned to break up his formation and pass in a well-spaced column.

The locals seemed enthralled with the aircraft carrier. Captain Albert K. Morehouse allowed visitors to come aboard the *Midway*. From Morocco to Malta, to Genoa and Naples, the ship was a marvel. As visitors, often comprising entire families, swarmed up the ladders, the scene in the nine-hundred-foot-long hangar deck soon rivaled opening day at Ebbets Field, the executive officer thought. The confusion of languages and customs eventually dissolved in an aura of mutual enthusiasm. Licensed peddlers littered the main deck with their laces, cameos, postcards, paintings, and silks, which, coupled with aircraft already crowding for room, made walking in this area difficult. "All these guests flattered us with their reluctance to leave the ship at the end of visiting hours . . . More than one young guest was snatched off the bridge just as he solved the operation of the chemical alarm," Ballentine said.

James Forrestal attached high strategic significance to the recovery of Europe. "You cannot talk about American security without talking Europe, the Middle East, and the freedom and security of the sea lanes and the hundreds of millions of under-fed and frustrated human beings throughout the world," he said in December. He considered the aid program an "essential part of the pattern of moral reconstruction" of a "deeply injured world society." For the new secretary of defense, the example of ancient Rome illuminated the risks to such injuries. The dangers of faltering public confidence and order could be mortal. "Rome had armies of hired legionnaires. She had wealth in the form of gold, and she had a strategic position in the Mediterranean. These were all powerless to prevent the fall of Rome before the swarming hordes of barbarians when the Roman citizens became unwilling to share in the defense of their own country, and the Roman economy became riddled with inflation and when there was no chance to maintain orderly government."

Order in Italy was ever fragile and had as much to do with the stability and standing of the Vatican as of Rome. Whenever Admiral Conolly or Bieri visited the capital city, they made a point of requesting an audience with Pope Pius XII. The United States had an ally in him, and the Mediterranean commanders knew his concern for the standing of the government. The pope approved of the Navy's role in encouraging stability. Eager for the fleet to show itself in every unsettled nation of the Med, Conolly secured Secretary of State Marshall's approval to send a destroyer, every six months, to every port in the Med that was big enough to take one. "You can't underestimate the importance of this," he said. "It isn't exactly a show of force. It's the show of the *existence* of force, and the show of a continuous interest on the part of the United States in what's going on. They were all scared to death of the withdrawal of the United States, not only physically. You might even say, they feared our *spiritual* withdrawal."

No one represented spiritual strength better than Eugenio Maria Giuseppe Giovanni Pacelli, the pope. Conolly thought that he and James Forrestal "were two of the few people that I had any contact with who realized that there was a Cold War, that we really were engaged in an out-and-out battle with the Communists. Others began to wake up a little later," Conolly said. "The pope made it plain you couldn't be a Communist and be a good Catholic." Such convictions always got a boost from the presence of a friendly cruiser nearby.

Deploying forward had always been the Navy way. The *Midway,* having proved herself as a denizen of the coming space age and a platform for atomic weapons, made a new sort of impression now wherever she appeared. As Ballentine's boss, Admiral Conolly in London, saw it, the appearance of the U.S. fleet in the Med in the fall of 1947 was all that kept Trieste from falling to the Communists. A few days before Thanksgiving in 1947, Truman approved a policy statement duly adopted by the National Security Council. It announced: "The security of the Eastern Mediterranean and of the Middle East is vital to the security of the United States. . . . The security of the whole Eastern Mediterranean and Middle East would be jeopardized if the Soviet Union should succeed in its efforts to obtain control of any one of the following countries: Italy, Greece, Turkey, or Iran. . . . In carrying out this policy the United States should be prepared to make full use of its political, economic, and, if necessary, military power in such manner as may be found most effective."

THE *MIDWAY'S* DEMONSTRATION of a missile-firing capability off Bermuda was linked to the debate playing out among the services regarding their respective roles in waging offensive atomic warfare. The previous July, within days of the underwater test at Bikini, Admiral

Blandy's special weapons office prepared a letter to the White House over the signature of the assistant secretary of the Navy, John L. Sullivan, suggesting that carriers be modified to handle atomic weapons. The final report of the Evaluation Board for Operation Crossroads explicitly recommended development of an offensive naval atomic capability as a deterrent to war.

That fall, in a projection given to the Joint Chiefs of Staff and the White House's Air Policy Commission for fiscal year 1949, Admiral Nimitz, as chief of naval operations, projected that the Navy would need sixteen aircraft carriers, enough for four task groups of four carriers. This number would allow the Navy to fulfill its part in the national war plan prepared by the Joint Chiefs of Staff, known as Charioteer, which specified what forces the United States would need in order to defeat the USSR in a general war fought seven years hence. As Charioteer envisioned the war going quickly nuclear, the United States would need to leverage its monopoly in atomic weapons to offset the Russian advantage in conventional arms. And yet the truth remained that the number of aircraft carriers that Nimitz sought exceeded the number of atomic weapons in inventory in 1947—nine—and that in the event of a Soviet thrust into Western Europe, the first mission of Admiral Conolly's Mediterranean command was not to rain nuclear destruction on Soviet armies, but to cooperate with the Royal Navy in evacuating all American and British civilians from the continent. The U.S. Navy hired Lloyd's of London to track all U.S.-flagged vessels in case Conolly might need to commandeer them.

Still, Admiral Gallery saw the day coming when the fleet would handle a full range of atomic strike operations. In December, he delivered a provocative memo to the deputy chief of naval operations for air warfare, Vice Admiral Donald B. Duncan, arguing that the fleet's traditional roles of hunting submarines, searching the oceans from the air, and landing troops from the sea was just the start. "It seems obvious that the next time our Sunday Punch will be an Atom Bomb aimed at the enemy capitals and industrial centers and that the outcome of the war will be determined by strategic bombing." Gallery wrote that "the war will be won by whichever side is able to deliver the Atom Bomb to the enemy, and at the same time protect its own territory against similar delivery. I think the time is right now for the Navy to start an aggressive campaign aimed at proving that the Navy can deliver the Atom Bomb more effectively than the Air Force can."

Even though many admirals considered Gallery a radical, there was little doubt that Operation Sandy was part of an institutional salvo aimed at the Air Force. Admiral Sherman's optimistic statements about the possibilities of the V-2 were assuredly meant for domestic consumption. The highest gray eminence of the Navy in 1948, Chester Nimitz, made it clear that the Navy was ideally suited to project offensive power.

In his final report upon retiring as chief of naval operations, made public on January 6, 1948, Nimitz touted the Navy's freedom of movement as a global striking force "able, without resorting to diplomatic channels, to establish offshore anywhere in the world, air fields completely equipped with machine shops, ammunition dumps, tank farms, and warehouses, together with quarters and all types of accommodations for personnel. Such task forces are virtually as complete as any air base ever established. They constitute the only air bases that can be made available near enemy territory without assault and conquest; and furthermore, they are mobile offensive bases that can be employed with unique attributes of secrecy and surprise—which attributes contribute equally to their defensive as well as offensive effectiveness." There was nothing truly revolutionary in this message. It was little more than a sober lesson derived from what the Pacific Fleet had done off Japan in the summer of 1945. And it was more than a little defensive. Nimitz made that clear when he pointed out that the Navy at that time had "little need to destroy combatant ships other than submarines." But he considered it a fallacy that major naval forces were superfluous at a time when no other nation had a large navy. It was control of the sea that made every other dimension of national power possible. America was the only nation to have that capacity.

As Nimitz entered a well-earned retirement in March, he wrote to Secretary of the Navy John L. Sullivan to summarize his views of the role of naval power in ensuring the future of the United States and peace in the world. "Sir Walter Raleigh," the first Cold War CNO wrote, "declared in the early seventeenth century that 'whosoever commands the sea, commands the trade; whosoever commands the trade of the world, commands the riches of the world, and consequently the world itself.' . . . Our interest in this control is not riches and power as such. It is first the assurance of our national security, and second, the creation and perpetuation of that balance and stability among nations that will ensure to each the right of self-determination under the framework of the United Nations organization."

The idea of an atomic-bomb-armed fleet opened offensive possibilities well beyond the traditional rubric articulated by the greatest American naval hero of World War II. The idea was a leap forward staged from the twin naval legacies of World War II. Carrier airpower had come of age, and aviation admirals such as Forrest Sherman, Arthur Radford, Donald Duncan, and Jocko Clark were entering positions of high responsibility as Nimitz and his peers began to retire from the scene. Progressive and forward-thinking—and conditioned by the ferocious existential struggle with the Air Force over roles and missions—they embraced the potential of "special weapons" and the tradecraft of the specialist in their design and delivery. They were supportive of the "weaponeers" such as Spike Blandy, Rear Admiral Horacio Rivero, and those two atomic bombardiers from the Navy's ranks during World War II, Deak Parsons and Frederick Ashworth. The latter had armed the Fat Man bomb in flight to Nagasaki in 1945, then set up the Atomic Energy Commission's Military Liaison Committee and served as its first executive secretary. The Bureau of Aeronautics, meanwhile, was designing carrier aircraft large enough to accommodate the payload of a Mark 4 nuclear bomb, an evolution of the Fat Man that weighed more than ten thousand pounds. The Navy's brand of atomic warfare in the near term would be waged by aircraft, not missiles. The evolution would accelerate under the admiral who was named to succeed Nimitz as CNO, Admiral Louis A. Denfeld, whom James Forrestal chose for his soft-spoken way and talent for compromise. Such traits would be helpful in managing relations with the willful U.S. Air Force, which urged production only of Fat Man–type atomic weapons, ostensibly for reasons of efficient use of scarce fissionables, though the Navy saw turf defense at work in its efforts to block development of smaller bombs.

The Navy's efforts to design naval aircraft capable of hauling a Fat Man bomb aloft were stillborn. The first such plane, the North American AJ Savage, had a piston engine on each wing and a turbojet built into the fuselage—"two turning, one burning," as pilots said. The hybrid propulsion plane generated the horsepower to lift a Mark 4 atomic weapon from a carrier deck, and was sufficiently controllable at low speeds for pilots to land back on board—the difficult feat of aeronautics uniquely required in carrier operations. But in the rush to get a nuclear capability to the fleet, the Navy decided not to send the Savage for test and evaluation at the Naval Air Test Center at Patuxent River, Maryland. Delivery to fleet squadrons was planned for the following summer; the first prototypes flew in July 1948. But the problems were so serious that the decision was finally made to adapt a land-based twin-engine maritime patrol plane, the Lockheed P2V Neptune, for the atomic-strike role instead.

To get airborne from a carrier, the thirty-ton aircraft needed a boost from a detachable rocket. The maelstrom of smoke and flame that was produced on a flight deck during jet-assisted takeoff (JATO) required the flight deck to be cleared of all other aircraft during flight operations. The choking effusions of the eight externally mounted auxiliary rockets rendered infeasible the traditional manner of launching "deck-load" strikes composed of diverse aircraft types in quick succession. And given the size and weight of the new types of bomber, it was quickly clear that even the *Midway*-class carriers were too small. Fortuitously, a new type of flattop, a supercarrier, was in the works.

At a special facility in Carderock, Maryland, scale models of an 83,000-ton, 1,090-foot-long aircraft carrier designated as the CVA-58 class were undergoing seakeeping tests in a gigantic bathtub. The experiments at the David Taylor Model Basin showed that a carrier designed without the traditional island superstructure or exhaust stacks gave the big planes room to taxi without obstruction. As World War II's premier carrier commander, Marc Mitscher had led the exercise to design a ship with an open flight deck expansive enough to handle multi-engine bombers. Though variants were still under review, Newport News Shipbuilding had been contracted to start the lead ship of the class in 1949. What had been an audacious novelty when the USS *Hornet* launched against Tokyo in April 1942 would be made a working state of the art, routine. Bombers would fly from the sea.

The admiral who was quarterbacking the Navy's initiatives in guided missilery had written a ten-page memo to the CNO, Louis Denfeld, arguing that the Navy was better suited than the Air Force to deliver atomic strikes, owing to the mobility and stealth of fleets. "I pointed out that big bombers flying from foreign overseas bases could never depend on their bases any longer than the next election or revolution in the countries concerned," Gallery later wrote. Somehow the memo leaked to the columnist Drew Pearson, the avowed foe of any cause championed by the malevolent corporatist and anti-Zionist James V. Forrestal. Pearson published the memo in its entirety and ran with the story for two days in different media. Secretary of the Navy John L. Sullivan "wanted to hang me from the top of the Washington Monument," Gallery wrote.

In recognition of its transformative role, and to encourage Congress to justify the appropriation, the CVA-58 was referred to not as an aircraft carrier but as an "atomic carrier." The new ship would be essential to the Navy's role in the emergency war plans that the Joint Chiefs of Staff had begun approving in 1948.

ON MARCH 10, 1948, the preferred Soviet method for influencing affairs with its neighboring countries asserted itself brutally in Prague. The Czech foreign minister, Jan Masaryk, was found dead in the courtyard of his office building, dressed in his pajamas. The Ministry of the Interior ruled that he had leaped to his death from a bathroom window. A joke that became popular in 1948 went like this: "Jan Masaryk was a very tidy man. So tidy that when he jumped out the window he remembered to close it behind him."

Admiral Richard Conolly had seen Masaryk in Paris a few months before his death, schmoozed with him about idle things. "He seemed in a fine mood then," said Conolly. Further inquiries in Prague would yield evidence tending to confirm that ducks look and quack like ducks. Masaryk's death would go down as a minor infamy, and Washington's relations with the Soviet Union entered free fall.

Ten days later, in Berlin, the Soviet representative to the Allied Control Council walked out of a working session, suggesting that the four-power system for administering postwar Germany had reached the limit of its usefulness. On the last day of March, the Soviet military governor in Germany delivered written notice to his Western counterparts that Russian troops would begin checking all Western personnel passing through their zones for identification and inspect all freight. When the United States rejected the notification, the Soviets sealed off highway, river, and rail routes to the German capital. The Berlin Crisis had begun.

Truman saw that Stalin was testing Western will. "In the face of our launching the Marshall Plan," Truman wrote, "the Kremlin tried to mislead the people of Europe into believing that our interest and support would not extend beyond economic matters and that we would back away from any military risks." At the end of the month, a National Security Council paper titled "The Position of the United States with Respect to Soviet-Directed World Communism," known as NSC 7, became the basis for America's counteroffensive against Stalin's apparent campaign to turn his neighbors into satellite states. Truman's policy had gained some iron after the Soviet Union arranged for Communists to seize power in Czechoslovakia in February and then invited Finland to enter into a mutual defense agreement—a gambit that Helsinki rebuffed. Secretary of State George C. Marshall cabled the U.S. embassy in Rome, "WE ARE ACTIVELY STUDYING WHAT U.S. GOVT MIGHT DO TO ASSIST IN CHECKING FURTHER COMMUNIST EXPANSION IN EUROPE THROUGH STEPS DESIGNED TO STRENGTHEN CONFIDENCE OF NON-COMMUNIST ELEMENTS AND DETER SOVIETS FROM FURTHER FIFTH-COLUMN ACTION ALONG CZECH MODEL. WE BELIEVE U.S. PUBLIC OPINION NOW PRE-

PARED SUPPORT STRONG MEASURES." A regional security agreement followed a week later, when Britain, France, Belgium, the Netherlands, and Luxembourg signed a fifty-year mutual defense treaty in Brussels. That month as well, the Act of Chapultepec, better known as the Rio Treaty, became effective between the United States and the nations of Central and South America. Writing in *National Geographic,* Nimitz touted it as reaffirming America's role as "a guardian of Western Hemisphere shores." The "peace dividend" of which historians would later speak did not *follow* the Cold War. From Truman's budget cutting to arrangements of mutual defense, it was a *feature of* the Cold War. Dozens of nations reaped the harvest, turning swords into plowshares while the United States pledged itself to their defense.

If AMERICA WENT crazy in the winter of 1949, should there have been any reason for James Forrestal not to? Something within him reached neuropsychic critical mass during that cold and fearful season. A little more than a year after his elevation from Navy secretary to become the first top civilian executive at the Pentagon, his mind and soul yielded to the weight of the seventeen-hour workdays that defined his tenure as secretary of national defense.

Walter Millis, who assembled Forrestal's diary for publication, wrote, "Everywhere around the vast periphery of the Eurasian continent the situation had been the same; everywhere there was the same sense of a pressure—acute in some places, latent but no less menacing in others; everywhere there had been the need for firmness, action, strength and coherence of policy in meeting this extraordinary threat. What was everywhere demanded was a far closer coordination between diplomatic and military arms; more and abler men in our foreign services; better use of the politico-military instruments we possessed. We should strengthen the Seventh Fleet in the Far East; we should keep the Marines in China; we should put naval power into the Mediterranean; we should be watchful of our sinking prestige on half a dozen threatened fronts. Such were the lessons Forrestal had brought back in his diary notes."

The pressures bearing on him were obvious to his friends. Drawn to Forrestal by his charm, independence of intellect, and competitive fire, the journalist Arthur Krock considered him a close friend. But it was Krock's wife, a Washington society columnist named Martha Granger Blair, who was the first to notice the change in him: an "irrationality and indecisiveness that was so completely at variance with the man I had known so well."

It may have been the result of the continuing persecution carried out against Forrestal by the radio commentator Drew Pearson, who began targeting the defense secretary in his syndicated Sunday broadcast. One salvo from Pearson hit Forrestal particularly hard. On January 16, the muckraker had questioned Forrestal's fitness to serve, on the grounds that more than ten years earlier he had supposedly hidden in his Manhattan townhouse while his wife, Josephine, was robbed at gunpoint outside. Pearson told his ABC Radio audience, "A man who runs out the back door of his house into the alley, leaving his wife to cope with a jewel robbery alone, would not appear to have the courage or chivalry to be the best Secretary of National Defense."

Krock knew Forrestal had done no such thing. He had stayed in the Forrestals' guest room that night. Forrestal had not fled. He was asleep while his wife was robbed of fifty thousand dollars' worth of baubles. As for Forrestal's home at 27 Beekman Place, it offered neither a back door nor an alley to the cowardly inclined. "To Forrestal's fervently expressed relief," Krock would write, "I volunteered to acquaint Pearson with the facts." Pearson never corrected the story. "From that time forward," Krock wrote, "I did observe a deterioration of spirit in Forrestal."

The ill effects on Forrestal of the incipient American culture of accusation did not go unnoticed at the White House. Though Truman had promised Forrestal that he would dismiss Stuart Symington upon request—the Air Force secretary was constantly in disagreement with Forrestal, his boss—Forrestal shrank from doing it. When news broke that Symington had made critical public remarks about Forrestal, again he demurred. His indecision was a sign that the competitive, willful, loyalty-valuing executive had changed in a fundamental way. When as a result Truman himself lost confidence in Forrestal, it was a far heavier blow.

The president had never particularly liked his secretary of defense. With his lack of higher education, Truman did not easily mix with Forrestal's refined extract of Princeton. Yet the president was aware of a decline in Forrestal's effectiveness. He felt increasingly that he was having to lead the Pentagon from the Oval Office.

One day Truman asked his naval aide, Admiral Robert L. Dennison, if he knew who the secretary of defense was. Dennison humored him: "Yes, sir, James Forrestal."

Truman said, "You're wrong. *I'm* the secretary of defense. Jim calls me several times every day to ask me to make decisions which are completely within his confidence and it's getting more burdensome all the time and it's something I shouldn't be called on to do."

"It was almost impossible ever to get an opinion out of him," Dennison said. "In the many talks I had with him I never really was sure I understood if he had a position, or, if he did, what it was."

Truman and his presidential campaign advisers were disappointed that Forrestal had not supported the reelection effort with his trademark aplomb. Forrestal claimed that officials should not involve themselves in partisan politics, and was also aware that he would need to position himself to deal with a likely Republican administration under Thomas Dewey.

Truman's other beef with the defense secretary was over Israel. Forrestal believed that the act of carving a new nation from Palestinian territory risked a costly war that would threaten crude oil supplies. It was a purely military objection arising from Forrestal's analysis of the Jewish state's adverse strategic geography. "He considered it a dangerous political concept, provocative of an eventual Third World War," Krock wrote, "to create a state surrounded by enemies and give it a guarantee of protection that someday, he predicted, the United States would be called upon to redeem." Though Forrestal was discreet with his public criticism, Truman was bothered by it.

For several weeks after the election, Truman froze Forrestal out of the Oval Office. "It was in the deepest dejection of spirit that Forrestal told me of this episode," Krock wrote. Many of Forrestal's friends "detected a steady decline in his mental state and his morale from that time forward." Neither Truman nor Dennison saw that Forrestal was in the grip of mental illness. "Why this escaped us, I don't know," Dennison said. "The president must have felt that what he was doing was not rational, but [Forrestal] just couldn't make up his mind apparently, couldn't make a decision, and that's why he was leaning on the president."

In January, Truman extended to Forrestal what seemed to be an olive branch, a lunch invitation at the Little White House in Key West, where the president was vacationing. Anticipating a one-on-one meeting, Forrestal was disappointed to find the town mayor joining them. A candid personal meeting was not possible.

Occasionally his public statements indicated the burden he was under.

"A recital of difficulties," Forrestal told the House Armed Services Committee during his first formal appearance before them on February 16, "is not always the best way to demonstrate the need for additional help." He was referring to the task of passing appropriations to build a "radar fence" to protect the continental United States against bomber attack and to establish a proving ground for the testing of guided missiles. But clearly personal difficulties were heavy upon him. "The entire weight of the military establishment focuses upon the office of secretary of defense and there is no way of deflecting those responsibilities," he said to the committee. If such words were innocuous in themselves, his friends sensed what was really going on. The tone of self-regard was out of character for such a broad-minded public servant. A friend wrote Forrestal concerning the complex task of streamlining the massive Defense Department: "There is so much dead wood that it constitutes a positive fire hazard."

"I saw for the first time the deterioration—you might say demoralization—of Mr. Forrestal when I went back there about 1 March 1949," Admiral Richard Conolly said. He hadn't noticed it when he saw Forrestal in January. In March, he said, "the handwriting was on the wall. He knew he was going to be relieved at the end of the month. It was very evident. He couldn't keep his mind on anything. I had a talk with him, and a little later in the same day he sent for me again, and I could tell he'd forgotten why he sent for me. That was quite unusual because he had a steel-trap mind. He was fidgeting and fussing around with his napkin at lunch. He was in a bad state."

Forrestal was shattered when Truman asked for his resignation. He had told associates he had decided to step down in March, but now circumstances no longer permitted him the dignity of retiring on his terms. He resigned by letter to the president on March 28. Truman named a top campaign honcho, Louis A. Johnson, to replace him. These sudden developments were said to have thrown Forrestal into a crisis of depression. His diagnosis, and Kennan's, of what ailed Europe now turned upon himself: "a profound exhaustion of physical plant and of spiritual vigor." For weeks he had not known the balm of unbroken sleep. His constitutional alacrity and quick, easy humor had left him. "The iron has entered deep into his heart and mind," Arthur Krock wrote, "and both the will and the strength to pluck it out were lacking."

Shortly after his resignation, a friend persuaded the weary, distracted man to go to a beach resort in Hobe Sound, Florida, where Josephine was vacationing, for a rest. Friends who saw him there described Forrestal as "quite depressed, sleepless and restless." He appeared completely exhausted, confused, even dazed.

A few days after he arrived in Florida, Truman told Dennison, "We've just had some strange calls from Jim Forrestal. He thinks his phones are tapped." According to Truman's appointments secretary, Matthew J. Connelly, Forrestal called him with the complaint. Connelly had the chief of the White House Secret Service detail check the phones at Forrestal's home and confirmed they were clean.

When Forrestal asked his good friend Ferdinand Eberstadt to summon a physician, Eberstadt contacted the famed psychiatrist William C. Menninger. Evaluating Forrestal in Florida, Menninger diagnosed the defense secretary with "reactive depression," akin to what some combat veterans exhibit after returning from war. Graying and gaunt, Forrestal was in a state of agita and fear. He said he saw threats around him. Zionist agents were watching his movements, targeting him, he thought, for opposing the creation of the state of Israel. Plausibly at such a fraught time there were foreign agents watching the movements of the top man in the defense establishment. And clearly some powerful men were bent upon ruining him. The nasty night work of Drew Pearson, his fabrications, innuendoes and lies, certainly qualified as a hostile disruption operation.

But Menninger concluded that Forrestal's prognosis was hopeful. The illness should be recoverable in three to six months, he told Eberstadt. They prevailed upon Josephine that hospitalization was advisable. Dr. George N. Raines, the chief of neuropsychiatry at the National Naval Medical Center at Bethesda, was dispatched by the White House to consult, and an agreement was struck to commit Forrestal to the facility. Raines made the arrangements, and Forrestal took up residence in a VIP suite on the sixteenth floor of the central tower on April 2.

8

THE ADMIRALS REVOLT

AS THE SOVIET UNION CONTINUED ITS SUBVERSIVE WORK IN vulnerable polities, from Poland to Czechoslovakia to Hungary, the United States and British high commands set aside their squabble over naval command relationships in the Mediterranean long enough to approve a new emergency war plan. Derived from the Pincher studies, the U.S. plan, known as Broiler, and its British counterpart, Doublequick, prescribed the immediate use of nuclear weapons to stop a massive Soviet assault on Western Europe. The response of the Allied commands, broadly overmatched by Moscow's conventional military power, prefigured the 1949 North Atlantic Treaty Organization (NATO) proviso that "an attack against one is an attack against all."

Assuming a continued U.S. monopoly on atomic weapons, Broiler/Doublequick envisioned their use to stop simultaneous assaults toward Norway, the English Channel, Denmark, the Pyrenees, and Italy, and deter a Soviet push into Greece, the Bosporus Straits, and the Far East. Thirty-five nuclear-capable B-29 Superfortresses based in the United Kingdom, the Suez, and Okinawa would drop fifty atomic bombs—likely the entire U.S. inventory at the time—on targets in or near twenty Soviet cities, with the goal of producing "immediate paralysis of at least fifty percent of Soviet industry." How or whether such a civilian holocaust would weigh on Soviet leadership in wartime was anybody's guess. In a modified version of the war plan known as Halfmoon, the Joint Chiefs framed an expansive ambition to destroy "the will of the USSR to resist" with an atomic air offensive "designed to exploit the destructive and psychological power of atomic weapons against the vital elements of the Soviet war-making capacity."

James Forrestal doubted an atomic attack would actually have such an effect. History offered no encouragement for the Air Force's belief in the psychologically devastating effects of strategic bombing, or its value as a deterrent to the type of Soviet conduct that concerned Forrestal and Kennan. The air campaign against Japan in 1945, including the two atomic bombings, was no precedent for the plan to subdue a continental power that had already shown a capacity for absorbing staggering casualties, as the USSR had in World War II. Concentrated aerial bombardment never succeeded in breaking Imperial Japan's or Nazi Germany's public morale either. And importantly, political leaders were aware of the sensitivity of announcing nuclear warfare as a basis for national strategy or policy.

When Forrestal asked the White House for guidance on what circumstances might call for the doomsday option, the response came from the National Security Council. A paper known as NSC 30, issued in September, clarified that only the president had authority to order the execution of an emergency war plan and that it was the military's duty to have it ready at all times.

The role of aircraft carriers in the nuclear offensive remained unclear: to "supplement and support the air offensive to the extent practical consistent with their primary task." Their primary task had traditionally been sea control—defeating other navies to ensure the flow of maritime commerce. Forrestal had gone to Key West in the spring of 1948 to broker an agreement that ended the dispute between the service chiefs about their roles and missions. The Air Force was granted the exclusive capacity to wage a strategic air campaign, with the Navy permitted to use atomic weapons as a "corollary" to its primary task of sea control, interdiction of enemy land and airpower, and close air support of U.S. troops.

But if Europe were ever to face the tread-rattle of Soviet armor and the heat of nuclear fire, the Navy's first task was to carry out an evacuation of Western personnel from French and Italian ports. The U.S. fleet would hold open the sea routes in the Med, not only to protect the evacuation but to defend the air bases in the Suez area that were supposed to launch retaliatory atomic strikes. In this nightmare scenario, Britain, under attack from Soviet bombers based in Germany, would be too busy fighting a jet-age replay of the Blitz to defend Cairo or the Suez Canal and keep oil flowing out of Iran and Saudi Arabia. The Joint Chiefs envisioned twenty aircraft carriers operating in the Med twelve months after hostilities began. Halfmoon thus served to make Admiral Conolly's Mediterranean command a primary forward area for offensive naval operations, even as the Navy was carrying out a major evacuation going the other way.

But if the armies defending Europe ever yielded, and if Soviet airpower were installed in southern Germany or Italy, control of the Med would slip from the U.S. Navy's grasp. Its mission would be to defend the United Kingdom and Gibraltar as stages for an eventual counteroffensive to retake the continent. That meant the United States would have to win a second Battle of the Atlantic against the Soviet submarine force, then carry a reconstituted army across the English Channel in a latter-day invasion of Normandy—whose occupier this time would not be diverted by the need to defend a collapsing eastern front. In August, Halfmoon was renamed Fleetwood, but the song remained the same. It was a funeral dirge for millions.

These war plans and their progeny were shaped more by fiscal constraints than by proven military doctrine. The Joint Chiefs had advised the White House that the cost of defending Paris and Rome while keeping the Navy in the Mediterranean would be at least $16.9 billion. But with $14.4 billion on the table and no more, the deficit seemed to require that the Pentagon leap straight to Armageddon as a way of saving Europe. The compromise was equally clear in the Pacific, where war plans in 1948 provided that Korea be abandoned while U.S. forces consolidated around the defense of Japan, Okinawa, and the Ryukyus.

Naval planners characterized the Air Force's confidence in an atomic bomber offensive as a form of mysticism. As chief of naval operations, Admiral Louis Denfeld saw neither sound strategy nor morality in handing Western Europe to the Soviets without a fight. He thought the strategy gave the Soviet Union far too much psychological power. A doctrine of preemptive retreat robbed the Western alliance of the capacity to inspire other countries to resist Soviet meddling and coercion. He questioned the wisdom of expending the precious U.S. arsenal of atomic weapons in a war plan that he regarded as poorly supported by intelligence on the state of Soviet air defenses. And he objected to the surrender not only of the European landmass, but of the Mediterranean Sea as well. Without a naval presence there, the United States could not access Southern Europe or North Africa, and would have only limited means of defending the oil regions of the Middle East.

Republican senator Arthur H. Vandenberg had successfully sponsored a resolution urging Truman to negotiate a defense treaty with all of Western Europe. It would adhere to the principles of the United Nations Charter but operate free of the veto enjoyed by the Soviet Union by right of its membership on the Security Council. As negotiations began in earnest for the North Atlantic Treaty, a bold internationalism outwardly characterized the viewpoint of Truman and his administration.

George Kennan had his doubts. He regarded the globalist vision as extravagant. He wondered how American interests could be defended "in the meshes of a sterile and cumbersome international parliamentarianism" whose deliberations seemed more show than substance. "The curtain is lifted; the lights go on for a brief moment; the posture of the group is recorded for posterity by the photography of voting; and whoever appears in the most graceful and impressive position has won," he had told an audience at the National War College in June 1947. Defending real American interests required more than gesture. It meant focusing resources and willpower in areas whose defense was worth American blood.

"Unpleasant as this may be," Kennan had said at the College, "we may have to face up to the fact that there may be instances where violence somewhere in the world on a limited scale is more desirable than the alternatives, because those alternatives would be global wars . . . in which all civilization would be dragged down. I think we have to face the fact [that] there may be arrangements of peace less acceptable to the security of this country than isolated recurrences of violence."

Truman was willing to take such a risk in the continuing crisis over Berlin. By the end of June, with the Soviets refusing to relax their blockade of roads into the former German capital, Truman took dramatic action. He pressed into service every available C-54 cargo plane in Europe to fly supplies to the blockaded western enclave of the city. The Berlin Airlift was under way. Though Truman understood that fighter escorts would not be able to overcome a determined effort by Soviet air forces to stop the airlift, he had no choice but to accept the test of his resolve. To underline his seriousness, he approved the deployment of four groups of non-nuclear-capable B-29 Superfortresses to Europe, two each to Germany and Britain.

For all the talk in Washington of atomic bombs—the Navy did some of it but the Air Force talked of little else—influential voices within the Navy preferred that the fleet recommit itself to mastering its traditional roles. As the airlift was beginning, the senior advisory group to the chief of naval operations, the General Board, delivered a direct rebuke to the administration's atomic war plan to defend Europe, concluding that "sole reliance on the complete success of violent and irretrievable departures from established concepts and techniques of war would be highly inadvisable." This study, led by a rising star, Captain Arleigh A. Burke, pointed to antisubmarine warfare (ASW) as the first priority of carrier task forces charged with keeping open the sea lanes to Europe. If the nation's fleet could not control the sea, it could do little else, the thinking went.

One postulate of the Broiler emergency war plan was that the Soviets, having secured the conquest of Europe, would seek to cut off Britain by means of a submarine blockade, rendering it untenable as a staging area for a 1944-style Allied amphibious counteroffensive into the occupied continent. The prospect of a major campaign of submarine warfare seemed likely, given the keen interest Moscow had shown in their captured U-boats. The Soviets eagerly exploited the advanced state of Germany's *untersee* art, mindful of the hard run that German U-boats had given the Allied convoys in World War II. Russians would by the early fifties have a robust production program building diesel-electric attack submarines based upon the German Type XXI U-boat. Moscow called them Project 613 submarines (the NATO code name was Whiskey-class).

The Soviets had reaped a windfall in advanced naval technology after Germany surrendered. Their force of 150 subs was supplemented by thirty common World War II–vintage IX U-boats and as many as twenty of the newer Type XXI. American intelligence estimated that seventy-five of the advanced Type XXVIs were in Soviet hands as well. In fact, when the war ended, the Red navy was completely submarine-centric. It operated 241 diesel-electric subs, dwarfing its surface fleet of four obsolete battleships, eleven cruisers, and sixty destroyers and frig-ates. While the history of Russia's wars and the lay of its geography discouraged Moscow from engaging in visionary thinking about the use of sea power, a large submarine force was a real threat to Allied naval plans. It suited Moscow's refined taste for the covert, and its stealthy offensive capability made it a cost-effective means of challeng-ing American control of the sea. Moscow dreamed of fielding an ar-mada of a thousand submarines.

George Kennan for one wanted to refine and reduce the extent of the burden imposed by the Truman Doctrine's notion of global perimeter defense. He identified certain power centers with a substantial indus-trial capacity as the core strategic areas that deserved to be paid for in American blood and treasure. There were four of them: first, "the At-lantic community"—Canada, Greenland, Iceland, Scandinavia, Brit-ain, Western Europe, Morocco to the French West African coast, and South America from the north coast of Brazil up to the Caribbean; sec-ond, the countries bordering the Mediterranean; third, the Middle East as far east as Iran; and fourth, in the Pacific, Japan and the Philippines. Their protection constituted "an irreducible minimum of national se-curity," he wrote in August 1948.

At the end of September, the Joint Chiefs seemed to acknowledge the primacy of the Navy in the Mediterranean by giving to Admiral Conolly, the commander in chief of U.S. Naval Forces Europe, Eastern Atlantic and Mediterranean, the responsibility of planning the joint operations of all three service branches in the event of a war emergency in that area. Such joint authority mirrored that of Pacific Command in Hawaii and Atlantic Command in Norfolk. Conolly's principal naval striking force, now known as the Sixth Task Fleet, under the command of Forrest Sherman, would defend the entire Atlantic community as it had been defined by George Kennan. Its mission would include everything from launching air strikes against Soviet forces advancing toward the Suez to protecting shipping convoys as they crossed the Atlantic.

The British once again were bothered that an exclusively American command would handle this important strategic project, but the Atomic Energy Act left the Pentagon with little choice. It required all nuclear-capable U.S. forces to remain under U.S. control. The Navy, keeping pace with the Air Force, was going full atomic. It was invested in the vision of a large new aircraft carrier that could perform a range of offensive roles, traditional and novel alike.

The CVA-58 "atomic carrier" project represented the future of the fleet. While the Navy Department was eager to preserve the traditional sea-control mission, including fighter aviation, the $190 million vessel was meant to serve as an atomic strike platform, the first carrier with the capacity to handle the heavy nuclear-capable bombers such as the AJ-1 Savage. Planners meant to use the CVA-58 to specialize in the atomic strike mission, fielding an air group equipped to deliver small atomic bombs while relying upon other smaller carriers to provide fighters for air defense. Though Truman had initially approved construction of five of the new carriers, his hard ceiling on military appropriations made the two new programs, the B-36 bomber and CVA-58 supercarrier, an either-or proposition. Secretary of the Air Force Stuart Symington viewed the new warship as a threat to the Air Force's mode of atomic weapons delivery, the heavy bomber. The Navy found the new carrier in an existential competition with the Air Force's top-priority weapon system for fiscal 1949: the Convair B-36 Peacemaker strategic bomber.

After Admiral Denfeld persuaded three of the four members of the Joint Chiefs to support the CVA-58—the Air Force chief of staff, General Hoyt S. Vandenberg, dissented—the other powerful Vandenberg,

Senator Arthur H., chair of the Senate Foreign Relations Committee, rebutted Denfeld by saying that U.S. airpower had practiced strategic bombing successfully against Japan and Germany, why couldn't it again now? But the CNO persisted in his belief, as did Forrestal, that the idea of evacuating Europe while blasting its Soviet invaders with fission weapons was "completely at variance with U.S. foreign policy." Certainly it made for awkward politics within an alliance, as ordinary Europeans contemplated their cities, schools, and homes being engulfed in a nuclear war. In the end, Air Force resistance led Congress to approve construction of only one of the new atomic carriers.

The B-36 was a monster of an airframe. It had a 230-foot wingspan, six piston engines mounted in an unusual "push" position on the trailing edge of its massive wings, a range of 9,100 miles, a service ceiling of 39,100 feet, and a bomb bay that, upgraded in the design process to something known as a "Grand Slam installation," could carry a payload of 86,000 pounds, enough for eight Fat Man–type atomic bombs. A later model boosted the aircraft's power plant by adding four General Electric J47 jet engines, one pair mounted outboard under each wing. As the Air Force went all in for the huge jet, which had first flown in August 1947 and entered service the following summer, naval officers testified that it was an albatross, vulnerable to fighter aircraft already in current inventory and unable to carry out its essential mission of penetrating enemy air defenses and delivering atomic bombs from high altitude, aiming by radar.

Arthur W. Radford, who as vice chief of naval operations had a prominent voice in the testimony before Congress, summoned technical witnesses to explain the difficulty of radar-guided bombing missions over Germany, and articulated the need for atomic bombs to be dropped with a high degree of accuracy in order to destroy particular targets, a counterintuitive fact well illustrated at Bikini Atoll two years earlier. The campaign against the B-36 turned nasty as Navy sources within the Pentagon began a whisper campaign that Secretary Symington and Air Force brass had personal financial interests in the contracts awarded to Convair.

On September 17, 1948, less than sixty days after the first squadron of B-36s began flying at Carswell Air Force Base near Fort Worth, Texas, flights of B-29s and B-36s passed at low altitude over more than a hundred U.S. cities. The extravaganza of Air Force Day, marking the first anniversary of the creation of the new Pentagon department, had a predictable effect upon an awed public. To amplify the impression, someone leaked to the press what was said to be a secret Air Force briefing to the Joint Chiefs of Staff that listed seventy strategic targets in the Soviet Union that were within range of the B-36. The breach led Senator Carl Vinson, the Georgia Democrat who chaired the House Armed Services Committee, a strong supporter of the atomic carrier project, to warn that further indiscretions would lead to a congressional investigation.

The politics of defense expenditures was front and center during the 1948 presidential campaign. On a six-state campaign swing, Truman announced that the country could not continue with military budgets approaching $15 billion a year. Numbers less than half that much would be a more sustainable burden on the American taxpayer, he said. Atomic airpower offered a windfall of thrift, it was said, and so the Air Force made its claim to exclusive ownership of the atomic mission. Efficiency required that the only service that fielded large four-engine bombers should deliver Armageddon's flame. Truman embraced economy as a proxy for strategic wisdom, eliding the fact that a bomber offensive launched from Great Britain, the Suez area, and Okinawa was vulnerable to interdiction, as conventional military power in all three areas was insufficient to assure the security of the air bases.

Both Forrestal and Denfeld urged the value of aircraft carriers as mobile, survivable air bases. They opposed the Joint Chiefs' recommendation in October to cut the Navy's carrier force from eleven to nine. Nine was the long-established minimum the Navy felt it needed to fulfill the mandate given it by the Joint Chiefs of Staff.

The president hadn't given up on fortifying the reserves either. On October 17, campaigning in West Virginia, he directed Forrestal by executive order to use "every practicable resource" to make sure the military reserves were at "appropriate strength and maximum effectiveness." With defense expenditures capped at $14.4 billion, plus $600 million for stockpiles of other materials, the president was insistent that the Pentagon find ways to win the next world war on the cheap. The expenditures for an expanded reserve waged war with the CVA-58 project on Pentagon ledgers. Penury in defense procurement would be the strategic bomber's trump card. And so, when Forrestal asked the Joint Chiefs to begin studying the prospects of an atomic air offensive to degrade the Soviet Union's capacity to wage war, the advocates of strategic bombing would have their way irrespective of the findings.

Returning to the White House amid all this volatility, the president faced long odds in the 1948 general election after Strom Thurmond, the South Carolina "Dixiecrat," threatened to split the Democratic vote. Still, Truman predicted a surprise when the votes were tabulated. The results on November 3 seemed to validate a foreign policy based on containing the expansion of totalitarian regimes and protecting "free peoples who were resisting attempted subjugation by armed minorities or by outside pressures." Truman was famously photographed holding high a copy of the *Chicago Daily Tribune* that announced a chimerical Republican victory—DEWEY DEFEATS TRUMAN.

ON DECEMBER 15, a federal grand jury indicted Alger Hiss on two counts of perjury in connection with charges that the former State Department official had committed treason against the United States as a member of the Soviet Communist Party underground. His accuser, a journalist named Whittaker Chambers, alleged that Hiss had passed to the Soviet Union sensitive papers on atomic energy, China policy, and military intelligence beginning in the late 1930s. Following closely on the news that the British had arrested a Los Alamos nuclear scientist, Klaus Fuchs, for stealing atomic secrets and passing them to Moscow, the Hiss-Chambers case made captivating blood sport out of the contest between the anticommunism of the Truman administration and the political culture of Franklin Roosevelt's New Deal, whose subscribers for a time made overt common cause with Joseph Stalin as a fellow enemy of Hitler.

For Truman, the Soviet Union was a treacherous and malignant betrayer. Champions of the New Deal had been conditioned to see the Soviets as gallant opponents of Nazism whose Communism was merely another flavor of their benign idealism. The controversy swirled through American life and deranged the nation's politics, consonant with the reality that the Soviet Union was no longer an ally in war. When "loyalty" became a relative term and patriotism acquired dark shadows as a cudgel against dissent, a wedge opened within America that the Soviet Union would exploit for another seven decades.

For Forrestal, Kennan, and the other strategists of the Truman administration, the covert mode of Soviet political warfare was a present and active threat, visibly at work around the world. Hiss and his supporters dismissed warnings of Moscow's subversions as paranoia. As the critic Sidney Hook noted, "All a Communist under threat of exposure need do was to cry 'Witch hunt!' to rally the innocent New Dealers to deny the facts of Communist penetration." Moscow took canny comfort knowing that its agents, when they were as successful as Klaus Fuchs was, could compromise important American state secrets, and that when they were unsuccessful, the recriminations would tear America apart.

9

The Man in the High Tower

On April 4, 1949, the North Atlantic Treaty was signed in Washington. It bound the United States, Canada, Belgium, Denmark, France, Iceland, Italy, Luxembourg, the Netherlands, Norway, Portugal, and the United Kingdom in a covenant of mutual defense and set the stage later in the year for a U.S. military assistance program that allocated $1.4 billion for the rebuilding of Western Europe's military defense.* But the realization of this long-sought internationalist project was overshadowed that spring by darker dramas in Washington. As Truman would record a few years later, "Something happened. I am of the opinion that Potomac fever and a pathological condition are to blame for the fiasco at the end. Louis began to show an inordinate egotistical desire to run the whole government."

"Louis" was Truman's new secretary of defense, Louis A. Johnson. When he was managing the president's fundraising, Johnson had been promised any job he wanted. He chose to run the Pentagon. The hard feelings crystallized almost immediately. The new defense secretary was an equal opportunity irritant, abrasive and arrogant and making no effort to filter it. Truman noted, "He offended every member of the Cabinet." Though Johnson understood well that Truman wanted atomic weapons production kept under civilian management at the

---

* Greece and Turkey would join NATO in 1952, followed by West Germany in 1955.

Atomic Energy Commission, Johnson made known his view that the AEC was little more than "a munitions maker that should fill military orders." The reputation he earned in the Navy Department was reflected in the view of Admiral Richard Conolly. "He was a complete opportunist, completely self-seeking," Conolly said. "I would say he was immoral, and that he was the most dangerous man we've had in public life since Aaron Burr."

On April 23, without forewarning, Johnson announced his decision to cancel the construction of the first CVA-58 class aircraft carrier, the USS *United States*. Though the rationale was specious—Johnson claimed that the ship's atomic strike capability duplicated the Air Force's strategic mission—it didn't matter. With the insistent politicking of the Air Force never relenting, the deck was stacked against the huge ship whose construction promised to save the private shipyard at Newport News, Virginia, and sustain its thousands of yard workers who had not built a ship since the March 1947 launching of the heavy cruiser *Newport News*. Johnson's animus toward the Navy was an open secret. He consulted neither the Navy secretary nor the CNO on the decision to kill the new carrier. The abrupt cancellation compelled Navy Secretary John L. Sullivan to resign, and the ensuing contretemps on Capitol Hill became a spectacle.

Johnson's decision to scrap the new carrier, whose keel plates had just been laid down at Newport News, escalated the debate over weapons procurement. The Navy's leading lights took up arms in congressional testimony that spring, attacking the Air Force case for the B-36 Peacemaker strategic bomber. While the chief of naval operations, Admiral Louis Denfeld, tried to stay out of the fray, the matter escalated in May when a Navy-friendly member of the House Armed Services Committee, Rep. James E. Van Zandt, a retired Navy captain, began investigating allegations that procurement of the aircraft continued only because Secretaries Johnson and Symington had personal financial stakes in it and owed favors to its manufacturer, Convair. The Committee braced itself for Navy witnesses who might substantiate the charges, but the issue was never broached. Far more vexing to the Defense Department were certain naval officers who freelanced as public critics of Louis Johnson's Pentagon.

Meanwhile, a major study of atomic warfare doctrine by a committee chaired by Lieutenant General Hubert R. Harmon was developing serious doubts about the ability of the B-36 to perform as advertised. Within three weeks of the cancellation of the CVA-58, General Harmon's board reported its conclusions to the Joint Chiefs of Staff that an atomic bombardment of Soviet industrial centers with weapons accurate to a circular error of three thousand feet would destroy up to 40 percent of Soviet industrial capacity and inflict 6.7 million casualties—but still not assure Moscow's capitulation. The lack of intelligence on the location of Soviet bomber bases was one key weakness of strategic war planning. Though the conclusions were shaded in gray—the act of capitulation being driven more by psychological factors than military ones—Truman thought the report cast doubt on the confident pronouncements of the Air Force brass.

The Navy seized the occasion to urge study of the tactical uses of nuclear weapons, the expansion of conventional air forces, and the rebuilding of Western European armies. CNO Denfeld, together with some of the leading visionaries at the Navy Department—Dan Gallery, Arleigh Burke, and others—urged all of this strongly. It was unclear how politically palatable any of these ideas would be in Western Europe, where the new alliance required the Pentagon to think seriously about defending the member nations of NATO against a Soviet onslaught.

The Soviet provocation over Berlin ended in May 1949 after the United States managed to do three things exceedingly well: sustain an airlift that flew 5,600 tons of food, coal, and other supplies into the former German capital; establish a sound currency for use in the western zone that defeated the Russian effort to flood it with worthless paper; and rally the besieged populace to rout the Communist Party at the ballot box. The U.S. victory in the test of wills settled the argument at the Department of Defense over whether war plans such as Broiler/ Doublequick should assume the use of atomic weapons. Though Truman hoped for an international ban on the bomb, after Berlin, the Joint Chiefs of Staff continued to draw up war plans predicated on the use of atomic weapons. Even as the Joint Chiefs began to doubt that the Soviets would be stunned into surrender by atomic strikes, Truman considered them as a trump card against Kremlin aggression.

AT THE NAVAL hospital at Bethesda, Forrestal was kept under sedation and constant watch by staff. His windows were screened and medical staff had orders to stay with him at all times. At night he was restless. "Throws himself around in bed," the nurse's notes indicated more than once. He talked in his sleep about "the Cabinet." He was kept on a regimen of subshock insulin therapy for about three weeks, during which time he was "obviously depressed," said the Navy psychiatrist who was on duty on the last night of the former defense secretary's life, Robert R. Deen. Thanks to the irrepressibly malicious Drew Pearson, false reports spread in the press that Forrestal had tried to kill himself at Hobe Sound, that he had run into the street shouting, "The Russians are coming!" Though Deen and the other doctors on Forrestal's case considered him potentially suicidal, none diagnosed him with paranoia. All stated that he was showing dramatic improvement and that as the calendar turned to May, nothing was amiss with his behavior or attitude. In spite of this, Dr. Raines gave medical backing to most any theory of Forrestal's behavior when he noted "how abruptly his condition would change at times in these undulating moments in the illness."

On May 1, the guard in Forrestal's suite was relaxed. He was allowed to take meals alone in his small bedroom until nine o'clock and retire without aid of sodium amytal to ease him into sleep. According to Raines, "He was in that stage of improvement. He was very close to the end of it. That, of course, is the most dangerous time in any depression."

When Truman and Robert Dennison visited Forrestal on May 20, both were surprised to find that the strict patient-monitoring protocols

Commander in Chief Pacific Ocean Areas Chester W. Nimitz signs the Instrument of Surrender marking the end of World War II on September 2, 1945. Aboard USS *Missouri* in Tokyo Bay, standing directly behind Nimitz (right to left), are Rear Admiral Forrest P. Sherman, Admiral William F. Halsey, and General of the Army Douglas MacArthur.

Home from war, USS *Missouri* anchors in the Hudson River for post–World War II Navy Day festivities, October 27, 1945. President Harry S. Truman visited *Missouri* to the highest military reception for a head of state, a 21-gun salute.

Secretary of the Navy James B. Forrestal presents newly minted Fleet
Admiral William F. Halsey with his fifth star on December 11, 1945.
Halsey joins the ranks of Ernest J. King (left), Chester W. Nimitz
(right), and William D. Leahy (not pictured).

James V. Forrestal, appointed
Secretary of the Navy in 1944, and
in 1947 appointed by President Truman
as the first U.S. Secretary of Defense.

George F. Kennan, American diplomat and
author of the February 1946 "Long Telegram,"
which greatly influenced post–World War II
U.S. policy toward the Soviet Union.

Admiral Forrest P. Sherman, Nimitz's
Deputy Chief of Naval Operations, who
later ascended to the CNO role himself
in November 1949.

Arleigh A. Burke as a captain in the
late 1940s, serving as Marc Mitscher's
Chief of Staff. Burke ultimately
became Chief of Naval Operations
in August 1955.

President Harry S. Truman (second from right) observes Eighth Fleet
exercises off the Virginia Capes on April 24, 1946. In this photo taken aboard
fleet flagship USS *Franklin D. Roosevelt,* Truman is surrounded by
(left to right) Fleet Admiral Chester W. Nimitz, Fleet Admiral William
D. Leahy, and Vice Admiral Marc A. Mitscher.

The Operation Crossroads "Test Baker" nuclear detonation conducted by
the United States at Bikini Atoll on July 25, 1946.

On November 7, 1946, Vice Admiral William H. P. Blandy and his wife
cut a specially designed mushroom cloud cake celebrating
Operation Crossroads, with Rear Admiral Frank J. Lowry watching.

Vice Admiral Richard L. Conolly, the U.S. Navy's representative to the 1946 Paris Peace Conference before taking command of U.S. naval forces in the Mediterranean.

Admiral Arthur W. Radford, Vice Chief of Naval Operations, later Commander of the U.S. Pacific Fleet, who became a strong voice in the so-called "Revolt of the Admirals" in April 1949.

President Truman signs the National Security Act Amendment on August 10, 1949. The original 1947 act merged the Army, Navy, and newly created Air Force Departments into the National Military Establishment, renamed the Department of Defense in the 1949 amendment. The act also created the National Security Council and the Central Intelligence Agency.

The aircraft carrier USS *Midway,* lead ship of her class, was selected in 1947 for experimentation as a seaborne rocket launching platform.

MIDWAY FIRING OF V-2 HERALDS NEW WEAPON

S EVERAL hundred miles off the East coast, the USS *Midway* recently tried something new in naval warfare. For the first time in history, a large bombardment rocket was launched successfully from the deck of a ship. For that matter, it was the first time a large rocket had ever been launched from a "rolling platform".

Leading military and civilian personnel in the field of guided missiles watched a captured German V-2 rocket as it was launched from the deck of the 45,000-ton *Midway* on Saturday, 6 September 1947. Immediately after the firing, the *Midway* conducted flight operations.

After being launched successfully, the V-2 travelled about six miles and exploded. But the experiment was successful so far as the Navy was concerned. Primary purpose was to ascertain whether large bombardment rockets could be fired from modern aircraft carriers without requiring modifications affecting flight operations. The *Midway*, the first CVB, did it.

A November 1947 *Naval Aviation News* article declares the September 6 V-2 launch from USS *Midway* a successful experiment.

An early design model for an atomic-capable carrier, the USS *United States* is tested at David Taylor Model Basin, Carderock, Maryland, circa late 1947. The carrier's superstructure had yet to be designed, but ideas of an elevating island and folding smokestacks were intended to maximize deck space to accommodate nuclear bombers.

A B-36B Peacemaker long-range strategic bomber circa 1948–49, before the addition of supplemental jet engines. Admiral Radford would call the B-36 program a "billion-dollar blunder."

The keel plate of USS *United States* is laid in a Newport News Shipbuilding construction dry dock on April 18, 1949. New Secretary of Defense Louis Johnson ordered the carrier canceled five days later.

USS *Carbonero* at the sea test range off Point Mugu, California, circa August 1949. The *Balao*-class submarine is preparing to fire an LTV-N-2 "Loon," an American copy of the German V-1, in continued experimentation with seaborne rockets.

Balao-class submarine USS *Cochino* departs Portsmouth, England, circa July 1949. She sank the following month after a battery explosion off Norway on August 26, 1949.

On June 27, 1950, two days after the Korean People's Army crosses the 38th parallel, President Harry S. Truman orders U.S. air and sea forces to support South Korea.

they expected were nowhere to be found. The doctors feared his progress might be hindered by the intrusions of close monitoring. Dennison said, "I think on balance they thought it would be more hazardous to put him in close confinement, so they gave him a certain amount of freedom. He seemed to be subdued and very quiet. He didn't have very much to say. He was glad to see the president but he obviously was ill. He wasn't vivacious at all. He didn't have very much to offer." Forrestal was certainly still upset over his president's decision to compel his resignation. Noting his sensitivity, Raines had been keeping him isolated from radios and newspapers. The doctor considered Forrestal's mood "rather directly related to his fear of further attacks by certain commentators who broadcast on Sunday evening"—a reference to Drew Pearson and Walter Lippmann.

According to Raines, "It so happened that these two individuals had been particularly vicious in their personal attacks and he was extremely sensitive about further attacks from them. He was so sensitive about these broadcasts that he refused to listen to them himself but asked that I keep an accurate record of what they said. As he improved he was quite disturbed, and reasonably so, over one Sunday night broadcast which had alleged that he was wildly insane and distorted in his judgment while still a member of the cabinet. The content of that particular broadcast, which I recorded, had no basis whatsoever in fact. Mr. Forrestal found that particular broadcast an especially hard one to deal with as he got better, because there seemed to be no way in which it could accurately be disposed of by him. The most difficult single problem in the management of the case was the wild attitude of certain sections of the press."

Night was the hardest time for Forrestal, the doctors noted. Said Raines, "His depression began to get deeper in the late evening and very frequently he needed someone to talk to and I felt he had enough of me during the day and there should be someone else during that time." And yet when night fell on May 21, the relaxed protocol left no one to watch Forrestal on a constant basis. The hospital apprentice who knew him best, Edward W. Prise, was on duty in the evening. Forrestal liked fresh air and often slept with the window open. That night he remarked to Prise that he thought it was stuffy in the room. Around eight o'clock, Forrestal went into the bedroom adjoining his, which was used by the attending night physician, raised the blinds, and lifted the window as far as it would go. When Prise entered, Forrestal "jumped aside," the hospital apprentice said.

Forrestal said, "Prise, I raised that window. If it gets you in any trouble, close it." Prise reported this to the newcomer to Forrestal's case, a hospital apprentice named Robert Wayne Harrison, Jr., who relieved Prise at the end of the four-to-midnight shift. Prise mentioned that Forrestal had been pacing the floor for nearly three hours before the shift change.

Harrison engaged with Forrestal several times during his shift but noticed nothing obviously amiss with him. He saw him getting a glass of orange juice in the small galley across the hall from his bedroom and later heard another hospital apprentice, Edwin Utz, bring him a cup of coffee.

The nurse on duty that night, Lieutenant Regina "Margie" Hardy, noted that Forrestal went to lie down in his darkened bedroom after drinking the coffee. Concerned that Forrestal had been so restless and hadn't taken his sedative, and with a new corpsman on duty, she decided to pay more attention to him. When she looked in on him at 1:30 A.M., she saw by the dim light of a night-light that he appeared to be sleeping. Harrison thought Forrestal was asleep too, but later told Hardy that he asked him who the woman was who had entered his room. Hardy instructed Harrison to ask Dr. Deen whether Forrestal should take his sodium amytal, as he had declined to take it earlier. Deen told Harrison that Forrestal could decide for himself whether to take the sedative.

Harrison last checked on Forrestal around 1:45 A.M. and found him apparently asleep, then went down the hall to the nurse's desk, where he updated Forrestal's medical chart. After Harrison finished, he returned to look in on Forrestal. After Harrison finished, he returned to look in on Forrestal, but saw that there was no one in the bed.

That was when a nurse working on the eighth floor, Dorothy Turner, came rushing up to sixteen. She told Nurse Hardy that a body had crashed to the roof of the building beneath the tower and that the person wasn't her patient.

Hardy awakened Deen, who came rushing into the hall. In the uproar that ensued, the staff ran to the small kitchen across the hall from Forrestal's bedroom, looked out the window, and saw his body, broken and still on the asphalt roof of the medical tower building thirteen floors below. He was in his pajamas and a bathrobe sash was tied around his neck.

Hardy and Turner were the first to enter Forrestal's empty hospital room. On his bed, the linens were half turned back. A few pieces of broken glass were on his bed and a razor blade was on the floor beside his slippers.

Down on the fourth floor of the tower, William Eliades, a hospital corpsman, heard a crashing noise and went to the window overlooking the third-floor roof. A body was lying there. He called for help, then climbed out the window, went to the crumpled figure, who was wearing pajamas, and felt for a pulse at the wrist. Finding none, he ran to find a doctor. When a doctor returned to make an examination, by the light of his flashlight beam Eliades noted that a bathrobe sash was tied around the man's neck.

Drew Pearson had claimed Forrestal had once tried to hang himself and also tried to slash his wrists. When he was in Florida, Forrestal himself had told Dr. Menninger that he had tried to hang himself with a belt while he was there. But Menninger and Raines were skeptical about the claim. "It was sort of a nightmare," Raines said. "The man had no marks on him and there was no broken belt. Very frequently a depressed person has a fantasy of dying and reports it as real. So far as I know he never made a single real attempt at suicide except that one that was successful.

"In the course of psychotherapy," said Raines, "he talked a great deal about his suicide; he would tell me when he was feeling hopeless and had to do away with himself. At those times we would tighten restrictions. He would tell me in symbolic language. One morning he sent me a razor blade which he had concealed. When I interviewed him I said, 'What does this mean?' He said, 'It means I am not going to kill myself with a razor blade.' Of course, he had the blade and could have done it. A man of that intelligence can kill himself at any time he desired and you can't very well stop him."

Several doctors on Forrestal's case would testify that he had never attempted suicide prior to his death on May 22. The glass found on Forrestal's bed and the razor blade on the floor were clean. There was no blood anywhere. An autopsy would find no sign of self-inflicted lacerations, or of asphyxiation.

And yet the figurative autopsy that newspapers conducted the following day in their reporting took a turn into the bizarre. Several articles, without citing sources, led with a macabre account of Forrestal transcribing a poem from an anthology that they claimed was found in his room immediately afterward. The book was said to contain "Chorus from Ajax" by Sophocles; a page of its morbid, death-wishing verse had been transcribed in Forrestal's own hand, seeming to foretell the former defense secretary's tragic end. An Associated Press story called it "a book of Greek poetry." A psychobiography of Forrestal published in 1963 cited an unnamed Navy corpsman who claimed that Forrestal was seen performing the transcription five minutes before he died. However, the proceedings of the Navy investigative board showed that in the hour during which he was supposedly transcribing the poem, Forrestal had been in bed in a darkened room. Though the board report does contain, without explanation or reference, an exhibit of a photostat of a handwritten transcription from Sophocles, the handwriting in no way resembles Forrestal's own, persuasively refuting the poetry transcription story. No witness testimony mentions such a document being found in Forrestal's room, nor the book from which it was supposedly copied. But the story had too much potency to submit to such ready refutation. Thus allegory became standard narrative. The writer's implication was clear: Forrestal must have meant it as a suicide note, though "it" did not exist.

Robert Deen and the other doctors testified that Forrestal's death had to have been a suicide, an impulsive act. "Self-destruction is a force that is so impelling," Deen would say, "that it is beyond the ability of the normal mind to comprehend its depth and intensity. The desire to die under those circumstances as I have witnessed it is only comparable to the desire of a normal, healthy person to live." But such speculation was no more dispositive of Forrestal's case than someone's supposed apocryphal sighting of the phantom book of verse. In the end, Raines seemed as mystified as anyone that his patient, on the verge of a complete recovery, should have died by his own hand. He considered it a "period of despondency" that was "very sudden in onset and probably the whole matter was on an impulsive basis." Neither Raines nor anyone else could explain why a man in such a state would trouble himself to tie a bathrobe sash around his neck when an open window beckoned.

The character of the investigative board proceedings—for example, it neglected to interview certain key witnesses who were on duty that night—suggests that Dr. Raines and the Navy were more interested in avoiding liability than in building a factual record that established what really happened. Accounts ever since that relied upon it have suffered for the Navy's decision to restrict access to the report and transcript of the investigative board. The transcript, released by the Navy only in 2004 after a researcher filed a Freedom of Information Act request, shows numerous physicians attesting to the quality of Forrestal's medical care. While these opinions were given by several doctors who were nowhere near Bethesda, four hospital corpsmen who were involved directly in Forrestal's care were never called to testify, nor were several friends who visited him, including Rear Admiral Clifford A. Swanson, the surgeon general of the Navy, who saw Forrestal fourteen times, the first time at Forrestal's urgent request. The board does not conclude that Forrestal took his own life, though several of its testifying physicians do. By keeping the report classified until 2004, the board ensured that misapprehensions would endure.

The testimony of Forrestal's brother Harry is unsettling. Long alienated from James and denied visitation by Raines, Harry finally prevailed by threat of a media campaign and a lawsuit. The day after

Forrestal died, Harry was due to come to the hospital to see his brother. Harry had planned to take him to convalesce at home. Harry said James was the last person in the world who would have committed suicide and that he had no reason for taking his life. James had told Henry that he was making plans for things to do after his release.

Suspicions would develop that Forrestal's death was foul play linked to his opposition to the creation of Israel, and also to his fervent anti-communism. A theory of murder based on circumstantial evidence would say that either Soviet or Israeli agents killed him. Motivation to murder arose, the theory supposes, from the fact that Forrestal would continue his political project after discharge. He was said to have plans to write books on foreign relations, and perhaps to edit *The New York Sun*. Years later, Hospital Apprentice Edward Prise's daughter surfaced, suggesting there was something dark about the case, that her father, as one of Forrestal's principal caretakers at Bethesda, "lived in fear of something happening because of information he knew about the case." Drawing conclusions from this, however, requires leaps worthy of Marvel Comics. There is no evidence to suggest that a killer had infiltrated the hospital tower on the night of May 22, 1949. But none can doubt that politics was behind his death.

Afterward, the journalist William Hillman, who was close to Harry Truman, thought Forrestal's most vocal detractors had poisoned American politics: "It should be the hour of deep soul-searching by Americans—of questioning of how far we can go in pillorying and crucifying men in public office. It is one thing to say that Forrestal made a mistake. . . . But to have subjected Forrestal to the charge that he was a tool of Wall Street, that he was a vicious warmonger, that he was using the crisis of the world merely to enhance his own power or his profit—and yet to have withheld proof of such a charge. . . . Washington and this country need a shaking up—a reorientation of our public life. . . . Rumors and gossip fill the air and the columns of newspapers to an extent that social historians someday will look upon with amazement. . . . Communism has no greater ally in this country than the half-baked hysterical charges against leaders of this country by political opponents." At Forrestal's burial service in Arlington National Cemetery, President Truman said, "This great American was as truly a casualty of the war as if he had died on the firing line." James Forrestal was a casualty of something, and it was not entirely clear which war the president meant.*

---

* One theory of Forrestal's death casts him as the victim of an assassination plot. See David Martin, *The Assassination of James Forrestal*. The conspirators, Martin concludes on the basis of inference from circumstantial evidence, were Zionists within the Truman administration who targeted Forrestal for his strong opposition to the creation of the Jewish state. He fingers "mysterious" Truman adviser David Niles as the "most likely coordinator" of the plot.

10

A TRUE SUBMARINE

IT WAS A COLD DAY IN NEW LONDON, CONNECTICUT, WHEN
General Maxwell D. Taylor stood before the eighty-third graduating
class of the U.S. Navy's Submarine School and declared, "I have never
understood why anyone ever wanted to be on a submarine." As a commander of airborne troops and the superintendent of the U.S. Military
Academy at West Point, Taylor should have had no other view.

World War II had been the submarine's proving ground. Of the nine
million tons of Japanese shipping sunk in the war, submarines accounted for 58 percent of it. Their next-best rival was naval airpower,
credited with 20 percent of the tonnage, and the Army Air Forces with
seven. Submarines had set a blockade such as no squadron of warships
ever had before.

But the submarines of the 1940s were little more than surface ships
with a special ability. They could disappear below for that brief period
of time when battery storage sufficed for propulsion. Underwater, the
diesel boats moved slowly, like sailing ships tacking in the doldrums.
Yet as far as Chester Nimitz was concerned, the world had yet to see a
true submarine. With his enthusiastic backing, the Navy's community
of technologists and dreamers were getting close. If ever there was a
time for someone to want to close a hatch, blow ballast, and disappear
into the depths, the decade of technological revolution that accelerated
toward fruition in 1946 was it.

The invention of a true submarine would require further break-throughs, such as developing an engine than ran without poisoning the crew with its exhaust. German innovations such as the closed-cycle engine, which used bottled compressed air, or a turbine that burned a high-test hydrogen peroxide solution known as ingolin, intrigued American and British submariners. This latter invention, the brain-child of Nazi engineer Hellmuth Walter, enabled a small coastal U-boat known as the Type XVII to operate submerged for six hours at unheard-of underwater speeds as high as twenty-five knots. The next generation of high-seas U-boat with a Walter engine, the Type XXVI, promised for a time to be the wave of the future. But ingolin tended to catch fire, and that constant danger was the death knell of that technology as far as Western navies were concerned. The Russians, less worried about safety, were thought to have captured seventy-five Type XXVIs in German shipyards after V-E Day and were studying them closely. Meanwhile, the streamlined Type XXI, with its improved acoustic quieting high-capacity battery and electric motors, outfitted with sensitive passive hydrophones, could speed along submerged at sixteen knots—a revolution unto itself, though only four were completed and made ready for action during the war.

Of the ten U-boats the Soviet Union received from Germany as post-war reparations, four were Type XXIs, all assigned to the Soviet navy's Baltic Fleet. As of January 1948, the U.S. Joint Intelligence Committee estimated that the Soviets had fifteen operational Type XXI submarines and could have another forty-one within eighteen months. The Navy feared a surge of Soviet construction. By early 1950 Moscow was thought to have 291 diesel-electric submarines of all varieties, 74 of them oceangoing types distributed among the USSR's four fleets, the Baltic, Northern, Black Sea, and Pacific.

But a "true" submarine would be an atomic-powered submarine, in the view of American experts, a vessel that could dwell beneath the waves. The lead author of a March 1946 technical report by the Naval Research Laboratory concluded that with enough support from Congress and the AEC, the Navy could build an "atomic-energy submarine" within two years. That visionary, Philip H. Abelson, and his boss,

Dr. Ross Gunn, had been at work for seven years on the problem of turning atomic heat into turbine-driving steam. In 1939, Gunn found a capable partner in Harold G. Bowen, the head of the Navy's Bureau of Engineering. Gunn recruited Abelson from the Carnegie Institution to come to the Clinton Laboratories in Oak Ridge, Tennessee, to work on the essential problem of producing fuel for an atomic pile: separating fissionable uranium-235 in quantity from uranium-238.

Whenever the early advocates spoke of the potential of the atom in naval propulsion, the limit of the human imagination was the first obstacle they had to clear. Edward L. Beach, a submariner who had worked for Rear Admiral Parsons in the Navy's Atomic Defense Section in 1947, recalled skeptics asking before the war, "So the thing can go underwater forever, but what good is it?" He responded, "It's the world's best submarine. You can do what we did in World War II, but twenty times as well." He told one doubter, "I think we could have won the whole damn war with ten of these things."

Cruising underwater free of the need for air and with a functionally limitless fuel supply, a submersible became a true submarine. Not only would it operate underwater, it would reside there. Enjoying unlimited range, and unlimited electrical power, the atomic submarine commander would enjoy the freedom to exploit the tactical initiative that was his birthright thanks to the World War II generation. The boundaries that confined him were the limits of his crew, not those of his machinery, and the hard edges of the coastline and sea floor, not the endurance of his fuel supply.

But when Philip Abelson left Oak Ridge and returned to the Naval Research Laboratory (NRL) after the war, he was "tired and disappointed," the legendary World War II submarine commander Charles A. Lockwood recalled. In the Manhattan Engineer District, which was an Army-run show, Navy ideas got low priority. The atomic bomb consumed the effort. Seeing some of his work in isotope separation get credited to others, he felt his energy flagging after almost five years of long hours. That was when he met Commander Robert I. Olsen. As a military liaison assigned to NRL and a World War II submarine commander of note, Swede Olsen was fascinated by Germany's advanced designs. He borrowed a set of captured plans for a Type XXVI U-boat from the Bureau of Ships and showed them to Abelson. According to Olsen, "I took them to Phil and made a big pitch based on two factors. One: We ought to be able to do it better than the Germans. And two: He would, at last, get a first that nobody would ever be able to take away from him."

Abelson was moved, telling Olsen that while his time was growing short, "he'd do it for the boys in the submarine service." Olsen promised him that he would see to it that nuclear power got into a submarine before it got into an aircraft carrier. As limited resources meant limited application, nuclear power would have to go to one type of warship or the other. Years into this revolution, the momentum seemed irresistible. Theory and application were in happy marriage. The rest was engineering, and the engineers at the Bureau of Ships were enthused.

Abelson's blueprints and diagrams were derived from a captured Type XXVI U-boat at the Engineering Experimental Station at Annapolis. He envisioned a vessel capable of twenty-six knots or more while submerged, driven by a shielded atomic pile mounted to the outside of the pressure hull. Eventually forty knots should be possible, he said, venturing further that atomic-powered subs operating on jet propulsion might be capable of sixty. "It read like something out of Jules Verne's *Twenty Thousand Leagues Under the Sea,*" Lockwood would say. "Our investigations and explorations ran from alpha to omega on the subject."

Abelson's imagination wasn't limited to improving on German technology. "To function offensively," he wrote, "this fast submarine will serve as an ideal carrier and launcher of rockets and atomic bombs." Innovation was part of the submariner's culture. Development of the atomic submarine hit a snag, however, when the Atomic Energy Commission, holding exclusive authority under law to license reactors to operate, announced it was undecided as to the feasibility of the atomic submarine. The AEC wasn't sure that either the funding or supply of U-235 would be sufficient for development to continue. This moved Chester Nimitz, an early-generation submariner himself, to declare the nuclear-powered submarine a "military necessity." Such a strong vote from the operating fleet invited the AEC Military Liaison Committee and ultimately James Forrestal to intervene. Forrestal notified the secretary of war that the

Navy wanted to tackle the engineering problem of naval atomic propulsion. When General Leslie Groves, head of the Manhattan Engineer District, suggested that Forrestal set up a naval technical team next to the Clinton Laboratories in Oak Ridge, Forrestal assigned eight midgrade naval officers and civilian engineers to collaborate with Groves's people. The head of the group was Captain Hyman G. Rickover.

Rickover had made his name designing shipboard electrical systems during the war. At Oak Ridge, he became convinced that nuclear power was a natural fit for a submarine. His team immersed themselves in the problems of nuclear propulsion for more than a year, collaborating with scientists, including the physicist Edward Teller, who saw great potential in naval atomic propulsion. Rear Admiral Earle W. Mills brought the group to the Bureau of Ships in September 1947, naming Rickover as his "special assistant on nuclear matters." Rickover did not want to go to Washington. He complained that such a posting would slow his career. But by the time he took up a barren fourth-floor space of the Navy building on Constitution Avenue, in an area that was once a restroom, Rickover found that his view of the opportunity had come around.

Though his job was to advise Admiral Mills, Rickover reported to a naval engineer who had been considered "Mr. Submarine" during the war, Captain Armand Morgan. Though technically his subordinate, Rickover effectively ran the office on the force of his abundant personal energy and nearly manic attention to detail. He worshiped the laws of physics with a front-pew fervor and dared his subordinates to pace him in chasing the ideal of engineering perfection that he felt those laws required. He wielded the lash at all times, not least his snapping tongue. As Rickover and the director of research at Oak Ridge, Alvin M. Weinberg, began work on the new pressurized-water fission reactor for the submarine, Rickover would ever after point to the humble trappings of his office in the renovated restroom as a moral mandate to upend a hidebound system that he held in contempt. While Rickover had never commanded a submarine, Mills thought he might well be the man to engineer a revolution. As the Truman administration held the line on defense expenditures for fiscal year 1950 with a hard ceiling of $14.4 billion, Mills managed to find the money to establish a Nuclear Power Branch within the Bureau of Ships. Soon thereafter, the Atomic Energy Commission created a Reactor Development Division under Dr. Lawrence R. Hafstad. In April 1948, Mills delivered what Lockwood called "a fine fighting address" at a classified symposium on new submarine designs at the Bureau of Ships. Lockwood would credit him for "getting the AEC off its duff" in the matter of actually building an atomic reactor for submarines.

But new tactical thinking was coming into the submarine service so rapidly that the cutting edge would not await the arrival of the first nuclear-propelled submarine. As the Bikini tests were under way in the summer of 1946, Chester Nimitz had approved Forrest Sherman's nomination of Rear Admiral Charles W. "Gin" Styer to head the only Navy Department billet devoted to submarine warfare at the time, the Coordinator of Undersea Warfare. Styer proposed the creation of two special units, Submarine Development Group One, based in San Diego, and Submarine Development Group Two, at New London, to serve as test beds for new technology and tactics.

Styer and his tribe thought their diesel-electric-powered fleet submarines had plenty of life left. Improving their underwater endurance was the purpose of the GUPPY (Greater Underwater Propulsive Power) program, which installed higher-capacity storage batteries in the old subs and streamlined their hulls. Specialized new prototypes proliferated on the rationale of simplicity and economy of production. Diverse variants included cargo carriers (SSAs), bombardment (SSB) and super bombardment (SSSB) boats, ammunition carriers (SSEs), guided missile launchers (SSGs), minelayers (SSMs), oilers (SSOs), and pickets (SSRs). The fleet boats *Cusk* and *Carbonero* were transformed into missile-launching SSGs with the addition of a topside hangar that could house a German V-1 buzz bomb clone known as a Loon. The first submarine-launched guided missile had to be fired while the sub was on the surface. A test carried out on February 12, 1947, off the Southern California coast went well enough to justify the continued investment in missile-firing submarines.

The SSO, a submarine oiler, resembled a pregnant whale with her

distended ballast and fuel tanks. It was envisioned as a mobile fuel supply at invasion beachheads or as a seagoing refueling base for seaplanes.

But the Navy's tacticians believed that the principal mission of U.S.
submarines should be the destruction of enemy submarines. The
hunter-killer boat, known as an SSK, could be built affordably and in
numbers. Both the Pacific and Atlantic submarine commands agreed
that such vessels, patrolling near Soviet harbors and listening with passive sonar, could be deployed in numbers large enough to bottle up
Moscow's submarine force. The technical and tactical challenges by
which one submerged craft would detect, fix, and destroy another became a generational project for the submarine community's best thinkers and operators. It would be known as Project Kayo.

When Captain Roy S. Benson took command of Submarine Development Group Two at New London, Connecticut, in March 1949, his
first meeting was with one of his sagest veterans, a fellow high scorer
from World War II named Henry C. Bruton. Benson invited his counsel. Captain Bruton, who had received three Navy Crosses, said to the
incoming commodore that the development group would have to show
dramatic results soon. "Otherwise it's all over," he said. "You're going
to have to depend very heavily on your underwater sound equipment.
You're going to have to listen to these enemy submarines. But the
equipment on these submarines is not equal to the task. They can be
made so if we give them some loving care. If we try that, we might be
able to get something going." And that's exactly what he did.

At New London in 1949, Benson had use of four submarines, the
Cochino, Tusk, Toro, and *Corsair.* With some of the sharpest minds in
the nation right down the Thames River at the Underwater Sound Lab
and at Woods Hole Oceanographic Institute in Massachusetts, Benson
enjoyed access to the scientific leading edge as well. But when the USL
technicians arrived to tune up the improved hydrophones on his four
subs, they found that their first order of business was simply to connect
the hydrophones to their receiver. The diesel-electric submarine was a
case of hardware not yet rising to the caliber of the minds contemplating its optimal use.

The *Toro* and *Corsair* were ordinary diesel-electric fleet boats. The

Cochino and *Tusk* had undergone modernization as GUPPYs, upgraded with snorkels and 250-ton arrays of lead-acid storage batteries. All that ballast and chemical potential energy yielded a modest return. Streamlined for high submerged speed, the GUPPYs had a top underwater speed of eight knots and could run for only an hour before they had to surface and recharge.

Benson knew from war experience how dangerous active sonar was. Throwing a sharp *ping* into the water and listening for the echo served to announce one's location as surely as did turning on a flashlight in a darkened room. So "passive" detection became the state of the hunter-killer's art. Submariners tracked their targets by listening with their sonar hydrophones, not broadcasting through them. Silence correlated with lethality. As improvements in the manufacturing tolerances of gears, shafts, motors, and pumps enabled submarines to operate more quietly and reduced ambient sound levels inside the hull, onboard hydrophones could hear more of what was happening in the surrounding ocean, and adversaries had less noise to listen for in return.

A better understanding of ocean science promised to extend the American advantage. The idea to pursue oceanography as a naval discipline belonged to Thomas Edison, who had advocated the formation of the Naval Research Laboratory in 1915. Eight years later it was a reality, carrying out research in underwater sound propagation and producing sonar sets, radio direction-finding devices, and the first radar equipment built in the United States.

Private universities were making creative contributions too. In 1937, a geophysicist at Lehigh University named Maurice Ewing had discovered something that would prove seminally important. While using underwater explosions to explore with sound waves the properties of suboceanic plates, he noticed that the waves bounced from the bottom to the surface in a regular, repeating cycle—and carried for great distances. Ewing posited the existence of a layer of water in the deep ocean that trapped, focused, and carried sound waves with minimal attenuation. It would become known as "the deep sound channel." Sound waves captured within it traveled as far as three thousand kilometers, or about eighteen hundred miles. Defined by a particular level of sea pressure, temperature, and salinity, the deep sound channel existed in the North Atlantic at a depth of twelve hundred meters, and in the Pacific at a somewhat shallower depth.

Using this finding, Ewing devised a system of long distance signaling that enabled pilots, shot down and adrift on the ocean, to communicate their locations to rescuers using miniature depth charges. It worked like this: The pilot, in his life raft, dropped an explosive charge set to detonate at the depth of the deep sound channel in his operating area. The sound waves of the charge, carrying through the channel, could be detected by hydrophones set at locations on the sea floor around the operating area. When the hydrophones detected the sound of a concussion, the differences in its arrival times at the various receivers enabled the pilot's position to be fixed by triangulation. Ewing called it Sound Fixing and Ranging, or SOFAR. Supported by the ocean-science community, the U.S. Navy would move to exploit the tactical uses of low-frequency sound waves and the deep sound channel phenomenon.

There remained so much to know about the ocean that the idea of submerging into its depths in a pressurized steel tube promised to be as exciting as venturing into outer space. Programs from coast to coast, from the Woods Hole Oceanographic Institution to the Marine Physical Laboratory (MPL) in San Diego, part of the University of California, helped the Navy to understand basic ocean science as it applied to naval operations. The Bureau of Ships commissioned MPL and the Scripps Institute in La Jolla to determine the axis of the deepwater sound channel off the West Coast and to survey the sea floor to determine the best places to install hydrophones to listen for Soviet submarines. Point Loma's Naval Electronics Laboratory researched sonar training and acoustic countermeasures as submarine commanders sampled seawater, studied ocean currents and sea ice, and explored chemical and biological ocean phenomena with an eye toward improving their chances in the next fight. In an extraordinary marine engineering project, arrays of hydrophones—acoustic receivers—were placed on the ocean bottom.

A thousand-foot-long horizontal line array of forty hydrophones laid on the sea floor at a depth of 1,440 feet was deployed off the island of Eleuthera in the Bahamas in January 1952. The hydrophones were connected by underwater cables to shore processing centers. It was the first prototype of a full-size SOSUS installation. Shortly thereafter, Captain Roy Benson of Submarine Development Group Two was asked to bring his four submarines to St. George's Island in Bermuda and find out how far the geophone could hear them—on the surface, at snorkel depth, at periscope depth, and at deep depth, as well as when the propellers' noises were heard directly and when the submarine was shielding some of the noise. The Navy decided to install similar arrays along the entire U.S. East Coast, the target of this set being the "Greenland-Iceland-UK gap," the natural bottleneck the landforms imposed upon the North Sea, making life difficult for any Soviet submarine transiting to the Atlantic. Two years later, the Navy decided to extend the system to the West Coast and Hawaii. These early SOSUS line arrays were located at the edge of the continental shelf looking out into the deep ocean.

At New London, the scientists helped Roy Benson and his commanders understand "the sonar equation," which modeled the performance of sonar systems based on oceanographic variables such as seawater temperature and salinity. The discipline originated during the search for the wreck of the *Titanic* in the early 1900s, but came into its own in submarine warfare after World War II. Older officers found the learning curve steep. "It was difficult to talk sonar equations to the senior people," Benson said. "They could follow the stock market, but they didn't want to hear about decibels and the sonar equation." Benson cultivated an "open-shop" attitude and a culture of truth-telling as he built his command into a center of tactical innovation. The demands of competence required every submariner to use his sonars at peak efficiency in different ocean conditions.

Because many of its major harbors were closed by Arctic ice for much of the year or permanently bottlenecked by the lay of the surrounding landforms, the Soviet Union was vulnerable to a well-executed submarine blockade. Newer passive sonars such as the BQR-4, mounted in a dome attached to a submarine's bow, would enable a hunter-killer to detect a submarine running on diesel engines at a distance of twenty or more nautical miles. So equipped, three to five SSKs—hunter-killer diesel boats—could form an effective barrier across enemy submarine transit routes, covering a hundred-mile stretch of sea as effectively as twenty-five to seventy surface ships could. The OEG calculated that ten new hunter-killer submarines could fully cover the avenues out of the Barents Sea, monitoring a rectangle of frigid water from Norway's North Cape all the way north to Spitsbergen, the summer boundary of Arctic pack ice at the time.

If the United States was going to check the Soviet Union's ability to deploy naval forces internationally, it could not rely upon ice fields as strategic bottle corks. It would have to operate proficiently on the open sea.

That was on Captain Roy Benson's mind when he received orders from COMSUBLANT, the commander of the U.S. Atlantic submarine force, to take four old subs to carry out a simulated war patrol in the cold seas north of Norway. On the afternoon of July 18, 1949, flying his commodore's flag in the *Toro,* under command of Robert K. Worthington, Benson led the *Tusk, Cochino,* and *Corsair* out of New London. Passing Montauk Light abeam to starboard, the quartet turned to open ocean and conducted several days of training dives and sonar tests before heading east toward Argentia, Newfoundland, and then to Londonderry, Ireland, and Portsmouth. A pair of Royal Navy frigates made contact under way for a friendly round of cat and mouse. With a boost of speed and some mild maneuvering, the submarines lost them utterly. HMS *Loch Tralaig* radioed Benson at the end of the exercise, "YOU WERE VERY ELUSIVE THAT RUN WHICH WAS A LITTLE TOO DIFFICULT FOR US." Benson and company enjoyed some R & R at Portsmouth before shifting his flag to the *Tusk* and getting under way again with the Royal Navy's top submarine officer, Rear Admiral Guy Grantham, on board for the busy duration of August 12. That evening after tea, the four submarines returned their VIP observer to Portland and headed to sea again. In the last hours of a clear, warm day with low swells and a light wind, they prepared for two busy weeks in Arctic waters.

Passage between Iceland and the Faeroe Islands was hazardous owing to relic minefields of World War II. Here the four boats split off, with *Toro* and *Corsair* patrolling north of Iceland, and *Tusk* leading *Co-chino* to the sea area south of Spitsbergen. Plunging north as the barometer fell, Benson's boats met winds and seas that grew heavier and angrier as they went.

The risks seemed justified given the nature of their mission: to gather data on very-low-frequency radio reception while submerged, to measure seawater salinity and temperature gradients in the cold northern waters, to chart the thousand-fathom curve, to test the performance of their sonars and underwater telephones, and to conduct a general reconnaissance of the Norwegian, Greenland, and Barents seas—the strategic seaways leading to Russia's Arctic ports. Though their orders prohibited them from operating east of the 30th meridian east of Greenwich, provocatively close to Soviet waters, they were rehearsing to wage war against Moscow's submarine force. The darkened boats proceeded on the surface, easily dodging the cargo ships and trawlers they frequently encountered. Separating on August 17, they submerged, continuing to track targets, treating cargomen as aircraft carriers and trawlers as destroyers while they surveyed with their sonars the shape of the thousand-fathom curve.

The *Tusk* crossed the Arctic Circle off Norway's northwest coast on the nineteenth at 4:30 A.M., two hours after sunrise. Radio weather reports indicated a falling barometer and the likelihood of polar storms. The winds shifted, coming from the west, and the sea dealt roughly with the surfaced boat, hammering her with waves as high as thirteen feet. Submerging then, still running on her diesels, her snorkel sucking air, the *Tusk* heaved with the swells, broaching to the surface and diving deep, occasionally so deep that her snorkel slurped water, forcing the engines to draw air from within the hull. Worthington and his crew felt it as a vacuum in their ear canals. The swaying air pressure played havoc with the ship's baker's yeast. The crew ate thirty loaves a day whether the bread rose or sank.

They were snooping, recording the frequencies, pulse rates, and strength of Soviet radar installations in the region. The surface traffic vanished as the weather became heavy. On the morning of the twenty-fifth, as the *Tusk* approached the eastward limit of the patrol area, Benson and Worthington changed course west. Eventually they made contact with the *Cochino*'s captain, Rafael Benitez, on the underwater telephone. The *Cochino*'s skipper reported his findings following four days of reconnaissance along the Norwegian coast.

The two captains were scheduled to rendezvous in order to make plans for their continued war play, but with the worsening weather making it unwise to surface, Worthington decided to hold the *Tusk* at snorkel depth. Violent seas shook the boat, causing unsecured items to slide and crash about. The planesmen in the control room struggled to maintain their trim as the wave bottoms shoved the shallow-running sub to and fro. Riding the unpredictable arcs, the crew stayed flexed at knee and waist, moving with the boat.

Just about noon, as Worthington closed to within a few miles of the submerged *Cochino,* zigzagging and tracking her with passive sonar, another message came from Benitez over the underwater telephone:

"Casualty. Surfacing."

This was a shocker. In seas this rough, a submarine captain did not lightly depart the safe haven of the depths. Benson looked at Worthington, caught his eye, and mouthed a dreaded word. "Gas?" The skipper nodded in agreement.

Three types of gas were mortal threats to a submerged submarine: diesel fumes, chlorine produced when battery cells got soaked with seawater, and hydrogen generated during a battery charge. The last was the worst of the three.

In extremely cold water, submarines collected dew on the insides of their pressure hulls. As the condensate pooled, the ocean movements could cause the water to splash about. Seawater entered the battery array, causing an electrical arc, a short circuit, between two of the batteries. During the recharging process, the by-product was hydrogen gas. Such "outgassing" was dangerous, as hydrogen in sufficient density was self-combusting. Without good ventilation, the hydrogen would begin burning and exploding. Experienced diesel boat hands knew the terror of occasional hydrogen flashes. Few survived to relate what happened if the gas was allowed to accumulate in greater density. The terse message from the *Cochino* suggested that such a catastrophe might be at hand.

11

ABANDON SHIP

No sooner had Captain Benitez shouted "Hydrogen! Put out the smoking lamp! Pull no switches!" than his submarine was seized by an explosion. As fire spread in the after battery compartment, smoke and heat welled. The door swung open and men rushed out, crowding into the control room. Poisonous smoke swirled in behind them until the door was slammed shut again.

Benitez shouted down the hatch from the conning tower to the control room, "Stand by to surface!" Swiftly the acknowledgment came.

"All vents shut, sir. Both plants running. Ready to surface."

As the captain triggered the alarm, calling "Surface, surface, surface," high-pressure air rushed into the main ballast tanks, shoving out water, and the bow planes were angled to full rise.

The violence of motion inside the *Cochino* was unmistakable as she rose from the waves. She broached the surface bow first at a high angle, then slumped level. Feet set, holding fast, Benitez spun open the hatch overhead and climbed from the conning tower to the bridge, greeting the squalls with his quartermaster, Joseph Stroz, alongside. The wind, whipping cold, threw rain and freezing seawater into their faces, and at intervals the waves crashed against the hull, washing them in spray.

Three decks below, the executive officer, Lieutenant Commander Richard M. Wright, reported over the intercom that the fire in the after battery compartment had been traced to a short circuit. Several men were unconscious from exposure to poison gas, Wright said. There were eighteen men in the engine and torpedo rooms. Wright said he was organizing a firefighting party to try to stop the short.

As the firefighters mustered, Lieutenant (j.g.) Frank Clifford drove his shoulder into the steel door. It did not budge. It was sealed shut either by heat or gas pressure built up within. Smoke laced with stibine and sulfuric acid seeped through the door seals, seizing throats with a stench like rubber afire. Benitez knew that if the short circuit could not be fixed, the outgassing of hydrogen would produce another bomb blast, likely destroying his sub.

Clifford came to the conning tower and shouted up to Benitez that the smoke had overcome several of the crew. The captain ordered all hands topside, tying open the conning tower hatch as the crew began to rise. Clifford wondered how dozens of men would fit in the tiny space of the bridge and the slick steel of the weather deck. But the captain was brooking no delays.

"Get them up here and on the lee side of the sail—and lively!" he told Clifford.

Yellow of skin, eyes rolled back into their heads, eight unconscious sailors were hoisted into fresh air by their shipmates and laid out on the deck, slippery with seawater as it yawed, rolled, and pitched with the swells. The worst off were given artificial respiration as more of the crew came topside.

As the deck had no handrail—the GUPPY boats had been streamlined for speed—sailors welded a handrail to the housing around the superstructure and fastened safety lines around it in order to tie down the wounded in place. A freezing wave washed over them, reviving a few to the point of miserable groans. More men came topside, dressed only in skivvies as they had moments before been asleep. Benitez feared the hydrogen more than he did exposure to the cold, so upward they came. The captain and a dozen men were jammed onto the bridge, and soon forty-seven more lay tied down and exposed on the weather deck.

That was when the huge wave came. It swamped the *Cochino* from astern. Dropping into a trough, the submarine was swallowed by green seawater, which surged over the wounded on the weather deck. When the water receded, one man was gone. Scanning the swells, Benitez spotted him to port, a striker named Joseph E. Morgan, bobbing in the numbing sea. Though held afloat by his life vest, he appeared to be unconscious.

COMMANDER WORTHINGTON NEEDED forty minutes to bring the *Tusk* to the surface and close to within sight of the *Cochino* through the squalls and high wind. He was greeted with a disturbing visual message from the stricken sub: "MAN OVERBOARD DEAD AHEAD X FIRE IN THE AFTER BATTERY."

Benitez was relieved to see the *Tusk* looming in the fog. The situation was quickly spinning beyond the captain's control. He had one man in the water and unresponsive, more at risk of being washed overboard, and a witch's brew boiling deep within his ship.

The rescue of Joseph Morgan was the work of several men who saw a shipmate in extremis and did not hesitate to go there themselves. Seeing Morgan floundering, Chief Torpedoman Hubert Rauch of Jamaica, Queens, climbed down from the weather bridge, removing his clothes as he went, and dived into the water. It was ten minutes out and back, and by the time Rauch was nearing the sub again with Morgan under an arm, he was too weak to keep his grip. Freezing seawater drained the strength from giants. The two men struggled.

Another sailor, Clarence Balthrop—the ship's cook and baker of the inconsistent bread—jumped in and began swimming toward Morgan, while five others formed a human chain and pulled Rauch up on deck. At that moment, the largest explosion yet rocked the *Cochino*.

Feeling the deck shiver beneath his feet, Benitez feared his submarine might be finished. He prayed. If the pressure hull ruptured, it would be a quick death for all. He felt in his pocket for his knife, in case he had to cut the wounded free from their lines.

Another large wave lifted the *Cochino* and dropped her to break deep. Morgan and Balthrop vanished beneath the surface. Benitez fixed his eyes on the swirl where they had disappeared, knowing that if his gaze drifted from that certain point of reference he might never find them amid the whitecaps. When the wave receded, though, Balthrop was visible again in the trough, holding fast to a protuberance in the hull, Morgan secured in a leg scissors. As the waves seemed to rest, men on deck re-formed the human chain and hauled them aboard. Morgan, barely conscious, was lifted to the conning tower for medical help. Balthrop, through chattering teeth and bluing lips, said, "If that d-damage control party doesn't p-put that fire out soon, that bread I got in the oven is going to be awful b-burnt."

Belowdecks, the firefighters were on the verge of a breakthrough. Electrician's Mate Oscar Martinez ran to the forward engine room to tell Commander Wright, the exec, that he had found the cause of the hydrogen outgassing. When he shut down all of the after electrical circuits, the ammeter showed that battery four was charging battery three. "We've got to pull the disconnects in the battery space," he said to Wright with no small amount of dread. The after battery compartment was sandwiched between the deck of the crew's berthing compartment and the bilges that contained the batteries and their lethal inferno. "They've been trying to get in from the other side, but they can't open the door from the control room."

Wright said, "Well then, I'm going in."

Wright pulled the mask of a rescue breather over his face, inhaled hard to initiate the flow from the canister, secured the harness, checked for leaks, and handed the safety line to another sailor, who knew the rules: one pull, give me more line; two, pull in the slack; three, drag me the hell out of here. From behind the steel door came a muffled, hollow *boom*. Wright told Martinez, "If we don't get to those switches quickly, it'll be good night for the *Cochino*."

When Wright grabbed the steel lever to open the door, it didn't budge. He pulled harder, until his right hand was burned through his heavy insulated gloves. He gripped the lever with both hands and laid his full weight into it. His flesh sizzled but the lever finally moved. Turning it and swinging the door open, he reeled backward as black smoke gusted out of the battery compartment and engulfed him. As he regained his footing and entered the burning compartment, his flashlight beam did not penetrate beyond arm's reach.

Wright moved with the care and deliberation of a blind man, feeling for the switches, hands sensing ahead. Through his mask he could smell the poisonous gases around him. Then the darkness turned white and orange, with a searing flash that struck like a sledgehammer. Flames poured from the blazing compartment and washed over him, throwing him back. As Wright fell to the deck in the forward engine room, his uniform was burned right off him, all but his shoes. Somehow the exec raised himself and staggered to the door. Lunging against it, burned across the whole front of his body, he muscled the door shut. He clasped the hot lever with his ruined bare hands and turned it, fancying for a moment that he had secured a gateway to hell.

But the engine room was ablaze too. The crackle of the fires was inaudible against the roar of the pair of ten-cylinder Fairbanks-Morse diesels in the compartment. With hydrogen mixing with their fuel supply, the engines had been kicked into overdrive, spinning up as if they had gone berserk. Wright could hear nothing above their howling metallic scream. The two enginemen on duty, William Payne of Groton, Connecticut, and George Fedon of Pennsauken Township, New Jersey, shut off the fuel intake, starving the engines, which quickly spun down.

Barely within his faculties, functioning on surging adrenaline, Wright shouted, "We gotta save her!" and went aft. Falling to the floor as fires licked at the bulkheads, Wright reached the door of the next compartment aft, the after engine room. He crawled through it and dogged it shut behind him. His eyes were glazed and his arms were like burnt stumps. The two petty officers on watch there guided him aft through the motor room and into the after torpedo room, the rearmost compartment of the boat, where they laid him in a berth. Wright was quiet for a moment, but as the adrenaline receded along with the numbing effect of his shock, he felt the agony of his burns and began softly to cry.

While the shutdown of propulsion momentarily saved the *Cochino*'s engines and prevented a catastrophic explosion, it left the sub helpless in a heavy sea. Just as the cresting swells had prevented Benitez from maneuvering to rescue men in the water, they kept Worthington from bringing the *Tusk* alongside. A collision with his squadronmate, adrift and at the mercy of the raging sea, would imperil both vessels and their crews.

Benitez saw what had to be done. He solicited a volunteer to run a certain gauntlet. To save Wright and the others trapped below, the captain had to get his senior hospital corpsman, Hubert "Doc" Eason, into the isolated space below. This meant someone had to take a safety line, tiptoe the hundred-foot length of the slippery after weather deck, and secure it near the hatch that accessed the torpedo room. The deck was almost constantly submerging and broaching by the action of swells and freezing waves.

Lieutenant (j.g.) Charles Cushman of Norfolk did not hesitate. Young and fit, he went to Benitez and said, "I'll start now, sir." Holding onto the housing of the bridge, he studied the waves, timing them, then sprinted out ten feet toward the stern. Dropping to all fours, he tied the line into the limber holes in the deck, then continued another ten feet, tying down the line again. A wave struck him. As he locked his fingers into the limber holes, the rush of sea swung him out legs first and he moved like a flag in an ocean wind. When the wave passed, he crawled farther aft, securing the line at ten-foot intervals all the way back to the hatch, then sprinted back to the conning tower with the help of the lifeline he had rigged.

Doc Eason then made his move. Running aft across the heaving deck, he reached the hatch, opened it, and descended through. The sound of Commander Wright's screams were met by a rush of seawater down the hatch.

Moving to the exec, Eason said, "Don't worry, baby, I'm going to take care of you somehow." He used the intercom to give his assessment to Benitez: "Captain, we've got to get medical supplies. My kit is in the inaccessible part of the boat. Mr. Wright may be dying, and the four others are in bad shape. I'm telling you, Captain, it's desperate."

Benitez had his signalman stand atop three other men and use semaphore to request help from Worthington: "REQUIRE MEDICAL ASSISTANCE X FIVE MEN INJURED X ONE BADLY BURNED."

As the sea state was still too rough to bring the *Tusk* alongside, Worthington directed his men to rig stanchions and lifelines on the forward deck, and to prepare to send over a rubber raft with a supply of medical kits. Deck hands used a line-throwing gun to fire heaving lines that were attached to heavier lines that were then hauled over and fastened to the raft. Worthington eased the *Tusk* into a windward position relative to the *Cochino,* attempting to calm the waters between the two submarines. He then flooded diesel fuel into the sea to produce a smooth surface more easily navigable by a rubber raft.

Benitez realized he had to give Benson, his squadron commodore, a fuller sense of the situation than semaphore signaling could allow. He asked Ensign John Shelton, "Do you think you can ride that rubber raft back to the *Tusk*?" Shelton accepted at once. The lone civilian on the *Cochino,* a Bureau of Ships field engineer named Robert W. Philo, offered to go with him. Shelton considered Philo brilliant and handy, a good man in a pinch, and was glad that Benitez approved the request without hesitation. As the raft arrived with the medical supplies, they contemplated their return trip.

The sea presented violently to Shelton and Philo as they stood on the fantail of their foundering submarine. Freezing seawater numbed them up to the calves. As they muscled the raft into a launch position, it was apparent that the high waves would demand good timing.

Shelton said, "Bob, when the water comes up to the deck level, we'll shove off. We'll ride this baby like a surfboard. Savvy?" But it was difficult to time the cross-cutting whitecaps. When they made their move, the wave did not behave as Shelton had predicted. As the raft launched from the *Cochino,* the wave continued to gain height. The raft met it at an unfortunate slope and instantly flipped upside down. The two men clung stubbornly to the grab ropes of the raft as the sailors on the *Tusk* hauled it in. It took about ten minutes to bring the would-be rescuers close aboard. Ten crewmen on the *Tusk* tried to form a human chain to haul them up to the deck. But in heavy seas, it was about as difficult to grab hold of men adrift as it was to keep one's footing on the slippery deck. Philo and Shelton had their raft between them and the *Tusk*. They were foundering and growing weak from cold, quickly in over their heads.

Seeing their lack of progress, an enlisted sailor on the *Tusk,* Norman

H. Walker, leaped into the water to assist. He grabbed Philo first. As he paddled with him around the raft and back to the submarine, a large wave caught them, pulling the technician free of Walker's strong grasp. Philo rode it headfirst into the hull and was knocked unconscious.

But at that point it was possible for the crew on deck to get hold of Philo and lift him aboard. Shelton, clinging to a lifeline that he was almost too weak to hold, was hauled up, and Walker was too. Walker was in good health. Shelton was conscious but numb from shock. Philo was still unconscious, and apparently drowned. A medic stuck him with adrenaline and began artificial respiration immediately.

Taken below, Shelton regained enough of his senses to describe to Worthington what had befallen the *Cochino*. The horror of hydrogen fires, the burning engine rooms, forcing abandonment of the lower decks, men choked out by gas, the crew escaping topside, forty-seven of them lashed to the forward deck and the handrail around the bridge, thirteen more jammed in the conning tower, five or six of these overcome by fumes, and five more men—Commander Wright and the four enginemen—hunkered in the only habitable compartment, the after torpedo room. The risk of explosion was still great, Shelton said, as one of the batteries was still short-circuiting with its neighbor. Worthington realized he would have only one chance to come alongside to rescue the crew of the dying submarine. He signaled his intent to Benitez and ordered the *Tusk*'s four engines ahead one-third.

Worthington found it impossible to approach safely. The two submarines plunged and rose, bow then stern, as if they were engaged in some sort of combat. The *Tusk*'s exec, Lieutenant Commander George Cook, gave it a try, as did Commodore Benson. But it was impossible to handle the ship to make a safe approach. Worthington retreated a few hundred yards from the *Cochino,* having ordered his crew to prepare another raft, when a large wave washed over her main deck from starboard to port.

The wave knocked down all fifteen men who were topside handling lines. It washed them against the lifeline that had been rigged on the port side. A second wave followed, equally violent and seizing. The weight of it slammed the human flotsam into the lifeline again, snapping it and bending four of the stanchions. Nothing was left to stop eleven of them from going overboard. Also swept away was Robert Philo, who had been receiving emergency care for nearly an hour but had not regained a pulse. Lying on the deck forward of the bridge, swaddled in blankets, he was suddenly carried overboard.

The greatest loss of life on this sad day would come not from the *Cochino,* but the *Tusk.* A heroic effort was made to retrieve the overboard men in the short window of consciousness that was left to them. Several were lost to sight right away. A few of the rescuees were forced to make an impossible choice: Hold on to the lifeline thrown from the deck or hang on to the unconscious man in his arms. Worthington did his best to handle the *Tusk,* timing his engine orders with the haphazard sea, avoiding hitting men in the water, and keeping them free of his churning twin screws.

Heroism was never a function of rank. George Cook, went over the side to rescue one young officer, and a seaman, Raymond J. Shugar, dived in to assist a petty officer, Ray Reardon, who was floundering alongside the empty life raft that had saved his life. As a wave capsized it, he had caught his foot in the line. Shugar wrapped a manila line under Reardon's arms, then took his knife, slashed his foot free of the raft, and helped him back to the *Tusk.*

On deck, dozens of sailors accepted the battering of the cold ocean to give their shipmates a chance at life. The last of the four *Tusk* sailors to be rescued, Petty Officer Reardon, returned to the ship more than two hours after going overboard. Seven men never made it back. With the terrible reckoning made, Worthington was able to respond to the *Cochino*'s message, that Captain Benitez was considering abandoning ship.

RAFAEL BENITEZ DID not know why the *Tusk* seemed to disappear. Worthington was so consumed by the sudden emergency on his own boat that he had sent no signal. Benitez's crew was beset by headaches, nausea, and fatigue from the fumes. The cold never stopped working on them. Eventually they no longer complained about it. Many were sullen. This was a dangerous sign, one brave chief petty officer decided. He thought it was worth the risk to go below to retrieve blankets from the abandoned forward torpedo room.

TMC Mahlon Woodward descended below, holding his breath against the burnt-rubber air. Two minutes later, an eternity on one breath, Woodward's arm appeared in the hatch, holding a stack of blankets. Red-faced and eyes bulging, he exhaled mightily, hoisting the full harvest of his bounty topside, where it was quickly distributed to the forty-seven freezing sailors, swaddling them against the cold.

The fires on *Cochino* had continued through the brightly sunlit evening and nighttime hours of August 25 off northern Norway. At seven o'clock, her engineers managed to start the diesel engine again and the *Cochino* began to move.

Steering with her engines, she fell in behind the *Tusk* and the two submarines chunked south through a moderating sea toward the nearest port, Hammerfest, about 140 nautical miles distant.

> 1537/25 August: Position 72-20' N / 23-53' E per USS Tusk,
> Report of Simulated War Patrol, 30-31
>   1950: Set course 175 at 10 knots; 0006: Cochino
> explodes.
>   Dist = 5.25 hrs x 10 knots = 52.5 naut miles
>
> 0209/26 Aug: Set course 175 at 17.5 knots; 0724/26 Aug:
> Entered Hammerfest Harbor
>   Dist = 5.25 hrs x 17.5 knots = 91.87 naut miles

For five hours they steamed together and Benitez thought he might have a chance. But then at midnight his diesels lost power. A series of concussions shook the ship from the battery compartment. These culminated in a large blast that caused the submarine to jump underfoot. The detonation was louder than the others, unmuffled, as though breaching out of the submarine into the open air. Smoke billowed from her snorkel mast. Benitez concluded that the *Cochino* had finally lost her race against time. He ordered the whole crew up on deck and contacted Worthington to close with him. The captain of the *Tusk* had seen smoke on the horizon and was already under way. Worthington knew it was time for him to make his move. Jettisoning the pair of armed torpedoes loaded in his bow tubes, he made his approach.

When the *Tusk* appeared within sight again, it was like a host of angels descending through parted clouds. Benitez considered it the end. He decided that if his executive officer, Wright, was doomed to die, unable to escape from the bowels of the sub because of his ruinous burns, Benitez would have no choice but to do what tradition expected captains to do: go down with his ship.

Below, in the *Cochino*'s after torpedo room, Richard Wright was laid out naked on a bunk, skin seared, blistered, ooze-crusted, and peeling. In a morphine fog, he watched the sailors who had been with him ascend the ladder topside.

"That leaves you and me alone, eh, Doc?" the executive officer said to the hospital corpsman who had been tending him, Hubert Eason.

"Yes, sir. But the Captain said to come to the bridge, and I already sent Fedon up to say we're coming."

"The Captain did?"

"Yes, sir."

Wright considered his burns, then dropped a leg from the bunk to the deck, holding his ruined arms high so that nothing would touch them.

"The Old Man ordered us topside, eh, Doc?"

"Yes, sir. Now try to get up. Hold yourself stiff."

At once, the men felt the shock of the *Cochino* hitting something heavy, steel sounding against steel. Their submarine had met the *Tusk* bow on bow, the better to hold at bay their exposed slashing screws. As the two vessels nestled into each other, coming to a stop hull against hull, they were tied fast with manila lines and the crews rigged a plank that spanned the twenty-foot gap between their decks. While they rose and fell with the swells, the *Cochino*'s crew began transferring over. Not one man was too cold to navigate the narrow brow with fleet footwork.

Below, in the after torpedo room, Richard Wright winced as Doc Eason pulled a too-small pair of dungarees over his blackened, seeping legs. He guided him to a standing position; then, one hand pressed gently on the small of his back, Eason showed Wright to the ladder. Step by careful step, the exec willed himself one rung to the next. What kept him moving was this realization, spoken out loud: "My God, I'm blocking Eason's chances."

He prayed for courage and felt almost weightless as he rose toward the light. On the deck he left behind, water was collecting higher and higher as the list continued to worsen.

As the *Tusk* took the *Cochino*'s crew on board, Rafael Benitez announced that he did not intend to leave the ship, that he wanted his sub to be taken in tow once the wounded were off. After his whole crew had made it across, many stood topside on the *Tusk* looking back at their boat, its deck awash. As water topped the captain's ankles, they raised an insistent chorus. "Skipper, *come on!*"

Benitez pondered the practices and rituals of the sea, the duties of a captain whose ship is lost. Then he considered his wife Nancy and their two children back in Groton. The conflict of duties bothered him only briefly. His deliberation did not last long. A calm came over him, a willingness to let go. He had known it before. One day during the Pacific War a Japanese destroyer had gotten a fix on his submarine, shellacking it with depth charges so heavily that he knew the end had come. It had not. But now, having succumbed to such a release once, he embraced it again.

It was the vision of his maimed executive officer emerging through the after topside hatch that changed Benitez's heart. With a push from Doc Eason below and a lift under the armpits from a sailor straddling the hatch, Wright made it to the deck. With that, the urging of the crew prevailed. When Benitez shuffled across the plank to the *Tusk,* he was the last man off his ship. Three minutes later, the *Cochino* sank stern first and disappeared in 158 fathoms, her grave fixed at coordinates 71-45' North, 24-20' East.

As Commander Wright was taken below and made comfortable in the captain's stateroom—a fresh dose of morphine helped—Rafael Benitez went to the bridge of the *Tusk* and found his counterpart. Taking Worthington's hand, he thanked him. Roy Benson embraced Benitez and said, "Sorry, skipper." He assured him that his men were getting excellent medical care as Worthington set course for Hammerfest.

Arriving about 0730, after the northern sun made its short dip through twilight, the crew took on board medical supplies at the pier. A Norwegian doctor arrived to help stabilize Wright and the others who were worst off. A U.S. Navy doctor dispatched by CINCNELM arrived that evening to take his report. The following day the *Tusk* got under way, escorted by a Norwegian patrol craft. Richard Wright stayed behind, hospitalized, while several badly wounded men were flown to Plymouth, England. The regional naval commander in northern Norway, Admiral Thore Horve, paid a visit. Horve, who impressed the Americans as "an officer of the highest caliber," Worthington noted, was on hand to meet the arrival in Tromso of the American vessel *Samuel B. Roberts,* which embarked the rest of the wounded and set course for Plymouth.

THE DIESEL-POWERED AMERICAN submarine force, which had come tactically of age in the Pacific just five years earlier, had yet to operate in Arctic waters. The sortie to the Barents Sea undertaken by the four boats of Submarine Development Group Two in the summer of 1949 demonstrated the limitations of the old breed. Had they been true submarines, atomic-propelled, these boats never would have made news and seven men likely would not have perished. As it was, the European press reported the novelty of the U.S. naval presence in northern waters, and the incident produced a stir. The Soviet navy newspaper *Red Fleet* condemned the "suspicious training" so close to Murmansk. "What draws American expansionists into the Arctic?" the Soviet editorialist asked. "A striving to scout our naval channels and airways of this area, which for some time has become one of the most important expansionist goals of the military." The first part of that assessment inarguably hit the mark. In his "report of simulated war patrol" written for COMSUBLANT, the *Tusk*'s skipper noted that "control of North Cape, Bear Island, and Spitsbergen determines mastery of ingress and egress from Northern Russian–controlled ports."

The Soviets, chastened by the failure of Stalin's gambit to blockade Berlin, read the friendly reception that the Norwegians gave to their accidental visitors as evidence of the abject subservience of the Scandinavian states to "imperial" America. But Moscow's notion of Norway as a vassal was nothing more than projection. The relationship between Oslo and Washington, fully reciprocal and secure within NATO, was based on the security needs of democratic Norway and the strategic value of its coast. As Worthington reported, the Norwegian fjords offered plentiful tactical advantages for an enterprising fleet commander. These included "ready concealment; year-round ice-free deepwater paths to the sea by diverse routes, easy protection from surface or ground forces, ideal antiaircraft gun protection possibilities, [and] large seaplane sheltered landing areas. Thus, bases in the fjords could be as advantageous to us as denial of them to the opponent would be disastrous to his plans." These insights would not be forgotten.

The Norwegian officers who met Roy Benson and his men were ready to meet Russia in war. "Within thirty minutes of declaration of war," a host officer boasted to the Americans, "every Norwegian male would be in uniform and under arms and in another half hour every Communist would be dead or in custody." Scandinavians had known recently the sound of the treads of Russian tanks and held no illusions about Moscow's continuing ambitions. They knew that Russia coveted naval bases in the fjords as a means of escaping the polar ice prison that constrained their potential to project naval power into the world. As Worthington put it, the Norwegians were "happy to see evidence that the U.S. Navy was thinking of their part of the world."

The loss of the *Cochino* illustrated the centrality of the periphery in Cold War geopolitics. Nations that perceived threats globally were compelled to operate on the outer membrane of the possible. Once, the idea of seizing the whole Pacific and moving a fleet into Tokyo Bay to begin a period of permanent forward deployment there would have been unthinkable. With America's principal rival busy consolidating its hold on portions of East Asia, Truman and his advisers considered it unthinkable to do anything else.

During the *Tusk*'s homeward Atlantic transit from Tromso, the need for U.S. forces to operate adventurously close to the Soviet periphery mushroomed in urgency. A few weeks after the submarine arrived in New London, Connecticut, on September 8, Worthington and his men received news that had deeply shaken Truman's White House. The Soviets had tested their first atomic bomb.

12

———————

THE REVOLT CONTINUES

THE AIRCRAFT THAT DETECTED THE SOVIET NUCLEAR TEST WAS a B-29 Superfortress flying out of Misawa Air Base in northern Honshu, Japan. On September 3, 1949, with First Lieutenant Robert C. Johnson at the controls, it had undertaken the thirteen-and-a-half-hour flight over the Bering Sea to Eielson Air Force Base in Alaska with the ostensible purpose of monitoring the weather. The bomber had had its weapons stripped away to save on weight. Unbeknownst to Johnson or any of the other "Pole Vaulters" of the 375th Air Weather Reconnaissance Squadron, their planes were fitted with external scoops that took samples from the atmosphere.

The mysterious "bug catchers," as the crews called them, captured air particles in paper filters, which were turned in for analysis at the end of each flight. Based on technology studied in the Crossroads tests at Bikini, the program had been urged by the head of the Atomic Energy Commission, David Lilienthal, and the first director of the Central Intelligence Agency, Rear Admiral Roscoe H. Hillenkoetter, whose interest in the concept of "strategic surprise" dated to the Pearl Harbor attack, when he was wounded while serving as executive officer of the battleship *West Virginia,* sunk by Japanese torpedoes. Later he served as the intelligence chief on Admiral Chester Nimitz's staff. The classified air-sampling program—the only truly effective component of an intelligence collection network that included acoustic, seismographic, radiochemical, and gamma-ray sensors as well as rainwater-sampling stations—was meant to ensure that no nation ever blindsided America again.

When Lieutenant Johnson landed at Eielson later that day, the paper filter was plucked from the bug catcher and flown to a Tracerlab facility in Berkeley, California, for analysis. It revealed that the eastward-drifting air masses he had flown through, just below the base of the stratosphere, contained debris from an atomic explosion. In the next two weeks, ninety-two additional sorties by the air-weather squadrons sniffed the skies from Guam to Great Britain looking for traces of fission isotopes of barium, cerium, and molybdenum. A third of the samples showed more than a thousand counts per minute. There was but one conclusion: For the first time, the Soviet Union had tested an atomic bomb.

The test of the fission weapon that the Soviets called Device 501 or First Lightning had been carried out on August 29 at a weapons range near Semipalatinsk in Kazakhstan, the site having been fixed by triangulating from recorded acoustic data. Code-named Joe-1 after the Soviet dictator, the test stunned the Truman administration. Stalin, for his part, was said to be equally surprised that the Americans had managed to detect it. After a naval research station in Alaska confirmed a high level of airborne radioactivity, Truman announced the news. His statement on September 23 was an embarrassment for the U.S. scientific and intelligence establishment, which believed the Soviets wouldn't have an atomic bomb for three more years.

Though it would be seven years before the Soviets fielded an aircraft that could take an atomic bomb to the continental United States, the end of the American monopoly in such weaponry produced a change in national psychology. Millions of American schoolchildren would become acquainted with the chewing-gum-spotted undersides of their desks as government agencies organized civil defense drills and built atomic air raid shelters. The news of the Soviet bomb would encourage the U.S. Navy, and its submariners in particular, to deploy far from home in order to keep the watch. CIA chief Hillenkoetter urged an expansion of technical surveillance of the Soviet Union. The movement to negotiate a pact to control atomic weapons gained momentum once again.

Fear of the Soviet bomb accelerated the unwinding of U.S. domestic politics in 1949. With George Kennan having shaped the maximalist case for resisting Soviet expansion, both in policy-making circles and in the rarified pages of leading journals, a partisan divide emerged that would harden with the trial of Alger Hiss and the rise of anticommunist sentiments in Washington. The American conversation over the nature of Soviet Communism burned hotter as the theatrics of Senator Joseph McCarthy came to stand for the government's effort to police Communist Party influence in American government. For years, the House Committee on Un-American Activities had worked to identify Moscow's subversive partners in labor unions and assist the FBI in dismantling actual spy rings. But soon its mandate was overshadowed by the opportunism and grandstanding of a U.S. senator from Wisconsin. Secretary of State Dean Acheson would refer to the phenomenon of Joe McCarthy as "the attack of the primitives."

But its excesses were matched by the moral idiocy of many New Dealers who saw little difference between the geopolitics of 1937 and of 1949 and had learned nothing about Joseph Stalin in the interim. "The Communists insisted that the interests of Russia and the United States were forever identical, and the majority of liberals collaborated in the hoax," wrote the literary critic Leslie A. Fiedler, a former naval intelligence officer, in *Commentary* magazine in 1951. The rhetorical trench warfare that characterized the controversy over the Alger Hiss case and the judgment of officials who questioned Truman's dim view of Stalin bled into other areas of national life. The Navy's intramural firefight with the two other services over strategy and missions was part and parcel of Russia's logic-defying transformation from ally to adversary in the dawning days of the Cold War.

With the mild-mannered chief of naval operations, Louis A. Denfeld, busy overseas helping to negotiate the command relationships among the new NATO partners, the task of making the Navy's case before Congress fell to Rear Admiral Arleigh A. Burke and Vice Admiral Arthur W. Radford, the new commander of the Pacific Fleet.

Burke was a rising star. As head of a Navy Department section known as OP-23, he coordinated the effort to conduct research supporting the Navy's case on Capitol Hill. His more publicly provocative sidekick was the missile entrepreneur Rear Admiral Daniel Gallery. Having staged the V-2 missile launch from the USS *Midway* off Bermuda, Gallery continued his practice of high-profile public advocacy by writing a series of pieces for *The Saturday Evening Post* pillorying the Air Force line on the B-36 and defending the need for a navy. Defying Secretary of Defense Louis Johnson's requirement to preclear any such articles, Gallery said Navy tradition placed no such prior restraint on an officer's ability to speak on unclassified matters. And speak he did, later comparing the Navy's howls of protest during the defense unification debate to those of a sexual assault victim. "Who does the screaming when a rape is being committed?" he wrote. Johnson was livid. Navy Secretary Francis Matthews darkly suggested to Gallery that he would be brought before a court-martial, and conspired to remove Burke's name from the list of officers receiving promotion to rear admiral before Truman reversed that bit of illegal meddling.

Gallery's reckless rhetoric served no one's cause, and he was caught in a controversy of his own making. But powerful men rallied to him as well. Gallery was interviewing a potential defense counsel when Admiral Ernest King, the furious force of will who had reigned over the Navy Department (and, on most days, the Joint Chiefs of Staff) during World War II, wrote to him: "I hope most people will read and reread it because you tell the truth, at least as I see it. The time has come for our people to understand that a proper officer does not like to be made a mere yes-man. Otherwise, as you have said, the police state is close at hand." In the end, CNO Forrest Sherman gave Gallery a letter of admonition, which he considered a victory, though he did not get the coveted promotion to a third star.

IN DRAMATIC TESTIMONY in early October, Radford panned the Air Force's theory of "cheap and easy victory" via atomic bombing, decrying the morality of atomic strikes against Soviet population centers and calling the B-36 bomber a "billion-dollar blunder." Another leading aviator, Vice Admiral Gerald F. Bogan, wrote Navy Secretary Matthews to say that after the scuffle over defense unification, "the morale of the Navy is lower today than at any time since I entered the commissioned ranks in 1916. . . . This descent, almost to despondency, stems from complete confusion as to the future role of the Navy and its advantages and disadvantages as a permanent career." Bogan poked at the expertise of Army and Air Force generals. When the letter was leaked to the press, along with news that Bogan's letter had been endorsed by Louis Denfeld, Defense Secretary Johnson threatened to disapprove the CNO's reappointment for another three-year term.

When Denfeld testified before the House Armed Services Committee, he faced a conflict between his duties as chief of his dissenting service branch and as a member of the Joint Chiefs of Staff, serving the president. He spoke moderately about the problem of "the improper operation of unification," but he backed Radford strongly, not merely defending the need for aircraft carriers but questioning the Air Force scheme for a strategic air offensive bereft of coordination with the other military branches or fidelity to an articulable national strategy.

Secretary Matthews, deeply stirred by the partisan activism that was rife within his department, thought it was all too much. On October 27, Navy Day, he wrote Truman charging that Denfeld had been insubordinate and asking that he be fired. Though he was prone to complaining about "the traitorous and sabotage press," the president left it to a radio network to give Denfeld the news of his relief as CNO. It was an undeserved end for Denfeld, often regarded as the heir to Chester Nimitz for his soft-spoken manner and talent for compromise. Hanson Baldwin of *The New York Times* lamented "the poisonous atmosphere and corrosive suspicions" in which "men in uniform fear that their telephone wires are tapped and their actions recorded; when bitternesses are so extreme that officers indulge in questionable practices to get their service viewpoints before the public; when fear and mistrust color service relationships."

The syndrome was evident after Truman named a successor. Taking the counsel of Nimitz, who recommended Richard Conolly or Forrest Sherman, Truman selected the latter. Though Conolly had a sure grasp of strategy and diplomacy as commander in chief, Europe, Eastern Atlantic and Mediterranean, and was the senior of the two, Sherman had cleaner hands in Washington, having avoided the partisan fisticuffs with the Air Force while commanding the Sixth Task Fleet in distant Naples. In November, at age fifty-three, Sherman returned from the Med to become the twelfth chief of naval operations. The hard feelings were in evidence when the senior officers attending the change-of-command ceremony filed out without congratulating him afterward. "There was sort of a feeling that Admiral Sherman had maybe hoisted [Denfeld] out of his job, which of course was not true at all," said John Ballentine, who took over for Sherman as commander of the Sixth Fleet.

Leaving the Pentagon, Denfeld embraced his evolution as a truth teller free at last to speak. In essays for popular magazines, he followed in Dan Gallery's footsteps, deriding Joint Chiefs of Staff chairman Omar Bradley and Air Force Chief of Staff Hoyt Vandenberg as ignorant of basic naval history and strategy. He called the canceled USS *United States* "the only carrier the Air Force ever sank." This was the tenor of the times, exacerbated by a broad-based fear of what the Soviet bomb portended for the free world.

If the military implications of Moscow's new weapon were ominous, even more disturbing was the revelation, which surfaced in 1950, that espionage was behind the Soviet breakthrough. Despite Truman's executive order attempting to block Communist Party members from government employment, in 1949 the Congress of Industrial Organizations brought charges against eleven Communist Party–dominated labor unions and expelled them from the organization. The American Civil Liberties Union, finding the commitment of Communists to the Bill of Rights "highly selective and decidedly unprincipled," had banned them from its leadership since 1940.

Ever since Truman's gambit to end the Chinese civil war had fallen flat, the culture of fear had been ascendant. After George Marshall returned to Washington, having failed to persuade Chiang Kai-shek and Mao Tse-tung to govern by coalition, it was clear that honest brokers had no place in wicked games.

SECRETARY OF STATE Marshall's reliance upon the good faith of China's rival warlords had been an act of sheerest optimism. Mao and Chiang wanted nothing more than to finish their eighteen-year war. Each believed he would prevail. Each used the American intermediary as his tool. Mao drew American blood whenever it served him, and the men who had made Marshall's diplomacy possible, the U.S. Marine Corps, never forgot that they were paying in that priceless currency. Platoons escorting supply convoys through Communist territory were more than once ambushed to deadly effect, but no reinforcement of road patrols could reverse the momentum Mao had gained in his decades-long war. The Marines had gone to China to help repatriate Imperial Japan's legions. They were neither equipped nor deployed to resist the Communist surge, and the political will back home did not exist to fortify them for such a task. They were forbidden to provide direct offensive support to Chiang's Nationalists, even though it was the policy of the United States to arm and equip him.

Marshall saw all too clearly that Mao and his brain trust were far from the "agrarian reformers" that many in the West wished them to be, but there was no reversing the humiliation of Marshall's failure. It was a blow to America's project to stabilize the world under United Nations auspices. In late 1948, after Mao's victory had turned China irretrievably red, the Seventh Fleet carried out the evacuation of U.S. troops from Tsingtao, the last American military outpost in China. It was an opening for Washington's most fervid anticommunists to discredit Marshall's idealism. Some took the politics a step further and tried to brand the general himself a traitor. "There have been rumblings and rumors," his colleague General Albert C. Wedemeyer warned him, "that you have been taken in by the Chinese Communists," and Senator McCarthy would try to make that flimsy case, although never by his choice of target did the Wisconsin senator distin-

guish himself as a greater fool. A fraction of the body politic cared
nothing for evidence or verdicts when they collided with their political
preconceptions. Those of a certain temperament and personality would
back Alger Hiss no matter how conclusively his deceit was established;
many more would condemn George Marshall for treason after Mao
Tse-tung's victory. The year 1949 was a trying one for the notion that
diplomacy could work if it were practiced in good faith. In a zero-sum
game, whatever was conceded was lost. With the actual guns silent, fear
of potential or even figurative guns proliferated.

The nascent Communist revolution in Beijing was more unsettling
than the one that Stalin had been consolidating for several decades in
the Soviet Union. Japan's ceremonial surrender aboard the USS *Missouri* had not yet taken place when the commanding general of U.S.
forces in China, Albert C. Wedemeyer, wrote, "I view Asia as an enormous pot, seething and boiling, the fumes of which may readily snuff
out the advantages gained by allied sacrifices the past several years and
may also definitely preclude realization of the objectives of the Atlantic
Charter, and the Teheran, Yalta, and Potsdam agreements." He feared
more that Japanese war matériel would fall into the hands of Chinese
Communists and preferred that the Soviets take it. Wedemeyer had
had a glimpse of the future.

In the Pacific, Communist China launched an amphibious invasion
of a Nationalist-held offshore island, Quemoy, on October 25, 1949,
which ended two days later in disaster for Mao. Chiang Kai-shek's
forces in exile destroyed the bulk of three Chinese regiments. Though
it was far from a decisive turn of fortune, the victory would be called
the Nationalist generalissimo's Battle of Midway for ensuring, at the
least, the continuation of a status quo, including his survival on his island freehold. While the victory seemed to move the Joint Chiefs to
reconsider offering some level of military assistance to Taiwan, the
United States invested itself in Japan as a base around which to protect
its East Asian strategic interests. Truman wanted a mutual defense
treaty with Japan in order to legalize the continuing U.S. presence
there. But what was the political nature of the former enemy empire?
In the space of just three years it had been transformed stunningly:

from an opponent in total war, to an object of conquest, a humanitarian project, a ward of security guarantees, and the anchor of a forward-deployed military posture. Might it, too, turn Communist? Japan was constitutionally compelled to "forever renounce war as a sovereign right of the nation." Its right to maintain military forces even for self-defense was a matter of some doubt. With significant military expenditures off the table, Prime Minister Shigeru Yoshida was content to invest in economic revival, and he looked to the United States for protection. Radford's Pacific Fleet in Hawaii and MacArthur's naval command, the Yokosuka-based Naval Forces Far East, had the mission of upholding Japan as the Switzerland of the Pacific and Taiwan as its West Berlin.

Yet the Basic Naval Establishment Plan for 1950 proposed to knock back the fleet's capacity for major combat, reducing the number of aircraft carriers from 11 to 8, battleships from 2 to 1, cruisers from 30 to 18, and carrier air groups from 36 (with about 2,500 planes) to 14 (with 1,500). Between the end of World War II and the summer of 1950, U.S. naval shipyards and the communities of steelworkers and other specialists that sustained them had little to do, working on a total of just fourteen new combatants—four destroyers and ten submarines. The Subic Bay–based Seventh Fleet operated a single aircraft carrier, the *Valley Forge,* until the Tsingtao evacuation briefly required the services of a second one.

The security of Japan and the Philippines were the primary strategic tasks of the Far East Command. The Eighth Army, headquartered in Tokyo, was meant to defend Japan in the event of war with the Soviet Union. Korea was an afterthought for Douglas MacArthur, its 38th parallel the relic of an administrative arrangement between U.S. and Soviet occupation forces in 1945. MacArthur's Far East Air Force was comprised of three numbered air forces: the Fifth (in Japan), the Twentieth (in Okinawa), and the Thirteenth (in the Philippines).

MacArthur's naval component had modest and essentially political tasks. Vice Admiral C. Turner Joy's Naval Forces Far East, important though it sounded, had just a cruiser, four destroyers, and six minesweepers to its name. Its business was clearing mines from harbors, training the Japanese merchant marine, operating naval stations at Yokosuka and Sasebo, interdicting smugglers between Korea and Japan, and keeping an ear to a hydrophone against Soviet submarines in the Sea of Japan. As onetime allies, the United States and USSR had never carried out their agreement under the United Nations mandate to unify the peninsula after the war. Having established a separate Communist Party government in the north, which they commenced to arm to the teeth for offensive warfare, the Soviets delayed all efforts at a settlement. From the start, Moscow made Korea both a subversive project and an act of open defiance.

The Soviet design to use offensive espionage to bring all of Korea under Communist control had been the subject of U.S. national intelligence reporting since January 1947. As many as ten thousand Soviet agents had infiltrated the south for this purpose, the Central Intelligence Group assessed. Admiral Hillenkoetter's CIA observed that "Soviet tactics in Korea have clearly demonstrated that the USSR is intent on securing all of Korea as a satellite. In pursuing this policy, the USSR has, since V-J Day, adhered to a definite program of infiltration, consolidation and control." The CIA was referencing Pyongyang's development of an underground in South Korea whose purpose was first to push the coalition government as far left as possible, then to engineer protests that would make conditions ripe for Moscow to demand the withdrawal of U.S. troops from the peninsula. At that point, agents provocateurs would stage a "state of emergency" that the North Korean army would have no choice but to move in to quell. The North Korean army had been so strongly built up under the Soviet-run political machine in Pyongyang that Stalin had nothing to lose by withdrawing his own troops. He knew there was moral high ground to seize in professing to be a peace seeker.

The gambit was straight from the Bolshevik playbook. Kim's regime, an offensively militarized, Soviet-backed monolith, faced down the South, whose political stability hung in the balance. Yet Kim promised to be the liberator of a puppet state. The thirty-eight-year-old dictator had been operating in the shadows for two years, staging insurrections with the counsel of Stalin. The United States was out of its league in such a game. The old OSS, forerunner of the CIA, might have had the moxie to operate in kind. But America did not have competent covert operations forces in 1950 and could do nothing to keep the regime of Syngman Rhee, South Korea's first president, from responding brutally to the Soviet-engineered riots. Months of violence in the southern island city of Jeju led to tens of thousands of deaths. Still Mao and Stalin urged caution upon Kim Il-sung on the question of when he might launch a war of forcible unification.

The American people seemed to find nothing more compelling than a righteous minority viciously besieged. In 1941, Franklin Roosevelt had acted in defense of hapless China as it was being overrun by Japan. In 1949, the escalation toward a new fratricide on the Korean peninsula seemed to be another case where the predations of outsiders urged the application of American power and will. Truman's attention was focused closely on the boundary area splitting the Korean peninsula at the 38th parallel. The arbitrarily established line of demarcation had become a double-sided Maginot Line in the superpower struggle in Asia. On one side, South Korea had been born under elections supervised by the United Nations. On the other, North Korea rose as an autocracy armed for conquest by Moscow, which proceeded to infiltrate covert operators to destabilize the south.

When a U.S. aircraft took off from Japan and sniffed out the first test of a Soviet atomic bomb, Washington's fear of Soviet intentions surged. After the Joe-1 test, the bomb and ideas about the bomb would color all American thinking on the waging of war and the maintenance of peace. Over every role and mission of the military, over every officer's career, and over every city, military base, and policy of state, stood the specter of a rising cauliflower cloud.

The famous epigram of a Frenchman, precisely a century old at the time, seemed applicable as ever: "The more things change, the more things stay the same." Always and ever, diplomacy would prove futile where it was backed only by the frail regiment of hope.

13

Problem on a Peninsula

WHATEVER HORROR THREATENED TO SWALLOW ASIA, AMERICA would understand and wage the ensuing conflict, unavoidably, as a naval war. The North American nation was bordered not by hostile states but by oceans. Its influence across the Pacific could not exist absent supreme naval power. Yet Secretary of Defense Louis Johnson still couldn't seem to help himself. He cared little for the sea services and made sure to stick his point where it hurt.

In December 1949 he flew to London, where he called on Vice Admiral Richard Conolly. After entertaining the British minister of defense, Viscount A. V. Alexander, Conolly and Johnson went to lay a wreath at a war memorial. En route, Johnson said to the admiral, "The Navy is on its way out. Now take amphibious operations. There's no reason for having a Navy and Marine Corps. General Bradley tells me that amphibious operations are a thing of the past. We'll never have any more amphibious operations. That does away with the Marine Corps. And the Air Force can do anything the Navy can nowadays, so that does away with the Navy." But Conolly, like all admirals of advanced careers and political talents, knew better than to argue too hard directly against the secretary of defense's bad-faith case. Louis Johnson, the Pentagon's boss of bosses, had a vindictive streak and had made enemies far more formidable than CINCNELM.

Johnson's dismissive view of the Navy's place in national defense, pushed upon Conolly in London, was implicitly contradicted by the policy of the Joint Chiefs of Staff, the U.S. Senate, the State Department, and the White House, which required a robust fleet. Johnson himself had just moved the National Security Council to endorse a comprehensive statement known as National Security Council Paper No. 48/2, which defined America's "basic security objectives" in Asia. These included "development of the nations and peoples of Asia on a stable and self-sustaining basis in conformity with the purpose and principles of the United Nations Charter," "development of sufficient military power in selected non-Communist nations of Asia to maintain internal security and prevent further encroachment by communism," "gradual reduction and eventual elimination of the preponderant power and influence of the USSR in Asia," and "prevention of power relationships in Asia which would enable any other nation or alliance to threaten the security of the United States from that area, or the peace, national independence, and stability of the Asiatic nations." The measures to be taken were nonmilitary. The levers of power were trade policy, export controls, and economic assistance, except "where clearly needed to supplement the resistance of the other governments in and out of the area which are more directly concerned." Truman approved NSC 48/2 on December 30, 1949. It was made moot thirty days later when the president convened a policy review group composed of Defense and State Department officials, instructing them "to undertake a reexamination of our objectives in peace and war and of the effect of these objectives on our strategic plans."

Chaired by Paul H. Nitze, the director of policy planning at the State Department, the group produced a new secret National Security Council blueprint, known as NSC 68. It offered a grave assessment of Soviet ambitions in the world, basically premised upon Dean Acheson's observation that "the priority given by the Soviet rulers to the Kremlin design, world domination, contrasted with the American aim, an environment in which free societies could exist and flourish." This premise had been borne out globally: in the Soviet blockade of Berlin, in its handling of Poland, Hungary, and any number of countries, in Moscow's recognition of the Communist regime of Ho Chi

Minh in Vietnam, Communist uprisings in Malaya, and most provocatively of all in Moscow's defiant establishment of an all-powerful Communist Party apparatus in North Korea and its rearmament with advanced offensive weaponry. A British balance of payments crisis in the summer of 1949, moreover, suggested that the Marshall Plan would be insufficient to restore Europe before it expired in 1952.

The defense of free societies, therefore, was the policy of the United States. Tyrants had no place in Washington's design for the world—nor in Washington itself. In a policy planning meeting at the State Department to discuss NSC 68, Louis Johnson lost his temper explosively. Secretary Acheson professed to being "scared out of my shoes," and Major General James H. Burns, the defense secretary's adviser on foreign affairs, was left in tears. After this, Johnson found himself frozen out of the discussions altogether and on the exit ramp to private life. None too soon for most at the Pentagon. Acheson thought Johnson was mentally unwell.

HISTORY HAD LONG showed that the foundation of a strategy to shape world events across oceans was the ability to command the sea. Navies were irreplaceable as instruments of a sovereign. This was the lesson of the most recent war. On a globe whose surface was 71 percent seawater, sea power is power itself. Supporting the reduced Pacific Fleet's ability to command the Central Pacific was at the root of the Senate's decision two years earlier to obtain influence by island chains. It ratified a UN agreement to organize the Marshall, Mariana, and Caroline islands under a trusteeship administered by the United States. James Forrestal had been the first advocate of the plan to expand the U.S. strategic preserve in the Pacific beyond the Territory of Guam in the Marianas. The trusteeship covered a modest amount of land—just seven hundred square miles—but a sea area the size of the United States.

Forrestal knew it resembled imperialism, and Truman too was sensitive to the point. The Soviets would repeatedly ask how what they had done in Poland, Hungary, Bulgaria, Czechoslovakia, Romania, or North Korea was different from what Washington had done on island bases such as Saipan or Ulithi. Seeing the difference needed more than a passing interest in the character of governance, some discernment in morals, and an interest in human problems, details of political process, and matters of rights. Stalin was shameless about masking his aggressive subversions as something else—a protective response to stop a threat to the popular good. In the Pacific, where the United States had established an unchallengeable mastery of the sea, Moscow showed a knack for exploiting the rhetorical blunderbuss named Douglas MacArthur.

In a March 1949 interview with a British journalist in Tokyo, MacArthur had referred to the Pacific as "an Anglo-Saxon lake." He had spoken these words with evident pride and the Soviet state press seized on the reference, calling it "something that his superiors in Washington usually try to conceal." Moscow had been keen to know what the U.S. strategy in the Pacific actually was, and in that interview MacArthur appeared to oblige them, tracing the boundary of his command: "It starts from the Philippines, and continues through the Ryukyu Archipelago, which includes its main bastion, Okinawa. Then it bends back through Japan and the Aleutian Island chain to Alaska."

Less than a year later, at the National Press Club on January 12, 1950, Dean Acheson repeated this construct, though in reverse. "This defensive perimeter runs along the Aleutians to Japan and then goes to the Ryukyus. We hold important defense positions in the Ryukyu Islands, and these we will continue to hold. . . . The defensive perimeter runs from the Ryukyus to the Philippine Islands."

Acheson professed surprise at the pushback he received. "With the authority of the Joint Chiefs of Staff and General MacArthur behind me," he would write, "it did not occur to me that I should be charged with innovating policy or political heresy." And yet there he stood, seeming to announce America's unwillingness to confront Communist aggression on the Asian continent.

Lest anyone overinterpret Acheson's remarks, he elaborated to remove all doubt: "So far as the military security of other areas in the Pacific is concerned, it must be clear that no person can guarantee these areas against military attack. . . . Should such an attack occur . . . the

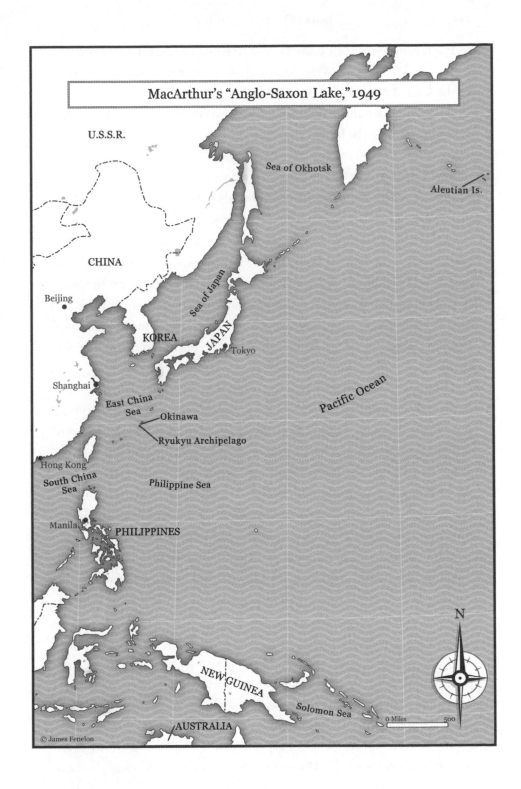

MacArthur's "Anglo-Saxon Lake," 1949

U.S.S.R.

Sea of Okhotsk

Aleutian Is.

CHINA

Beijing

Sea of Japan

KOREA

JAPAN

Tokyo

Shanghai

East China
Sea

Okinawa

Ryukyu Archipelago

Pacific Ocean

Hong Kong

South China
Sea

Philippine Sea

Manila

PHILIPPINES

N

NEW GUINEA

Solomon Sea

0 Miles   500

AUSTRALIA

© James Fenelon

initial reliance must be on the people attacked to resist it." Thereafter, he said, it would be up to the "entire civilized world under the Charter of the United Nations."

Though he would disclaim both innovation and heresy, Acheson's echo turned out to be louder than MacArthur's report. The secretary of state had seemed to make a startling case for U.S. indifference to a renewed Communist attack against Taiwan, or a new one against South Korea. "I concluded that old relationships between East and West in Asia were ended," he would write. "If new and useful ones were to succeed them, they must be based on mutual respect and helpfulness. We were ready to be helpful but could be so only where we were wanted and where conditions of help were sensible and possible. So the new day just dawning could go on to a glorious noon or darken and drizzle out. Which would come about would depend on decisions of the Asian peoples, which no friend or enemy from the outside could make for them."

His apparent indifference to the triumph of sun or storm was a departure from the foreign policy of his president and of the new national policy that Acheson would have a hand in devising. Though Acheson saw that "it was a supercharged moment to be speaking on Asian matters," he set aside the many drafts he and his staff had prepared and spoke from "a page or two of notes." The exclusion of Korea and the rest of the Asian mainland from America's defensive zone made an impression upon Communist dictators. "In North Korea, Kim Il-sung, who had been pressing Moscow and Beijing to support an invasion to 'liberate' the South, began to find his patrons more compliant." In Acheson's improvisations and flourishes Stalin heard not an echo of MacArthur but the splashes and splatters of a washing of hands.

IN FEBRUARY 1950, the chief of naval operations, Forrest Sherman, landed in Tokyo with the rest of the Joint Chiefs of Staff to meet with Douglas MacArthur, the commander of Far East Forces, and Arthur Radford, commander of the Pacific Fleet. The CNO had last seen MacArthur on board the *Missouri* on September 2, 1945, and the two men indulged a moment of nostalgia on greeting. The world they had known less than five years earlier had been made anew. Power blocs driven by leaders wielding the motive power of ancient resentment or the latest political or cultural conceit were constants in history, but their permutations and vectors changed a few times every century. After Stalin's humiliating failure to sever Berlin from the West, the Joint Chiefs believed he might be looking to test the Americans, perhaps in Asia. The former commander of the Seventh Fleet, Admiral Charles W. Cooke, who was serving as a technical adviser to Chiang Kai-shek in exile, noted that China was receiving Russian military assistance and believed that Mao would order a new attack on Taiwan imminently. With the exception of General Omar Bradley, their chairman, the members of the Joint Chiefs opposed Truman's policy, announced the previous month, that the United States would refrain from confronting Communist China militarily over the problem of Taiwan, the island redoubt of China's defeated Nationalists.

The question of whether to give direct military support to Chiang Kai-shek was made moot, for the time being, by the fact that China did not have credible amphibious naval forces. Mao's clodhopping attempt to invade in 1949 had proved as much. Though even MacArthur described the strategic value of Taiwan in terms that were explicitly naval—he called it "the equivalent of an unsinkable aircraft carrier and submarine tender"—the idea of losing the island paled next to fears that the Philippines or Japan, which hosted important U.S. bases, might see their governments turn Communist.

Forrest Sherman and the other members of the Joint Chiefs agreed that U.S. troops did not belong in Korea. There simply were not enough to go around. The Eighth Army, based in Japan on occupation duty since the surrender, was at only partial strength, barely adequate to fulfill its principal mission of defending Japan from a Soviet invasion. South Korea's small army was being counseled by a group of U.S. advisers numbering fewer than five hundred. George Kennan, whose voice had been so commanding when amplified by James Forrestal, found himself convinced by the example of China that Asian politics was beyond America's ability to control. Neither the Joint Chiefs nor

MacArthur's intelligence staff nor Acheson at State considered South Korea a likely direct target of Moscow. Acheson rated Turkey, Greece, Iran, and Berlin as places where "the balance of convenient operation dipped in favor of the Soviets" and thus as potential objects of mischief.

The naval threat posed by the Soviet Union in the Far East was manageable, Sherman noted. Though Stalin's naval manpower was impressive, totaling six hundred thousand men, almost half were coastal defense troops. His deployable sea forces consisted of just 15 large ships, 123 light combatants, 2,000 landing craft and minor combatants, and 275 submarines. Radford said his Pacific Fleet could cope with its rival's seventy-five diesel subs based in the Far East, though he had only six of his own and the training of destroyer crews in antisubmarine warfare had fallen on hard times.

Elsewhere, the spring of 1950 began hopefully for the worldwide outlook of free societies and the ability of U.S. naval forces to bolster them. Tito's Yugoslavia, though Communist, remained independent and even defiant of Soviet influence. Berlin, sustained from the air during Stalin's blockade, remained free. In March, Vice Admiral Jocko Clark's Sixth Fleet carrier task force arrived in Athens to celebrate the victory of the Greek royalist government over its Communist insurgency. Clark reveled in the festivities, social calls, and church services. He met with the king and the queen, robed in golden raiment. "The most queenly of queens," he called the queen consort of the Hellenes, the former Princess Frederica of Hanover, granddaughter of Germany's kaiser—personal background that the Communists tried to exploit. "Rarely has there ever been assembled such a magnificent display." Yet even in victory a feeling of vulnerability persisted.

Conferring with Lord Mountbatten and other allies during his travels, Clark had the sense that the fleet was in the Med "more or less under sufferance, because if the Russians really wanted to cut loose with modern weapons, either you'd have to have a tremendous air umbrella over your carriers or you better get them out of there quickly." Facing an enemy equipped with jet aircraft, an aircraft carrier task force defended by World War II–vintage F4U Corsair fighters might be driven from the Med entirely. But that same month, Clark's parent command, the Atlantic Fleet, showcased another Navy birthright of the Pacific War: the ability of heavy amphibious power to overpower an enemy at the boundary of land and sea.

With Forrest Sherman and Louis Johnson both in attendance, the Norfolk-based naval command carried out a large exercise in the Caribbean, with 160 ships and more than 65,000 men of all services rehearsing a seaborne and airborne assault on the island of Vieques. Though the umpires judged that losses among the invaders would have been heavy, and though a pair of submarines damaged fourteen ships in simulated torpedo attacks (including the battleship *Missouri*), the exercise, known as Portrex, demonstrated the mobile offensive power of U.S. naval forces in the atomic age. The Marine Corps had developed new methods of coping with the threat of atomic weapons at the beachhead—moving infantry ashore in helicopters from carrier decks as opposed to landing boats from transports. Although the Joint Chiefs had planned to simulate the use of nuclear weapons in the exercise, the idea was finally canceled, in part because the Strategic Air Command took little interest in the maneuvers. Perhaps they feared an embarrassing setup. The exercise finally produced no data to refute the conviction of Marine Corps leaders that air mobility and dispersion would make their assault forces unprofitable targets for atomic bombs at the beachhead.

The Navy's new nuclear strike plane, the AJ-1 Savage, entered fleet service at Moffett Field, California, before flight testing had been completed. Pressure from Washington to rush atomic weapons to the fleet led Commander John T. "Chick" Hayward, the skipper of the Navy's first atomic heavy attack squadron, to bypass the usual route through service testing at the Naval Air Test Center at Patuxent River, Maryland. The big plane made its first carrier takeoff in April. Its bombing and navigation systems didn't work, and defects with the hydraulics, flight controls, fuel systems, and turbochargers led to crashes and lives lost. The planes flew awkwardly at best from the *Midway*-class aircraft carriers that were too small to handle them properly. The breakdowns in maintenance and training that ensued defeated the value of the plane's devastating new capability.

When Dick Ashworth took command of the second heavy attack squadron, he again recommended to Hayward that the aircraft be removed from service to complete testing. Pressure from Admiral Radford compelled Hayward to reject the idea, and the AJ-1s finally were deployed to the Mediterranean, where they were based ashore, at Port Lyautey, Morocco. For all the Navy had invested in developing an atomic strike capability, it did not yet really exist. At a time when few missions concentrated minds at the Pentagon more than the aerial delivery of atomic weapons, that capability had more impact in notion than in fact.

AS THE PORTREX exercises were playing out in the Caribbean, Stalin and Mao signed a thirty-year "Treaty of Friendship, Alliance, and Mutual Assistance." The agreement, by which Stalin officially recognized China's Communist government and returned control of occupied port cities to the People's Republic in exchange for a $300 million loan and political and military backing, including combat aircraft, was often interpreted in Washington as evidence of a unified Communist bloc and a bold step toward the fulfillment of Lenin's worldwide ambitions for the Communist International, or Comintern. But in fact Mao's interests were largely nationalist. He needed time to consolidate power. The nuances of China's motivations would remain obscure to American leaders. Communist leaders in turn would be poorly served by their own crude estimations of U.S. intentions based on the speeches they heard.

Case in point was the apparent exclusion of Korea from America's strategic perimeter. Such a notion was inconsonant with the sweeping mandate of NSC 68, which put teeth into the Truman Doctrine in many ways, not least by calling for a buildup in conventional and nuclear arms. The exclusion also disregarded George Kennan's influential articulation that the United States should apply "unalterable counterforce" to Communist aggressions worldwide. Though it had not been declared by MacArthur or Acheson, almost five years of diplomacy had underscored that South Korea's security was elementally part of Japan's. In June 1950, a senior diplomat who had been critical of Truman's "timidity," John Foster Dulles, visited Seoul to assure Syngman Rhee that he had U.S. support beyond the modest detachment of American advisers that was trying to make a fighting force out of the army of the Republic of Korea (ROK). That same month, the president himself addressed Congress, speaking of Korea as "a testing ground" of adversarial political systems and a "beacon" to the people of northern Asia whom Communism was seeking to overrun. "We will not fail to provide the aid which is so essential to Korea at this critical time," he said.

At home, Acheson lobbied for the new policy. He considered it a performance, made necessary by what he viewed as the ordinary American's lack of sophistication in international politics. His attidude was on display in Dallas on June 13, where he foreswore isolationism as a general matter. "We should not pull down the blinds and sit in the parlor with a loaded shotgun, waiting," he said. "Isolation is not a realistic course of action. It does not work and it has not been cheap." Acheson and Paul Nitze, who led the interagency policy group that had produced NSC 68, put the price of rearmament in the neighborhood of $50 billion a year, more than a tripling of the White House's previous hard cap for defense spending. The need for it would arrive with the heat of summer.

Seven hundred miles west of Tokyo, Korea's demilitarized zone trembled on the other side of the strategic boundary that MacArthur and Acheson had seemed to draw. Their apparent disclaimers reached wishful ears, inviting the North Korean dictator to act on his conviction that the arc of history was bending his way. Only encouraging that conviction were Mao's victory in the Chinese civil war, and Syngman Rhee's brutal response to the political agitations and rioting instigated by Communist Party agents in South Korea.

Stalin approved of Kim's plan, so long as the Chinese didn't object. On May 13, Kim flew to the Chinese capital with his foreign affairs minister and informed Mao that Stalin had blessed his plan to "reunify" Korea. Old regimes were crumbling. Emboldened by the Kremlin's

backing, by the fast progress of his army, and by evidence that the campaign of subversion had weakened Rhee and his regime of "dogs," Kim
judged conditions in Seoul ripe for a revolution.

Western critics of the White House's anticommunism saw paranoia
in policies such as NSC 68 and in the popularity and influence of books
such as Ambassador William C. Bullitt's *The Great Globe Itself,* which
warned of Soviet authoritarianism on the march. Unimpressed by the
blunt public statements of Truman and his cabinet—Acheson would
admit that "we made our points clearer than truth"—they would de-
ride the idea that Lenin's expansive ambitions from the 1920s, demanding the allegiance of the worldwide proletariat, were still operative. But
Kim seemed to heed nothing more faithfully than the call of the
Comintern. On June 25, 1950, he considered what faced him south of
the Demilitarized Zone—a frayed society, ready for unification by
arms—and seized his moment. Spearheaded by Soviet-built tanks and
self-propelled artillery, the North Korean army poured across the
38th parallel.

SEOUL WAS SITUATED just thirty miles south of the 38th parallel, as if
to invite invasion. That the peninsula's railroad lines converged from
the north at the capital before diverging toward the opposite coasts
heading south—leaving Seoul at the nexus of a giant standard-gauge
X—ensured that the path of invasion led directly to the city. Facing
direct assault by the main body of the North Korean army, and gradual
envelopment by the other three prongs of the advance as it spread south,
the city was immediately in the balance. For MacArthur, it was an
awful echo of 1941, when his positions on Luzon were suddenly set
ablaze. "It couldn't be, I told myself. Not again!" he would write.

Vice Admiral C. Turner Joy wasn't sure Washington would do
much about it. It did not surprise him that the United Nations quickly
called upon Kim to halt the North Korean aggression, but he thought
it would end there. Acheson mobilized the international body at once,
and with the Soviet representative on the Security Council absent, the
secretary of state's proposal for a collective response received no veto.

Truman took executive action in the name of the international body, and the United States Congress became superfluous. Joy was stunned to see Truman's order for Far East Command air and sea forces to "cover and support" the South Korean troops, and for the Seventh Fleet to sortie north from Subic Bay, and MacArthur was as surprised as he was. According to Joy, MacArthur called Truman's decision "a complete reversal of our Far East policy" and admitted, "We had no plans for this type of war."

Truman was visiting family in Missouri when it started. The public statement he issued strongly echoed forewarnings of James Forrestal, George Kennan, and Ambassador Bullitt. The president's rhetoric owed a debt to FDR as well. "The attack upon Korea makes it plain beyond all doubt that communism has passed beyond the use of subversion to conquer independent nations and will now use armed invasion and war," the president said.

Truman flew back to Washington the following morning and met at Blair House with the Joint Chiefs of Staff and his diplomatic advisers. It was clear at once that generalized intelligence warnings of a possible invasion by North Korea, which had been staples of State Department, CIA, and military reporting since late 1949, should have been taken more seriously. More urgent threats, those agencies thought, confronted the United States at other potential hot spots—Indochina, Turkey, Berlin, Iran. With the French reeling in their Indochinese war, suffering fifty thousand casualties, conditions were ripe for a covert hand to tip the balance, and China filled that bill. France, like the other European nations, was committing little to the collective defense of Europe, where the Soviets maintained twenty-five well-equipped divisions, with another fifty to sixty-five in reserve. But if the French brought home their troops to fortify NATO, Dean Acheson feared Indochina would "go to pieces overnight." The loyalty to the West on the part of West Germany, which was not a member of NATO, was far from certain.

Facing dangerous contingencies around the world, Washington had not read with a high degree of alarm indications that Pyongyang was stockpiling munitions near the 38th parallel. Rather, Truman was focused on Soviet intentions with respect to the Korean peninsula. He

ordered his intelligence stations worldwide to reassess them and asked
the Joint Chiefs to study how much airpower would be needed to destroy Soviet air bases in the Far East in the event their aircraft intervened in a war for the peninsula.

General J. Lawton Collins, the Army chief of staff, advised Truman
that saving Syngman Rhee meant U.S. troops would have to return to
the Asian mainland. Unfortunately, all four divisions of the Eighth
Army stationed in Japan were under strength, and no war plan existed
for the defense of South Korea. Admiral Sherman, the CNO, and Hoyt
Vandenberg, the Air Force chief of staff, argued that air and naval
power alone could do the job. Sherman advised the president that the
Seventh Fleet's carrier task force—with its single carrier, the *Valley
Forge*—could be quickly moved up from the Hong Kong area to operate off Korea. The president, however, was not yet ready to throw U.S.
forces directly into the fray. For the time being, his goal was to prevent
the outbreak of a wider regional war that risked becoming World
War III. Escalation alarmed him more than did the prospect of a South
Korean defeat.

Both Omar Bradley, the Joint Chiefs chairman, and Forrest Sherman told him the Soviets were not ready for a new world war. Truman
concluded that Korea was "the Greece of the Far East. If we are tough
enough now, if we stand up to them like we did in Greece three years
earlier, they won't take any next steps." Communists in Greece, like
Communists everywhere, Truman believed, "thrived on the continuing
conditions of misery, starvation, and economic ruin." While he did not
see the invasion as signaling a *casus belli* with the Soviet Union, he was
concerned that Mao might exploit the opportunity presented by Pyongyang's aggression to settle old business. On June 28, after directing the
Navy to support South Korean forces below the 38th parallel, he ordered the Seventh Fleet to establish a patrol in the Taiwan Strait to
deter another Chinese attack on Taiwan.

Admiral Joy undertook the dual mission on behalf of the Far East
Command, ordering the *Valley Forge* to depart Hong Kong and set
course for Subic Bay, where it would refuel and reprovision, then to
steam north toward Sasebo on Japan's western coast. The port would

be a principal staging area into Korea and would serve as the head-quarters of the South Korea Support Group, a cruiser and destroyer force dedicated to blockading the peninsula's coasts. The destroyers *De Haven* and *Mansfield* carried out the U.S. Navy's first operation of the emergent war, evacuating American nationals from the port cities of Inchon and Pusan. Joy then threw his support into the ground fight, directing his destroyers to escort two ammunition ships ordered by MacArthur from Tokyo into Pusan. Small surface units were involved in the ground fight at once. On the first day of hostilities, a South Korean submarine chaser intercepted a North Korean steamer loaded with six hundred soldiers and sank her off Tsushima Island. The Communists were soon to rue their complete incapacity to operate at sea.

While the *Valley Forge,* the cruiser *Rochester,* and eight destroyers were under way to Sasebo, under command of Rear Admiral John M. Hoskins, the Joint Chiefs placed the Seventh Fleet under the control of the Far East Command. It was the first time MacArthur had ever enjoyed operational command of a fast carrier task force. He wanted the carriers, known as Task Force 77, off Korea at once, but that was not to be. It impressed Forrest Sherman and Turner Joy alike that Sasebo was just seven hundred miles from the Soviet Pacific Fleet base at Vladivostok, and that the State Department had warned through diplomatic and military channels, "POSSIBLE THAT KOREA IS ONLY FIRST OF SERIES OF COORDINATED ACTIONS ON PART OF SOVIETS." Vice Admiral Sir William Andrewes noted that Admiral Joy "was anxious not to have too many ships in Japanese mainland ports as he did not know what the immediate Russian reaction might be to any direct intervention by United Nations forces." According to the official British historian of the war, "The lesson of Pearl Harbour was not lost upon the American admiral." Joy diverted the ships to Okinawa instead.

After Admiral Sherman announced that combat operations would not begin until a second carrier could reach the Far East, Joy was pleased to hear from the Royal Navy commander in Hong Kong, Admiral Sir Eric J. P. Brind, that HMS *Triumph,* a light carrier visiting Japan, would be placed at his service. The Australians offered him what they had there as well, and New Zealand promised a pair of frigates. With his modest command overtasked and underequipped, Joy gladly accepted the help. These vessels, to be joined later by the Dutch destroyer *Evertsen* and a number of Canadian light combatants, would supplement UN forces and alternately serve as a separate British Commonwealth squadron that would operate off the Korean west coast, under command of Admiral Andrewes, Brind's number two.

For Japan-based U.S. naval forces, the plan of the day was catch as catch can. This was reflected in Admiral Joy's order authorizing his submarine captains, with other ASW elements, to attack and drive off unidentified submarines at will. While such an order was in contradiction to international law, Forrest Sherman took the position that self-defense was an inherent right of a naval force in international waters. He rebuffed a request from the British ambassador to reduce the risks of sinking a "neutral" Russian sub by announcing a general warning to noncombatant nations. Sherman believed issuance of a warning would be an unjustifiable restriction of his commanders' freedom—which Joy promptly removed from his small submarine force anyway. He assigned the commander of his submarine task group, Commander Francis W. Scanland, Jr., to serve as an antisubmarine warfare adviser to Task Force 77's carrier commander rather than run his command independently. The commander in chief of Pacific Fleet submarines, Rear Admiral John H. Brown, called this "a most unsatisfactory situation."

The city of Seoul fell to the North Korean army on June 28, putting up no semblance of the robust defenses that great cities through history had offered when transformed into urban battlegrounds. As South Korean soldiers fled across the Han River, relentless North Korean artillery kept them from holding the far bank as a defensive barrier. MacArthur watched the city burn from just a mile away and saw Korean refugees stream by, carrying all their worldly goods. "I watched for an hour the pitiful evidence of the disaster I had inherited. In that brief interval on the blood-soaked hill, I formulated my plans. They were desperate plans indeed, but I could see no other way except to accept a defeat which would include not only Korea, but all of continental Asia."

Turner Joy, meanwhile, placed his modest naval force—the light cruiser *Juneau* and the destroyers *Mansfield, De Haven, Collett,* and *Swenson*—under Rear Admiral John M. Higgins, and ordered it to harass and interdict North Korean troops. In the midnight morning hours of June 29, the *Juneau*'s radar detected three bogies. Believing that no friendly naval forces were in the area, the *Juneau* lofted illumination rounds and opened fire, sinking a target that turned out to be a South Korean minelayer.

On June 30, President Truman approved the commitment of American troops to the peninsula. It was fortuitous that Admiral Joy had a well-qualified amphibious commander in Japan when the war broke out. Rear Admiral James H. Doyle, lean, tall, and acerbic, was the Navy's leading expert on amphibious warfare, having been a protégé of the boss of the Pacific Fleet's "alligator navy" during World War II, Richmond Kelly Turner. The next afternoon Doyle received an order from Joy's headquarters to carry Major General William F. Dean's 24th Infantry Division from Fukuoka and Sasebo, and from there by sea, 140 miles north past Tsushima Island to Pusan.

Empowering the Navy to exploit the sea control it enjoyed, Truman approved Forrest Sherman's request to declare a naval blockade of North Korea's ports—east and west coast alike—and authorized the Seventh Fleet, under the command of Rear Admiral Arthur D. Struble, to strike targets in North Korea.

14

LOSING SEOUL, HOLDING PUSAN

FAR EAST NAVAL FORCES WOULD SCRAMBLE THROUGHOUT TO fulfill two simultaneous missions: projecting power into the ground fight in Korea while guarding Taiwan against another Chinese invasion. When Admiral Turner Joy's Sasebo-based Japan-Korea Support Group diverted the heavy cruiser *Helena* and several destroyers to patrol the Taiwan Strait with Task Force 77, Rear Admiral John M. Higgins found himself in direct command of ships in two fleets eight hundred miles apart. As U.S. and British Commonwealth warships began enforcement of the blockade, Far East naval commanders kept one eye on Korea, another on China, and reptile fears centered on Moscow. Not since the Guadalcanal campaign would the working surface navy chase so many fleeting hares in the course of so many chaotically evolving days.

Facing a shortage of shipping to handle these disparate missions, Admiral Struble brought forward Pearl Harbor– and Guam-based maritime patrol aircraft—P2V Neptunes, PBM Mariners, and PB4Y Privateers, a variant of the B-24—to assist as his long-range eyes in the Taiwan Strait, operating from bases in Japan and Okinawa. With a shortage of destroyers to assign to patrols and sweeps, submarines filled the gap. Although the Yokosuka-based submarines *Catfish, Greenlet, Pickerel, Remora,* and *Segundo* had a primary mission of antisubmarine warfare, Admiral Joy would use them and the boats that came later to reconnoiter the coast from China to the Soviet Union's far eastern coast. The primary purpose of the diesel submarines and patrol aircraft squadrons in July would be to monitor the Taiwan Strait while operations were escalating off Korea amid Typhoon Grace's wind-driven rains.

On the night of July 2, Higgins's command redeemed itself. The *Juneau,* in company with newly arrived HMS *Jamaica* and the sloop *Black Swan,* carried out the initial shore bombardment of the war, hitting North Korean troop formations near the town of Chumunjin. The UN ships were cooling their barrels early the following morning when four North Korean torpedo boats and a pair of gunboats approached. Quickly and bloodily they discovered the efficacy of modern cruisers firing rapid partial salvos. Three of the torpedo boats and both gunboats foundered under a shellacking from U.S. five-inch/38s and British six-inch Mark XXIIIs. As that was playing out, Struble's carrier task force, with USS *Valley Forge* and HMS *Triumph,* was steaming north from Okinawa, preparing their air groups, totaling 130 planes, to undertake the first U.S. naval air combat operation of the Cold War.

AT 5:45 A.M. on July 3, the carriers began launching from a position in the Yellow Sea about 150 miles from Pyongyang and less than two hundred miles from the Soviet base at Port Arthur. The *Triumph*'s air group led the way in. Twelve Fairey Fireflies and nine Supermarine Seafires, naval variants of the famed Spitfire of World War II, took off fifteen minutes ahead of the group from the *Valley Forge*. As with the British, the first American element of the flock was a relic of the last war: Vought F4U Corsairs. Pilots would complain that the famed gull-winged fighter-bomber was about as well suited to the emerging jet age as the death-trap TBD Devastator had been in 1942. But it was available in numbers when war summoned it to action, and to action the old birds went.

Lieutenant Commander Douglas K. English set out for the North

Korean capital with sixteen F4Us. Joining him were a dozen Douglas AD-4 Skyraiders, single-engine powerhouses with an ordnance capacity as great as a four-engine bomber. En route, the propeller-driven strikers were overtaken by a formation of dark blue aircraft blowing fire from their tails. These were the first carrier-based jets ever to sortie for war, twenty-two Grumman F9F Panther jet fighter-bombers led by the skipper of Air Group Five, Commander Harvey P. Lanham.

Lanham's two futuristically equipped squadrons, VF-51 and VF-52, had raised eyebrows on their arrival in Pearl Harbor, and again at Guam, where the *Valley Forge* relieved the *Boxer,* which had only Corsairs and Skyraiders on board. Still, the *Valley Forge*'s air boss was leery about the untested jets, fearing accidents during training. The fear was self-fulfilling. "We were flying only four hours a month," said Donald E. Engen, a pilot with Fighter Squadron 51. "*That* was dangerous."

After all the public attention generated by the B-36 bomber controversy, fighter aviation's transition to the jet age was taking place in relative obscurity. The testing and evaluation of the new generation of planes was under way at the Naval Air Test Center at Patuxent River, Maryland. The Navy chose the right man to direct the effort at a critical time. Frederick M. Trapnell was by acclamation the greatest flight-test engineer in the Navy in the 1950s. Having served as a dive-bomber pilot during World War II, Captain Trapnell was quick to tease out the virtues and foibles of an unfamiliar airframe, and equally adept at identifying pilots with a similar skill set. He recruited a team of all-stars to Pax River, combat veterans and test pilots like Marion Carl, Thomas F. Connolly, John J. Hyland, Jr., and Apollo Soucek. They were dynamic and innovative and had hearts that pumped engine coolant.

Jets had problems in carrier operations. The difficulty began with the aeronautical peculiarities of turbojet propulsion. Ordinary aircraft propellers produced thrust inversely proportional to an aircraft's speed. At low speeds, a prop-driven aircraft generated peak thrust. This was helpful on a short flight deck, where quick access to full power was essential. As the plane got airborne and accelerated, its propeller moved less and less air, reducing its thrust. But it had thrust where it really counted, down on the deck. On a carrier, it was essential for aircraft to handle well at low airspeeds, as when approaching to land, or "trap," as catching an arresting wire was known.

Jets maximize their thrust when they're flying fast but struggle to build thrust from a stop. To get aloft, the early jets needed a boost from a catapult. Only after they had been grubstaked with sufficient speed could they zoom heavenward. But since jets flew faster than propeller-driven planes did when landing, the shock to the plane was considerably greater, and the jet's airframe had to be reinforced to handle the extra impact. This added weight, as did the larger fuel load needed to accommodate a jet engine's voracious appetite for aviation gas. And since flying at transonic speeds tended to freeze an aircraft's control surfaces, powered flight controls and dive brakes were essential too. All such modifications added more weight, complicating the performance equation in the unforgiving limits of an aircraft carrier.

An aircraft that worked well for the Air Force might be a dud in the fleet. Through the years, one new jet after another would show up at Pax River bidding for Fred Trapnell's heart. He and his flight-test engineers evaluated Germany's groundbreaking Messerschmitt Me-262 Swallow, the Lockheed P-80 Shooting Star (the U.S. Air Force's first successful combat jet), the McDonnell XFH Phantom (the first jet to fly from a U.S. aircraft carrier), and its successor, the XF2H Banshee (a versatile but mediocre stopgap). The Chance Vought XF6U Pirate and XF7U Cutlass, a flying wing, were utter failures. The swept-wing North American FJ-1 Fury, the Navy's first operationally deployed jet fighter, showed promise before leaving the fleet and evolving into the Air Force's successful F-86 Sabre. When Grumman's XF9F-2 Panther arrived at Patuxent River in early 1948, the chief of flight testing, Fred Trapnell, identified the next-generation Navy fighter as a keeper.

Putting the bullet-nosed, straight-winged experimental jet through its paces at the Grumman test range in Bethpage, Long Island, Trapnell gave it a fine review. In level flight, he noted, the Panther tended to oscillate, a strange "snaking" motion that became more pronounced at higher air speeds. It turned out to be the sloshing of fuel in the tanks. In November of the following year, he assigned test pilot Corwin "Corky" Meyer to demonstrate the F9F at an airshow at Idlewild Airport in

New York.* Lieutenant Meyer's 625-mile-per-hour flyover of the grandstands sent a haunting roar across Queens and produced a shock collar of condensation that trailed him to impressive visual effect, enthralling the crowd of half a million. Among them was President Truman. Grumman had itself another winner. By the time the *Valley Forge* took the Panther to war for the first time on July 3, 1950, the Navy was on the way to ordering fourteen hundred of the new plane.

Angling downward, straight wings tipped with teardrop fuel tanks, Commander Lanham's Panthers struck the North Korean airfields before many of the piston-engine Yakovlev Yak-9s could get off the ground. Forty to fifty of the Russian-built fighters were scattered around the revetments, hangars, and runways around Pyongyang. The Panther's four 20 mm cannons, pulling belts that alternated an armor-piercing tracer, a high-explosive incendiary, and a ball round, could blow apart locomotives and sink ships. It was overkill for grounded airplanes. "The goal was to hit many targets, to announce in no uncertain terms that the United States had entered the war," Don Engen said. Behind the jets came the Skyraiders and Corsairs, bombing parked planes, ammunition dumps, fuel storage, hangars, and other buildings.

Engen spotted a yellow convertible racing down a road. He took it for a flag officer's staff car. "We were told to get anything that moved on the roads, because it was going to be Army-related, even yellow convertibles." He lined up on it, eased it into his gunsight, and turned the Chevy to parts.

Two of a handful of Yaks that got airborne fell to the guns of Lanham's pilots. Breaking off their strafing runs over the airfield to chase the enemy interceptors, Ensign Eldon W. Brown and Lieutenant (j.g.) Leonard H. Plog of Fighter Squadron 51 became the Navy's first air-to-air killers in the jet age. Having gained air superiority, Lanham released a few Skyraiders and Corsairs to bomb some ships he had seen in Pyongyang harbor during the run in. Flak was light during the day and no planes were lost. As the strikers returned to the sea, a gray-black pall rose from the North Korean capital city, visible for miles.

* Now known as John F. Kennedy International Airport.

Task Force 77 planes struck Pyongyang's airfields again the next day, losing a Corsair and three Skyraiders to flak. Concerned about the threat of Soviet submarines, the commander of the Seventh Fleet, Vice Admiral Arthur D. Struble, limited the carriers to two consecutive days of hitting enemy targets. The antisubmarine capability of his destroyers was low. Though a handful of friendly subs were available at Yokosuka to work with destroyers in training exercises, sonar teams had not rehearsed since June. Under the pressure of war operations, their ships could "seldom be spared for refresher work," a Navy report stated, imposing "a virtual suspension of training services because of the departure of combatant vessels from the Yokosuka area."

In spite of the two-consecutive-day limitation, the carriers remained as active in the following weeks as their need for replenishment allowed, targeting road and rail traffic in support of the heavily pressured front. The strikes, finishing on Independence Day, would keep Pyongyang's Soviet-equipped, Soviet-trained air force from joining the rout of the reeling South Korean forces in the first days of the war. The naval aviators suffered no losses.

ON JULY 5, a battalion of the 24th Infantry Division made the first U.S. contact with the North Korean People's Army (NKPA) thirty miles south of Seoul, as a Communist element advanced along the highway crossing from the capital to Pusan on the east coast. The enemy troops, fresh from overrunning the South Korean capital, outflanked the Americans and pushed them back. The commanding general of the division, Major General William F. Dean, stressed to MacArthur that they would underestimate the enemy at their peril and begged for more armor and artillery. MacArthur asked the Joint Chiefs for five full-strength divisions and three tank battalions. He was refused on grounds that commitments in other parts of the world could not be shirked, and that shipping was scarce in any event. He would have to make due in the near term with forces on hand in his theater. The workaday echelons of the Navy set about delivering U.S. troops to the war zone from Japan.

The first problem faced by Admiral Doyle was to find enough vessels for a large-scale lift. Doyle relied on Japanese-crewed merchant ships to bring the bulk of the Eighth Army to the peninsula. The 24th Division completed its movement to Korea by July 6. Next down the ramps were the 25th Infantry Division, coming from Moji, the Inland Sea ports, and Sasebo. On the following day, the UN Security Council established a unified UN command with the United States serving as its "operative agent," entitled to appoint an overall commander. The Joint Chiefs named MacArthur commander in chief, United Nations Command, or CINCUNC.

Admiral Joy had ordered the Korean coasts blockaded as far north as possible, stressing the need to destroy the tunnels that enabled rail and road transport on the fringe of the mountainous peninsula. On the night of July 11, the *Juneau* and the destroyer *Mansfield* stopped half a mile off the beach, ten miles south of the North Korean city of Songjin. The destroyer lowered a whaleboat containing a nine-man demolition party led by the cruiser's executive officer, Commander William B. Porter. Motoring ashore, Porter's team—the first U.S. servicemen to enter North Korea—located their target, a train tunnel, rigged it with a pair of timed charges, and spirited back out to sea. The following day, radio intercepts suggested the charges had worked as designed. Naval interdiction, improvisational and opportunistic in many cases, kept the advancing enemy off-balance and swivel-necked, helping the U.S. and Republic of Korea (ROK) forces avoid being overrun along the coast.

The Eighth Army's commanding general, Lieutenant General Walton H. Walker, was a Texan who had served as one of George Patton's principal corps commanders during World War II. From his headquarters in the city of Taegu, where he arrived on the twelfth, he oversaw the three U.S. and five Republic of Korea divisions under the United Nations flag. The threat was most serious to his west, where the understrength regiments of the 24th Infantry Division had been falling back, staging one futile delaying action after another until they finally dug in near the city of Taejon.

As the North Koreans advanced, MacArthur hosted General Lawton Collins, General Hoyt Vandenberg, and Admiral Radford at

CINCFE (Far East Command) headquarters on the sixth floor of the Dai-Ichi Life Insurance Company building in downtown Tokyo and briefed them on the state of the war. Launching into his reflexive mode of argument, he explained why his command deserved primacy over all other areas. The outcome of the Cold War, he contended, would be decided in the Far East. He announced his intention not merely to hold against the North Koreans but to destroy them. MacArthur said he could hold with the three U.S. divisions he had in country, but that to win, he would need eight. The stakes as he saw them were just as Truman had explained. The war in the Far East was the ultimate test of containment. "We win here or we lose everywhere," the president said, and MacArthur agreed. Once reinforcements arrived, MacArthur would take the offensive. The Second Infantry Division was already mounting up in Hawaii, and a Marine regimental combat team was not far behind. The Marines were essential, MacArthur said, because his scheme for a counteroffensive was amphibious. Exploiting his uncontested control of the sea and the well-cultivated talents of the Corps, he meant to stage an amphibious landing near Seoul on the peninsula's west coast.

For now, however, nothing was going to save General Dean's 24th Division against an enemy outfitted with Russian-built tanks, not without close support from aircraft. Dean simply could not maintain his scattered blocking positions. His men were overmatched at every point, as Soviet-built T-34 tanks spearheaded river crossings at night while guerrilla elements infiltrated the refugee stream and struck like heat lightning in the rear. The division suffered 30 percent casualties while yielding one hundred miles to the North Koreans, losing more than twenty-four hundred men and almost all of the division's heavy equipment along the way.

In the battle that ensued within the city limits of Taejon, T-34s roamed at will. Corralling a bazooka gunner and his assistant, his aide and his Korean interpreter, the division commander went hunting tanks. At a city intersection they found an idle T-34 unaccompanied by infantry. Creeping up close, the bazookaman disabled it with three shots to the base of the turret. In the chaos of the enemy counterattack that followed, the command post was finally overrun. Dean ordered it evacuated. He helped load some trucks with wounded before jumping in and trying to get back to American lines. En route east they encountered a North Korean roadblock. Dismounting quickly from their vehicle, Dean, with seventeen U.S. soldiers and one terrified South Korean civilian, spent the night alternately hiding and marching toward UN lines.

LIEUTENANT GENERAL WALTON Walker's besieged command received a boost on July 18, when Admiral Doyle's amphibious attack force appeared in the roadstead off Pohang. A team of Navy frogmen from Underwater Demolition Team Three, under Lieutenant Commander William R. McKinney, reconnoitered the beach, then the Japanese-crewed LSTs of Captain Norman W. Sears's tractor group began delivering the First Cavalry Division to the breakwaters and jetty walls. They were unopposed.

Facing eight North Korean divisions supported by armor, Walker welcomed more than ten thousand troops, two thousand vehicles, and three thousand tons of cargo—a volume of matériel that Pusan's port simply could not have sustained, congested as it was with soldiers, arms, supplies, and war refugees looking to depart.

With Taejon fallen, and General Dean missing in action, Walker moved the First Cav into the breech left by the defeated 24th Division. On July 23 they were confronted by a North Korean assault led by more than two dozen T-34s and major elements of the NKPA's Third and Fourth divisions. The Americans were enveloped and overrun. Seven light tanks fell to the dated but still-powerful Soviet models, the mere rumor of which compelled some of the cavalrymen to abandon their positions and weapons. Two companies simply disappeared in the desperation and confusion. The First Cav took more than a thousand casualties, some by friendly fire. There were shameful incidents of cavalrymen shooting Korean refugees in the panic. A battalion of the 29th Infantry advanced toward contact under command of the former chief of staff of the South Korean army, Major General Chae Pyongduk. They ran into a well-prepared element from the North Korean Sixth Division and were destroyed utterly. General Chae was among more than three hundred killed in action.

MacArthur could see the hand of Moscow and Beijing at work. "The pattern and density of the enemy's supply and reinforcement movement," he wrote, "showed that heavy tonnage was coming from Chinese Manchuria and Russian Siberia, through Seoul, in spite of our bombing and strafing. It moved habitually at night." Walton Walker focused now on holding the three-sided perimeter around his own nexus of supply, the port of Pusan. Harry Truman would write, "A small band of heroic youngsters led by a few remarkable generals was holding off a landslide so that the strength for the counterpunch could be mustered behind their thin curtain of resistance."

15

NEW WAR FOR THE OLD CORPS

ON HIS BAD DAYS AT CAMP PENDLETON, THE COMMANDER OF the First Marine Division, Major General Graves B. Erskine, could identify with the lamentable state of readiness of the UN ground forces in the Far East. The Eighth Army's infantry divisions—serving occupation duty in Japan—were at two-thirds strength. Fewer than one in five of Syngman Rhee's infantry and reconnaissance battalions were more than 50 percent combat-effective, and none had been trained to defend against an armored assault. In the age of Louis Johnson, the Marine Corps was not much better off. Erskine's regiments, battalions, and companies were all at two-thirds strength as well. That July, with his entreaties for more men and more equipment routinely denied by Fleet Marine Force, Pacific, Camp Pendleton's annual carnival and rodeo seemed just the thing to boost morale. Erskine's assistant, Colonel Edward A. Craig, was overseeing the setup of the rodeo area, taking delivery of horses and cattle, laying dirt and sand—when he received word from Washington that there had been an incident in the Far East and that all liberties had been canceled. The carnival ran for a night, but the Marines never got their rodeo.

As Kim Il-sung was sizing up his opportunity to unify Korea by force, Lieutenant General Lemuel C. Shepherd, newly tailored with a third star, was taking the slow coach from Quantico to San Diego to Honolulu to become the new commander of Fleet Marine Force Pacific. Since Admiral Radford had approved his request to tarry, Shepherd took his family to Yellowstone National Park on the way. He was in Colorado Springs when the morning papers reported a North Korean attack on the south. Shepherd thought, *Well, that's MacArthur's bailiwick. There aren't any Marines in Korea.* In Cody, Wyoming, he thought he might do some fishing. Shepherd was rowing a boat on a lake when a young woman appeared on the beach, hollering and waving a piece of paper. She was from the local telegraph office. The dispatch was from Radford. It read, "PREFER YOU COME BY AIR RATHER THAN BY TRANSPORT. TAKE THE REST OF YOUR LEAVE SOME OTHER TIME." The Marines were going to have work to do overseas. Shepherd and his wife were in Salt Lake City by midnight. On arrival in Honolulu, he received from his chief of staff an order to mount his brigade and prepare to send it to the Far East.

Douglas MacArthur was delighted when Turner Joy confirmed the availability of the Marine brigade. With Seoul lost and the combat front descending south like a curtain, MacArthur knew the defense of South Korea would be an all-hands effort. The general was making plans, and his plans called for the Marines.

At Pendleton, Eddie Craig assembled the choicest elements of the understrength division: the Fifth Marine Regiment, under command of a decorated World War II veteran, Lieutenant Colonel Raymond L. Murray. Craig helped him load out the unit, raiding the division armory for some late-model bazookas and M-26 Pershing heavy tanks, and made contact with Marine Air Group 33, part of the First Marine Air Wing based at El Toro. Its Corsairs and Grumman F7F Tigercat twin-engine heavy fighters were an integral part of the Marine Corps "air-ground team." Craig and the assistant wing commander, Brigadier General Thomas J. Cushman, brought together their seven-thousand-man ad hoc outfit, attaching medical, supply, motor transport, ordnance, and repair elements in typically self-sufficient Marine combat team style. They called the unit, which was the whole available strength of the First Marine Division, the First Provisional Marine Brigade. The two commanders then flew to Tokyo while the body of the brigade mustered at San Diego. The escort carrier *Badoeng Strait* took them on board along with MAG 33's allocation of Corsairs for her westward transit, which began on July 14.

Under way, their orders changed. The brigade wasn't going to Japan. The deteriorating situation on the ground left no time. While Craig established his command post in a vacated Army billet near Osaka, his Marines went directly to Korea. The president would call it a "police action," but the Marine Corps knew there was a war to be won. A peninsular war was tailor-made for their kind of combat, and the enemy had no direct experience standing on its receiving end.

A week later, as Typhoon Grace began to lash the beach, elements of the 29th Infantry Regiment began arriving from Okinawa. General Walker had no luxury to accumulate a reserve, so he used the newcomers to re-form his lines in the west. Though he could feel the prospect of being thrown into the sea diminishing, his strength in the southwest was sparsest of all. There, along the road to Masan, his intelligence reported, a North Korean division was quickly moving east.

The sea was a limit on a soldier's freedom to retreat. When the tide of battle was going out, the waterfront was oblivion itself. Owing to the thoroughgoing manner in which Turner Joy controlled the seas, they would be Walker's lifeline.

ON JULY 19, Eddie Craig and Tom Cushman reported to Far East Command headquarters at Tokyo. MacArthur, Admiral Joy, and the chief of the Far East Air Force, Lieutenant General George E. Stratemeyer, were glad to see the Marines arrive. When Craig and MacArthur met in private, the theater commander said, "They tell me I have a reputation for not liking Marines. But I'm proud of the fact that the First Marine Division served under me in World War II." MacArthur said he intended to carry off a dramatic counterstroke: a west coast amphibious landing near Seoul. It would cut the fast-moving North Korean army's lines of supply, he said, turning grape to raisin by severing the vine. MacArthur told Lemuel Shepherd that if the whole First Marine Division were at his disposal, he could carry off such a landing at Inchon, the port that served the South Korean capital. It was a tricky target, he noted, accessed by a winding channel that was subject to severe tidal swings, but a division of three full regiments could pull it off, MacArthur thought. He asked Shepherd to write the Joint Chiefs and ask that the division be sent to the Far East.

It put Shepherd in an awkward spot to make such a request without the knowledge of his commandant, General Clifton B. Cates. But Cates was forgiving when the two finally met in San Diego a few days later. Cates said he didn't think there were enough men to go around, given that he was trying to raise a Marine division to serve in Europe with NATO. Shepherd said, "Clifton, we're fighting a hot war over there in Korea. NATO is something they're just forming on paper. We belong in the Pacific. The Western Pacific is our theater." Both men were delighted when President Truman ordered the activation of the reserves in late July. Most Marine leaders saw themselves as engaged in a fight for their existence with Louis Johnson's Pentagon and on Capitol Hill. Brigadier General Harry B. Liversedge, a legendary combat Marine from World War II, oversaw the activation as director of the Marine Corps Reserve. He brought a large number of fellow veterans back into the fold. "They were good people. They just needed shaking down," General Oliver Smith said. Activation of the reserve would raise the strength of the Marine Corps from 75,000 men to more than 260,000 by the end of 1950, half of whom would be reservists.

Stratemeyer seemed "very anxious," Craig thought, to bring the Marine brigade's aviators under Far East Air Force command. Craig knew the value of an integrated air-ground team and told MacArthur that if his pilots were given to the Air Force, the fighting potential of the whole outfit would be cut by 99 percent. Overstatement being something MacArthur could appreciate, he reassured Craig that he would keep his pilots and that he would so advise Stratemeyer. When he met with the Joint Chiefs in Tokyo, MacArthur said nothing about close air support. His demands for more airpower were focused on strategic bombers. He wanted thirty more B-29 Superfortresses in theater, noting that Korea's tunnels and bridges invited "a unique use of the atomic bomb." But he met his promise to Craig, and aviation would stay with the Marines all the way to the end.

On July 22, while HMS *Triumph* retired to Sasebo for a ten-day rest, the *Valley Forge* moved off Korea's west coast to avoid the ravages of Typhoon Grace and began launching air strikes in support of Eighth Army forces retreating south of Seoul. The North Korean Sixth Division was advancing fast through the southwestern part of the peninsula, with little to stand in their way. An emergency dispatch from Eighth Army announced an "urgent requirement" for immediate naval air support.

The capacity of a single aircraft carrier to affect the ground war would be tested on this day. The F9F Panthers of Air Group Five struck airfields and road networks in the greater Seoul area, while the Skyraiders and Corsairs placed themselves at the disposal of Fifth Air Force airborne tactical air controllers who were directing the close support of the ground forces.

On low-level sweeps, the Navy planes faced heavy antiaircraft fire, and two of their pilots paid the price. A Skyraider flown by Ensign Don R. Stephens of Attack Squadron 55 was shot down near Kangyong-ni. Three days later, Ensign Keith E. Thomson's Corsair was holed in the engine and lost oil pressure, leaving the pilot to crash-land fifteen miles northeast of Posong, where he was taken as a POW.

The Navy's inaugural interdiction strikes had gone well enough, destroying much of Kim Il-sung's air force at Pyongyang and damaging Wonsan's refinery installations. But the first close air support mission of the Korean War was a disappointment. It went awry as the Navy aircraft, unable to reach Army controllers on the given radio frequencies, searched for targets of opportunity—whatever they could find with their own eyeballs. The afternoon sorties were equally frustrating. In the *Valley Forge* ready room, Lanham's pilots raged at their powerlessness to make an immediate impact and save lives on the ground.

Walton Walker's Eighth Army was holding gamely against the persistent North Korean advance. Still, MacArthur and his willful number two, Major General Edward (Ned) M. Almond, wanted Walker to perform more boldly. MacArthur considered every unit assigned to help Walker as one less that would be available for his amphibious landing on the west coast. With the First Marine Division's other two regiments, the First and the Seventh, bound for the Far East, he would soon be ready to carry out the amphibious invasion that was code-named Operation Chromite. But Walker's first order of business was his own survival. He requested an audience with MacArthur, who flew to meet him at Eighth Army headquarters, along with General Almond, on the morning of July 27.

MacArthur rejected Walker's otherwise sound suggestion that Eighth Army headquarters, in danger so close to the front, be relocated from Taegu to the coast at Pusan. Believing it would signal an expectation of defeat, MacArthur told Walker to hold his headquarters in place, regardless of the risk. Walker carried this attitude of resolve into a series of meetings with his division and regimental commanders. While it wasn't in his character to perform publicly, as his theatrical theater commander did, Walker channeled some MacArthurian bluster during a conference with his division commanders at the 25th Infantry Division command post at Sangju on the twenty-ninth. "There will be no more retreating, withdrawal, or readjustment of the lines or any other term you choose," he declared.

> There is no line behind us to which we can retreat. Every unit must counterattack to keep the enemy in a state of confusion and off balance. There will be no Dunkirk, there will be no Bataan. A retreat to Pusan would be one of the greatest butcheries in history. We must fight until the end. Capture by these people is worse than death itself. We will fight as a team. If some of us must die, we will die fighting together. Any man who gives ground may be personally responsible for the death of thousands of his comrades. I want you to put this out to all the men in the Division. I want everybody to understand that we are going to hold this line. We are going to win.

Walker's words made for dramatic headlines—*The New York Times* called his remarks a "stand or die order." They turned the predominant pessimism into a bracing clarity: The fighting in Korea was a real war and that resolve must be summoned to win it. With the enemy committing his full strength in the south, gaining ground rapidly as Pershing tanks broke down amid the general retreat, American combat correspondents filed pessimistic dispatches.

On August 2, a convoy of transports carrying the First Provisional Marine Brigade arrived at Pusan as a Korean military band played the thumping strains of the Marine Corps hymn. General Craig was dismayed to see his men leaning over the rails of the lead ship, the attack transport USS *George Clymer*. He had ordered the Marines to land ready to carry out an assault. That would come soon enough. The Marines were given to the 25th Infantry Division, which was receiving a newly arrived regiment of its own as well.

A few days later, the commanding general of the U.S. 25th Infantry Division, Major General William B. Kean, ordered the combined Army-Marine task force to advance to a contested hot spot ten miles down the coast from Masan, the village of Chingdong-ni, where UN forces were braced for a North Korean assault. General Kean put Eddie Craig in command of the troops in that area, and the Marine general commenced preparing the disorganized American units to advance.

On the night of August 4, Admirals Joy and Doyle called upon their frogmen once again, this time putting a UDT force ashore in boats to demolish a rail tunnel near the South Korean town of Yosu. The purpose of this mission was to divert the North Korean army from focusing its entire effort at the front. A detachment from UDT-3, just flown in to Sasebo, embarked in the high-speed transport USS *Diachenko* and set out toward the enemy coast.

Transferring to a small landing craft carrying RB-10 inflatable boats, the frogmen motored toward shore after midnight on the fifth, a full moon rising behind them. Lieutenant (j.g.) George C. Atcheson and Boatswain's Mate Third Class Warren Foley were the first in, swimming ashore ahead of the team. They found a fifteen-foot rocky beach fronted by a thirty-five-foot sea wall. Climbing it, they found the tunnel and sized up the trestle leading out of its north end. Atcheson directed Foley to bring in the team, and the petty officer went back down to the beach by the dangerous light of a rising moon.

Without warning, a handcar carrying a squad of North Korean soldiers came squealing out of the tunnel. Atcheson lay motionless under the trestle. He willed himself small as the enemy soldiers, ten feet above him, studied the seacoast and panned a flashlight across the beach. Foley led in the inflatable holding his team and their explosives, then noticed the threat to his leader. Grabbing a Thompson submachine gun, he and two other frogmen went to assist their stranded teammate.

Up top, Atcheson took matters into his own hands. He carried a waterproofed pistol and four hand grenades. Moving undetected up a slope to get a better angle, he lofted one toward the handcar, and sent another bouncing into the tunnel. The young officer, running crouched toward the embankment, was taken under fire by the enemy patrol—and by his teammate, Foley, from down below. His teammate missed. The North Koreans didn't. Bullets hit Atcheson in the hand and thigh, and his tumble down the sea wall left him with a smashed kneecap, unable to reach the water. One of his teammates, McCormick, scrambled to him and hoisted him over a broad shoulder. All four men who went ashore made it back to their inflatable and exfiltrated through the surf back to the landing craft. With a fractured knee and wounds in his hand and thigh, Atcheson—Beijing-born, the son of a senior diplomat to China who had served as a political adviser to MacArthur—returned to safety but became the first U.S. Navy UDT casualty of the Korean War.

The ranks of the frogmen would swell in the coming year. Admiral Doyle's Special Operations Group, or SOG, based at Camp McGill, twenty miles south of Tokyo, operated four fast transports supporting a team of frogmen from UDT-1 with a detachment from a Marine reconnaissance company. Nighttime demolition raids along the Korean east and west coasts became a staple mission once MacArthur's headquarters discovered the utility of seaborne covert raiders. His chief of staff, Major General Ned Almond, took volunteers from the U.S. Army, the Royal Navy, and the Royal Marine Commandos and organized the Provisional Raider Company, which became the primary element of the Special Activities Group (SAG), under command of Colonel Louis B. Ely, USA. Although the underwater demolition teams were developing their most-advanced submarine infiltration techniques on the East Coast, with little contact with their San Diego–based brethren, the submarine transport *Perch* carried off a daring insertion of British SAG commandos to sabotage the rail lines leading south from Vladivostok. The expanded capacity for amphibious special operations helped the CIA develop its kinetic capabilities in Korea. UDT personnel would help CIA agents establish overland escape and evasion corridors for downed pilots, and carry out special missions developed by CIA officer Frank G. Wisner's blandly named Office of Policy Coordination. From a small island headquarters connected by a causeway to Pusan, the CIA's operations in the Far East would develop as part of a worldwide covert effort guided by George Kennan and the State Department.

If Navy frogmen made an inauspicious debut as tunnel blasters, the heavy cruiser *Toledo* redeemed them two nights later when it laid into the coastal transport network around Samchok with her eight-inch rifles, sealing a road with a rockslide. Some missions were best accomplished from six thousand yards with flat-trajectory AP.

The aircraft carriers *Triumph* and *Valley Forge* had stood in well when UN aviation was first announcing itself on the battlefield. With the arrival of the carrier *Philippine Sea* at Sasebo on August 5, Task Force 77 gained two squadrons of Panthers, two of Corsairs, and a squadron of Skyraiders. But the aviators of Air Group Eleven would have been far more effective if MacArthur had not placed them under control of the Fifth Air Force's Joint Operations Center for missions that were not primarily naval, such as antisubmarine patrols. On their first close-support missions, pilots found their radio circuits were overloaded, so only one division of Corsairs and Skyraiders from the *Philippine Sea*—four planes out of sixty—managed to link up with an Air Force controller. They did their best against troop concentrations, supply columns, and storage depots for ten critical days in August. But in the vital work of supporting Walker's troops along the front, carrier pilots applied no more than 30 percent of their potential, a journalist reported.

Marine aviation was the story of the siege of Pusan. It was not until a pair of small "jeep" carriers, the USS *Sicily* and *Badoeng Strait,* arrived that the ground battle was tilted by application of tactical airpower in the close-support role. When the sixty F4Us and fifteen hundred men of Marine Air Group 33 entered battle from these two small flattops, General Walker gained a force multiplier in his contest against North Korean armor. The aircraft would give him a fighting chance to hold his perimeter.

Admiral Joy ordered the Marine aviators into action as soon as they arrived in Japan in early August. Short of spare parts, the crew of the *Sicily* scrounged the waterfront for surplus items that might be useful on a Corsair. Then the carrier cleared her lines and was under way for Korea at flank speed. Marine Fighter Squadron 214 (VMF-214), under Lieutenant Colonel Walter E. Lischeid, landed with their Corsairs the next day. Two days later, the other squadron from Marine Air Group 33, Major Arnold A. Lund's VMF-323, flew out to the *Badoeng Strait*. As Colonel Murray's Fifth Marine Regiment jumped off down the road to Chinju, the Marine pilots covered them, set up to demonstrate what the Navy had been carrying on about for so many years before Congress, insisting that aviation and naval landing troops be integrated as a fighting team.

Half of their missions were hunts, armed reconnaissance, roaming in search of targets of opportunity. Taking off from the *Sicily* on the morning of August 8, Major Kenneth L. Reusser was flying at treetop level when he spotted what appeared to be a factory complex guarded by North Korean vehicles and antiaircraft emplacements. The volume of flak that met him on his first pass convinced him that it held something valuable. Directing his section leader to orbit while he made another run, Reusser passed low enough to see through the large windows of the complex. For the cost of a few more bullet holes in his Corsair's blue gull wings, he saw several tanks in various stages of maintenance. He returned to his carrier. "There's a jackpot there," Reusser said to Captain John S. Thach, who was always in the ready room to hear his pilots' reports. The pilot asked for permission to return to the target, and Thach and the air group commander approved.

Loaded with napalm and a fresh load of rockets, Reusser's flight, in spite of accurate antiaircraft fire, destroyed the plant, six enemy tanks,

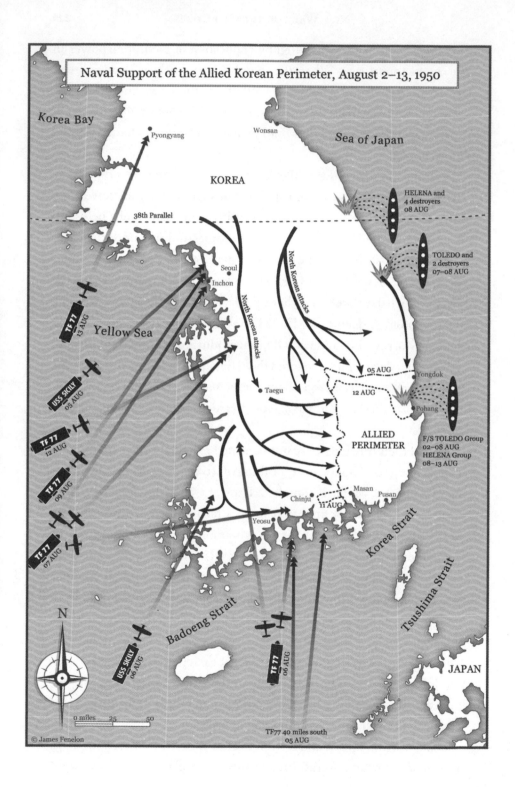

Naval Support of the Allied Korean Perimeter, August 2–13, 1950

Korea Bay

Sea of Japan

Pyongyang

Wonsan

KOREA

38th Parallel

HELENA and
4 destroyers
08 AUG

TOLEDO and
2 destroyers
07–08 AUG

TF 77
13 AUG

Yellow Sea

Seoul

Inchon

North Korean attacks

North Korean attacks

USS SICILY
05 AUG

TF 77
12 AUG

TF 77
09 AUG

05 AUG

Yongdok

12 AUG

Pohang

F/S TOLEDO Group
02–08 AUG
HELENA Group
08–13 AUG

Taegu

ALLIED
PERIMETER

TF 77
07 AUG

Chinju

Masan

11 AUG

Pusan

Yeosu

Korea Strait

Tsushima Strait

N

USS SICILY
06 AUG

Badoeng Strait

TF 77
06 AUG

JAPAN

0 miles   25   50

© James Fenelon

TF77 40 miles south
05 AUG

and a quartet of trucks in the factory courtyard. Continuing west, the Corsairs attacked the heavily fortified harbor area at Inchon, burning out an oil storage facility and strafing a tanker. The detonation of the ship damaged Reusser's plane, but he maintained control and landed that afternoon on the *Sicily*. Reusser, the son of an Oregon minister, would go on to become the most decorated combat pilot in the history of the Marine Corps. Once the battalions in the field received their tactical air control parties, the Marine aviators would be set up to save the Pusan perimeter, and thus keep the United Nations Command from losing a war in less than sixty days. The pilots of VMF-214 were a tribe of veteran hands. Made famous as the "Black Sheep" by the reporters who lavished attention upon the unit's colorful leader, Major Gregory "Pappy" Boyington, during World War II, the unit had plenty of older pilots, married with children. Thach called them "the top pros in the business." Each of the pilots knew his tactical air controller personally, having rehearsed drills together at Camp Pendleton.

Walton Walker placed the newly arrived Marine brigade under Army Task Force Kean, named for the commanding general of the 25th Division, whose performance had yet to impress Walker. He ordered the Marines to march to Masan and prepare to meet the North Korean push against the southern anchor of his perimeter.

Murray's men pushed forward twenty miles from Masan and took Kosong on the eleventh. Corsairs from Marine Fighter Squadron 323 shredded a column of North Korean vehicles fleeing the assault. As bullets ripped into trucks belonging to the elite North Korean 83rd Motorized Regiment, the column telescoped to a stop as soldiers dived for cover in roadside ditches and fled into the hills.

But as Murray's Marines continued down the road toward Chinju, they ran into a North Korean ambush. The NKPA's Sixth Division had been reinforced by a mobile regiment equipped with motorcycles, scout cars, and small trucks, which supported the Communist advance. Facing a collision with North Korean armor, Craig got Walker's blessing to wait until Marine fighter squadrons were on hand before engaging. But the battle did not wait for American support. Murray's lead battalion came under crossfire from enemy tanks. Airpower on call was particularly well suited to saving such a situation. The Marines, pinned down and isolated in pockets, used their airpower to cover their medevac. As battalion tactical air controllers knew where the medevac was needed, they directed a quartet of Corsairs from the *Sicily* to ride with it. "Here comes this ambulance tearing down the road and the Corsairs weaving right across it," Thach said. Carrying single five-hundred-pound bombs and four rockets under each wing, the aircraft pounced on anything that threatened that four-by-four angel of mercy, scouring the roadside ditches and embankments with their fifties and dropped ordnance. The ambulance reached the Marine triage station and got all the wounded out. Still, the morale of Colonel Murray's regiment flagged as they gave up their gains, retracing their advance back to Masan and north.

Boarding Walker's personal aircraft at Eighth Army headquarters at Taegu, General Craig appreciated how vulnerable the UN perimeter was, and how threadbare were the troops defending it. Its broad arc ran from its north coast anchor at Pohang around Walker's headquarters to the southern tip of the peninsula at Masan. Walker had about 92,000 men in his Eighth Army. Though it nominally outnumbered the estimated 70,000 attackers, the North Koreans deployed not in a continuous line but in a series of columns that probed roads and mountain trails in a ceaseless effort to penetrate and outflank the Americans. The enemy thus held the initiative at each point of attack, forcing Walker's battalions to move about constantly, putting out fires and staging counterattacks where opportunity allowed. Well drilled in fire and movement, confident enough in their leadership to hold and fight when ordered, the Marine brigade proved to be General Walker's best quick reaction force, and was effective wherever it went.

The Army regiments operating with the Marines, however, were not as well trained or equipped and often ran into serious trouble. The Fifth Regimental Combat Team was reeling on August 12 after an important road was left unguarded, allowing the North Koreans to surround and destroy a pair of exposed field artillery battalions. The 90th Field Artillery and the so-called Triple Nickel, the 555th Parachute Infantry Battalion, a segregated African American unit, had had

its gun pits overrun by North Korean armor and infantry and its personnel slaughtered nearly to a man. High-angle-firing howitzers were
no match for Soviet tank armor. While armored reconnaissance units
from the 25th Infantry Division tried to advance into the area to search
for survivors, they were repeatedly repelled. The few artillerymen that
did escape could thank for their lives the furious support of counterat-
tacking Air Force Mustangs and Marine Corsairs, as well as their luck
to avoid capture, the consequence of which, for many of the Americans,
was to be forced to kneel and take a bullet through the head. The drive
to Chinju failed, producing another tactical victory for North Korea's
army. Opportunistic and eager to seize their moment, Kim's generals
looked to advance on all fronts.

The collapse of Task Force Kean's position in the southwest, together with the news that North Korean forces were pushing the Pusan
perimeter farther north, near Taegu, threatened Walker with a double
envelopment. Two North Korean divisions had crossed the Naktong
River, coming within thirteen miles of his Taegu headquarters and im-
periling its lifeline to the port of Pusan. As a bulge formed in U.S. lines
near Naktong, owing to the Communist penetration, a general evacuation was ordered for the city's half million residents. There was talk
that President Syngman Rhee should join the exodus, but he finally
held firm and refused, staying in the provisional capital. The famed
newsman Edward R. Murrow prepared a national broadcast blaming
MacArthur for the defeat of Task Force Kean, but CBS management
spiked it. Murrow's protests inflamed the idea that the U.S. government was censoring war news in order to hide the fact of an impending
defeat.

Anchoring the northern flank of Walker's perimeter, the city of Pohang on Korea's eastern seacoast was at risk of being overrun. The
town had seemed secure after the First Cavalry Division arrived, but
the First's fast inland march to join the defense of Taegu left the South
Korean Third Division on its own to hold Pohang. Now the South
Koreans were being flanked and infiltrated. With Air Force spotter
planes unable to find targets in the wooded areas around the city, F-51
Mustang pilots operated on their own wits, without communication

with the Joint Operations Center. Admiral Higgins's cruisers and destroyers, throwing salvos at enemy troops, lacked communications with
shore fire-control parties. The South Korean division held on longer
than many thought possible, but by August 12, the envelopment was
complete and nothing could stop the North Koreans. Control of the
strategic city was at risk of being lost. If the enemy could exploit any of
his three potential breakthroughs, the UN perimeter might collapse.

Though MacArthur had plans to use Eddie Craig's Marine brigade
for the amphibious masterstroke he was planning, an assault landing at
Inchon, near Seoul, General Walker needed the Marines to stabilize his
perimeter. Craig received orders to support the 24th Infantry Division
by confronting the new threat of the "Naktong bulge." Moving about
by helicopter to confer with other field commanders, General Craig
directed the brigade to go by rail north to Naktong, where the Marines
formed up with a half-strength Army regiment on either side. When
they had assembled, Walker ordered them to attack the bulge head on.
On the night of August 17, Craig's men faced an enemy well dug in
atop a ridge called Obong-ni. The initial push was repulsed and a
North Korean counterattack produced a stalemate. In the morning the
Marines tried again, this time with their aviation "linebackers" piling
in behind them.

When Colonel Lund's VMF-323 checked in with Marine tactical air
controllers, Craig was in position to observe from the air. Through an
opening in the clouds, he could see Murray's men entrenched in ditches
along the road tracing the ridge. The first pass by the Corsairs was a
high dummy run, orienting themselves to the front and making radio
contact with their tactical controllers on the ground. On the second
pass, with targets marked with smoke, the pilots delivered five-
hundred-pound bombs in whistling earthbound parabolas. As the
planes struck, North Korean soldiers rose from their trenches, taunting
the Americans and waving their arms. "They were the damnedest
bunch of people I ever saw," Craig said. "They were very cocky and
were sure they were going to win, because they had been pushing the
American troops back ever since the war started." Craig wished his

pilots had some napalm on hand, the better to cleanse the ridge. As it happened, the high explosives did the trick.

The enemy troop positions were swallowed in concussive paroxysms of flames and shrapnel. The taunting ceased. The air attack broke them. "You could see the smoke and fire flash of the rockets leaving the wings," a war correspondent wrote, "and then would come the great tearing sound the rocket made in flight, and then the roar of its bursting against the hill. And after the rockets had gone, you would see the little round dots of smoke in the sky as the wing guns fired, and all the crest of the hill . . . was a roaring, jumping hell of smoke and flame and dust and noise." The Marine Corsairs finished their work in nine minutes and the ridge was clear in thirty. The Fifth Marines advanced quickly to exploit their opening, and that same day the area was in UN hands, the Naktong bulge punctured and deflated. The Marine pilots from the two jeep carriers, maintaining a 92 percent aircraft availability ratio, claimed thirteen tanks destroyed along with thirty-five boxcars and 197 vehicles.

Brigadier General Joseph L. Stewart, the Marine brigade operations officer, called it "the best air-ground show that you'd ever see. An entire enemy mechanized regiment was destroyed without ground forces becoming involved hardly at all. It was all air." An Army regimental commander would write to a superior, "The Marines on our left were a sight to behold. Not only was their equipment superior or equal to ours, but they had squadrons of air in direct support. They used it like artillery. It was, 'Hey, Joe, this is Smitty. Knock the left off that ridge. . . .' They had it day and night. . . . General, we just have to have air support like that or we might as well disband the infantry and join the Marines."

What made Navy and Marine pilots effective in close air support was related to a distinguishing feature of Marine battalions. Unlike their Army counterparts, each one had a tactical air control party assigned to it. Located with the frontline units, the seven-man teams led by an aviation officer, who was a qualified pilot, could feel the pressure of the enemy and determine how aircraft should respond. It was an essential fact, easily grasped from a foxhole concussed by fire, that if air support failed to arrive within ten minutes, it might just as well not arrive at all. And when the planes struck, they struck close, often bombing within a hundred yards of the front line. Because Marine pilots were riflemen before they learned to fly, they tended to insist upon operating this way. Corrections radioed to them from the ground were measured in tens of yards, and their accuracy followed to scale. The Air Force put their tactical air controllers above the battlefield, flying in "mosquito" aircraft such as the North American T-6 Texan. Given the persistent communication problems and centralized control at Taegu, the mosquito controllers were unresponsive to the needs of ground troops in life-or-death real time.

Though the Air Force flew more than fifteen thousand close-support sorties from the start of hostilities through September 15, its generals were neither strongly interested in nor its planes adept at the art of close air support. The Fifth Air Force's Joint Operations Center at Taegu was organized to handle requests for close air support from the field efficiently and not urgently. Fast response times, helpful though they were to the troops, were expensive in terms of resources at the supporting command. The Air Force valued thrift and efficiency in the delivery of air ordnance more than anything else. "At times they appeared to be actually *prescribing* the needs of the ground forces for close air support," noted one of Admiral Doyle's amphibious group commanders. The Air Force Joint Operations Center was slow in responding to requests for fire. The captain of the escort carrier *Sicily,* John S. Thach, was "amazed that it could be so bad." His returning pilots told him, "We couldn't help. We wanted to. We were there and we couldn't get in communication with people."

Air Force wings preferred an independent strategic mission, targeting the enemy's deeper heartland. General Stratemeyer's twenty-two B-26 Invader medium bombers, twelve B-29 Superfortresses, seventy F-80 Shooting Stars, and fifteen F-82 Twin Mustangs (twin-boom heavy fighters) had been trained to defend Japan from Soviet air attack or to strike Soviet air bases. The war in Korea was a localized variation of their preferred theme, "battlefield interdiction." During the critical days of August, Stratemeyer used B-29s to "carpet bomb" the front from six thousand feet. The results, though "efficient" on paper in terms of weight of ordnance delivered, did little to save infantry battalions in extremis at the front. To swing momentum there, Air Force ground-attack doctrine emphasized cutting off the battlefield from its sources of enemy support, to isolate it with strikes against distant but critical infrastructure and lines of supply. Such operations had a valuable payoff, but it was redeemed in a longer term. Marine pilots, on the other hand, were trained to operate *in* the battlefield. At Naktong, the Corsairs were in the battlefield.

With the Fourth Division of the North Korean People's Army in a pell-mell retreat across the river, artillery was zeroed on road junctions and bridgeheads while low-flying Marine aircraft chased and strafed at will. Joseph Stewart said, "I actually observed for the first time in my life the panicked retreat of an enemy force, with our tanks taking pot shots into scores of fleeing troops. Then the air caught the remnants going back across the river and, I repeat, that division was never heard from again."

With the rout under way in the west, the crisis on the coastal city at Pohang in the north required a different solution. With the Korean defenders surrounded and under siege, Walton Walker had no choice but to order an evacuation by sea. It fell to Admiral Doyle's amphibious group to stage a Dunkirk-style rescue. Three LSTs appeared off Pohang that day to evacuate Air Force ground personnel and heavy equipment from the air base. Under sniper fire from the beach, the amphibious navy went to work. The ROK division maintained its perimeter long enough for the destroyer *Wiltsie* to lead the Japanese-crewed LSTs to the landing area, navigating by headlights of vehicles on the beach. With the cruiser *Helena* and her consorts harassing North Korean troops, Doyle's beachmasters finished their work. By morning of August 17, six thousand South Korean soldiers and twelve hundred civilian refugees had been spirited to safety.

WHEN CORRESPONDENTS EMBARKED with the Seventh Fleet heard about the trouble Navy pilots were having communicating with Air

Force controllers during ground-attack missions, they reported the problem in detail. A series of newspaper articles illuminated the problem of close air support during the ten-day stretch in which the Pusan perimeter was under threat, quoting Navy pilots as well as Rear Admiral Edward C. Ewen, the commander of Task Force 77, on the inadequacies of the Air Force tactical air control system.

General Stratemeyer thought his sister service was waging an offensive campaign of a different sort. The admiring press given to Navy and Marine Corps close air support drove him to enraged distraction. He considered it "another step in a planned program to discredit the Air Force and the Army and at the same time to unwarrantly [*sic*] enhance the prestige of the United States Marines." If the Air Force was still smarting from its fight with the Navy over the B-36—as it would for years—the Army had moved on and was focused on more immediate problems. The Korean peninsula's most avid customer for air-dropped ordnance, General Walton Walker, told Stratemeyer that he endorsed the Marine approach to close air support and that the Army ought to "emulate" it.

Stratemeyer was incensed. He regarded Walker as in the tank for a "conspiracy" run by "Navy masterminds" such as Captain Walter Karig, the chief of Admiral Turner Joy's public information office. Stratemeyer asked MacArthur that "something be done at your level," meaning that he wanted the theater chief to raise the issue of bad publicity with Admiral Sherman and General Collins when the two members of the Joint Chiefs were next in Tokyo. The Air Force chief found it easier to ask for five-star interference in a press relations matter than to untangle the complex problems of a mission he regarded as unimportant. Registering such a complaint at the very moment the fate of Eighth Army headquarters stood in the balance revealed more than Stratemeyer would have liked about Far East Air Force priorities in the summer of 1950. The life or death problems of troops on the ground were for someone else to worry about.

★   ★   ★

ON THE RUN since his defeat at Taejon, Major General William F. Dean and his patrol of walking wounded continued their trek to reach friendly lines. Having ducked a North Korean roadblock, they endured for weeks in mountainous terrain, subsisting on handouts from sympathetic but wary locals and surviving on their wits. One night, his men thirsty and with empty canteens, Dean went in search of a water source. Attracted by the rush of a stream, he proceeded down a steep slope in the dark, lost his footing, and tumbled. He landed headfirst and hard. When Dean did not return, his men searched for a time but were finally forced to assume the worst. They decided to march south and reached American lines the next day.

Dean awoke alone. Bleeding from the forehead and disoriented, he resumed his forlorn wandering until he met a lieutenant from the 25th Division whose company had been scattered. Dean introduced himself. "I'm the SOB who's the cause of all this trouble." The overstatement dissolved the barrier of rank between the two men, and they evaded capture for another several days, collecting information on North Korean strength and dispositions that they were eager to bring to headquarters.

Hungry and increasingly desperate, they took refuge in a house where they were finally betrayed to the Communists. As the enemy approached, the Americans escaped through a rear door and fled into a rice paddy, where they separated. The lieutenant, Stanley Tabor, was captured, never to emerge from the notorious red prisons. Dean evaded for several more days, until August 25, when he was given up by a pair of Koreans he encountered just a two-day march from General Walker's command post at Taegu. Dean was taken to Seoul and paraded through the streets, the highest-ranking U.S. prisoner of the war.

General Dean's odyssey, like that of the South Koreans who made their narrow escape by sea at Pohang nine days earlier, stood as a reminder of what the Marine Corps had argued for years: Without wings on his shoulder and a fleet behind him, no soldier can long stand and fight.

16

STRIKE FROM THE SEA

THE NORTH KOREANS HAD MISSED THEIR CHANCE, MACARTHUR thought. Had Kim Il-sung's army not attempted to land a roundhouse right hook by swinging far south before pushing east, but instead jabbed short and hard, striking immediately and with full force at the disjointed American front along the Naktong River, the war might well have been over. The dilatory Communist offensive had given MacArthur what he needed most: time. He used that precious commodity well, building a secure base at the port of Pusan. On July 19, he wrote Truman, "The desperate decision to throw in piecemeal American elements as they arrived by every available means of transport from Japan was the only hope to save the situation."

The rapid naval movement would go down in history, MacArthur thought. "I do not believe that history records a comparable operation which excelled the speed and precision with which the Eighth Army, the Far East Air Force, and the Seventh Fleet have been deployed to a distant land for immediate commitment to major operations," he wrote the president. Though he professed to be fond of the Marines, MacArthur did not mention them. But they and the fleet, he saw, had the expertise to land what he believed would be the crowning blow. For the enemy before him had become overextended. His lines of supply were exposed. A peninsula was open to amphibious assault most everywhere a wave lapped upon a beach. He had relished the possibility of striking from the sea long before the victories of August secured the United Nation's toehold in the south of South Korea.

As he prepared to brief the Seventh Fleet and the First Marine Division on his cherished plan of a west coast amphibious landing at Inchon, the carriers and their air groups softened the target. Road, rail, and bridge connections feeding the city of Inchon's defenders were subject to a ferocious series of strikes. Airfields within supporting range of Inchon received a shellacking too, and with Corsairs and Skyraiders roaming in pairs and quartets across the mountains north and east of Inchon and Seoul, Korea's roads—which one pilot called "comparable to those fine highways found in the mountainous areas of Kentucky"— became killing fields for North Korean trucks and armored vehicles, which "frequently avoided detection by the simple expedient of driving through the wall of the nearest house and parking in the dining room."

Pilots flew three times a day, starting before dawn and ending at dusk. The flak-dense areas around Pyongyang were physically draining. The aviators began their dives at twenty-five thousand feet, plummeting through a welter of flak explosions that were often dense enough to obscure the target, diving down to thirty-five hundred feet to release bombs, closing out the dive brakes, pulling out steeply while screaming aloud to tighten their stomach muscles against the rush of blood from their heads. They flew interdiction, close air support, combat air patrol, photo recon, night attack, and airborne early warning missions.

But the *Valley Forge* and the *Philippine Sea* risked further losses with each of the strikes they sent out around the clock for weeks through August and into September. Half of these were hunting sorties that the pilots enjoyed almost as recreation. Their favorite aircraft for strike missions was the propeller-driven AD Skyraider, a versatile air-to-ground weapon system with fifteen external hardpoints for bombs, torpedoes, rockets, mines, and gun pods, and an eight-thousand-pound capacity. With four 20 mm cannons, it was well suited for hunting trucks, locomotives, grounded aircraft, and power stations. Armed reconnaissance missions, undertaken by pairs and quartets of planes, were especially popular in the ready room. "It has all the elements of going hunting," Commander Harvey Lanham of Air Group Five wrote. "You go out and look for game and when you pick up some game you have the test of shooting accuracy, and it's a great deal of sport."

Destroying bridges was altogether different. Striking the heavily defended fixed targets required detailed planning and a rigorous adherence to the script. The Skyraiders carried thousand-pound bombs with delay fuzes to allow penetration, and two-thousand-pounders with radar-activated proximity fuzes that detonated above the ground.

The carrier air groups, versatile as Swiss Army knives, were constantly in demand and thus operated to the limit of their capacity. The continuous operations were a grind, exhausting pilots through their mundanity—dwindling fresh produce, tired reruns of old movies, freezing temperatures redeemed only by the sophomoric pleasure of an occasional snowball fight on the flight deck, punctuated by occasional terror—deck fires, explosions, crash landings, and the often unwitnessed tragedies of pilots in extremis over distant targets, manifested finally by an empty seat in a ready room and rumors of attempted escapes, evasions, and rescues. MacArthur had offered a prize to the squadron that knocked out a particularly important bridge near Seoul. On August 19, the skipper of the *Philippine Sea*'s Air Group Eleven, Commander Raymond W. Vogel, Jr., pulled off the trick on his last of several runs. With his final bomb, he dropped the west span of the huge bridge into the river. Flak struck Vogel's Corsair and set it afire. He was killed while bailing out. The carrier task group commander, Rear Admiral John M. Hoskins, said, "The whole of North Korea isn't worth the tip of his little finger."

While the air strikes continued to prepare Inchon for invasion and target the North Korean army troop concentrations wherever they could be found, Navy underwater demolition teams, supplemented by Marine reconnaissance operators, scouted alternative landing sites south of Inchon on the night of August 21. Though the commando operations were an open secret, Admiral Arthur D. Struble, who would have overall command of the operation, intended for the enemy to notice them. He wanted to divert their gaze from the actual target. Inchon was the one and only plan. By the third week of August, MacArthur was ready to brief his Washington superiors on Operation Chromite, his cherished plan of carrying off an amphibious assault at Inchon.

On August 23, at his headquarters in Tokyo, MacArthur, together with Admirals Joy and Doyle, briefed Forrest Sherman and Lawton Collins of the Joint Chiefs of Staff, as well as Admiral Radford representing the Pacific Command, on how they would carry off the main event. MacArthur said he would revive the Navy's tradition of amphibious warfare in order to break the North Korean army once and for all. The Communists had neglected their rear and were "dangling on a thin logistical rope that could be quickly cut" by a strike behind the lines near Seoul. "I can almost hear the ticking of the second hand of destiny," he said, his voice dropping to a whisper. "We shall land at Inchon and I shall crush them."

The naval officers doubted Inchon's suitability as a landing site, as did General Collins. Reaching the chosen location required the assault force to navigate a meandering estuary known as Flying Fish Channel. With tidal variances of thirty-two feet, the critical passage was constricted at low tide and dangerously shallow, leaving the landing beaches of Inchon buffered by impassable mudflats. Struble, who did not attend this final meeting although he would have overall command of the operation, likened the long approach through an easily defensible passage to "coming into the capes and up into Baltimore from the Atlantic Ocean." Even if they reached the landing beach, there remained plenty of known unknowns, from the height of the sea wall to the sufficiency of the piers.

With the arrival in Japan of the First and Seventh Marine regiments, the First Marine Division was available at full strength to carry out Operation Chromite under the command of Major General Oliver P. Smith. It was odd that neither Smith nor his boss visiting from Pearl Harbor, General Shepherd, was invited to attend the August 23 meeting. Smith sensed that General Edward Almond, whom MacArthur had tapped to serve as commander of the landing force in spite of his lack of expertise in amphibious warfare, "didn't want a lot of Marines around." Almond treated the august Smith with supercilious condescension, probably because he was still smarting after Admiral Joy read him off Navy-style during a staff conference for proposing to substitute a poorly trained South Korean regiment for Ray Murray's crack Fifth Marines in the assault plan. Admirals Struble and Doyle had plentiful expertise to handle Inchon's complexities, however, being veterans of major amphibious campaigns under MacArthur and Nimitz respectively. Their combined expertise, working within the tradition-rich combination of the Seventh Fleet under MacArthur, made the challenging plan possible.

MacArthur anticipated skepticism from the Navy. In early planning, a consensus of doubt had formed within Doyle's staff. One officer said, "We drew up a list of every conceivable and natural handicap, and Inchon had 'em all." As his staff weighed the complications, including their preference for several days of preinvasion bombardment to neutralize defenses emplaced on the island, Wolmi-do, that commanded the center of the harbor, Admiral Sherman interrupted. "I wouldn't hesitate to take a ship up off Wolmi-do after a day of bombardment." MacArthur, surprised by the CNO's dissent, said, "Spoken like a Farragut."

As Forrest Sherman was an aviator, not an expert in amphibious warfare, Doyle chafed. He stood, turned to MacArthur, and said, "General, I have not been asked nor have I volunteered my opinion about this landing. If I were asked, however, the best I can say is that Inchon is not impossible."

Doyle's hedge drew uncharacteristic conciliation from MacArthur. "If we find we cannot make it," he said, "we will withdraw."

Doyle said, "No, General. We don't know how to do that. Once we start ashore we keep going." Doyle later regarded his reply as "a bit John Wayneish," but he conceded that the idea of failure never entered an amphibious sailor's mind as a contingency.

MacArthur ended the meeting with a stem-winding oration in which he embraced the many doubts as reason to believe the North Koreans would be utterly surprised. "The only alternative to a stroke such as I propose," he declared,

333

will be the continuation of the savage sacrifice we are making at Pusan, with no hope of relief in sight. Are you content to let your troops stay in that bloody perimeter like beef cattle in the slaughterhouse? . . . It is plainly apparent that here in Asia is where the communist conspirators have elected to make their play for global conquest. The test is not in Berlin or Vienna, in London, Paris or Washington. It is here and now! It is along the Naktong River in South Korea. . . . Actually, we here fight Europe's war with arms, while there it is still confined to words. . . . Make the wrong decision here—the fatal decision of inertia—and we will be done.

He added that the Navy had never let him down before and that he was not bothered by long odds.

While Turner Joy found himself moved, his qualms dissipating, Forrest Sherman admitted that he might not be a David Farragut after all. After meeting privately with MacArthur the following day, the CNO admitted to Joy, "I wish I had that man's confidence." On his way back to Washington, Sherman called on the commander in chief of the Pacific Fleet, Admiral Radford, who persuaded him that Turner Joy needed a combat-seasoned hand in Tokyo to coordinate such a critical wartime operation. Sherman dispatched his star protégé, Arleigh Burke, equipping him with a special encrypted key to report directly to the Pentagon. Burke opened the steam valves at Joy's headquarters, actualizing MacArthur's urgent schedule. The window for action was narrow. A major typhoon was moving toward the area from the Philippines, and the landing would have to take place at the highest of high tides, which would next occur at Inchon on September 15. If that date could not be met, the next hydrographically suitable one was nearly a month away. Although there would be no time for important rehearsals, Burke would not wait.

As Admiral Joy's representative, Arleigh Burke visited Far East Command headquarters, pushing past Chief of Staff Ned Almond to see the top man himself. He explained the risks of missing the narrow window. MacArthur asked him, "What do we do?" Burke said, "We sail early."

MacArthur said, "All right. You prepare the dispatches."

"I just happen to have them right here." Burke understood MacArthur's great combat intuition in that moment, and was glad he had not let himself be stalled by the general's chief of staff.

When Admiral Doyle received his orders, he didn't like them, but he understood the restrictions. In the ensuing days, a covert mission to confirm the critical hydrographic data near Inchon was undertaken by a plucky young intelligence officer on MacArthur's staff. Lieutenant Eugene F. Clark, working with two highly capable South Korean intelligence officers, set up a command post on an offshore island fourteen miles from the invasion beach. They made contact with resistance elements in the occupied capital and developed a network of volunteers to collect data on Inchon's defenses and ascertained the schedule of tides. The North Koreans got wind of their mission and mounted several attacks on the island, but Clark's platoons, operating a heavily armed junk, repelled the assaults long enough to confirm the operational parameters. Tides produced navigable sea levels at the beach every twelve hours. But with low tide on D Day set to fall at night, when the channel to the landing area would be no deeper than ten fathoms, Admiral Doyle's preferred nighttime approach would be impossible. He would have to make it during daylight, with the landings to follow on the evening high tide, before darkness fell. But General O. P. Smith and his Marines were used to long odds and prepared to adjust to any reality that confronted them.

ON SEPTEMBER 11, Vice Admiral Struble ordered the fast carriers to sea from Sasebo. Flying his flag in the heavy cruiser *Rochester,* he was in overall command of the joint task force of 230 ships, including vessels from seven nations. Doyle departed Kobe in his flagship, the *Mount McKinley,* with MacArthur on board as well. Fully a third of Doyle's attack force were borrowed or chartered from U.S. or Japanese merchant firms. The diverse fleet movements perplexed prying eyes. The bustle of UN naval forces in Japan was so widespread and visible that Operation Chromite had an unofficial nickname: Operation Common Knowledge. Though Lieutenant Clark claimed that "confused Red spies that swarmed the Japanese ports had reported the fleet headed for seven different points" and that "at Seoul, everything was normal," a joint U.S.-Japanese counterintelligence team verified in September that Pyongyang had been tipped off to the operation and had issued orders to consolidate its Seoul and Inchon defense commands. But those commands had no time to put those orders into effect. MacArthur's sense of urgency left Kim Il-sung unable to reinforce Inchon in the few days available. In the days before the assault landings, Task Force 77 and the Fifth Air Force applied themselves with a vengeance behind enemy lines.

As the *Valley Forge, Boxer, Philippine Sea,* and HMS *Triumph* launched their Corsairs, Skyraiders, Fireflies, and Seafires to strike far and wide on deep support missions, sweeping roads of vehicles and troops, cratering road and rail junctions, the planes from the escort carriers, meanwhile, burned Wolmi-do island ahead of the assault landings by a battalion of the Fifth Marines. The Corsairs of VMF-214 and VMF-323 delivered double loads of napalm until the small garrison there was wrecked. The pace of operations chewed up the carriers' flight decks. The blast of turbojets scorched teak and melted caulk, the heavy F9Fs and Skyraiders digging divots as they landed, causing tailhooks to bounce and miss wires and complicating the recovery of aircraft.

Doyle's invasion force merged under way from Yokohama, Kobe, Sasebo, and Pusan, reaching the transport area on the morning of the thirteenth. The destroyers *Mansfield, De Haven, Swenson, Collett, Gurke,* and *Henderson* started up the shipping channel on the flood tide. It was a calculated risk, as Struble's seven minesweepers, steaming with the transport group, had not yet done their work. Following the destroyers came the *Rochester* with Struble embarked, the *Toledo* with

Admiral Higgins, and HMS *Jamaica* and HMS *Kenya*. Since Wolmi-do was a blackened wasteland after the air strike, Inchon received the bombardment group's fury. North Korean shore batteries scored more than a dozen times in return, hitting the *Collett* and *Gurke,* but the only fatality on the morning came from a near miss on the *Swenson,* which killed one of her officers.

The massive landing ship dock *Fort Marion* delivered a trio of tank-loaded utility landing ships, while the fast transports *Bass, Diachenko,* and *Wantuck* landed the Marines on Wolmi-do. The four-hundred-man garrison on the conical island sentinel was annihilated after a forty-five-minute firefight, with more than a hundred taken prisoner. Twelve hours after the tide receded, the opportunity to assault drained away with the neap tide, leaving supplies-laden LSTs to sit on the mud until the lunar cycle refilled the anchorage. The interval was filled with continued preinvasion bombardment.

Midnight struck on D Day, September 15. Riding in with the tide came the invasion force. Preceding Tenth Corps into the roadstead was a trio of floating platforms jammed with rocket launchers. Those who went to war in the thousand-ton, two-hundred-foot-long ugly duck-lings known as LSMRs, or "landing ships medium, rocket," considered it "one of the most uncomfortable and unlivable ships in the U.S. Navy today." Their designation as landing ships masked their function as heavyweights in fire support, which was reflected in their installations of ten rocket batteries and the five-inch/38-caliber gun mount sitting oversized just forward of the pilothouse. Assembly of each ship's store of five thousand spin-stabilized five-inch rockets for these weapons was a herculean all-hands task, requiring five days for each 133-man crew. They shot them all off in thirty minutes in a cacophony of igniting pro-pellant gas.

While the ground smoldered after the rocket attack, the aircraft re-sumed their strikes and boats carrying two battalions of the Fifth Ma-rines went ashore at Red Beach, facing the city's industrial district, while the First Marines, under Colonel Lewis B. "Chesty" Puller, landed about four miles to the south at Blue Beach, near the junction to the highway to Seoul, twenty miles east. As Lieutenant Clark and his

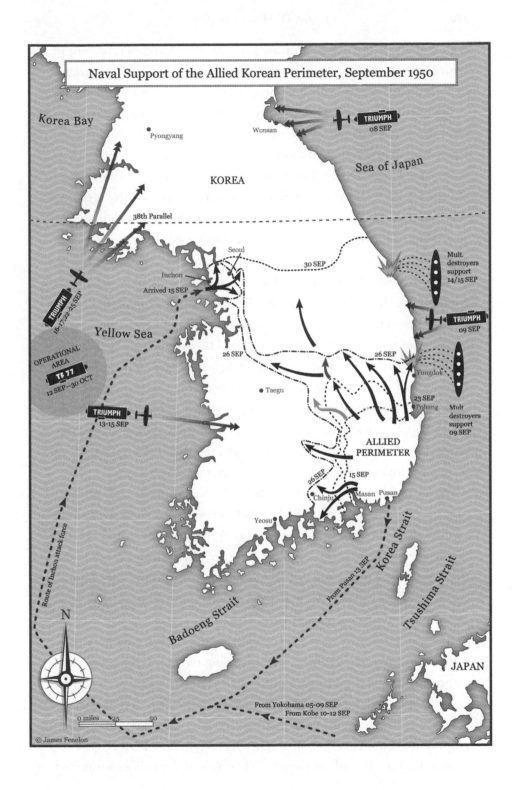

Naval Support of the Allied Korean Perimeter, September 1950

Korea Bay

Pyongyang

Wonsan

TRIUMPH
08 SEP

Sea of Japan

KOREA

38th Parallel

Seoul

30 SEP

Mult.
destroyers
support
14/15 SEP

Inchon
Arrived 15 SEP

TRIUMPH
16-17/22-25 SEP

TRIUMPH
09 SEP

Yellow Sea

OPERATIONAL
AREA

TF 77
12 SEP—30 OCT

26 SEP

26 SEP

Yongdok

TRIUMPH
13-15 SEP

Taegu

23 SEP
Pohang

Mult
destroyers
support
09 SEP

ALLIED
PERIMETER

26 SEP

15 SEP

Chinju

Masan Pusan

Route of Inchon attack force

Yeosu

Korea Strait

From Pusan 13 SEP

Badoeng Strait

Tsushima Strait

N

JAPAN

From Yokohama 05-09 SEP
From Kobe 10-12 SEP

0 miles   25   50

© James Fenelon

men had taken the measure of the seawalls, the landing craft went in with ladders mounted to their forecastles, giving them the appearance of swimming insects with long antennae. The men of the first wave rushed with their ladders to the wall and began climbing while others scrambled through breaches opened by the naval bombardment. Enemy small arms chattered and mortar shells plunged to the beach as eight rust-bucket LSTs commandeered from Japan's fishing trade churned close to shore in the hour-long window before the receding tide foreclosed any entry. The LSTs, laden with ammunition trucks and drums of gasoline, came under withering fire. Several were set ablaze. Their crews returned fire into the heights facing the beach with a vigor that put the advancing Marines in a bind. Enfiladed by their friends from the sea, they were forced to advance faster than their commanders preferred. Casualties resulted. But within twenty minutes, an amber flare rose from the top of Cemetery Hill overlooking Red Beach, indicating that A Company of the 1/5 Marines, under Captain John R. Stevens, had secured the high ground commanding the lodgment. His unit suffered eight men killed among thirty-six battle casualties. Stevens's battalion commander, Lieutenant Colonel George S. Newton, had offered him a reward if he could take the Asahi Brewery with its fermented inventory intact. Second Platoon took the honors.

While the carrier air groups undertook close-support and interdiction strikes unopposed by enemy aircraft, the assaulters entered Inchon against sharp but vanishing resistance. Almond's other division, the Army's Seventh Infantry Division, followed the Marines ashore, and the corps commander established his headquarters in the city. As successive waves landed, South Korean marines interrogated the local populace about the movements of Communist forces and the location of its cells. At dusk, Inchon glowed with the fires of burning buildings.

General Lemuel Shepherd, disembarking on D Day plus one, was impressed by the high morale of his men. Though the men who had carried the day were led by seasoned war veterans such as Ray Murray, their ranks were filled out with reservists who until lately had been employed as bankers and businessmen. As weekend warriors, they responded to the call and did the job. When Admiral Struble approached the beach in a small boat to assess progress, an older Marine, not recognizing his rank at a distance, hollered sharply, "What the hell are you doing out there?" The admiral smiled. "It was obvious to me that there were some damned good people on the beach."

The war correspondent Marguerite Higgins, who had come down the ramp with the third wave of the Fifth Marines, filed a dispatch that ran in the *New York Herald Tribune* on September 18. Their success was a sound rebuke to President Truman, who, as victory at Inchon was being secured, found himself taking heat for his recent remarks about the Marine Corps. When a U.S. senator proposed that a Marine serve on the Joint Chiefs of Staff, Truman had responded, in part, "For your information, the Marine Corps is the Navy's police force, and as long as I am president that is what it will remain. They have a propaganda machine that is almost equal to Stalin's." It did not amuse the public to see Truman compare his victorious sea soldiers to the dictator whose designs made necessary their latest battlefield sacrifice. And the Marine leadership didn't care for his subscribing to the sharpest of Army talking points: "When the Marine Corps goes into the Army it works with and for the Army and that is the way it should be," the president wrote to the senator. There's little other evidence that Truman, who often had a snappy edge in correspondence, actually meant these things to the degree his critics perceived, but there wasn't a dogface anywhere who could have expressed it better himself.

It was well that MacArthur landed at Inchon when he did. While securing the city's railyard, U.S. troops found several flatcars full of Russian mines. Their installation in the channel could have ended Operation Chromite before it began—with dire consequences not only for Doyle's attack force but for the entire UN presence in Korea. Now the momentum belonged to MacArthur. He exploited it to the hilt.

The short campaign of house-to-house combat in Inchon was vigorously supported by shore- and carrier-based aviation. The arrival of the *Boxer,* relieving the *Philippine Sea,* put four fast aircraft carriers at Admiral Ewen's service. They laid into the North Korean transportation network and reverted it to antiquity. With the ammunition ship *Mount Katmai* on hand to replenish their magazines, the carriers sustained an aerial assault that left the enemy without operable heavy equipment, trucks, or trains, taking delivery of food and supplies by handcart, ox-cart, or not at all. With the luxury of complete air superiority and sea control, Tenth Corps faced only a single air attack on the anchorage. A pair of Yaks put six near misses near the cruiser *Rochester* and strafed HMS *Jamaica* as they lay at anchor south of Wolmi-do. One sailor on the *Jamaica* was killed in exchange for one Yak shot down. The *Boxer* exhausted its stock allowance of two hundred aircraft drop tanks by using them as napalm weapons.

The Marine aviators from the escort carriers *Sicily* and *Baeong Strait* did what they did best, sending Corsairs to fly direct close air support by day, and flare-dropping night hecklers after dark. The Black Sheep squadron paid a tragic price when the commanding officer of VMF-214, Lieutenant Colonel Walter E. Lischeid, was shot down and killed over Seoul.

In the fight for the capital, the Fifth Marines repulsed a counter-attack by two hundred North Korean troops, destroying six T-34s, then advanced all the way to the Kimpo airfield, calling down naval fire on pockets of resistance as they advanced. On the evening of September 17, the airfield was theirs. Two days later, as the regiment prepared to cross the Han River, two more fighter squadrons from Marine Air Group 33, VMF-212 and VMF(N)-542—a night squadron accoutred with radar-equipped Grumman F7F Tigercats—landed at Kimpo while the Fifth Air Force airlifted in their ammunition and fuel. General Cushman's fliers pushed toward the front almost as fast as the infantry did. They flew their first strikes the very next day.

By September 29, Seoul was in UN hands after an intensive effort that saw heavy and sustained house-to-house fighting. First Marine Division losses since the landing were 350 killed and 1,786 wounded in action. More than four thousand North Koreans laid down their arms as President Syngman Rhee prepared to make Seoul his seat of power once again.

The landings at Inchon changed the dynamic of the entire battle-field. The North Korean army's rush south toward Pusan had left it with supply lines stretched and undefended, inescapably vulnerable to the type of mobile jolt that had fallen upon it from the sea. With the lines cut, the offensive capacity of Kim Il-sung's legions vanished. They retreated into the central mountains of the Korean peninsula to regroup. The pressure on Walker's perimeter ceased. Saved from being driven into the sea, the Eighth Army pivoted to the offensive. With UDT teams, Marine Raiders, and British commandos staging raids from the sea, South Korean troops under General Walker advanced from Pusan.

As U.S. troops pushed through Seoul and secured the main highway to Pyongyang—the First Cavalry Division arriving and passing through the Fifth Marines—North Korean positions along the east coast shook under bombardment from a newcomer to the Far East, the battleship USS *Missouri*. In preparation for the Eighth Army's advance, the battleship, joined by the heavy cruiser *Helena,* laid into their targets with the guidance of fire-control parties on the front lines. Captured North Korean soldiers referred to the *Helena* as "the hell ship" after the Fifth Division took almost 200 tons of eight-inch naval ordnance from her over a two-week period.

On September 15, Turner Joy received an emergency call for assistance from a position on the beach well north of Pohang. The peril of amphibious amateurism was made clear after General Walker, overruling the objections of the naval commander at Pusan, decided to stage an amphibious assault of his own. He sent an LST to land seven hundred South Korean guerrillas behind enemy lines. The ship broached at the beach, leaving the Koreans stranded and under concentrated enemy mortar fire. Joy was forced to recall the *Missouri, Helena,* and a division of destroyers from their fire missions supporting the Eighth Army front and send them to plaster the enemy formations menacing the castaways. When the evacuation was complete six days later, the LST was lost and sixty South Koreans were dead on the beach. Audacity was never a substitute for sound practice in the difficult tradecraft of invasion from the sea.

MacArthur had meant to follow up his landing at Inchon with an amphibious assault at Wonsan—the largest city on North Korea's east coast. The Marines embarked and sailed around the peninsula, but the landing was canceled in the eleventh hour following the discovery that the Soviets had helped the North Koreans seed the harbor with thousands of mines. The fields of moored two-ton devices packing a 550-pound charge of TNT included many with advanced "influence" fuzes, triggered not only by contact but by acoustic waves, magnetic fields, or hydrostatic pressure.

This revelation may have been the handiwork of the submarine *Segundo,* which conducted a special mission along the northeast Korean coast on September 23 for which records have been destroyed. At the time, the *Segundo* was part of a rotation of six Yokosuka-based submarines that Admiral Joy was using to monitor Soviet cargo shipping in the La Pérouse Strait, the choke point between Sakhalin Island and Hokkaido. Her diversion to the northeast Korean coast at the height of this other high-priority reconnaissance operation suggests a mission of importance.

The news that Wonsan's valuable harbor was closed to shipping reached Turner Joy mere days before the Marines were to land. Reports from Navy patrol planes in mid-August that an unusually large number of barges were in Wonsan might have suggested a mining project, but Joy's staff had not connected the dots. It was a serious matter. In World War II, U.S. mines had sunk one Japanese ship for every sixty laid and produced a casualty for every twenty. Given the postwar atrophy of U.S. minesweeping capability, the risks were significant.

The first ships to enter Wonsan's harbor on October 10 were not assault transports, but minesweepers assisted by helicopter spotters. Their work in this neglected trade was made easier after a minesweeping specialist, Lieutenant Commander Don C. DeForest, went ashore and located and recruited the North Koreans who had assisted the Soviets in mining the harbor. It was a lifesaving coup in human intelligence. The Koreans showed him the arsenal where the mines had been built and described the secret nighttime operations that had sown the harbor with about three thousand of them. More than two dozen Russians who had supervised the operation had disappeared the week before the Americans arrived, the informants said.

Though two minesweepers, the *Pirate* and *Pledge,* struck mines and sank, with ninety-two casualties, the timely discovery spared him a disaster of the first order. When the First Marine Division arrived in the harbor on October 26, the city had already been taken from the landward side. The planned assault became an "administrative landing," the urgency and peril of which were indicated by signs posted on the beach for the benefit of the Marines, THIS BEACH IS ALL YOURS THRU COURTESY OF MINE SQUADRON THREE.

Chesty Puller could see no reason beyond politics to explain why the First Marine Division was ordered to reembark at Inchon and sail all the way around the Korean Peninsula to land on the opposite coast. "The Marines captured Seoul, didn't they?" Puller asked a colleague. "If you were MacArthur, would you let the Marines capture Seoul *and* Pyongyang?" An Australian colonel could have provided the affirming vitriol Puller sought; on October 18, just thirty miles south of Pyongyang, the commander of the U.S. First Cavalry Division, Major General Hobart R. "Hap" Gay, met the Third Battalion, Royal Australian Regiment—leading the advance toward the North Korean capital as part of the 27th British Commonwealth Brigade—and ordered them to move to the shoulder of the road so the Americans could pass and take the honors.

MacArthur, alive to the strategic opportunity at hand, had ambitions larger than sidelining Marines or Australians or laying claim to taking a particular capital. He wanted unconditional surrender from the North Koreans, but failing that, he wanted to destroy its government utterly. He would not be content with a mere restoration of the status quo ante bellum. The UN allies agreed that to decline pursuit would merely allow the North Korean army to withdraw and rebuild. With a multinational fleet that now included ships from Canada, Colombia, Denmark, France, Great Britain, the Netherlands, New Zealand, and Thailand, and a ground force that included soldiers from those nations plus Belgium-Luxembourg, Greece, the Philippines, South Africa, Turkey, and eventually Ethiopia, MacArthur would destroy the army of the Korean Communists even if it meant marching all the way to the border of China.

And the Joint Chiefs seemed content to give him the freedom of action to accomplish this goal and more. MacArthur directed Walker's Eighth Army to link up with Almond's Tenth Corps and go all the way to the Yalu. He received emboldening words from the new secretary of defense, George Marshall: "We want you to feel unhampered tactically and strategically to proceed north of the 38th parallel."

17

War with China

When Captain Edwin T. Layton arrived in Tokyo to join Admiral Turner Joy's intelligence apparatus in October, he was appalled by what he found. Joy's communications intelligence branch, known as the Naval Security Group, produced standard fare for Far East naval commanders—data on ports, harbors, coastlines, and beaches; interpretations of captured documents and equipment; interrogations of prisoners of war; and photos of anything of interest. Layton was shocked to discover that the intel shop could not translate what they heard on Russian, Korean, and Chinese radio frequencies, and that their human intelligence sources were suspect. Aerial photo reconnaissance units were poorly staffed and outfitted. Carrier air groups had special-mission-capable composite squadrons, but their principal eyes in the sky, camera-equipped Corsairs, were in short supply and their lenses were inadequate. Admiral Joy relied on long-range patrol aircraft and submarines not only for tactical intelligence, but for photographic and observational reconnaissance of shipping moving along the East Asian coast. Naval patrol squadrons were stationed in Atsugi and Iwakuni in Japan, and on Okinawa. And there was a Royal Air Force Sunderland flying boat wing, and a detachment of long-range seaplanes at Sangley Point naval station near Manila.

In parallel to Joy's own intelligence effort, Navy and Air Force units stationed in the northwestern Pacific carried out an all-hands project to locate Soviet bases that housed their first-generation atomic-capable bomber. The Tupolev Tu-4 was a straight knockoff of the atomic-bomb-carrying Silverplate version of the B-29. It had a three-thousand-nautical-mile range and thus the ability to strike Strategic Air Command bases from Washington State to South Dakota. When jet-stream winds were cooperating during winter, Joint Chiefs of Staff analysts feared, even Chicago or New York might be in range of an aerially refueled Tu-4 regiment based in the polar region above the 64th parallel. For war-planning purposes, it was critical to locate air-fields in the Kuriles, Siberia, and even on drifting ice floes and un-charted "ice islands" in the Arctic. Given how little was known about the locations, capabilities, and technical characteristics of Sino-Soviet bloc radar systems, and the state of development of Soviet surface-to-air missiles, then in testing, the collection of electronic intelligence on these systems became a high priority in early 1950. Truman asked the Joint Chiefs to oversee a program of strategic aerial reconnaissance that employed Navy and Air Force aircraft to fly in international airspace around the Soviet periphery, taking photos and intercepting electronic signals.

An airborne intelligence collection program, however, required so-phisticated electronics, the largest share of which the military had sold as surplus after World War II. Having received Truman's directive, the Navy sent two chief electronic technicians to locate and buy back the liquidated equipment. Wearing civilian clothes and carrying suitcases full of cash, the two chiefs rooted through war surplus stores in New York City, acquiring all the intercept receivers, direction finders, pulse analyzers, and other electronic reconnaissance equipment they could find.

The missions of the specially equipped "ferret" planes would persist in spite of significant loss of life. On April 8, 1950, a Soviet fighter inter-cepted and shot down a Navy PB4Y Privateer off the Baltic coast of Latvia, killing the crew of ten, including a cryptologic technician from the Naval Security Group.

Supporting the effort to discern Moscow's strategic intentions in Korea, the crews of the submarines *Remora, Catfish, Segundo, Pickerel,*

Tilefish, and *Diodon* took turns braving the seven-knot currents of La Pérouse Strait to report on Soviet seaborne traffic in the northwestern Pacific choke point. In a three-week patrol ending on October 5, the *Pickerel* reported one hundred contacts passing through the strait, including three Soviet subs, noting that it marked a 50 percent increase in westbound Soviet cargo shipping.

The United States was still chagrined over China's entrapment, the previous year, of five officials at the U.S. consulate in Shenyang on dubious charges that they had assaulted a fired Chinese employee. Editorialists at *The New York Times* fulminated, "If the Chinese Communists are illiterate in the language of international diplomacy and decency we will have to draw them a picture that they can understand." *The New York World-Telegram* opined on the case for six of seven days, proposing ultimately that the U.S. Pacific Fleet draw that picture for them. MacArthur drew his own indelible picture, visiting Taiwan in late summer, where he expressed outright support for Chiang's ambition to retake the mainland kingdom. Truman was so angry at this that he asked the secretary of defense, Louis Johnson, to demand a retraction from his freelancing general. Johnson balked and it cost him his job. Truman appointed George Marshall as the new secretary of defense in September.

But the U.S. Navy had unwittingly drawn another picture for Mao: that America meant to invade and conquer the Middle Kingdom. As U.S. troops were moving to Korea, Mao announced that the presence of the Seventh Fleet in the Taiwan Strait had "torn to shreds all international agreements regarding the nonintervention in China's internal affairs." Zhou Enlai, his press secretary, called the U.S. actions "a violent invasion of Chinese territory." This belief was fantasy, but it was apparently sincerely held.

The Shenyang consulate staff had left the country in December 1949. Now lacking diplomatic relations with China, the United States had no official apparatus from which to stage espionage operations that might forecast the consequences of these public clashes. The CIA considered its veteran OSS "China hands" not as valuable assets but as relics of an old guerrilla war. The OSS's rivalry with the Sino-American Cooperative Organization, or SACO, a covert liaison group organized by the Department of Naval Intelligence during the war, produced a legacy of frustration that culminated with Chiang's defeat and hampered U.S. intelligence on China for decades. Mao was ruthless in purging or banishing groups suspected of any association with the former regime.

Dining in Beijing on September 25, the Chinese army chief of staff, General Nieh Yen-jung, had told India's ambassador, Kavalam Panik-kar, "We cannot sit with folded hands while the Americans come to the Manchurian border. We know what we are in for. . . . But they cannot defeat us on land." The ominous remark did not impress U.S. intelligence analysts. Zhou Enlai issued an express warning in a speech six days later, saying the Chinese people "will not tolerate foreign aggression and will not stand aside should the imperialists wantonly invade the territory of their neighbor." Analysts at the CIA, Joint Chiefs, and State Department dismissed this statement as public posturing, believing the victorious but regrouping Chinese revolutionaries would not seek a new war. Already the Americans and Chinese were involved in a proxy war in Indochina, furnishing arms and finance to France and General Vo Nguyen Giap's People's Army of Vietnam respectively. Realists asked: Would Beijing risk a hot war in Korea at the same time?

On September 30, when the South Korean Third Division advanced north of the 38th parallel, in the van of UN forces exploiting the North Korean collapse following the Inchon landing, MacArthur demanded of Pyongyang an unconditional surrender. When it did not come, he directed Almond's Tenth Corps and Walton Walker's Eighth Army to destroy North Korea's ability to wage war entirely. He had no idea that his success at Inchon had solidified Mao's conviction that China was being surrounded by aggressors, with U.S. naval forces threatening it in the Taiwan Strait and armies approaching the Manchurian border. Focused on the risk of Soviet intervention, the Truman administration and MacArthur's UN command both missed the signals of danger emanating from Beijing.

Kim Il-sung turned first to Stalin for military assistance, then to Mao. As Stalin feared the outbreak of World War III, and Mao perceived a security threat to his nation, it is unsurprising which of the two rose to fight. At two A.M. on October 2, Mao summoned his Politburo and military planners to Beijing. Then he ordered his Northeast Border Defense Army, 255,000 strong, "to complete its preparations ahead of schedule and to await the order to carry out operations against new enemies." Mao named as its commander General Peng Dehuai, the dictator's loyal comrade in arms since 1928. In a telegram to Stalin sent the same day, Mao requested Soviet tanks, heavy equipment, small arms, trucks, and, above all, air support to offset the U.S. technological advantage.

The silver-tongued Zhou Enlai was candid with India's ambassador to Beijing on October 3. "The American forces are trying to cross the thirty-eighth parallel and to expand the war," Zhou said to Ambassador Panikkar. "If they really want to do this, we will not sit still without doing anything. We will be forced to intervene." On the fifth, Mao met with General Peng, who said he supported intervention because it "not only combined the ideal of internationalism with considerations of patriotism, but was also critical to the safety of China's northeastern borders." When Mao reconvened his Politburo that afternoon, Peng said the intervention would rescue North Korea, advance an Asian and world Communist revolution, and defy U.S. "arrogance" as well. Mao christened Peng's force the Chinese People's Volunteers.

The term "volunteer" was a fig leaf; they were nothing of the kind. The forces assembling were the cream of the People's Liberation Army's regular reserve. While they did not have the mechanization, heavy firepower, or supporting air forces to match the United Nations units, he felt he could count on their "absolute political superiority" as a difference maker. A two-month campaign of ideological education had produced "a reliable group with high political awareness," the director of the border army's political department, Major General Du Ping, said. He invited soldiers who had fought alongside Americans in Burma during World War II to talk about the characteristics of the U.S. soldier. "These arguments proved that American troops were not invincible but were absolutely defeatable," Du continued. The Americans, fighting far from home with extended lines of supply, no powerful allies, and a limited appetite for foreign wars, were beatable, Mao argued. They were a "paper tiger," he felt, and not even the atomic bomb would save them. "It was men, not one or two atomic bombs, that determined the outcome of war," Du would write. Besides, the United States would tread cautiously with its atomic monopoly a thing of the past.

On October 5, Stalin wrote Mao that he did not fear "a big war" with the United States. "If a war is inevitable, then let it be waged now, and not in a few years when . . . the USA and Japan will have a ready-made bridgehead on the continent in the form of the entire Korea run by Syngman Rhee."

When Zhou met with Stalin at the Soviet dictator's villa on the Black Sea on October 11, he lobbied for fulfillment of the terms of their non-aggression pact. Stalin was eager to see China intervene in Korea. He warned Zhou of a reverse "domino effect." If the Communist revolution failed in Korea, Moscow's and Beijing's own backyard, where else could it ever succeed? But Stalin was cagey about such commitments. He finally balked at Mao's most important demand: He refused to provide Chinese forces with air cover south of the Yalu River. Zhou said this was a treaty obligation, but his timing in pressing the case was poor. Stalin was privately disturbed that a pair of U.S. Air Force F-80 Shooting Star jet fighters had strayed into Soviet air space three days earlier. Having been blown off course over the peninsula's far northeast coast, they had strafed an airfield near Vladivostok. The excuse Stalin offered was that the Soviet Union's recovery from the Second World War left it ill prepared to fight a third. This Mao considered a betrayal. His representatives would come to resent how the Russians "talked to us in an oversimplified and patronizing way, which we could hardly tolerate," and "satirized our huge requirements." But for China, Russian arrogance was the lesser of two evils. The Middle Kingdom's fear of America could be expressed in terms of raw meat. As General Peng put it, "The tiger always eats people, and the time when it wants to eat depends on its appetite. It is impossible to make any concessions to a tiger." This was the Chinese general's view of the United States. While Mao and Stalin shared the ideology of advancing the spread of international

Communism, ultimately Mao's decision to intervene in Korea stood on his assessment of Chinese national interest.

Indoctrinated intensively in the righteousness of their cause, the Chinese army along the Yalu, Du Ping said, "was just like a dry haystack soaked with gasoline; it might become a raging flame ignited by a single spark." So, with or without Soviet air cover, the Chinese were going into Korea.

MacArthur foresaw a quick victory following his success at Inchon. He was surprised, shortly after the Air Force's accidental attack on the Soviet airfield, to receive a summons from the White House to meet Truman on Wake Island. The accident, which had made alarming headlines, was of gravest concern to Truman. He suspected MacArthur of trying to provoke a wider war. The president decided then and there that a face-to-face meeting with his theater commander was necessary.

When the two met, the general promised his commander in chief that victory would be in hand by Thanksgiving. MacArthur was confident that China would not enter the war—so much so that he told Truman an entire Army division (twenty thousand strong at wartime strength) was available to be released for service in Europe. MacArthur suggested the president "make a clarion declaration of a Truman Doctrine of the Pacific." None of this made much of an impression on the president, who had already lost confidence in MacArthur. At dusk on October 18, the advance elements of eighteen Chinese divisions crossed the Yalu River, about 180,000 men.

THE ROAD NORTH from Wonsan tracked the seacoast railway line to the port of Hungnam, then turned inland, winding through sloping farmlands until finally, thirty miles along near the village of Sudong, the mountains began. It was a new world for naval infantrymen. The traditional domain of the Marine Corps consisted of beaches, lagoons, islands, and harbors. The Corps trained constantly in the diverse methods of assault. Trundling up winding dirt roads into the hills, seeing each one beyond the curve ahead grow higher and higher, the Marines became mountain infantry, and some of their habits were no longer useful. "It was ambush country," a Marine from the First Regiment remembered. "We had to struggle against the impulse to take the high ground, which would have overextended us. We had to accept the fact that we were always under observation."

Who might be observing them was indicated by some South Korean troops who met them coming the other way. Grinning weirdly and pointing north, they declared "Many *Chinesu!*" Apparently their unit had met a strong enemy force of some kind. A Marine first lieutenant who was Chinese American spoke with the Koreans and discerned that they were rank-and-file men with little good information. One of Colonel Homer Litzenberg's battalion commanders, Lieutenant Colonel Raymond G. Davis, sent forward a fire team in a trio of jeeps to reconnoiter the road ahead. The Marines met an enemy patrol and won the sharp firefight that developed. The several enemy dead appeared to be Chinese, and searching them for intelligence, the Marines found telltale souvenirs such as towels embroidered with Chinese ideograms. Shortly thereafter they came upon a South Korean command post that had custody of Chinese POWs. Oliver Smith's intelligence chief, Colonel Bankston T. Holcomb, Jr., had grown up in Beijing, served as a Chinese linguist and radio intelligence officer for the Pacific Fleet, and led Nationalist guerrillas during World War II. When he saw the prisoners, he knew who he was looking at. They attested to belonging to the Chinese army's 124th Division, and he reported this to General Smith. General Almond was soon persuaded.

Though it was common knowledge among the Eighth Army's field commanders that Chinese regular infantry were in the fight, MacArthur's headquarters remained in denial. As UN troops came within a few dozen miles of the Chinese border, the theater commander was in a celebratory mood. But when his troops made first contact with the Chinese, it did not go well. Just a hundred miles to the west of the Marines, at Chosin Reservoir, several regiments of South Korea's II Corps, attached to Walker's Eighth Army, were surrounded and routed by Peng's advancing troops. Reordering the breached lines to prepare a counterattack, the U.S. I Corps called forward its reserve, the First

Cavalry Division, the conquerors of Pyongyang. As they advanced on November 1, one of Hap Gay's regiments, the Eighth Cavalry, marched into an envelopment just fifty miles from the border.

The Chinese devised novel tactics to give their infantry a chance against the amply equipped and robustly supported UN divisions. Mao had cabled General Peng, the latter recalled, "instructing us that our mouths should not open too wide when fighting the American forces. We must adopt the tactic of 'eating sticky candy'—bite by bite." The Chinese units escaped aerial detection and attack by moving at night, avoiding roads, and starting gasoline fires in forests to produce smoke-screens by day. Their attacks focused on small UN elements wherever they could be isolated, surrounded, and rushed, supported with bar-rages of rockets and heavy mortars.

Near the town of Unsan, two battalions of the Eighth Cavalry met such a fate, holding out atop a mountain, sustained by their own des-peration and that of the pilots who struck at the elusive, dispersed Chinese troops and dropped pallets of supplies and ammunition. A breakout to the south resulted in the regiment's becoming dispersed. The Eighth's Third Battalion was left holding a hill surrounded by an entire Chinese division. In the hills and riverbanks, scattered pockets of cavalrymen scavenged for ammunition and food and called in aircraft to drop medical supplies and attempt an aerial medevac that proved to be too hazardous to carry out.

The three-day fight at Unsan, which a unit historian would call "the most painful chapter in the proud history of the First Cavalry Divi-sion," cost the Eighth Cav more than six hundred officers and men and all of its respect for Douglas MacArthur. In the ensuing weeks the gen-eral held to the fiction, against all the evidence, that the Chinese had not entered the Korean War. He and his intelligence chief, Willoughby, discounted the incoming reports of an intervention. The foundation for their view was the Far East Command's intelligence summary for Oc-tober 14, which had concluded that "CCF and Soviets . . . have decided against further expensive investment in support of a lost cause." In-vested in that position, MacArthur discounted anything that seemed to contradict it. Though Lieutenant Eugene Clark, who had so fruitfully

reconnoitered Inchon, and had repeated his feat, establishing reconnaissance camps up the Yalu River, now reported Chinese infantry
crossing into North Korea from Manchuria in strength, his radioed reports to Tokyo were considered unreliable and duly ignored. Even after
dozens of captured Chinese "volunteers" confirmed their unit affilia-
tions, and even after General Almond himself had interrogated some of
the prisoners, the UN Command still considered the Chinese to be volunteer reinforcements for North Korean units. As Command reckoned
with the dawning of the unthinkable, Mao was drafting a cable to Stalin requesting a massive increase in ammunition for infantry weapons.
The scale of the need suggested the size of the Chinese troop commitment to Korea. Mao informed the Soviet dictator that thirty-six divisions, totaling 380,000 men, had crossed the Yalu River.

18

To the Yalu

As the First Cavalry Division was facing its Alamo in the west, General Oliver Smith's First Marine Division moved north, obeying General Almond's directive to march all the way to the Yalu River at full speed. Smith ordered his regiments to proceed with utmost caution and prudence. As Homer Litzenberg's Seventh Marines reached the high inland plateau holding the Chosin Reservoir, Smith worried about the dispersion of his battalions, which were two hundred miles apart. Almond was unmoved by the idea that they were exposed. "His idea," Smith said, "was there was nobody out there." Not wanting Litzenberg to persist with open flanks, Smith ordered Ray Murray's Fifth Marines to move from their location east of the reservoir to join the Seventh. Chesty Puller's First Marines were far to the rear, defending the division's lifeline, the road leading up from Hungnam.

On November 1, 1950, in his first engagement with Chinese troops, Litzenberg, with a regiment of fewer than three thousand men, faced a whole Chinese regular division. Well emplaced, supported by tanks and artillery, the Seventh decimated the People's Liberation Army's 124th Division. The firefight in the Sudong Valley left seven hundred Chinese dead on the battlefield and countless more removed for burial per the custom of the PLA. Smith decided his regiments would hold at the reservoir and allow time to accumulate supplies and ammunition. Pressured by MacArthur to advance, Smith ordered Litzenberg to take the town of Yudam-ni on the west side of the reservoir. Litzenberg's encounter convinced Almond that the Chinese army had entered Korea in force.

Mao enjoyed Stalin's commitment of frontline Soviet airpower beginning in November, when the first Mikoyan-Gurevich MiG-15 jet fighters began appearing over North Korea. On November 9, Lieutenant Commander William T. Amen, the skipper of Fighter Squadron 111 on the *Philippine Sea,* destroyed a MiG-15 in air-to-air combat. Nine days later, USS *Valley Forge*'s Lieutenant R. E. Parker got a MiG-15, as did Ensign F. C. Weber from the *Leyte*'s VF-31.

Meanwhile, the fighting in the north had taken an unsettling turn for the worse. On November 3, almost three weeks after Chinese soldiers began crossing the Yalu, MacArthur told the Joint Chiefs that it was "impossible at this time to authoritatively appraise the actualities of Chinese Communist intervention in North Korea." The CIA, whose leadership had passed from Admiral Hillenkoetter to General Walter Bedell Smith on October 7, was dismissive of testimony of Chinese POWs indicating Beijing's entry into the war. But Dean Acheson's dispatch to the British foreign secretary, Ernest Bevin, on November 6 revealed that Washington saw through not only Mao's gambit of calling his regiments "volunteers," but the long-standing fiction of Soviet noninvolvement. "We have officially ignored Soviet arms and advisers 'volunteers' from Manchuria and other assistance in the past, even though the whole world knew the facts," Acheson wrote. "We did so in order to leave the other side a way out. I doubt that it is possible to treat organized Chinese units on the same basis, even though there has not been an official espousal of these units by the [Beijing] government."

That same day, MacArthur's eyes seemed to open. He informed the Joint Chiefs, "Men and matériel in large force are pouring across all bridges over the Yalu from Manchuria. This movement not only jeopardizes but threatens the ultimate destruction of the forces under my command."

The surge of China's peasant army into Korea would pit their numerosity and superiority in "political training" against modern mechanized infantry supported by artillery and airpower that had refined its ability to deliver its throw weight against ground targets from afar. MacArthur ordered General George Stratemeyer to exert a maximum effort to destroy all military targets along the Korea-Manchuria border. Citing "military necessity," MacArthur did not seek approval of this move from the Joint Chiefs of Staff. He ordered Stratemeyer to focus on the bridges over the Yalu but exempted several major power plants on the theory that such infrastructure would be needed by victorious UN forces. Air crews were to fly "to exhaustion if necessary." Dean Acheson was outraged at MacArthur's arrogation of supreme executive authority on the battlefield, but the general, flushed with his recent successes, was conditioned by experience to accept nothing less than victory in its fullest form.

Aircraft carriers would be thrown into the bridge-busting effort too, but there were delays in reactivating flattops mothballed in the Pacific Fleet Reserve at Bremerton. Important modifications to strengthen flight decks to handle heavier modern planes, authorized before the ships were put into "deep freeze," had not been completed. But four carriers were surged into the area to support MacArthur's soldiers. At the beginning of October, the *Essex*-class carrier *Leyte* was the first of them to reach the Far East from the Atlantic, having carried out four deployments with the Sixth Fleet giving muscle to the NATO alliance. Detached from the Sixth Fleet, she arrived in Yokosuka with her own air group and a detachment of Sikorsky HO3S-1 helicopters, which CINCPAC, Admiral Radford, had ordered surged into theater because of their usefulness in medevac, minesweeping, and combat rescue work. The *Princeton* was reactivated in record time, departing Alameda on November 9 with a hastily gathered complement of reservists. She would carry out strikes on North Korean targets just three months after her activation, a record turnaround for a fleet carrier. The escort carrier *Bairoko* left San Diego on the fourteenth carrying a large load of Air Force F-51 Mustangs as well as VMF-311, the first Marine fighter squadron to receive F9F Panthers fitted for close air support missions with rockets rails and bomb racks. The Marines based the newly arriving squadrons at Wonsan Airfield, close to the advancing front. The U.S. Pacific Fleet would finally make available eleven *Essex*-class carriers and a half-dozen light carriers to Turner Joy's command, making it possible to keep three to four carrier air groups continuously operating in support of UN ground forces in North Korea while retaining sufficient strength in the Far East to deter or stop a Chinese attack on Taiwan.

The incapacity of the CIA to discern Beijing's plans remained a grave concern of the White House. On November 14, the National Security Council announced, "It is of the utmost importance that the real intentions of the Chinese Communists be ascertained as soon as possible" and recommended that the United States "intensify covert actions." As it turned out, whatever operations were undertaken proved ineffective in determining Chinese intentions.

Offshore, on the destroyers, cruisers, and other UN warships plying Korea's littorals, the wintry winds whipped mist from the wavetops and lashed the bulkheads and decks, where it froze, layer after layer of ice accumulating two, three, four inches thick as temperatures fell. General Oliver P. Smith's First Marine Division, marching north from Wonsan as the vanguard of General Almond's Tenth Corps, experienced winter as it existed only in Korea's mountainous interior. It descended in late November like an extremity-numbing contagion. Medics carried morphine syrettes in their mouths to keep them from freezing. Oil lines seized, stalling vehicles. O. P. Smith summed it up: "Napoleon never had anything worse than that, getting out of Moscow."

With a broken enemy fleeing before him, MacArthur meant to push the entire UN front all the way to the Yalu River, which traced North Korea's boundary with China. He meant for Smith's Marine division to serve as the northern pincer of what he described to the Marine general as a "massive compression envelopment" aimed at destroying the North Korean army as a predicate to the optimistic end of unifying the entire peninsula under Syngman Rhee. Though Smith's men never quite reached the Yalu, in the end they marched much farther than that. When it was all over, as it would be all too soon, the First Marine Division in Korea, by the penumbra of its exploits, would reach the mythic shores of Tripoli and the fields of Belleau Wood, at least measuring by the grid coordinates of legend and lore.

Though MacArthur's radio snoopers were intercepting plenty of Chinese voices, they were, in the moment, oblivious to the envelopment of the UN Command. "Almost every frequency carried Chinese transmissions, and we knew the Chinese were out there," General Stewart said. *New York Times* journalist Hanson W. Baldwin, who was wise in the ways of military headquarters, considered MacArthur's staff "ingrown with mediocrity" and blinded by "an almost idolatrous worship for their chief," whose charisma cowed them. Independent assessments of intelligence and strategy did not flourish in such a culture. MacArthur had traditionally stonewalled civilian agencies seeking to conduct paramilitary or intelligence operations in his theater. In World War II, he kept the Office of Strategic Services (OSS) out of his operations to the extent possible. He did not want the CIA setting up shop in Korea, though the agency had been running agents in Communist China and North Korea since 1947.

Smith and MacArthur merged their regiments, setting their lines near the town of Yudam-ni west of the frozen reservoir while regimental engineers began construction of an airstrip. "Apparently pressure was put on General MacArthur by the Joint Chiefs of Staff to get closer contact between the Tenth Corps and Eighth Army," Smith said. More than that, MacArthur wanted his combined armies assaulting northward. As Walton Walker's Eighth Army advanced north of Pyongyang, the Marines pushed cautiously up the road to the Chosin Reservoir. With only a single battalion at a time able to advance up the winding mountain trace, Smith, unwilling to allow his vanguard to advance so poorly supported and with an open flank, instructed Litzenberg to slow down and allow Murray to catch up with him. Though the decision irritated Almond, Smith was not willing to gamble with his men's lives.

As the Marine regiments joined up, Almond arranged for an Army regiment to take the place of Murray's unit east of the Chosin Reservoir. About an hour later, Chinese hit the Marine positions with seven or eight full divisions. Moving at night, the Chinese avoided roads instead traveling across ridges and hillsides. The Marines held their lines and trusted their training. Hal Roise's 2/5 and Robert D. Taplett's 3/5 absorbed the brunt of human wave attacks that sought to flank and surround them, giving far better than they got. The next morning Smith knew enough to know that the situation was not good.

With the Air Force committed to a bombing campaign along the Yalu, and Fifth Air Force fighter squadrons rising to meet an emergent intervention by Soviet MiG-15 jets, it fell once again upon naval aviation to protect the Marines under combat conditions such as none of them had ever seen before.

Marine and Navy pilots, having showcased the power of concentrated and well-coordinated close air support at Inchon, where battalion commanders had summoned air strikes that arrived in minutes, turned their shoulders to the task again as the nine divisions of the Chinese Ninth Army Group made their bid to overrun UN positions at the reservoir. The First Marine Air Wing and the carriers put out thirty-five hundred sorties of close air support in thirteen days, coordinating the strikes through a twin-engine transport that General Field Harris had arranged to be stuffed with high-power communications gear in order to defeat the mountainous, signal-interrupting terrain. According to O. P. Smith, "North Korean refugees told us that these Chinese were holing up in huts in the daytime and moving at night. They had no tents and the only way they could keep warm was to hole up in these huts and by body heat keep themselves warm. These North Koreans suggested we burn the huts. So we put Field Harris to work on burning huts five miles on either side of the road. They were in there all right. The poor devils had no shelter. We captured documents with their bitter complaints about the cold. We found that in one of the Chinese corps, which had thirty thousand men, ten thousand were disabled by cold." Hard though the cold was on the Americans, Smith continued, "we had nothing like that in the division."

Mao Tse-tung suffered a terrible personal loss on November 25, when UN B-26 medium bombers struck Peng's headquarters complex at Taeyudong with napalm. The Chinese commander's lead

Russian language translator, Mao Anying—Mao's oldest son, aged twenty-eight—was killed after Peng and others had retreated to a fortified cave.

Two nights later, in a cacophony of bugle calls, whistles, and shepherd's horns, Chinese troops attacked across the entirety of the Tenth Corps area of operations. Colonel Allan D. MacLean's regimental combat team from the Seventh Infantry Division, numbering thirty-two hundred men, had moved into positions east of the reservoir as the Fifth Marines moved west to join the Seventh. MacLean's units were dispersed and strung out. The fighting quickly became a brute, raw hand-to-hand affair. With well-coordinated Marine close air support, the Marines, vulnerable though they were, held fast and inflicted heavy losses on the attackers, but they could not stop finally the Chinese from enveloping the U.S. soldiers.

On the morning of November 28, General Almond flew to the reservoir area to confer with his Army commanders. He had drawn up plans for MacLean to lead a Tenth Corps push toward the Yalu in the coming days. In spite of the Chinese attack he intended to keep the rapid timetable. Because of the Marines' setback at Yudam-ni the previous day, he canceled the Marine component of the offensive, but he notified MacLean that the Army task force, despite its perilous situation, would attack northward the next day, after the expected arrival of another line battalion. "The enemy who is delaying you for the moment is nothing more than remnants of Chinese divisions fleeing north," Almond told them, voicing the prejudice of the era. "We're still attacking and we're going all the way to the Yalu. Don't let a bunch of Chinese laundrymen stop you."

Colonel MacLean, seeking to make contact with a presumed friendly battalion to his rear, was confronted with a Chinese assault and was wounded in a hail of small-arms fire and captured. Command of the army task force passed to Colonel Don Carlos Faith, who then sent out search parties to look for MacLean, with no luck. MacLean was declared missing. General Peng sought a spectacular opportunity: to destroy the vaunted First Marine Division on the field of battle. On November 29, the commanding general of the First Marine Air Wing,

Major General Field Harris, urged a maximum sustained effort by Task Force 77 in the Tenth Corps zone of action. In Washington, shortly after Truman began his press conference on November 30, more desperate measures seemed suddenly to be in the offing. Truman was asked whether UN deliberations would bear on future air attacks on Manchuria. "We will take whatever steps are necessary to meet the military situation, just as we always have," Truman replied.

"Will that include the atomic bomb?" the newsman asked.

"That includes every weapon we have."

"Does that mean that there is active consideration of the atomic bomb?"

"There has always been active consideration of its use," the president snapped. "I don't want to see it used. It is a terrible weapon, and it would not be used on innocent men, women, and children who have nothing to do with this military aggression."

Another correspondent circled back around: "Mr. President, I wonder if you could retrace that reference to the atomic bomb? Do we understand you clearly that the use of the atomic bomb is under active consideration?"

"Always has been," Truman repeated. "It is one of our weapons." He began to flounder. "It's a matter that the military will have to decide. I'm not a military authority that passes on these things." Later, when he attempted to clarify himself before Congress, saying that "only the president can authorize the use of the bomb, and no such authorization has been given," he appeared to contradict his earlier response. Newspaper headlines dramatized the flip-flop, construing his clodhopping articulation as a "warning" to use the bomb and a muddying of the roles of civilian and military authority—that is, the decision to use the atomic bomb as opposed to the decision of what to target once the use was authorized. Truman, with his shaky performance in the original question-and-answer, bungled his messaging at a critical moment regarding a matter of considerable gravity. His performance convulsed public opinion.

That January, the editors of *Collier's* magazine were moved to imagine what an all-out nuclear war against the Soviet Union might actually

A Grumman F9F-3 Panther from squadron VF-52 readies to catapult from USS *Valley Forge* bound for Korean targets on July 19, 1950. Operating as the flagship of the Seventh Fleet, *Valley Forge* became the only U.S. carrier on station at the outset of hostilities.

Vice Admiral C. Turner Joy, Commander Naval Forces Far East, 1949–52.

Rear Admiral James H. Doyle, Commander Amphibious Group One and Transport Squadron One, 1950–51.

Major General William F. Dean, commander of the 24th Infantry Division, was awarded the Medal of Honor for valorous action during the Battle of Taejon in July 1950. He subsequently became the highest-ranking U.S. officer captured by North Korea.

Lieutenant General Walton Walker, Commanding General U.S. Eighth Army, 1948–50. He was killed December 23, 1950, in a traffic accident in theater.

The first waves of landing craft approach Red Beach in the early morning of September 15, 1950. Smoke pours from the Inchon industrial area.

U.S. Fifth Marines use scaling ladders to disembark an LCVP over the Red Beach seawall during the Inchon landings of September 15, 1950. On the ladder is Lt. Baldomero Lopez, wounded and then killed in action in the following minutes. Lopez was posthumously awarded the Medal of Honor.

Douglas MacArthur and senior U.S. commanders inspect the Inchon port area, September 16, 1950. To MacArthur's right is Vice Admiral Arthur D. Struble, Commander Joint Task Force Seven; to his left is Major General Oliver P. Smith, Commanding General, First Marine Division.

Major General Oliver P. Smith, commanding general of the First Marine Division, 1950–51.

Two commanding generals: Major General Edward M. Almond, Tenth Corps (left), with Lemuel C. Shepherd, Fleet Marine Force, in August 1950.

LVTs carry elements of the First Marine Division across the Han River to join the fight for Seoul, late September 1950.

MacArthur and Truman meet for the Wake Island Conference on October 15, 1950, amid Truman's concerns that MacArthur is seeking to expand the war. Six months later, Truman would fire the general.

USS *Philippine Sea* preps a bomb-laden Douglas AD-4 Skyraider of squadron VA-115 for launch circa October 19, 1950.

USS *Missouri* fires her 16-foot main battery in a shore bombardment of
Chongjin, North Korea, in late October 1950.

A Navy Skyraider (center top) bombs bridges over the Yalu River
at Sinuiju, North Korea, in early November 1950.

Jesse LeRoy Brown, the first African American aviator to complete U.S. Navy flight training. Recipient of the Distinguished Flying Cross, Ensign Brown died from wounds sustained during a mission supporting the Battle of Chosin Reservoir on December 4, 1950.

Thomas Jerome Hudner, Jr., was awarded the Medal of Honor for his actions in trying to save the life of his wingman, Ensign Jesse L. Brown, during the Battle of Chosin Reservoir.

Clearing snow from the flight deck of USS *Valley Forge* in early 1951. As the war dragged on, *Valley Forge* carried out her second of four Korean War deployments.

On September 1, 1952, Marines were moved from ship to shore for the first time by a new method. HRS-1 helicopters carry Marines into the Inchon area off escort carrier USS *Sicily*.

The 82-ton "Ivy Mike" hydrogen bomb, housed in a corrugated aluminum building on the small island of Elugelab in Eniwetok Atoll, circa October 1952.

look like. They commissioned an entire issue to portray a dramatic fictive Armageddon scenario. Alarmed over the creeping pessimism of the free world as it faced the threat of "an unending series of Koreas," the editors wrote, "*Collier's* planned this unprecedented project. Its purpose was no less than this: (1) to warn the evil masters of the Russian people that *their* vast conspiracy to enslave humanity is the dark, downhill road to World War III; (2) to sound a powerful call for reason and understanding between the peoples of the West and East—before it's too late; (3) to demonstrate that if 'The War We Do Not Want' is forced upon us, we will win.

"An appeal to the reason of Joseph Stalin and the men around him is the ultimate purpose of this issue of *Collier's,*" the editors added. "We believe that it is the most important single issue that any magazine has ever published."

Later that year, the October 27, 1951, issue of *Collier's* would hit the world's newsstands with this spellbinding four-color phantasmagoria just two days ahead of the UN General Assembly's meeting in Paris at the Palais de Chaillot. The first to protest it was an American official. The U.S. representative to the UN's 1951 General Assembly, Chester S. Williams, writing to Edward R. Murrow, accused the magazine of "blatant warmongering" and called the special issue "a gift from the Gods" to the Communists. "*Collier's* has done to our country, the United Nations, and world peace in general a great disservice," Williams wrote. "Its effect in Europe has been to weaken confidence in American leadership, to frighten our friends rather than our enemies, thus weakening our capacity for collective action, and to obscure the real issue of preventing war by practical cooperation."

The friendly fire from Williams was mere prelude to the fusillades of indignation and conspiracymongering that followed from the Soviets, who treated the presentation less as the product of a free press published for stated reasons than as a U.S. conspiracy cum secret war plan unearthed and revealed to the world.

The magazine's self-described liberal editors had of course invited such accusations by declaring their anti-Soviet motive so forthrightly: to "warn the evil masters of the Russian people" back from the brink and describing how "our overall conception of this issue was confirmed in study and consultation with top political, military, and economic thinkers." And the magazine editors' multilayered flight of fancy never had its intended effect of scaring the Soviets into changed behavior. It merely seemed to enhance Moscow's sense of persecuted victimhood— the insecurity and paranoia that live near the core of all true tyrannies.

The fractious talk of peace played out against a backdrop of war, actual and potential, in the spring of 1952. As U.S. casualties in Korea surpassed 106,000, with 18,458 dead, a NATO naval task force completed a nine-day exercise in the Mediterranean. Involving more than two hundred ships from nine Western navies, including major units such as the *Midway* (CVB 41), *Franklin D. Roosevelt* (CVB 42), *Wasp* (CV 18), and the battleship *Wisconsin* (BB 64), Exercise Grand Slam was the first large-scale exercise carried out by the Allied Command Atlantic under its commander of Allied Forces Northern Europe, Admiral Sir Eric J. P. Brind, Royal Navy. In the Norwegian, Barents, North, and Baltic seas, carrier and amphibious forces demonstrated offensive strike and amphibious ops, as in a simulated land battle on NATO's northern flank, Norway and Denmark. The exercise concluded with hundreds of aircraft from land bases and carriers bombing targets on the island of Stromboli, off Sicily, in conjunction with Marine Corps landings. Admiral Robert B. Carney, who presided, said afterward, "Perhaps the most important thing we have demonstrated is that the senior commanders of all the four powers can successfully take charge of mixed task forces and handle them effectively as working units in spite of language barriers."

19

NERVES OF ICE

IN KOREA, THE FIRST MARINE DIVISION FACED A MOMENT OF truth as they repulsed repeated Chinese attacks while encircled at the Chosin Reservoir. Fox Company of Litzenberg's Second Battalion faced a prospective Alamo in the Toktong Pass west of the reservoir. Fortunately the Marines' fighting spirit and capacity to hold were considerably magnified by the angels on their shoulders: the well-drilled Marine-Navy air-ground team, whose maximum effort started on November 30 and carried on daily for weeks, tearing, with concentrated fury at low altitude, into Chinese troop concentrations wherever they were found during the day.

To plan the offensive, Colonel Litzenberg conferred at his command post with Lieutenant Colonel Ray Davis, whose First Battalion was in combat several ridgelines over from the main road. The regimental commander intuited that the Chinese had judged the Americans to be entirely dependent on roads and unwilling to hazard overland maneuvers. So he suggested that Davis carry out an overland movement, crossing ten miles of unknown terrain against uncounted enemy strength, and make an assault to relieve Fox Company. The stoic Georgian considered the mission risky but accepted the urgency of its objective: not only to save an embattled company, but to open the road through the Sudong Valley and hold it long enough to bring the entirety of the two surrounded Marine regiments out of a trap.

Litzenberg apprised Fox Company's commander, Captain William Barber, of the plan, and Barber pledged to hold. That night, Davis's battalion began its ten-mile push through waist-high drifts over three frozen ridges. The snapping wind, positively numbing at 24 below, masked the footfalls of Davis's men crunching through the snow and ice. At times they came so near Chinese troops in the dark that they could smell their cooking and hear them talking. They advanced for twenty-four hours before colliding with the rear echelon of a Chinese company along the road. After ambushing their would-be ambushers, Davis got his first look at Barber's hot perimeter. Some 450 Chinese corpses were splayed out around it, many of them stacked and used by the Marines for cover. Over the course of six days, Fox Company's 220 men had suffered 26 killed, 89 wounded, and 3 missing.

But Davis's bold dash spared the rest of them. Over four days and three nights this epic march and attack enabled the larger elements of the Fifth and Seventh Marines to push the fourteen miles back down to Hagaru, fighting through seven Chinese roadblocks along the way. A British combat correspondent asked General O. P. Smith whether the move south should be called a retreat or a withdrawal. Smith replied that it was neither, the division being surrounded and thus required to fight its way out. "Retreat, hell. We're just advancing *in another direction*" was the epigrammatic masterpiece ascribed to Smith. The general's foresight in ordering his engineers there to prepare makeshift airstrips in the frozen earth at Koto and Hagaru would save any number of lives by enabling rapid resupply and medevac. More than forty-three hundred wounded or frostbitten U.S. troops were flown out from the rough-hewn airstrips.

After loading out the wounded, the ground elements that remained mobile got moving south. Smith ordered forward Colonel Chesty Puller's First Regiment, which had been deployed to defend the Division's main supply route to the rear. As Puller drew close to Hagaru, General Smith requested a situation report. Puller responded, "Fine! We have enemy contact on all sides."

On December 4, Radio Peking had announced that "the annihilation of the United States First Marine Division is only a matter of time."

No international body roused itself in protest of the warmongering press standards thus displayed. That morning, a flight of Corsairs from the USS *Leyte* arrived over Yudam-ni to provide close support for the Marine column. Commander Horace Epes of Fighter Squadron 33 made radio contact with a battalion close air support liaison officer and they strategized per their air-ground playbook. "I'm in the lead jeep," the officer said to him. "I have a fluorescent panel marker on my hood. Fly over me and rock your wings.

"Now come over me on a heading at 180 degrees. Now push over, commence firing." Eight Corsairs from the *Leyte* hit a Chinese platoon with their fifties and braces of antipersonnel bombs, then returned to drop napalm. "Move it closer," the radio voice told Epes after the first F4U released, tearing a raging black scar in the frozen ground.

That same day, naval aviation saw one of its most wrenching losses of the war as well as one of its most notable cases of individual heroism. Two divisions of Corsairs from the *Leyte* were part of a strike targeting a reported Chinese troop encampment west of the reservoir. On his first run, Ensign Jesse L. Brown's airplane took ground fire that hit its Achilles heel, its poorly protected oil cooling system. As the Corsair lost power, Brown guided his plane down to a snowy meadow, hitting the ground like a gull-winged six-and-a-half-ton bobsled. The impact knocked Brown for a loop. He found the wherewithal to slide open his canopy, and his squadronmates in VF-32, passing overhead, saw him waving from the cockpit of the aircraft, which was beginning to burn. After a rescue helicopter was summoned, Lieutenant (j.g.) Thomas Hudner, discerned that Brown was trapped in the plane. With Chinese patrols in the area and ground temperatures below negative thirty degrees Fahrenheit, Hudner realized time was short. He knew Brown well and liked him, having served with him at Quonset Point early in their careers, then on the eventful Mediterranean deployment bolstering the Greeks and the *Leyte*'s long interoceanic passage to the Pacific.

Hudner had learned as well from the Marines he had served with on board the carrier. Their most fervently held ethos was "Leave no man behind." Hudner saw what he had to do. Toggling his mic, he informed his division leader, "I'm going in." Descending toward an open pasture near Brown's wreck, he cut his throttle, pulled back on his stick, and set his plane belly-first in the snow. His windscreen shattered and his big triple propeller shed its blades as his Corsair ground to a stop. Lifting himself out of the cockpit, his jarred spine throbbing, Hudner lurched through the snowdrifts to Jesse Brown's aircraft. He discovered that his friend, the son of Mississippi sharecroppers, who had won the distinction of being the Navy's first African American fighter pilot, was trapped by cockpit wreckage and bleeding badly. His eyes were hooded and showed little light. Packing snow and ice into the cockpit, cowling, and bulkhead to retard the flames and heat, Hudner patted him on the cheeks and offered some encouraging words, then shambled back to his own aircraft, using his radio to request that the inbound helo make haste and bring an ax to free Brown, who was by then passing in and out of consciousness. On arrival, the rescue crew went to work, hacking at the tangle of metal pinning Brown in his cockpit before yielding to the fact that they needed a cutting torch and that one was not available. Noting that Brown was not breathing, and with hostile troops in proximity, they made the wrenching decision to depart. For the carrier air wings and their squadrons, the air campaign was a dismal, draining grind punctuated by concussions of sudden, personal loss. Hudner, distraught, returned in the helicopter to his carrier. He would receive the Medal of Honor for his selfless attempt to save the life of a fellow aviator.

Napalm strikes and strafing of Chinese blocking positions by carrier and Marine aircraft enabled General Smith's trapped division to push through a crossfire of Chinese artillery and mortars. Marine controllers guided 239 close-support sorties, two in three of them originating from Seventh Fleet carriers, the rest from General Harris's land-based First Marine Air Wing. The two Marine regiments needed twenty-two hours to cover the nine miles to reach Koto and its emergency airfield. Repelling attacks by Chinese who tried to toss phosphorous grenades into trucks bearing the wounded, they muscled through roadblocks, repairing damaged bridges as they went, finally delivering the wounded and frostbite cases into waiting OY Sentinels, TBM Avengers, and Air

Force C-47 and Navy R4D transport planes. Care of the wounded was Smith's overriding concern.

At one critical pass, the Chinese had blown a bridge, leaving the road cleft by a fifteen-hundred-foot gorge. Smith's caravan of several hundred vehicles stalled, stuck with their considerable payload of wounded. The division engineer, Lieutenant Colonel John Partridge, devised a plan to lay down prefabricated treadway bridge sections by aerial drop. Smith, dubious, questioned Partridge about it, asking how he knew it would work, whether test drops had ever been conducted, what would happen if some sections were damaged while being parachuted in, and whether there was a backup plan. Partridge admitted that the Air Force had never done such a thing before. Finally tiring of the inquisition, he snapped at his boss that the arrangements with the Air Force were in place. "Sir, I got you across the Han River! I got you the airfield! And I'll get you a bridge!" Smith chuckled, nodded, and told the engineer to carry on.

On December 7, eight C-119 Flying Boxcars appeared over Koto, each hauling a one-ton bridge module. The segments, clattering to the ground and secured in place, spanned the gorge and enabled the column to trundle south.

Though the prohibition imposed by the White House on striking targets in Manchuria hampered the effectiveness of the air campaign to "isolate the battlefield"—i.e., to cut off enemy frontline units from their sources of resupply (Radford called this "the crux of the situation and the reason our army was being pushed back")—the Marine aviators and their fleet counterparts under Admiral Edward C. Ewen did what they could, striking directly at the spear tip of the Chinese army wherever it could be found. "Without air we would have never made it out. I am convinced that air really saved the day for that operation," Radford said.

American reporter and war correspondent Marguerite Higgins had become deeply endeared to the Marines she had been writing about since she had landed with them at Inchon in September. When she informed General Smith of her wish to march out with them, he told her he wouldn't hear of it. He took her by the hand and delivered her to Chesty Puller, who brought her to General Shepherd. "Maggie, it's too bad," he said. "I can see how General Smith doesn't want another burden on his chest during the withdrawal."

As the last of the stretcher cases were loaded into a C-47 and the aircraft began to taxi, North Koreans and Chinese began lobbing mortars from the west end of the airstrip. Shepherd took Higgins into the plane and buckled her into the navigator's seat. Seated facing her, he watched tracers flash over and under the plane. As they gained altitude, he said, "If we get hit, we will die in each other's arms." To his men Ray Murray said, "We are going to come out of this as Marines, not as stragglers. We're going to bring out our wounded and our equipment. We're coming out, I tell you, as Marines or not at all." On December 9, battered, exhausted, bone-chilled, but proud, the pair of weary Marine regiments marched into Hungnam. Smith and his chief of operations, Colonel Alpha Bowser, were in a tent at Hagaru one night, working on the issue of how to replace a blown bridge on their line of withdrawal toward the seacoast, when they heard a swell of voices. It was Davis's lead element coming into camp, singing. The sight of Ray Davis's men and Barber's Fox Company singing the Marine Corps hymn as they arrived brought an eruption of cheers. For Oliver Smith it was "quite an emotional experience."

Bowser looked at Smith and said: "Our troubles are over. We've got it made." With their dashing "advance in another direction," the First Marine Division had carried off an escape that would go down as one of the Marine Corps' signature feats of arms, even if the taciturn O. P. Smith never ascended the peaks of personal fame or public adoration for orchestrating it.

On December 9, MacArthur summoned the Navy to complete the great escape, directing that Almond bring the entirety of Tenth Corps to the seacoast for evacuation to the Pusan area. Turner Joy ordered the amphibious units of Admiral Doyle's Task Force 90, supported by Seventh Fleet air and gunfire support, to carry off the maneuver—an amphibious landing in reverse.

Arleigh Burke, a skeptic of reports that the Chinese had not massively intervened, had sent a dispatch to the CNO, Forrest Sherman, asking permission to retain every fifth transport at Hungnam after it was unloaded in case the Chinese did come in. As a result of this foresight, ninety transports were on hand for Doyle to use in the evacuation. When the Marines began reaching the port, the battleship *Missouri,* cruisers *Rochester, Helena,* and *St. Paul,* and numerous destroyers and missile-launching vessels operating with the carriers loosed a barrage of high-capacity airbursts upon the pursuing Chinese. Within about eight miles of the port, destroyers were prolific with their five-inch/38s. The cruisers interdicted, aided by air spotting, out to ten miles. *Missouri*'s main battery could reach out effectively to twenty. Fire support ships fired more than twenty-three thousand rockets and various-sized main battery rounds at Communist units. But it was not enough to save the Seventh Infantry Division's Task Force Faith, which found its southward march thwarted by blown bridges and Chinese roadblocks. Colonel Faith himself led an attack against one enemy roadblock and was killed in action. Thereafter his unit disintegrated into a leaderless mass whose survivors—fewer than half its complement—found their way across the reservoir's thick ice and joined other Tenth Corps elements at Hagaru.

Overseeing the operational timetables of the amphibious extraction from Hungnam was a hardened World War II combat veteran with nearly twenty years of service, Colonel Edward H. Forney. The Task Force 90 evacuation control officer oversaw the removal of 80,000 Americans and their equipment, supplies, and vehicles. His transports, cargo ships, and LSTs accommodated 30,000 civilians as well in the week before Christmas. With 105,000 U.S. and South Korean troops, 91,000 refugees, and 17,500 vehicles hauled away in the end, it was a feat akin to Britain's great evacuation from Dunkirk in 1940.

The exodus of forces invited a refugee problem of massive dimensions. Surrounded by tens of thousands of Chinese soldiers determined to forcibly conscript North Korean military-age young men—or capture, intern, imprison, or execute any who showed sympathy for the "imperialist" Americans—terrified local farmers, shopkeepers, and factory workers sought to evade the Reds and await developments.

"They waded across icy streams and crawled painfully across broken ridges rather than stay at home and face the Communists," Marguerite Higgins recorded. Colonel Holcomb, the First Marine Division's intelligence officer, was asked by several families to burn their homes lest the Chinese take them. "Of course he did not do it," Higgins wrote, "but it was an interesting insight into the depth of feeling." Many North Koreans feared they had made a terrible mistake in siding with the Communists, revealing their willingness to leave behind the deprivation-racked north for South Korea's more hopeful pastures. A pervasive feeling of panic had settled over the city of Hungnam.

As the Americans slipped from his grasp, the Chinese commander in Korea, Peng Dehuai, flew to Beijing. Meeting with Mao, he confronted the despot angrily, telling him bluntly that his forces were woefully underequipped, undertrained, and undersupplied. The attack on the Marines had been a disaster, Peng declared. His divisions at Chosin had suffered twenty-five thousand dead, twelve thousand wounded, and tens of thousands of frostbite cases. These units, withdrawn from the theater for rehabilitation, would not return to action until March of the following year.

Mao was not entirely moved. He needed no lecture in the pain of loss. He understood from the start that his troops were entering a hard campaign in which the enemy enjoyed complete control of both air and sea. Bereft of air cover and heavy antiaircraft weaponry, his troops could not maintain long lines of supply featuring typical concentrations of vulnerable depots. Their solution was to embrace the primitive. Chinese troops subsisted by relying on stuffed rucksacks and well-toned quadriceps, hauling the food they ate and the bullets they fired, loading onto mules the components of their pack howitzers and heavy mortars. A Chinese soldier, his planners calculated, could survive on five pounds of supplies and provisions a day, or twenty-five tons for a division. American troops consumed ten times that. Foreknowledge that the Chinese peasant troops would suffer severe deprivation under fire was part of the logic of their indoctrination in propaganda. Peng and his planners, anticipating the air campaign to destroy the Yalu River's bridges, had moved forces and supplies across from Manchuria in mid-October.

The larger ambition of UN air forces in Korea was to do more than just blunt the sharp end of the Chinese spear at the point of attack. General Stratemeyer wanted to achieve battlefield interdiction and isolation—to cut off forward-deployed enemy armies from their supplies altogether. But Mao's approach to unit logistics ensured that that campaign would fail: A soldier was not easily deprived of that which he hauled on his shoulders or guided along on the back of a mule. Airpower's destructive effect upon the Chinese divisions would be significant, but never in itself decisive.

By the end of December, U.S. Navy and Marine Corps aircraft were given credit for fully half of an estimated forty thousand casualties suffered by Chinese ground forces in Korea that month. When the supply ship USS *Mount Katmai* came alongside the *Leyte* on the night of December 8, ammunition replenishment proceeded through careful organization and old-fashioned "Norwegian steam" at a pace of eighty short tons per hour. Such displays enabled the *Philippine Sea*'s air wing in the fall of 1950 to pile up more than 8,600 combat sorties, 23,000 flight hours, and 4.6 million miles flown (equivalent to 185 times around the world), consuming 3.7 million gallons of fuel and dropping 4,800 tons of bombs on Chinese targets in the reservoir combat zone.

Yet the campaign by the Far East Air Forces to destroy the bridges spanning the Yalu River was beset by many challenges: the intrinsic difficulty of achieving the level of bombing marksmanship to collapse heavy abutments and spans; dense-packed antiaircraft gunnery; the anthill efficiency with which peasant laborers repaired and replaced fallen bridges, their fear of delay-fuzed American bombs surmounted at gunpoint by work-party "political" supervisors; the increasing activity of Soviet-piloted MiG-15s operating from Soviet and Manchurian air bases, which darted into North Korean airspace to disrupt bombing attacks, then scooted back to base, protected by the moratorium placed upon U.S. pursuit.

Whatever his campaign's shortcomings, Mao assessed that a strategic victory was nearly at hand. His illiterate, unmechanized peasant army had pushed the Americans, led by one of the world's most prominent generals, Douglas MacArthur, the conqueror of Japan, out of North Korea. The "political superiority" cultivated in the People's Liberation Army had given the Communists a chance of victory. Their ability to endure was akin to the useful fanaticism that Tokyo's leaders had cultivated in the Imperial Japanese Army during World War II, a psychic boost to overcome inadequate clothing and equipment, deficient mobility and firepower, unhealthy rations, and the generally desperate prospects of legions beholden to an autocratic system unequipped to feed them. "The Soviet-directed Oriental taught us a great deal about himself in the period between June and December 1950," Marguerite Higgins observed. "Their system of intensive political indoctrination has certainly paid off. The fanaticism of the officers often kept the North Koreans and Chinese fighting under circumstances in which enlisted men were eager to surrender." Whatever it took to keep a man facing forward as the Siberian freeze blew down and settled over the field, dropping temperatures below zero and biting nearly as hard as the enemy's air strikes, the enemy forces seemed to have it.

In this winter of setbacks, on December 23, the Eighth Army suffered a gratuitous tragedy as it stabilized itself near the 38th parallel, when General Walton Walker, touring the front lines in his jeep, suffered a collision with a South Korean army vehicle that killed him instantly. General Matthew B. Ridgway was named to take his place. Harry Truman overcame his hesitancy to provoke Stalin and authorized, after securing agreement with British prime minister Clement Attlee, the first photographic reconnaissance overflights of Soviet territory to determine what the Soviets had deployed in their Pacific frontier.

20

AIR SUPERIORITY?

AS A DETERMINED CHINESE OFFENSIVE PUSHED TO RETAKE Seoul, RAF and U.S. Air Force crews began flying strategic reconnaissance bombers RB-45Cs, RB-29s, and RB-50s on missions to obtain radar photography of potential targets in Soviet territory adjacent to the Sea of Japan, and in North Korea, Manchuria, and Communist China.

On February 11, 1951, the Chinese, now reinforced by a reconstituted North Korean army, launched what Peng called the Fourth Offensive. Once again the initial attacks struck ill-prepared South Korean divisions, and again the UN Command gave ground. Again the Eighth Army fought back methodically, holding and regaining the 38th parallel after two months.

Turner Joy's headquarters, however, was closely watching for a renewal of the Chinese threat to Taiwan. Before the war began, an estimated one million Chinese troops were massed as if preparing to assault the island. As the war continued, large numbers of motorized junks were detected near Foochow, on China's coast. Informants spotted soldiers using the lightly armed vessels, which were painted with the Chinese characters for "destroyer," "cruiser," and "battleship," carrying out amphibious rehearsals. In mid-September, intelligence reports noted, these troops began to leave the area, heading inland to Shangrao, where they boarded trains for destinations unknown. Those troops, when they appeared again, would deliver America's first great intelligence surprise of the Cold War. The CIA simply failed to connect the dots as a guide to Beijing's intentions in the fall of 1950.

What might have happened had the national intelligence services detected Mao's intention to order several hundred thousand Chinese troops into North Korea is ripe for speculation. But the failure began with the Truman administration's lack of diplomatic relations with, or even a rudimentary ability to comprehend and communicate with, the new Communist regime. Beijing did not seek diplomatic recognition outside the Communist sphere, and the United States said it would not entertain it unless Mao's regime recognized the previous government's treaty obligations, a nonstarter for the Communists. For China, U.S. support for Taiwan was in any event a barrier to establishing formal relations.

Meanwhile, over Korea, frontline Soviet fighter regiments equipped with the best jet fighter in the world at the time, the Mikoyan-Gurevich MiG-15, turned in a determined and occasionally shockingly effective effort to blunt the Far East Air Forces' bombing campaign against Yalu River bridges and airfields. On April 7, 1951, B-29s from three groups hit a bridge complex at Sinuiju; MiG-15s from Antung intercepted. Undeterred by the escort of Air Force F-84 Thunderjet fighter-bombers, slower than the MiG-15s and underpowered, the Soviet pilots slashed into the formation, downing two bombers and an F-84. Only six of the 30th Squadron's dozen B-29s returned safely to Okinawa, and the bridges at Sinuiju stood. Five days later, further large raids by the Superfortresses met an even bloodier fate, with twenty-five B-29s lost or heavily damaged over two missions, a 25 percent loss rate. Confronted with these setbacks, General Stratemeyer suspended all further daylight raids by the Far East Air Forces.

As suggested by the results, the Moscow-headquartered fighter unit that carried off these feats of bomber interception, the 324th Fighter Air Division, was elite, world-class. It had deployed to China in March 1950 to train Chinese pilots in the MiG-15, and featured some of the most skilled fighter pilots in the Soviet Union. It was an all-star team of air show exhibitionists and test pilots under command of Stalin's top-scoring ace of World War II, Colonel Ivan N. Kozhedub (sixty-two aerial victories). Facing showers of 20 mm cannon fire in what the U.S. Air Force began calling MiG Alley—the airspace over the Yalu River that forms the boundary between Manchuria and North Korea— Kozhedub's pilots dispelled the myth of the invulnerability of the B-29 Superfortress and put a deep dent in the sunny assumptions of the Air Force's cherished atomic war plans as well as its faith in the B-36 bomber. A total of fifty-two Soviet pilots became aces over Korea, scoring five or more confirmed kills.

As U.S. B-29s were coming to grief over Manchuria, the ground forces of General Matthew Ridgway and Lieutenant General James Van Fleet were conducting a sound and competent defensive campaign, ably blunting the Chinese spring 1951 offensive and preparing to go on the offensive again to recapture Seoul. MacArthur in public statements pointed to the failure of the Chinese to cope with modern Western weapons while lacking control of the air and the sea. He mocked China's "complete inability to accomplish by force of arms the conquest of Korea," declaring that "The enemy, therefore, must by now be painfully aware that a decision of the United Nations to depart from its tolerant effort to contain the war to the area of Korea, through an expansion of our military operations to its coastal areas and interior bases, would doom Red China to the risk of imminent military collapse." So speaking, MacArthur had directly addressed Mao's greatest fear.

Mao still saw a chance at outright victory. "After we have consumed hundreds of thousands of American lives in a few years," he wrote Stalin in March as hundreds of thousands of new Chinese troops prepared to pour into Korea, "the Americans will be forced to retreat, and the Korean problem will be settled."

Truman, who was keen to negotiate a cease-fire in order to secure South Korean independence, took MacArthur's declaration as a threat to push the war beyond the president's stipulated boundaries: a localized victory secured by a stable peace settlement. The next day, April 11, MacArthur met his personal Waterloo when he authorized Ridgway's Eighth Army to advance as far as twenty miles (32 kilometers) north of the 38th parallel. Truman was outraged. "I was ready to kick him into

the North China Sea," he wrote. "I was never so put out in my life. . . .
It was an act totally disregarding all directives to abstain from any dec-
larations on foreign policy. It was in open defiance of my orders as President and as Commander-in-Chief. . . . I could no longer tolerate his
insubordination." Securing unanimous approval from the Joint Chiefs
of Staff, Truman relieved MacArthur of his command, stripping him
of his positions as Supreme Commander, Allied Powers; Commander
in Chief, UN Command; Commander in Chief, Far East; and Commanding General, U.S. Army, Far East, and replacing him with General Matthew Ridgway, who in turn handed command of the Eighth
Army to General Van Fleet.

That night, in a televised speech from the White House, Truman
placed his limited-war strategy in Korea in the context of a sweeping
global mission. He excoriated "the communists in the Kremlin [who]
are engaged in a monstrous conspiracy to stamp out freedom all over
the world." Nevertheless, he explained, it "would be wrong—tragically
wrong—for us to take the initiative in extending the war. . . . Our aim
is to avoid the spread of the conflict." The president continued, "I believe that we must try to limit the war to Korea for these vital reasons:
To make sure that the precious lives of our fighting men are not wasted;
to see that the security of our country and the free world is not need-
lessly jeopardized; and to prevent a third world war." MacArthur had
been fired "so that there would be no doubt or confusion as to the real
purpose and aim of our policy."

Speaking a few weeks later at Washington's Statler Hotel, Truman
said, "The Kremlin is trying, and has been trying for a long time, to
drive a wedge between us and the other nations. It wants to see us isolated. It wants to see us distrusted. It wants to see us feared and hated
by our allies. Our allies agree with us in the course we are following.
They do not believe that we should take the initiative to widen the conflict in the Far East."

As MacArthur packed out of Tokyo for a hero's return to the States,
Ridgway's outnumbered United Nations forces checked the Commu-
nist advance on Seoul. Two Commonwealth battalions—the Second
Battalion of the Princess Patricia's Canadian Light Infantry Regiment

(2PPCLI) and the Third Battalion of the Royal Australian Regiment (3RAR)—bore the brunt of the attack, and their defense of the Kapyong River valley against an entire Chinese division helped halt the Chinese spring offensive.

Piston-engine planes continued to perform an outsized share of the notable feats of the Korean air war. On May 1, 1951, well to the south of where the Soviet MiG-15 regiments roamed, Navy Skyraiders from Attack Squadron 195 hit an unusual North Korean target. Armed with torpedoes, the planes twisted and dived around four-thousand-foot ridges to reach the short curving leg of the freshwater lake created by the hydroelectric dam at Hwachung. The North Koreans had been releasing excess water from the dam's spillway to disable floating bridges installed by the UN Command downstream. With barely enough room to level off at low altitude, they released their torpedoes and pulled up sharply to skirt the cliff faces and high-tension wires over the dam. Scoring three hits on the dam's sluice gates, VA-195 carried out what was the first combat use of aerial torpedoes by the Navy since World War II. Unusual though the strike was, it offered a higher-percentage result than did more conventional naval ordnance against critical infrastructure.

In his flagship, the heavy cruiser *Los Angeles,* the commander of Cruiser Division Five, Arleigh Burke, was assigned to destroy a Communist railroad bridge in support of a South Korean regiment. Captain Robert MacFarlane was preparing to open fire on it with the cruiser's eight-inch main battery when Burke said, "Bob, you'll be wasting your bullets. You can't hit a bridge with eight-inch guns. The thing to do is to knock out the abutments at each end."

"I can hit it," replied MacFarlane.

"I'll make you a bet," said Burke. "I'll bet you can't hit that bridge with your first ten shots. If you hit your first shot, I'll buy you nine cases of scotch. If you hit it with your second, you get eight cases of scotch, and so on to ten shots. But for every shot over ten that it takes you to hit it, you have to buy me a bottle of scotch," said Burke. Thirty shots later, MacFarlane was making out an IOU to his division commander for twenty bottles of scotch.

The next shoe to drop was a diplomatic gambit out of Moscow. The Soviet ambassador to the UN, Jacob Malik, proposed terms for a cease-fire. The White House engaged the suggestion, and the UN Command named as its senior delegate to the talks the old cruiser sailor who had been running the naval campaign in the Far East, Vice Admiral C. Turner Joy. The first parley took place in July at the North Korean town of Kaesong. Mao had personally asked Stalin to handle the negotiations but Stalin replied, "It's up to you to lead, comrade. The most we can give is advice on various questions."

From the first day of the parley on July 10, Admiral Joy sensed a deep insecurity in his Communist counterparts, from the size and height of flags displayed in the conference hall to the length of time allocated for opening statements to the height of chairs around the conference table. "The Chinese were the real bosses," Joy wrote. From Washington, a Soviet hand was visible. Speaking in New York on May 18, Assistant Secretary of State Dean Rusk said, "We do not recognize the authorities in [Beijing] for what they pretend to be. The [Beijing] regime may be a colonial Russian government—a Slavic Manchukuo on a larger scale. It is not the government of China. It does not pass the first test. It is not Chinese. It is not entitled to speak for China in the community of nations." In fact this was a considerable overstatement of the bond between Moscow and Beijing. Although Chinese government officials were euphoric that history seemed to be on the side of Communism in Asia, that sentiment did not a conspiracy make.

Rusk's remarks certainly undercounted China's sense of threat from the United States. He wrote years later, "We had to learn that in negotiating with Communists, there is no substitute for the imperative logic of military pressure." He took the Chinese willingness to negotiate as a sign of the successes of UN forces on the battlefield. China's latest offensive had crumbled and stalled north of the 38th parallel as Ridgway's defensive reorientation stabilized the combat front, leaving General Peng's troops with some two hundred thousand total casualties. Rusk concluded, "The net results of my ten months of meetings with the Communists convinces me beyond a shadow of a doubt that in dealing with them there is no substitute for power."

ON JULY 22, 1951, Forrest Sherman, the chief of naval operations, died suddenly at age fifty-four in Naples, after having met with Generalissimo Francisco Franco about security assistance to Spain. Pressed about naming a successor on July 27, the president demurred. "I don't like to discuss things like that when the great man is lying in his coffin."

Eisenhower, at SHAPE (Supreme Headquarters Allied Powers Europe) in Belgium when he heard the news, saw the magnitude of the loss and was distraught—"Why the hell didn't that happen to one of us old fuds instead of somebody like Forrest?"—rating Sherman's contributions to the sustenance of the Atlantic alliance as comparable to his own. Eisenhower called Sherman "a tower of strength in the Joint Chiefs of Staff" who had prevailed with his case to authorize an immediate naval buildup for Korea. Sherman had been able to persuade General Omar Bradley, the chairman, that the marginal utility in combat of additional aircraft carriers was more a geometric than arithmetic progression, and before the war was at its midpoint, eight carriers were on station in the Far East.

VICE ADMIRAL JOCKO Clark, who took command of Task Force 77 in September, called the battlefield interdiction mission "one of the toughest jobs I think the Navy's ever taken." Given that his carriers faced no threat from enemy submarines, aircraft, or naval forces, Clark's words reflected the intensive operational wear and tear sustained by the carrier air wings in the task. USS Boxer's air wing alone mustered 1,250 sorties from March to October, taking credit for destroying 175 bridges, 140 trucks, 125 railway wagons, and several hundred buildings. The North Korean practice of pre-positioning railroad rail and ties and pens of logs to replace damaged abutments enabled them to repair many cuts within hours, and the goal of isolating the Chinese army from its source of supply could not be effected as the Communists shifted to nighttime supply. The Navy's failure to accomplish battle-field interdiction, as with its failure to destroy the Yalu River bridges, would be a powerful impetus for innovation and change as the war's lessons came into focus.

The desperate proxy air war between frontline Soviet fighter regiments and the Fifth Air Force carried on with a vengeance. Owing to the F9F Panther's shortcomings in speed and range, naval fighter squadrons could do little to support the bombing campaign. The famed Japanese fighter ace Saburo Sakai, claimant of sixty-four air-to-air victories in World War II, appeared at Yokosuka on October 3, boarding the *Boxer* with a group of Japanese aviation writers to marvel over the F9F. But the Grumman-built jets were not the difference makers. The Air Force F-86 Sabre proved to be the best counter to the MiG-15, and the Fourth and 51st fighter wings took the lead in the air superiority role over North Korea. Ridgway wanted eight groups of F-86s in country, but North American Aviation's factories had a capacity problem, able to turn out only eleven planes per month. Senator Lyndon B. Johnson's defense preparedness committee investigated the problem, and the Joint Chiefs, chastened, purchased sixty F-86Es built in Canada. By the end of the war, more than four hundred F-86s would be in service in the Korean theater.

Still, the MiGs, with their speed and superior climbing ability, were usually able to blow past a high escort and make effective high-side attacks on the American bombers. With UN and Chinese armies opposing each other on a fixed front, Admiral Clark commenced that fall a campaign of "Cherokee strikes," self-promotionally named after Clark's oft-touted Native American heritage. These targeted Communist supply concentrations within twenty miles of enemy lines, locating and fixing targets in advance via photo reconnaissance.

When human intelligence came to bear in targeting as well, the results were occasionally spectacular. In mid-October an intelligence group of underground North Korean assets operating out of Pusan reported that a meeting of several hundred Communist Party leaders was to take place at a munitions complex near the town of Kapsan. On

October 29, the air wings from the USS *Essex* and *Antietam* visited the site laden with proximity-fuzed thousand-pounders and napalm. After a flight of F2H Banshees strafed the antiaircraft emplacements around the complex, the attackers began their runs. High-capacity airbursts and liquid fire devoured sixteen buildings, killing as many as five hundred party officials. This feather lodged in his cap, Clark rotated home, ordered to San Diego to take the helm of the First Fleet, while Rear Admiral Apollo Soucek boarded the *Boxer* as commander of Task Force 77. Six months later, Clark returned to Japan as the new CO of the U.S. Seventh Fleet.

21

HEAVY METAL

ON FEBRUARY 20, 1952, THE NORTH ATLANTIC COUNCIL (NAC) held its summit meeting in Lisbon, Portugal, to set up the structure of the new Alliance as NATO became a permanent organization with a headquarters in Paris. The appointment of an American, Vice Admiral Lynde D. McCormick, to be NATO's first Supreme Allied Commander did not assuage French fears of German nationalist revanchism, a concern that finally scuttled the prospect of a Berlincentric European Defense Community. The "community" of the Western European continent moved forward more as an economic bloc than a military alliance.

The following month, Chinese state media leveled spurious charges that U.S. planes had dispersed biological warfare agents over Manchuria. On March 6, Zhou Enlai issued a radio broadcast warning that UN pilots captured after flying such missions would be treated as war criminals.

The propaganda offensive "has but little to do with Korea," commented General Mark Clark, who had replaced Ridgway as the head of the Far East Command. "Korea was but the setting for the play. The Communist purpose was far more comprehensive than this little war on this little peninsula. The Communist purpose was to create an issue which would strengthen world Communism and weaken the forces of freedom globally in preparation for a far greater test of strength than

Korea." Clark went on to say that the basic objective "was to plant the idea in men's minds that Americans were the new Nazis. American airmen were butchers, that American bombardiers aimed at schools and hospitals and reveled in a bloodbath."

The UN Command did its best to confront the Communists about the lies they were spreading. Clark's headquarters issued furious denials, while the State Department urged the Red Cross and World Health Organization to investigate. Soviet representatives to the UN repeated the accusations—but then vetoed a pair of U.S.-sponsored resolutions authorizing the investigations. When the Red Cross and WHO approached the Chinese and offered to investigate independently, the Chinese rebuffed them as tools of U.S. military intelligence. One theory was that China might be setting up a pretext for a Pearl Harbor–style surprise attack with their own chemical/biological stockpile. As a result, General Clark requested additional stockpiles of biological and chemical munitions for potential retaliatory use. Meanwhile, Soviet and Chinese agents, cooperating with the North Korean government, fabricated evidence, producing fake "infestation maps" and injecting condemned political prisoners with cholera and plague bacilli. They then buried their septic corpses where they could be unearthed and demonstrated for propaganda effect. In May, Radio Peking and *Pravda* publicized the "confessions" of two captured U.S. pilots, one of them a colonel and chief of staff of the First Marine Air Wing. After coercion and torture, he admitted to dropping "germ bombs" for the "warmongers of Wall Street."

In July, the CIA apprised Truman and the Joint Chiefs that enemy fighter strength had more than doubled over Korea, operating with "good to excellent" combat effectiveness. "Soviet participation in enemy air operations is so extensive that a de facto air war exists over North Korea between the UN and the USSR." Naval aviation's contribution to that campaign was proving to be marginal at best as the Air Force's F-86 wings took point against the Soviet Union's fighter regiments over "MiG Alley."

* * *

ON JULY 14, 1952, at Newport News, Virginia, the nation's heartland of major naval construction, Deputy Defense Secretary William Chapman Foster took a small hammer and tapped a brass nameplate displaying the name FORRESTAL to a forty-foot-wide keel plate suspended from a crane. He inscribed his signature on the plate, then watched as the crane swung it out and lowered it to the working floor of the shipway, where steelworkers in white coveralls laid it on a wooden cradle and fastened it to another long steel plate. A foreman activated a buzzer and a red light began strobing, indicating that construction of the country's first supercarrier was underway. Foster said, "I'm happy to report the keel has been well and truly laid."

Nearly every state in the union would contribute raw materials to build the USS *Forrestal,* the lead ship of a new class of supercarrier. As hundreds of guests watched from a canvas-covered grandstand— including former secretary of the Navy John L. Sullivan; Admiral William Leahy, representing President Truman; Admiral McCormick; and John Ballentine, Commander of Atlantic Naval Air Forces—Navy yard workers gathered on the decks and sponsons of the carrier USS *Randolph,* an *Essex*-class ship undergoing modernization in the neighboring shipway, to witness the laying of her keel. The *Forrestal* would weigh in at 61,000 tons, the sixteenth flattop to be built at Newport News. If she measured up in sea trials, more such ships would be coming Norfolk's way, so long as Congress found the money and management and labor in the steel industry could sort out a deal.

Nationwide that summer, half a million steelworkers were on unemployment lines, worried about food for their families as strike negotiations resumed. Prestrike, the dangerous trade of steelworker had paid $1.88 an hour. But wages were a lesser point of contention than were rules controlling union enrollment and membership and steel prices.

United Steelworkers negotiators met with representatives from the principal steel companies in a Pittsburgh hotel, pressed by the White House to settle their differences in a stoppage that had delayed delivery of 13.5 million tons of steel over the previous forty-three days.

While Army depots were growing short on artillery ordnance, Navy steel inventory was secure. The second *Forrestal*-class carrier, USS *Saratoga*—the sixth U.S. warship named for the Revolutionary War battle—would have her keel laid at Brooklyn's New York Naval Shipyard on December 16, 1952. Showpieces of capital naval construction, the two new supercarriers, along with the angled-deck upgrades to *Essex*-class flattops under way at several yards, promised to exploit the development of the steam-powered catapult, a British innovation that the Navy was testing in Philadelphia and the Patuxent River Test Center on the Chesapeake Bay. The thirty-three-knot behemoths, though too wide at the beam to use the Panama Canal, were equipped with four such devices to serve an air wing of a hundred of the latest jets. The *Forrestal*-class carrier portended new capabilities in naval operations. The fleet's traditional mission of power projection would be advanced to a new frontier once carriers of the size and capacity of the *Forrestals* were wedded to air wings equipped with next-generation nuclear-capable jets.

MEANWHILE, THE DYNAMICS of the ongoing propaganda war bore little relation to the actual task of sustaining the air interdiction effort against the Chinese army. It was pure hard work—and "plain damned drudgery," the commander of Carrier Division One, Rear Admiral John Perry, called it. For flight deck crews, plane handlers, ordnance crews, and catapult operators, the nonstop day-and-night flight operations were a draining grind, hard physical duty opposed by wind, ice, and cold, requiring footspeed and a head on a swivel, and plenty of dead-lift strength on the bomb carts.

The pure danger of it all came to light early on the morning of August 6, as the carriers swung into the wind to begin flight operations off Korea. A flash fire started in the hangar of the USS *Boxer*. As dozens of men leaped overboard and others rushed to remove bombs and rockets from overheating aircraft, smoke filled the hangar. Lieutenant W. J. Norton, the hangar deck officer, lowered the carrier's number three elevator, rolled an F4U Corsair onto it, and started the engine. As the roaring Pratt & Whitney drew smoke out of the hangar deck, the firefighters were able to make quicker work of putting out the conflagration. Still, nine sailors were killed, thirty-two injured.

Three weeks later, the *Boxer* launched five F6F-5K Hellcat drones, controlled by pilots flying two-seater AD-2Q Skyraiders equipped with TV cameras. The World War II–era warbirds carried off the first guided-missile attack from an aircraft carrier. The experiment with remote-dropped two-thousand-pound bombs went down as a failure; one hit an undefended bridge, but the other drones crashed as a result of either control casualties or pilot error. The program carried out by Guided Missile Unit 90 on the *Boxer* was thereafter discontinued.

If glory was unavailing for the exhausted ships' companies, pilots managed to find it in flashes, as on September 10, when Captain Jesse G. Folmar, a Corsair pilot with Marine Attack Squadron 323 from the USS *Sicily,* saw a MiG-15 pass in front of him. With a five-second burst from his 20 mm cannons, Folmar became the first pilot of a piston-driven naval fighter ever to destroy an enemy jet. He watched the Soviet pilot bail out and begin descending beneath a burning parachute, a thrill that was quickly superseded by the shudders and death rattles of his own plane—another MiG shot down Folmar mere seconds later, leaving him to bail out and splash down to await retrieval by an Air Force SA-16 Albatross flying boat.

ON NOVEMBER 1, 1952, the Pacific Ocean was seized by an elemental power such as had never before been manifested on earth. Neither of the atomic bombs that exploded over Japan, nor the two fission blasts that shook Bikini in 1946, nor any sum or product of the effects of those four events, matched the magnitude of the cataclysm of the "Ivy Mike" test, the world's first detonation of a hydrogen fusion weapon. Testing the super bomb had been a top priority of the Truman administration ever since the Soviets carried off the Joe-1 test in 1949. The physicists Edward Teller, Hans Bethe, and Stanislaw Ulam teamed up to brainstorm and engineer the process of using a fission reaction to trigger hydrogen fusion. Teller's notion of "radiation implosion" was "largely accidental" but nevertheless "a stroke of genius," Bethe confessed. The eighty-two-ton device was housed in a corrugated aluminum building called the "shot cab," eighty-eight feet long by forty-six feet wide and sixty feet high. A three-hundred-foot signal tower received the impulse from the shot control room on the USS *Estes,* where the firing party was located.

The 10.4-megaton explosion destroyed the island of Elugelab at Eniwetok Atoll in the Marshall Islands. The Pacific Fleet's forward fleet anchorage during World War II, an asset once so great that the Pacific naval war might never have moved past the Philippines without it, was shaken, uprooted, incinerated, destroyed, by a force so mighty it was unprecedented. Elugelab was gouged away, replaced by a sea-floor blast crater more than a mile in diameter and 165 feet deep. The surge of seawater produced an expanding ring of twenty-foot waves that remained visible from the air an hour after the mushroom cloud and its steam had dissipated. Radioactive hunks of coral landed near ships anchored thirty-five miles away.

Three days later, Dwight D. Eisenhower and Richard M. Nixon swept to victory in the U.S. presidential race over Adlai Stevenson with a 431-electoral-vote landslide. Two weeks after Election Day, on November 18, a direct showdown with Russia beckoned off the coast of North Korea as Task Force 77 radar operators reported seven unidentified aircraft heading south toward them from the Vladivostok area. On the cruiser *Helena,* a special National Security Agency SIGINT (signals intelligence) group used its classified technical capabilities to eavesdrop on the enemy's tactical communications, confirming that the marauders were Soviet. Continuing south toward the carrier task force, the aircraft urged an immediate response. Scrambling to the *Oriskany*'s flight deck went four F9F Panther pilots of Fighter Squadron 781. *Oriskany* radar controllers alerted them to high bogeys and directed them to an intercept bearing.

Lieutenant E. Royce Williams and the three other Panthers flew north, climbing, finally spotting contrails of what he soon visually identified as seven MiG-15s flying loosely abreast high above him, near fifty thousand feet. Apparently sighting the Americans, the enemy element split up three to the left side and four to the right, as if to bracket the

Navy fliers. The U.S. division leader suffered a fuel pump casualty, forcing him and his wingman to return to base. Losing sight of the MiGs as he reached twenty-six thousand feet, Williams, followed by his wingman, Lieutenant (j.g.) David M. Rowlands, proceeded to close the range and engage. Leveling off, he saw four MiGs make a firing pass at them at ten o'clock level.

Williams broke hard left, frustrating the enemy gunnery while beginning a wide high-G turn that brought him around onto the tail of the trailing MiG. He placed the pipper of his radar-computing gunsight on the MiG and triggered his four 20 mm cannons. The MiG-15, smoking, went into an uncontrolled plunge. The three other MiGs split away, then turned toward Williams on a high-side run. He countered by turning straight at them, firing head-on as Rowlands followed the smoker down to confirm the terminus of the Russian's graveyard spiral.

Jerking his stick into his thighs, Williams stomped his rudder pedals to jink and roll, evading cannon fire in his solo contest against the pair of Soviet trios. Such rapid maneuvers gave Williams plenty of fleeting opportunities to take deflection shots and head-on to near-head-on bursts against his numerous opponents. One of the ablest marksmen in the squadron, Williams used his radar-ranging gunsight and quartet of 20 mm cannons to deadly effect. He did not often miss. Operating at full throttle for the duration of the thirty-minute encounter, he experienced no emotion or exuberance, just a monofocus on the rigor of his training, Pensacola by way of El Centro's gunnery ranges, doing what Navy pilots had always done with battleworthy Grumman-built hardware.

When Williams found the haphazard geometry of the swirling fight putting him astern a MiG, he fired a long burst that hit home. The MiG's dive brakes, the twin panels that straddle the tail swinging out to slow the jet, flared, forcing Williams to break right and pull up to avoid a collision. As two MiGs circled high to make a firing run on him, he chased the wingman of his first victim, who climbed hard into the sun, blinding Williams with its corona. The attacking pair met him head on then, and Williams fired at the leader, then passed the wingman belly to belly, firing a long burst that set the Soviet jet on fire. The Russian section leader came around on Williams, who fired point-blank, tearing wreckage from the MiG that he had to "porpoise" to avoid. At that point another MiG—there was no tracking them all—gained Williams's tail and opened up with the heavy, slow *thump-thump* of its 37 mm cannon. The shells tore up the hydraulics of Williams's jet, and he felt his rudder control go dead. As he dived toward cloud cover, the MiG cannon still jackhammering, Lieutenant Rowlands cut in and saved him, driving off the Soviets with a firing pass.

Passing through the clouds and emerging at just four hundred feet altitude, Williams was too low to eject. Finding that his Panther was still flyable—albeit laboriously, absent hydraulic assistance—he decided to return to the *Oriskany*. Approaching the task force, he drew antiaircraft fire from plane-guard destroyers before the task force commander ordered them to cease fire. Williams's riddled Panther, with 263 Soviet shell holes in its wings and fuselage and out of ammunition, caught the number three wire and jerked to a stop. The *Oriskany*'s captain and the air wing intelligence officer summoned Williams to the captain's quarters for a debriefing. When the carrier reached Yokosuka, the commander of Naval Forces, Far East, Vice Admiral Robert P. Briscoe, saw him and informed him that he had destroyed four Soviet fighters in the remarkable two-versus-seven encounter. The *Helena*'s SIGINT spooks had heard the distress calls in Russian, confirming the outlandish result and raising fears from Tokyo to Washington of an incident that could spark World War III.

On December 4, the U.S. president-elect, Dwight D. Eisenhower, arrived in Seoul for his well-publicized visit to the fighting front. Ending the unpopular war had been a promise of his campaign, and so had been the visit. The Secret Service combed his schedule of visits to headquarters, airfields, and frontline units amid reports that Communist agents were infiltrating Seoul with an eye to assassinating him. In company with General Omar Bradley, chairman of the Joint Chiefs, and the new defense secretary, Charles Erwin Wilson, Ike flew to Iwo Jima, where he met with CINCPAC's Admiral Radford. The president-elect visited General Van Fleet's Eighth Army headquarters to meet senior air, naval, and ground commanders, where Briscoe suggested that Ike meet the Navy's hottest MiG killers. He gladly assented. Jocko Clark was on hand to show Lieutenants Williams, Rowlands, and Middleton into Van Fleet's office, where the presidential staff had set up a bar with a selection of rare scotches. Ike proceeded to push the premium offerings upon the naval aviators. "Being a convinced bourbon man, I stuck to my guns," Williams said. Ike "was delighted to meet the three pilots," General Mark Clark observed, "and put them so much at ease that before they left they had given him a blow-by-blow account of their battle, complete with hand gestures and body English." At the end of it, Admiral Radford joined the meeting. He swore Williams and his cohort to a lifetime of secrecy regarding their fight against the Soviet pilots. Moscow all along denied that its pilots were fighting over Korea, and to avoid a provocation, the Truman administration never accused them otherwise. The MiGs Williams destroyed had carried no markings—most featured a North Korean red star inside a red and blue double circle. The Soviet pilots who fought in Korea wore Chinese uniforms and were instructed to use Korean radio calls. In the stress of this desperate and lethal encounter, however, Russian language flew in red streaks. Snoopers from NSA Detachment 254 in the *Helena,* meanwhile, intercepted the evidence indicating that Soviet Pacific Fleet air controllers had vectored the MiGs to intercept and ordered the attack.

The United States kept a lid on the fact of its direct combat against Soviet pilots, though Williams's fight made the front page of *The New York Times,* albeit without revelation of the nationalities of the Communist pilots killed. Decades later, the Russian government confirmed the loss of the four MiG-15s and disclosed the names of the pilots Williams and possibly Rowlands had shot down.

As the only fleet pilot approaching five kills, Williams was the closest the Navy had to a legitimate air-to-air jet ace in the Korean War. It would be eight long months before the fleet produced an official one. On July 16, 1953, a USS *Princeton* pilot flying a radar-equipped F4U-5N Corsair, Guy Pierre Bordelon of Ruston, Louisiana, operating from the K-16 Marine airfield south of Seoul, shot down a North Korean–piloted Polikarpov Po-2 biplane. With his "seal-clubbing" spree against North Korea's obsolescent night-heckling biplanes, Bordelon became the only

Navy ace in Korea and the last fighter ace to fly a piston-engine aircraft. Williams's more notable feat left him one kill short of ace status, and the great sensitivities of the head-on engagement against Soviet pilots required the engagement to lie under cover of secrecy for upward of fifty years. By picking his spots and engaging smartly with conviction, with a squirrel hunter's shooting eye, Williams had shown in microcosm how competence and commitment to air combat maneuvering training could pay off in matching superior Communist numbers.

As his air wing commander concluded: "It is felt that the success of what is believed to be the Navy's first jet dogfight with MiG-15s is attributable to the following factors:

a. Defensive tactics developed and practiced by the air group in countering at the right moment when a high-speed jet is definitely committed to his run.

b. Continual practice of a sound lookout doctrine.

c. Aggressiveness of the pilots and their ability to fly the airplane to the maximum of its potentiality.

d. Excellent performance of the 20 mm guns and APG-30 radar-ranging gunsight.

e. The seeming inexperience of these particular Communist pilots in their failure to take greater advantage of their high-performance aircraft.

Elements of the analysis applied just as surely to the First Marine Division's performance at Chosin Reservoir. It was a universal in any combat scenario: What mattered was firepower and the ability to effectively apply it first. With the jet age dawning in carrier aviation, the *Essex*-class carriers and their piston-engine air wings faced dusk. The British innovation of the angled flight deck would transform carriers for better efficiency and safety. The old flattops had served well in opposing the Communist aggression in Asia, but the days of the straight-deck carriers and their droning swarms of blue propeller-driven aircraft were brought to an effective end with the advent of the Korean War–era swept-wing jet. The evolution carried an unmistakable message:

Nimitz had been proved right. All maritime nations had vital interests beyond their borders and required robust forward-deployed fleets as peace insurance. But not for much longer would the ships America sent to sea resemble the Navy of Chester W. Nimitz.

FOLLOWING A PARTY on the afternoon of January 20, 1953, at Alice and Dean Acheson's elegant red brick townhouse at 2805 P Street NW in Georgetown, Harry Truman climbed into his private car. Five thousand people assembled at Union Station to see him off as he boarded the 6:30 P.M. train to Independence, Missouri. In one unwieldy voice, the crowd belted out "Auld Lang Syne." Earlier that day President Eisenhower had taken the oath of office.

Eisenhower's visit to Korea, the *New York Times* editorial board thought, held "worldwide importance," and they noted the president's pledge to "see it through" there. How he might do so would derive from a clear assessment of the nature of the opponent. The new president's inaugural speech, delivered in front of the U.S. Capitol after he took the oath of office from Chief Justice Fred M. Vinson, featured a sharp indictment of Communism's essence that could have come only from observation from close aboard.

"We are persuaded," Eisenhower said, "by necessity and by belief that the strength of all free peoples lies in unity; their danger in discord. To produce this unity, to meet the challenge of our time, destiny has laid upon our country the responsibility of the free world's leadership." He spoke of "a purpose of strengthening our dedication and devotion to the precepts of our founding documents, a conscious renewal of faith in our country and in the watchfulness of a Divine Providence."

Eisenhower went on to measure the character of the Communist apparatuses he knew around the world, rendering stern and unambiguous judgment:

> The enemies of this faith know no god but force, no devotion but its use. They tutor men in treason. They feed upon the hunger of others. Whatever defies them, they torture, espe-

cially the truth. Here, then, is joined no argument between slightly differing philosophies. This conflict strikes directly at the faith of our fathers and the lives of our sons. No principle or treasure that we hold, from the spiritual knowledge of our free schools and churches to the creative magic of free labor and capital, nothing lies safely beyond the reach of this struggle. Freedom is pitted against slavery; lightness against the dark.

To fulfill an oft-sounded campaign commitment to craft a prudent, affordable national security strategy, Ike sought to unify the thinking of his senior staff. Questions about Soviet behavior were the talk of the free world after March 5, 1953, when Joseph Stalin died of a stroke at his heavily fortified personal residential compound in a birch forest outside Moscow. After four days of national mourning—Eisenhower sent condolences, but not an appreciation—Stalin was given a state funeral and was interred in Lenin's mausoleum.

On the morning of July 27, United Nations, Chinese, and North Korean delegates at Panmunjom signed an armistice agreement establishing a "complete cessation of all hostilities in Korea by all armed forces." It was to be enforced by military commanders on both sides of a 2.5-mile-wide fortified demilitarized zone between the two Korean nations. A Neutral Nations Supervisory Commission was established to prevent additional military personnel or new weapons from entering Korea, and supervisory commission teams from Czechoslovakia, Poland, Sweden, and Switzerland operated as inspectors throughout the country. If not officially ended, the three-year Korean War was placed on permanent pause.

22

COURAGEOUS IMPATIENCE

ON THE NIGHT OF MAY 31, 1953, IN THE DESERT ABOUT AN HOUR'S drive west of Idaho Falls, Captain Hyman G. Rickover entered the control room of a $30 million installation of pumps, valves, heat exchangers, turbines, electrical generators, thermometers, steam lines, and control panels. Accompanied by the head of the Atomic Energy Commission, Thomas Murray, Rickover directed him to grasp the handle of a particular valve and slowly to turn it. Somewhere within the complex of the experimental atomic fission reactor, liberated steam hissed and began blasting turbine blades, spinning them. When a propeller shaft connected to the turbine began to spin, a celebration was deemed in order. The era of nuclear naval propulsion had begun. Hasty champagne was concocted from some fruit soda mixed with grain alcohol from the chemical lab. As he and Murray enjoyed the poor man's Dom Perignon, Rickover directed Commander Edwin E. Kintner, the project officer of the Submarine Thermal Reactor, to proceed with a simulated transatlantic voyage.

Rickover had hung charts of the North Atlantic on the walls of the control room, with a Great Circle course from New London, Connecticut, to Ireland plotted over it. Kintner updated his position with the change of every four-hour watch. Every mark indicated a new frontier. No submarine had ever covered more than twenty miles submerged at full speed before.

Born in Poland in 1900, the son of a tailor, Hyman Rickover was single-mindedly dedicated to actualizing his philosophy of naval revolution: "Radical technologies require conservative engineering." His breakthrough was to engineer a reliable nuclear reactor that would fit within the twenty-eight-foot beam of a standard naval engine room. Obsessed with every detail of his program, the better to guarantee safe reactor operation, Rickover established a cult of personality within the Pentagon, building the nuclear navy around his own personal creed of devotion to engineering excellence and unending work. Flamboyant, confrontational, often insulting, and unsurpassed as a workaholic, he became known for his aphorisms on innovation and high performance:

"Good ideas are not adopted automatically. They must be driven with courageous impatience."

"Every hour has sixty golden minutes, each studded with sixty diamond seconds."

And thus: "Only Heaven is blessed with perfect rest. The blessing of earth is toil."

For the naval nuclear propulsion program, Rickover generally selected the top performers in science, math, and engineering at the Naval Academy. Nuclear power school became Rickover's monastery, and the nuclear engineers his monks. He told a journalist that if he could rule the nation, he would transform the power relationship between the American people and their intellectual class. Perhaps only Plato, in the fever dream of composing *The Republic,* that bible of meritocrats, could have envisioned such a social arrangement.

With his "dual hat" arrangement as both head of the Navy's nuclear reactor systems and also of the Naval Reactors Division of the Atomic Energy Commission, Hyman Rickover held the exclusive statutory authority to certify and license all operators of naval reactors. This once-obscure engineering duty officer who never qualified for command held power that neither depended upon nor derived from the military hierarchy. His attachment to the AEC gave Rickover personal administrative and regulatory control over the nuclear Navy. It was a club he wielded freely in battles within the Navy, using AEC money, for instance, to fund so-called research facilities that he put to use for training.

If only for that bureaucratic trick, Rickover would go down as one of the most influential technology transformers of his generation. But it was his high-wattage intellect and will that made him one of the most notorious but celebrated change agents of any U.S. public institution in modern history. An expert in playing Congress and the media in his battles with his opponents, he disdained procedures and protocols. His battlefield of dominance was the congressional briefing. Under Rickover's tempestuous forty-year tenure, nuclear propulsion became the signature innovation of the U.S. Navy.

After the reactor in Idaho had run safely at full power for forty-eight hours, Kintner's engineers announced their intention to shut down the plant. Rickover immediately overruled them. He had visualized that if the forty-eight-hour run went well, they should continue the exercise, carrying out a simulated submerged cruise across the Atlantic. Such an exploit would prove that nuclear propulsion was feasible in ships. It would give the project the momentum and breathing space needed to carry on the development without constant harassment from Congress until the first atomic-powered submarine, the *Nautilus,* then under construction in Groton, Connecticut, could finally go to sea.

As the reactor reached full design power, Rickover's obsessively rigid safety parameters held. But how long could the machinery withstand extended full-power running? Rickover was pleased to find no indication of overheating in the reactor fuel elements. Radiation levels were less than half of those his team had calculated, indicating the efficiency of the plant's radiation shielding. In Washington, the technical directors of the Navy's Naval Reactors Branch were so concerned about Rickover's cowboy manner of extending the demonstration that they called a meeting of senior personnel and urged Rickover to terminate the test. Rickover insisted it continue until an unsafe situation developed. "If the plant has a limitation so serious," he said, "now is the time to find out. I accept full responsibility for any casualty," he said.

At the sixty-hour mark on the simulated transit from Newfoundland to Ireland, a condenser tube began to leak. Near it, a spike in radiation was soon detected. A steam generator then began to leak. Reps from Westinghouse debated shutting down the reactor, but since personnel safety was not implicated, the run continued.

Then the control for one of the steam generators failed, causing the water level to drop and the reactor power level to become erratic. The debate about shutdown became more heated. The crew inserted the reactor control rods to reduce power output to half. In the end, the reactor "crossed the Atlantic" in ninety-six hours, though not quite maintaining full power. Still, it was victory enough for Rickover's fledgling program. The crew in Idaho had managed the problems, showing that nuclear propulsion was feasible and not just a pipe dream. Rickover was no longer merely an irascible, didactic tyrant. He was an irascible, didactic *proven visionary*. With his successful demonstration of the Mark I Submarine Thermal Reactor, Rickover had set course to change irrevocably the role of the submarine in naval warfare. A replica of the Submarine Thermal Reactor in Idaho was under construction at Westinghouse, soon to be delivered to the General Dynamics Electric Boat shipyard in Groton, Connecticut, and installed in the *Nautilus*. A second atomic submarine, the *Seawolf*, was under construction alongside. Their design did not appear to be a dramatic departure from the past. Their hulls were novel, but not radically evolved from the old World War II *Gato-* or *Balao*-class fleet subs, whose service lives were being fruitfully extended under the GUPPY program.

On January 21, 1954, *Nautilus* SS-571, named after Jules Verne's imaginary vessel from *Twenty Thousand Leagues Under the Sea*, was christened and slid into the Thames River, under command of her prospective skipper, Eugene Parks "Dennis" Wilkinson. Displacing 4,000 tons, the 320-foot-long submarine had a bow with unusual vertical lines, giving her the aspect of a wedge. The streamlined "sail" structure housed the periscopes and retractable masts. She was mounted with no deck guns, a feature that improved her hydrodynamic characteristics, permitting her high submerged speeds.

Rickover, standing alongside Wilkinson on the bridge, had long asserted direct personal control over every aspect of nuclear propulsion, interviewing each man who aspired to join the program. Every one of these sessions turned into an ordeal of antagonism in which particulars would be eagerly compared with those of other interviewees over the years, a test of pressure and hazing that would make Rickover a figure of near-legendary dimensions. After being kept waiting for several hours, the candidate would be ushered into the admiral's office and seated in a chair that had had its front legs sawed short to keep its occupant from leaning back and getting comfortable. Having been intensively prepped on the academic background of the man before him, be it at Navy nuclear propulsion school or at the Naval Academy, Rickover would quiz him on his major and interrogate him about his performance in each class. If Rickover did not like what he was hearing, he sometimes asked a candidate to step into a coat closet for a disconcertingly long while. The admiral's purpose in employing this strategy can only be speculated about. Some said he wanted men who could think on their feet and perform in surprise adversity, or to follow rules no matter what—or break them when circumstances required.

The future CNO Admiral James L. Holloway, who headed the Bureau of Naval Personnel when Rickover was running Naval Reactors, funneled him the best engineering talent to man new ships such as the *Nautilus*. Such favoritism likely contributed to the resentment Rickover faced in other corners of the Navy, especially in the ranks of engineering duty officers, whose resources he was commanding and whose jobs he was in the process of transforming. Holloway said, "I think Rick had his heart on his sleeve a long time because [as] a little Jew in the Naval Academy, and funny looking at that, [he] probably got kicked all over the place, and he had to be overaggressive to overcome it, which he was. He's got plenty of guts. And I think his compatriots in the [engineering duty officer] group were probably jealous as hell of him. So he was passed over, and just raised hell because he had a terrific following in Congress. There's no doubt in my mind that he got *Nautilus* built five years ahead of what it would've been without him just by being a little ornery pusher and fighting and giving them hell and so forth."

Rickover vetted the *Nautilus*'s crew from the ranks of its sharpest nuclear technicians and engineers. He directed that two of these junior officers and a high-performing group of enlisted personnel go to the

Westinghouse Atomic Power Division in Pittsburgh to begin a training study of the newest model atomic power plant. The so-called "school of the boat" was a tradition in submarines. It required each man to learn enough about all the equipment and watch stations that he could take over any station in an emergency and do a competent job. The ship's prospective engineers spent six weeks in Pittsburgh mastering the warren of reactor spaces while the non-engineers went to Arco, Idaho, for eight weeks of lectures on engineering systems.

Rickover picked Eugene Parks Wilkinson to be the *Nautilus*'s first commanding officer. Unusually, Wilkinson was not a product of the Naval Academy, but of the University of Southern California. In Rickover's eyes, the lack of Annapolis pedigree was an asset. He liked pragmatic, no-ego attitudes in men he chose for plum assignments. With considerable wartime experience as a junior officer in submarines, Wilkinson had commanded the USS *Wahoo,* one of the few conventional attack submarines built after the war. He personified Rickover's insistence on meticulous technical training. He also had a gift for capturing the historic moment. On the morning of January 17, 1955, as the *Nautilus*'s reactor control rods were raised and her atomic heart stirred to life and her lines were cast off, as Wilkinson put steam to her turbines and moved down the Thames River, he had the privilege of uttering words that would ring in naval history almost as loudly as Neil Armstrong's "One small step" soliloquy did more generally. By blinker signal to a tugboat escorting the submarine, Wilkinson announced, "UNDERWAY ON NUCLEAR POWER." The dawn of a new age in naval operations, the age of Chester Nimitz's "true submarine," had finally arrived. Senator Ralph Flanders of the Armed Services Committee marveled to President Eisenhower that atomic energy in ship propulsion "is really here." A whole new way of being a sailor was implicit in the revolution. Galloping along on a nearly inexhaustible supply of fuel, and thus endowed with a near-limitless supply of generated electricity, an atomic-powered submarine had scant need ever to surface.

23

ALLIANCE OF RIVALS

WHEN EISENHOWER TOOK OFFICE, HE HAD RESUMED THE TRU-
man administration's parley with European countries over strategy
and command relationships within NATO. In Lisbon and Rome, at
meetings of the North Atlantic Council, the alliance's executive body,
U.S.-UK relations were a complicating overlay to the politics of the
expanding Western alliance. When Greece and Turkey joined NATO,
Admiral Robert B. Carney, as the commander in chief of Allied Forces,
Southern Europe, envisioned taking them, along with the British, under
his control, thus placing most everything in theater under General
Matthew B. Ridgway as Supreme Allied Commander in Europe
(SACEUR), expanding the American-controlled portfolio in the Med.
The previous June, CNO William M. Fechteler had proposed to create
a Royal Navy–led Naval Forces Mediterranean command alongside a
U.S.-run Naval Striking Forces Med (comprised of the Sixth Fleet),
both under Carney's CINCSOUTH (Allied Forces Southern Europe)
headquarters at Naples, which would also command Allied air forces
as well as Italy's, Turkey's, and Greece's ground forces. The Joint Chiefs
approved the setup for submission to the North Atlantic Council.
Three days later, the British proposed that their Mediterranean Naval
Command report directly to NATO's Standing Group, leaving Carney
without control of it.

Churchill's having to cede Atlantic Command to the Americans had been a blow to British pride and may have moved the aging PM to try to preserve British primacy in the Mediterranean. He had complained to Fechteler that it had been "a deep humiliation for the British Navy."

But for the United States, deferring to the British in the Med created the risk of being drawn into uniquely British strategic problems, namely the colonial administration of the Suez Canal, which was poised to vex all parties involved as deeply as had the problem of Israel and Palestine. Since its construction in 1869, the Suez Canal had been irretrievably positioned on Whitehall's world map as the pulmonary artery of the Eastern empire. In 1936, England had acquired by treaty the right to occupy the Canal Zone with troops and air stations in exchange for promises of eventual Egyptian political independence.

Eisenhower cabled the First Sea Lord, Admiral of the Fleet Sir Rhoderick McGrigor, that most any arrangement in the Med could work if Sixth Fleet striking forces could remain under SACEUR, since U.S. law required any force equipped with atomic weapons, as the Sixth Fleet's carriers were, to be under U.S. control. The final agreement, establishing a British-led Allied Forces Med, whose helm Admiral of the Fleet Lord Louis Francis A.V.N. Mountbatten would take in March at Malta, as well as a U.S. carrier striking force under independent American control, met all needs. Mountbatten's command relationship with the Sixth Fleet was left undefined, and Carney thought the setup muddied his waters, but as Churchill said laconically to an inquiring member of Parliament, "I expect they will help each other."

The task of cooperation among NATO nations would be made easier once they agreed on a common strategic design. During the critical transition to an activated NATO alliance, this task was greatly facilitated under a U.S. president with Eisenhower's proven talent for alliance leadership.

"NATO was always very near to [Eisenhower's] heart, and he stressed NATO all the time," said Arleigh Burke, who worked for the CNO as director of strategic plans. European bases needed political stability. Eisenhower's Joint Chiefs prized northern Scotland, where the harbor town of Faslane offered a site from which submarines could base in order to confront Soviet naval forces in the Norwegian

Sea. In the Med, Spain and Portugal offered bases outside the confines of the Mediterranean Sea proper, but that were close enough to bear on trouble. Gibraltar and Rota, Spain, were chosen for major development. "By that time I had extremely close relationships with all the chiefs of the other navies," Burke said. "Having them over, talking over their problems, and seeing what we have in common and how we can help each other, but mostly to make sure that you learn to trust one another."

The fundamental trust issue at the heart of NATO was the question of where the alliance would finally spill blood in defense of a Soviet invasion of West Germany. In November 1951, the Joint Chiefs of Staff had approved plans contemplating a U.S. retreat to the Pyrenees and an evacuation of Europe to the United Kingdom from the French port of Cherbourg. When the proposal was shown to SACEUR, it was delivered on a NOFORN basis—no foreign recipients. Indeed, the politics of making Spain into Europe's Alamo was difficult to embarrassing. The last-stand-at-the-Pyrenees strategy pointed up the irregularity of Fascist generalissimo Francisco Franco's membership within democracy's coalition of the willing. An unreconstructed admirer of Hitler was the irreducible defensive kernel of the Atlantic alliance?

Back in October 1952, at a meeting of North Atlantic Council, the Standing Group had muscled up its thinking, expressing a preference for a robust "continental" defense strategy—defending Germany as far as possible to the east of Denmark and Norway; defending Italy and Greece as far north and east as possible; and defending the Turkish Straits as well. The prospective use of nuclear weapons precipitated an argument between Omar Bradley, the Joint Chiefs of Staff chair, and Sir John Slessor, marshal of the RAF. Slessor thought atomic weapons would stop a Soviet onslaught cold. Bradley saw "wishful thinking" in this, citing insufficient atomic stockpiles and the recent example of Nazi Germany's ability to endure years of strategic bombardment. No one seems to have brought up the butchery that Soviet MiG-15s had inflicted on well-escorted formations of B-29s over Manchuria in spring and fall of 1951, but that incident deserved to bear on the debate about the efficacy of atomic deterrence as well.

In the summer of 1953, at the National War College, Ike convened a top secret strategy review seminar known as Project Solarium, under the auspices of the Joint Chiefs of Staff. The exercise was held under cover of the rubric "First National War College Round Table Seminar," its subject delimited as "American Foreign Policy, 1953–1961." The president convened three task forces of experts, giving each a distinct mission to analyze in support of a particular U.S. policy toward the Soviet Union. Working from common reference documents and intelligence assessments, each task force met individually or in plenary format between June 10 and July 15, 1953, reporting finally to the National Security Council and the president.

The chairman of Project Solarium's Task Force A, George Kennan, had flinched at the bombardment of press comment generated by his previous authorship of "the X article," but it did not deter him from doubling down on its most robust policy prescriptions, which were focused on prevention of general war in the context of containing the Soviets in Europe.

Task Force B, led by the officer who had been the naval attaché to Moscow at the time Kennan was chargé d'affaires, Vice Admiral Leslie Stevens, and including General Jimmy Doolittle and State Department councilor Douglas MacArthur, Jr., looked at containment options based less on forming Western alliances than upon the threat implied by U.S. atomic weapons deployments.

Task Force C, chaired by J. J. McCloy, a Wall Street lawyer who had advised Secretary of War Henry Stimson, included two notable Asia hands, Lieutenant General L. L. Lemnitzer, who had commanded the Seventh Infantry Division in Korea, and Edmund A. Gullion, a member of the Policy Planning Staff who had served recently advising the colonial force in Indochina, as well as an influential naval commander, Admiral Richard L. Conolly. This group had an aggressive mandate drawn straight from NSC 68: "to diminish Soviet power—and Soviet-controlled territory—everywhere and by any means available."

The summary report resulting from the exercise was highly consequential. It formed the basis for NSC 162/2, approved by Eisenhower on October 30, extending and clarifying the prevailing Truman administration policy to "contain" the Soviet Union in accordance with generally understood policy and doctrine. Incorporating the conclusions of all three task forces, the report placed a premium on the importance of alliances, military mobilization, and a buildup of the nuclear arsenal, proposing to meet the Soviet threat without seriously weakening the U.S. economy or undermining American "fundamental values and institutions." In effect it was no dramatic departure from Truman's policy, NSC 68. The Soviet threat, 162/2 held, arose from the combination of "basic Soviet hostility to the non-Communist world, particularly to the United States," and "great Soviet military power." The United States, then, should develop and maintain "a strong military posture, with emphasis on the capability of inflicting massive retaliatory damage by offensive striking power." It required, further, "U.S. and allied forces in readiness to move rapidly initially to counter aggression by Soviet bloc forces and to hold vital areas and lines of communication," as well as a "mobilization base and its protection against crippling damage, in the event of general war."

Eisenhower would develop this ability for quick response and staying power under what would be dubbed the New Look strategy. While it was branded as new, and while some would see it as a foreboding departure in U.S. policymaking toward an embrace of an antidemocratic "military-industrial complex," it is easier to recognize its straight continuity back to George Kennan's "X article" and the Long Telegram from Moscow. Not for nothing had the man who had urged the United States, "without being provoked or unseated," "to confront the Russians with unalterable counterforce at every point where they show signs of encroaching upon the interests of a peaceful and stable world," been placed effectively in charge of the Solarium exercise, the important high-strategy council of the new administration.

Nothing in the strategic mandate had changed with the passing of the Soviet dictator in March of that year. "The authority of the Soviet regime," the report noted, "does not appear to have been appreciably impaired by the events since the death of Stalin. The transfer of power may cause some uncertainty in Soviet and satellite tactics for some time, but will probably not impair the basic economic and military strength of the Soviet bloc.

"In the face of the Soviet Threat," the report continued, the security of the United States requires "an intelligence system capable of collecting and analyzing indications of enemy intentions," and "manpower training in scientific and technical training and military production and stockpiles," and a "feasible balance" between expanding peacetime economy and defense requirements. The report gave a telling nod to the fact that a major Asian land war had just been engaged in an area the United States had not established as within its strategic core, and in this same vein, it included a disclaimer that seemed not to rule out a future all-hands U.S. military effort in a peripheral arena: "The principle of collective security through the United Nations, if it is to continue to survive as a deterrence to continued piecemeal aggression and the promise of an eventual effective world security system, should be upheld even in areas not of vital strategic importance."

By stating the need to maintain overseas bases from which to launch strategic airpower against the USSR, the United States obligated itself to maintain potentially far-flung vulnerabilities around the world. Holding overseas air bases, as experience had shown, depended upon keeping them safe from attack. Aircraft carriers roamed international waters of the world with impunity, imposing no such costs of diplomatic overhead.

Where relationships with host countries did have to be secure, which meant maintaining troop strength adequate to protect bomber bases from being overrun, the implications of the New Look weighed heavily on the Navy. Holding "vital areas and lines of communication" required it to perfect the mission of sea control in order to move and supply troops by convoy. The imperative to maintain sea control had been the impetus to keep the Norfolk-based Atlantic Command a U.S.-controlled headquarters. It would run antisubmarine operations as the Sixth Fleet did naval aviation in the Med: from a position of lock-stock-and-barrel ownership.

★   ★   ★

THE WAR IN Korea revealed that America could do nothing on the far side of an ocean without control of the sea. Mahan's view was Nimitz's view was Arleigh Burke's view, pressed forcefully upon Congress. "If we fail to command the seas, we cannot support our war effort overseas," he said. "In other words, every U.S. airfield and U.S. division stationed overseas is a vote of confidence in the U.S. Navy's ability to supply and maintain it."

During the Eisenhower years, the Navy's seat at the table of national strategy was secured by, of all things, Ike's deep pedigree as an Army man. In 1946, the rolling of the caissons had brought him along in support of partisan Army schemes to discredit and marginalize the sea service in the name of defense unification. But William Fechteler as CNO and Arleigh Burke, his perspicacious director of strategic plans, were welcome voices in Eisenhower's council room, which became a harmonious salon of strategic insight and counterpoint. As Ike came to rely upon Burke, engaging him among others in regular private sessions, Burke developed admiration for Ike's methods and character. "I might question his judgment but I'd never question his integrity," Burke said. "How do you get a feeling for a man like that? What does he do to cause you to have a feeling like that for him? I think it's mostly informal conversation on, well, any subject, so that he gradually gets his views across and how he formed those views."

Eisenhower did not extend himself to match Burke's fifteen-hour days—Burke came to see the president as "kind of lazy." But it was not a disqualifying laziness. "He wasn't a great hardworking man," Burke said. "But the man had integrity and he had good judgment, and he had high standards. That is the most important attribute a president can have. He knew a lot about the Navy without knowing why the Navy had to do things the way it did. But he would listen, more than most Army officers would listen, [to] why you can't do things that are done habitually in the Army, why you can't do them in the Navy. And it was nice to find somebody who would listen."

Burke learned to be wary when the president's steward brought around a crystal decanter. "He liked to serve old-fashioneds. It was a great big old-fashioned—double, triple, I think—so I never finished an old-fashioned, because I wanted to walk out, and I wanted to *think*."

Burke joined the task of crafting the New Look strategy for the administration. The State Department performed its usual role, coming up with U.S. policy with respect to a given country's political, economic, and military dimensions. State's policy proposals would go to the president for approval, and military plans would evolve to accommodate them. Under the relative austerity of the postwar spending reduction Ike sought, military planning emphasized nuclear deterrence, along with "bang for the buck."

All maritime nations have vital interests beyond their borders. All maritime nations, then, to the extent that they project power over an international commons, are empires. But the degree of that projection, its character and the actual motives animating it, matter. The United States was an empire not for the purpose of subjugation or exploitation, but for the aspiration of advancing the expressly articulated ideals of the United Nations, the Atlantic Charter, and NATO: namely, the right of nations to stand free from outside coercion or subversion of peoples to chart their own destiny. Adherents of moral equivalence saw their arguments founder on the example of U.S. treatment of the powers of the defeated Axis. Japan and Germany were as soon as possible rehabilitated, and given as much of a privilege of self-determination as a consensus of the free would permit.

The problem inherent in striking a peace on the Korean peninsula had to do with what new adventurous imperial or revolutionary task the Chinese would find for their "volunteers" in Korea once the war ended. A metastasis—this was the fear that occupied Eisenhower, Dulles, Kennan, and the rest—that France's loss of Indochina would expose Thailand and Burma to the Communist insurrection, casting shadows over British Malaya and complicating London's own security problem there.

The threat of the Communists' overtaking Indochina required a weighing of American interests in Asia relative to the rest of the world. "If it is our carefully considered conclusion that, due to the demands for military assistance from other areas of strategic importance to the United States," Assistant Secretary of State for Far Eastern Affairs Dean Rusk cabled his colleague, Deputy Under Secretary of State Matthews, on January 31, 1951, "we cannot follow through on the military program which our political program foreshadows, then we must trim our sails accordingly. In a word, the United States has in Southeast Asia reached the point where we must decide whether we shall put up or shut up."

This fearful view traveled beyond the world of defense hawk officials to executive branch agencies and the Joint Chiefs of Staff. Leading journalists emerged from the ordeal of bearing eyewitness to the carnage in Korea as convinced anticommunist watchdogs. "If we cede the Asian mainland to the communists, without a fight," Marguerite Higgins wrote,

> we will greatly strengthen our enemy. We will give the Chinese military dictatorship time to build an even stronger and better army. We'll give them the opportunity to "liberate" the rich prizes of Indochina and Thailand. But we will not be giving them only manpower and raw materials. We will be giving them something of great strategic importance. "Pull out of Asia," we say to the Soviet world. "Your eastern flank is now comparatively secure, go ahead and concentrate on Europe." If we do the Soviet world this favor, then Europe will eventually go under, and when that happens, if America continues to sit back naively, maybe waiting for the Soviet dictatorships to crack from within, it is only a matter of time before the entire world will become a string of Soviet Socialist dictatorships.
>
> The word "alarmist" has come into disrepute in America. Perhaps this is because we like what we've got, and don't want to believe that we should be alarmed. I think the word should come back into good standing; we need more alarmists. My great worry is that the alarm won't be sounded in time. It seems to me that our leaders should've started preparing us

for possible war the moment Russia slammed down the blockade in Berlin in 1948. Russia showed then that she was prepared to use force. It is a mockery for Truman to tell us that
three and a half million soldiers can protect us when every responsible officer knows that it will be closer to fourteen million if we want to win.

Ike was alive to the Chinese imperialist impulse. In his first State of
the Union Address, given before Congress on February 2, 1953, Eisenhower placed France's struggle in Indochina in the context of the larger
campaign against Communism in the Far East. He called the Korean
War "the most painful phase of Communist aggression throughout the
world. It is clearly a part of the same calculated assault that the aggressor is simultaneously pressing in Indochina and in Malaya, and of the
strategic situation that manifestly embraces the island of Formosa and
the Chinese Nationalist forces there." Appreciating an enemy's actual
intentions was often little more complicated than heeding his publicly
stated goals. Mao, in his Christmas 1947 report to the Chinese Communist Party Central Committee, had urged that a Communist International comparable to the one established in Belgrade be set up "to
coordinate the liberation movements of the billion people of the Far
East."

As Harry Truman saw it, the Korean War had to be fought "for the
simplest of reasons: because free leadership failed to check and turn
back Communist ambition before it savagely attacked us. The Korean
War—more perhaps than any other war in history—simply and swiftly
followed the collapse of our political defenses. There is no other reason
than this: we failed to read and to outwit the totalitarian mind."

The tension of simultaneously building integrated national military
capabilities and strong alliance relationships was a constant problem of
the Eisenhower years. Prior to his death, Forrest Sherman had established alliance building as part of his legacy by supporting the permanent forward presence of two combat-credible fleets, the Sixth and the
Seventh, from politically stable bases. While underway replenishment
reduced the fleet's dependency on bases, and use of forward bases sim-

plified logistics and kept operating costs down, there was no going back to the days of holding the fleet to the U.S. coasts and surging it forward as needed.

Multinational NATO naval exercises, CNO visits, planning conferences, war games, personnel exchanges, and foreign military sales all blossomed during the Eisenhower administration, with the U.S. Navy in the lead of a global coalition of Western navies. The president meant for this strategy to be part of a mission to defend overall Western security. "Our policy will be designed to foster the advent of practical unity in Western Europe. The nations of that region have contributed notably to the effort of sustaining the security of the free world. From the jungles of Indochina and Malaya to the northern shores of Europe," Ike said, "they have vastly improved their defensive strength. Where called upon to do so, they have made costly and bitter sacrifices to hold the line of freedom."

Later that year, in December 1953, the heads of state and foreign ministers of the United States, United Kingdom, and France met in Bermuda to discuss Soviet relations in the post-Stalin era. Winston Churchill thought an opportunity might be at hand for a rapprochement with Moscow. Speaking to the assembled diplomats in the white stucco oceanfront luxury of the Mid Ocean Club, Eisenhower dismissed such optimism. "Russia," he said, "was a woman of the streets and whether her dress was new, or just the old one patched, it was certainly the same whore underneath. America intended to drive her off her present 'beat' into the back streets." The president then adjourned the conference. British foreign secretary Anthony Eden, lamenting that the whole meeting had been "just about wrecked," asked Eisenhower when he thought the next one might be. Ike said, "I don't know, mine is with a whisky and soda," and stomped off.

IN MARCH 1954, the French garrison in Indochina found itself surrounded and quaking from concentrated artillery bombardment at its stronghold of Dien Bien Phu. The U.S. prepared a plan, known as Operation Vulture, a scheme to use concentrated American airpower and even atomic weapons to save the French position in Indochina, and specifically to rescue the French forces engaged in the Battle of Dien Bien Phu.

On March 19, the chief of naval operations, Admiral Robert B. Carney, ordered First Fleet Commander Vice Admiral William K. Phillips's carrier force to maintain a twelve-hour alert and to prepare to steam near the entrance to the Gulf of Tonkin, ready to launch airstrikes in support of the French on three hours' notice. On March 22, Phillips was ordered to make flank speed to a position a hundred miles south of Hainan Island.

Three days later, CINCPAC Felix Stump recommended that aircraft from Phillips's force carry out a reconnaissance of the roads and trails over which Chinese artillery and other supplies had been flowing to the Viet Minh rebels to support the siege of Dien Bien Phu. Two days later, Admiral Arthur Radford, the chairman of the Joint Chiefs of Staff, said to the president, "I am gravely fearful that the measures being taken by the French will prove to be inadequate and initiated too late to prevent a progressive deterioration of the situation. The consequences can well lead to the loss of all of southeast Asia to communist domination. If this is to be avoided, I consider that the US must be prepared to act promptly and in force possibly to a frantic and belated request for the French for US intervention."

The use of nuclear weapons by naval forces had been on the table as the French position in Indochina crumbled throughout 1953. The urgency of the moment now impressed itself upon Radford. Eisenhower did not want the United States to intervene unilaterally against Chinese-backed forces in Indochina, but Radford reinforced his earlier remarks by commenting that "atomic weapons would be automatically used to counter blatant Chinese intervention."

On March 29, Secretary of State John Foster Dulles delivered an address titled "The Threat of a Red Asia" at the Overseas Press Club of America in New York. He described the Viet Minh as a component part of the Communist imperialist movement headed by the Soviet Union and Communist China. Stalin, Mao, and Ho had, after all, met in Moscow in 1950 to map out the strategy for an eventual takeover of

Indochina. Dulles warned that should the Viet Minh prevail, they "would subject the people to a cruel Communist dictatorship taking its orders from Beijing and Moscow." The secretary further contended that "if Communist forces won uncontested control over Indochina or any substantial part thereof, they would surely resume the same pattern of aggression against other free peoples in the area."

Such a domino theory was nothing new in history. Its operation was nearly as predictable and mechanical as the game metaphor suggested. The ancient Greeks needed little imagination to discern what awaited them after Xerxes crossed the Hellespont, nor the Britons after Rome conquered Gaul. On April 1, Secretary of Defense Charles Wilson asked Radford to solicit the views of the individual service chiefs about using atomic weapons to support the French. They met in Radford's office the next day. Most forceful in opposition was Army Chief of Staff Matthew B. Ridgway, who feared the execution of Operation Vulture would provoke a general war with the Chinese and Soviets. Lemuel Shepherd, commandant of the Marines, was opposed as well. The Air Force chief of staff, General Nathan Farragut Twining, voiced a qualified approval of the strike, but "with so many caveats [that] it rendered his assent moot." According to General John W. Vogt, Jr., of the NSC planning board, "It was Radford's view that we ought to respond to the French problem with a massive dose of nuclear weapons to eliminate the Communists' artillery positions." The Joint Chiefs' Advanced Study Committee concluded that three mushroom clouds "could successfully accomplish this destruction."

The French stood to accomplish little with the squadron of old Hellcat night fighters they had in Indochina. Delivery by the light carrier USS *Saipan* to Haiphong of a load of Marine Corsairs, duly transferred to the French aircraft carriers *Arromanches* (formerly HMS *Colossus*) and *Bois Belleau* (the former USS *Belleau Wood*), did little to expand French prospects to hold. However, ninety-eight B-29s were on hand on Okinawa and in the Philippines to drop incendiary weapons on demand. And Phillips's Fair Weather Training Force stood in the Yellow Sea, ready to stun the world. Radford wanted to carry out an atomic strike. To provide the means to accomplish it, the Joint Chiefs transferred the attack carriers *Essex* and *Wasp,* whose air groups had atomic weapons capability, from Naval Forces Far East to Admiral Stump. Stump then gave the carriers and their escorts to Phillips, the commander of the San Diego–based U.S. First Fleet. Phillips flew out to Subic Bay in the Philippines to take tactical command of the Fair Weather Training Force and undertake a series of exercises rehearsing the delivery of "special weapons."

Stump described the situation: "There are some people who felt that it would be very simple for us to have dropped three atomic weapons around the periphery on the far side of the crests of the mountains, which would have wiped out most of the Viet Minh and not done any damage to the French. This attack could have been launched within ten minutes of receiving orders from Washington." The supposed simplicity of this plan might well have been disputed by Lieutenant Commander J. Gallagher and his "Ghosts" of Fleet Composite Squadron 35, Detachment Able, whose AD-4B Skyraiders gave the *Essex* its nuclear strike capability. The onerous climbing maneuver by which a Skyraider lofted a seventeen-hundred-pound Mark 7 atomic device from its reinforced centerline rack, never having been tested live, left little assurance that a pilot's rollover and dive away from the target area he was obliterating would save him from a messy fratricide in the air.

With Dien Bien Phu falling, Eisenhower saw more prudent and defensible ways to stop Communist expansion in Southeast Asia, an untidy collection of current and former European colonies with limited political resilience and capacity for self-defense. Unwilling to commit ground forces in Asia again, Ike saw a collective security framework as the best way forward. The Far East Division of the State Department urged a pact "that would bring in India, Burma and Indonesia, along with the Philippines and Thailand" and allow Asians to bond in anti-communism without their European protectors. "A chain with links of moderate strength is much more useful than a chain with some strong links and some missing links," the Far East hands at State argued, not without merit.

On May 1, 1954, Ike finally took the measure of the Navy's mad atomic strike plan and said to Cutler, his national security assistant, "I certainly do not think that the atomic bomb can be used by the United States unilaterally. You boys must be crazy. We can't use those awful things against Asians for the second time in less than ten years. My God." With this, Phillips's carrier task force returned to the Philippines, and six days later the French garrison at Dien Bien Phu surrendered.

AT THE TIME of *Nautilus*'s launching back in January, the Caribbean Sea Frontier, an area command with bases in San Juan, Trinidad, Guantánamo, and Aruba-Curaçao, had begun running air-sea patrols in the Gulf of Honduras after the leftist government of Guatemala requested arms from the Soviet bloc in reaction to a U.S. decision to give covert support to an antigovernment "liberation" movement. To protect Honduras from invasion and to monitor and regulate arms shipments into the region in violation of the Monroe Doctrine, which had since 1823 warned European powers against meddling in the Western Hemisphere, the United States airlifted arms to Honduras. On May 20, the first Soviet arms shipment arrived in Guatemala. A few days later, the commander in chief of the U.S. Atlantic Fleet ordered a contingency evacuation force into the area comprised of an antisubmarine carrier and five amphibious ships with a Marine battalion embarked. On June 18, the United States announced an arms embargo against Guatemala. The crisis ended eleven days later with a U.S.-backed coup that installed a new government under the dictator Carlos Castillo Armas.

THE CONQUEST OF Dien Bien Phu seemed to embolden Chinese Communist forces near the Nationalist island of Taiwan. In July, Communist aircraft attacked a Seventh Fleet P2V Neptune patrol plane in the Taiwan Strait. Two weeks later the Chinese Communists shot down a British passenger airliner en route from Bangkok to Hong Kong. U.S. First Fleet units raced to the scene to conduct search and rescue operations. Less than a week later, Chinese Communist fighters attacked a flight of U.S. search planes, and at least two Chinese fighters were destroyed.

It was galling to Mao that Chiang Kai-shek's Nationalists, soundly beaten in the civil war, had taken refuge on Taiwan and were receiving diplomatic recognition and military support from the United States. The Nationalists maintained garrisons on some far smaller islands in the Taiwan Strait situated very close to the coast of Communist China, including Quemoy, site of their 1949 stand. While they were named collectively after their largest member, they were also known as the Kinmen Islands or just the Offshore Islands. Chiang, with plenty of U.S. help, had turned Quemoy into a minor fortress. Although defense of the Republic of China, better known as Taiwan, against Communist invasion had been U.S. policy for the better part of two decades— President Truman had declared its neutrality back in 1950, when China was mauling MacArthur in Korea—Washington was bound by no treaty-level commitment to defend the Offshore Islands.

In August 1954, the Taiwan-based Nationalist Republic of China placed fifty-eight thousand troops on the island of Quemoy and another fifteen thousand at Matsu, building defenses. On September 3, Communist Chinese forces massed on the facing coast of China bombarded the U.S.-supported Nationalist-held redoubt with heavy artillery, killing two U.S. Army colonels who were stationed there with the U.S. Military Assistance Advisory Group. Nationalist guns responded in kind as the garrison braced for an invasion. Within the U.S. Joint Chiefs, discussions again turned to employment of nuclear weapons. Eisenhower refused the nuclear option just as he had with Dien Bien Phu months before.

In January 1955, a House Joint Resolution gave congressional authorization to step up American commitment for U.S. forces to protect Taiwan against attack. Seventh Fleet forces patrolled the strait thereafter.

ON DECEMBER 11, 1954, the festive day of the USS *Forrestal*'s christening at Norfolk's shipway number 11, fifteen thousand spectators were in attendance to see the largest seagoing vessel ever made by man slide into the harbor. James Forrestal's widow, having shattered the customary bottle of champagne against her bow, watched the Blue Angels demonstration team flying F9F Panthers trail red, white, and blue smoke over the ship. A sense of the future prevailed.

It was increasingly clear that U.S. naval forces needed the capability to perform a permanent transoceanic mission. The Harvard professor and political strategist Samuel Huntington saw that "a world divided into one major land power and one major sea power is different from a world divided among a number of rival sea powers." "The new doctrine of the Transoceanic Navy," he wrote, "required a robust interpretation of the traditional power-projection mission by a fleet oriented towards the land masses on the far side of the nation's boundary seas.

"Command of land could be asserted from the sea," Huntington argued. "The locale of decisive action has switched from the sea to land: not the inner heart of the land mass, to be sure, but rather to the coastal area," portending a "drastic change in the mission of the Navy," all of it part and parcel of the Korean "police action" on the far side of the world and the further entanglements that threatened to arise from it.

CNO Robert Carney's insistence on maintaining a private, secure communications link with Admiral Stump at Pearl Harbor and also the right to counsel the president as his chief naval adviser—a role that Eisenhower explicitly endorsed—bothered Defense Secretary Wilson, and he declined to reappoint Carney at the end of his two-year term in the spring of 1955. On May 10, Charles Thomas offered the Chief of Naval Operations position to Rear Admiral Arleigh Burke. Burke was startled and dismayed by the offer, for he knew there were ninety-two active duty flag officers senior to him on the Navy Register, more than eighty of whom were potential candidates for the post, and he thought his sudden rise might hurt department morale. Burke did not top anyone's list of candidates. But he was on everyone's list.

No admiral in the twentieth century had spent more time contemplating and practicing strong, effective leadership than Arleigh Albert Burke. An outstanding destroyer combat commander whose willingness to delegate command to subordinates led to a string of victories in the South Pacific in 1943, Burke had completed a total reassessment of the surface warfare tactics employed in the night actions off Guadalcanal the previous year. The fruit of his study were his victories in the Battles of Empress Augusta Bay and Cape St. George, earning him the Navy Cross and the only Presidential Unit Citation awarded to an entire destroyer squadron. Burke completed his glittering war record as Vice Admiral Marc Mitscher's chief of staff in Task Force 58—a fast-carrier task force, the heart of the Pacific Fleet—during the Navy's great Central Pacific offensive, making him one of the first surface officers to master naval aviation's operational intricacies. He served smartly in Korea in major staff and diplomatic postings, concluding with an education in diplomacy as part of the negotiating team that worked out the armistice with the Chinese and North Koreans.

All this had been a heady life for the son of a humble Colorado farmer, but he had taken integrity, self-discipline, and strong principles from his father and his mother, a teacher. In 1923, the year he graduated from the U.S. Naval Academy, the faculty had just compiled the first textbook on naval leadership. It listed the "essential qualities" of a naval officer as personal dignity, honor, courage, truthfulness, faith, justice, earnestness, assiduity, judgment, perseverance, tact, self-control, simplicity, and loyalty—to country and to service, to both one's seniors and juniors. "Loyalty up and down was important because of the natural independence and self-reliance of the American sailor," and naval officers had to earn the respect of their men through their personal merit and example. Burke had been trained as a specialist in ordnance, earning a master's degree in chemical engineering and becoming a design and production specialist in explosives. This background exposed Burke to the most advanced naval technologies of his time and would prepare him as CNO to promote the development of nuclear weapons, nuclear power, and guided and ballistic missiles.

Meeting with Secretary of Defense Wilson soon after his appointment, Burke admitted he had a bad habit of speaking his mind. But Wilson and most everyone in the Navy thought well of his accomplishments, and Burke was quickly approved to become the fifteenth Chief of Naval Operations.

But Burke quickly got crossways with Thomas and Wilson over the issue of the draft. Burke considered compulsory service the best way for the Navy to meet its manpower goals in the face of declining enlistments and retention after the war, even as the administration was announcing that the draft would not be reinstated. He requested an Oval Office meeting to make his case. He did so, and Eisenhower agreed to reverse his decision, but afterward he warned Burke never again to put him in such an embarrassing position. Eventually the president developed a warm relationship of trust with his willful top naval honcho.

Where Burke made his name was in driving major technology innovation. First off, he well understood the power of a force of nature on the loose. He backed Hyman Rickover's effort to will naval nuclear propulsion into being. Burke announced that two more nuclear submarines would be included in the 1956 shipbuilding plan and, moreover, that all new submarines would be nuclear-propelled. He also directed a study of using nuclear propulsion in frigates, cruisers, and aircraft carriers. Nuclear power was the future: On May 10, 1955, the same day Arleigh Burke was offered the CNO role, the world's first atomic submarine departed her home waters of Long Island Sound and headed south for a shakedown cruise. The *Nautilus* made the run to San Juan, Puerto Rico—1,381 nautical miles—in less than ninety hours, maintaining a record-setting submerged speed of more than fifteen knots.

24

THE GADGETEERS

IN 1952, LIEUTENANT WALLY SCHIRRA SHOWED UP AT NAVAL
Ordnance Test Station China Lake in Southern California, deeply disappointed to have been given a job in the desert. He had wanted a slot as a test pilot at Maryland's Patuxent River Naval Air Station. That was the hot stuff, and having flown ninety combat missions in Korea, he felt he deserved it. The China Lake base experimental officer, Commander Tom Moorer, hearing the young pilot's lament, pulled him aside and explained that the fighter pilot's life wasn't what it used to be. Machine guns and cannons were becoming obsolete. A new day was coming, Moorer said. He showed Schirra to a complex of buildings housing the station's test laboratories. The duo entered one where a couple of scientists were working on a small glass dome that, Moorer explained, had been designed to be mounted on the tip of a rocket. As he walked across the room, Schirra noticed that the mechanical eyeball was tracking him—or rather, the burning ember at the tip of the cigarette in his hand. Seeing his surprise, Moorer smiled and said, "This is your new toy." A new toy that almost destroyed the future Mercury, Gemini, and Apollo astronaut's own aircraft when Schirra later test-fired and was forced to outfly it.

A design team at the station was making fast progress on an infrared heat-tracking missile known as the Sidewinder. Initially known as "the weapon nobody asked for," it became one of the most lethal and cost-effective missiles ever built. But early test firings of the new device had produced mixed results. An Air Force detachment was providing remote-controlled B-17 Flying Fortress bombers for use as targets in the tests. In a January trial, the missile tracked the hot exhaust of the drone's number one engine, but it failed to hit or detonate by action of its radar-activated proximity fuze. The Sidewinder did come close enough to pass within the radius of the propeller. An explosion of sparks was produced as the blade hacked into the missile, destroying it and leaving the famously durable bomber lumbering along with a broken propeller. For the February test, the Air Force drone technicians turned over the aircraft to the Navy guys with a dismissive attitude— "Go ahead, knock yourselves out." They scoffed at the undersized Sidewinder—a toy indeed, it appeared—doubting that it would do any serious damage to the famously stout four-engine aircraft.

"Sure enough, we clobbered the thing," a Navy technician remembered. "It was a very dramatic thing with all kinds of cartwheels, flames, and engines flying off. It went on and on and on and we thought the [plane] would never hit the ground."

That week a telegram had arrived at China Lake from the Pentagon stating that it had been proved that infrared homing would never work. Following the successful test, the telegram was pinned up on the bulletin board in the Sidewinder development team's main lab. After the films of the B-17 shootdown were taken to Washington, however, the telegram mysteriously disappeared, as did the skepticism that had provided the impetus for its composition and dispatch. The principal objective in air-to-air warfare, as the Pentagon saw it, was killing Soviet bombers. The 3M Myasishchev M-4 Molot (Bison-B), the successor to the M-4, and the Tupolev 95M Bear were the first Soviet bombers with intercontinental reach. The new trick would be to ensure that the likes of Wally Schirra didn't end up with the missile chasing the firing plane's heat signature in the process.

As head of the aviation ordnance division, the Navy physicist William Burdette McLean found himself immersed in air-to-air fire-control problems. The most critical one was how to engage, target, and destroy a Soviet bomber armed with atomic weapons. Long-range missiles were seen as the answer. A huge Air Force radar tracking system was in place to vector fighters to the path of incoming enemy bombers, using radar and all-weather radar-guided missiles to intercept and kill them from a long distance.

The first missile designed for the task was the radar-guided AIM-4 Falcon. The Hughes Aircraft Company was the principal contractor for the missile. Convair produced the supersonic fighter designed to carry it, the F-102 Delta Dagger. Introduced in April 1956, the Dagger was widely purchased by the Air Force, which bought about a thousand of them. One feature of the new jet was typical of the new generation of fighters: It lacked a gun. The Dagger was a disappointment to those who wanted actual supersonic performance, but that summer, two hundred Sidewinders were sent to the fleet for testing by the first two Navy squadrons to receive the missile. Commander Glenn Tierney, a test pilot stationed at China Lake, articulated the new paradigm in air combat. "Fighter pilots," he said, "are only chauffeurs whose job it is to deliver the ordnance into the enemy." The Sidewinder, with its "fire-and-forget" capability, contributed to the transformation arising from the fact that missiles could be independent killers. General Gordon P. Saville, who had helped write the specifications that led to the creation of the P-38 Lightning and the F-86 Sabre and who had encouraged the Hughes contract for the Falcon missile, was the authority on air defense in the U.S. Air Force. In his view, the dexterity of the dogfight—"air combat maneuvering," as it was formally known—had been overtaken by missile technology. The Red Baron's art, carried forward by the likes of Butch O'Hare, Dick Bong, Paddy Finucane, Erich Hartmann, and David McCampbell, was passing into history, Saville and others thought.

Dr. McLean, the head of the Sidewinder development team, was a leading naval scientist of his day. The son of a Presbyterian minister from Portland, Oregon, a world-class tinkerer, he was taught by his mother to knit, crochet, and sew before he went to kindergarten. From his father he learned to fix cars and repair household plumbing and electricity, and the habit of frugality, which became deeply ingrained. He felt an "overwhelming" attraction to simplicity in design, a colleague said. He had thrived at Caltech, studying electrical engineering, then physics, and rolling straight into the Ph.D. program after commencement. Entering the Navy during the war as an ordnance specialist, McLean eventually recruited his Navy weapons team from the school. He became China Lake's technical director in 1954.

McLean had seen as early as 1946 that the fire-control system on a missile should not be external to it. It should not be dependent upon a tracking system housed in the aircraft that carried it. The early AIM-4 Falcon and AIM-7 Sparrow missiles relied on a tracking system in the airplane to keep a fix on its target as the pilot maintained contact and illuminated the target with radar. However, a system contained inside a missile would have to be small, and light. McLean designed the Sidewinder to use a lead sulfide photocell to detect infrared radiation. The sensor was linked to a gyroscope that produced electrical signals that turned the missile's fins to keep its axis aligned to the point of heat representing the target. The simplicity of the system accounted for its light weight, which in turn permitted the use of a warhead in the Sidewinder large enough to produce a thirty-foot kill radius. The Falcon missile would fail because its guidance system was complex and therefore heavy, leaving no room for a warhead large enough to enable a kill by proximity. The Falcon had to actually hit its target to bring it down.

Working on fuzes and ordnance-arming mechanisms taught Bill McLean about design in the context of the imperatives of affordable production. Reliability of better than 90 percent was always the physicist's goal. Good design involved minimizing the number of parts and maximizing a mechanism's reliability. The result, manifesting in the Sidewinder missile, was one of the most efficient weapon systems in Pentagon history.

In spite of opposition from the Air Force, McLean benefited from the fact that a brilliant gadgeteer will generally recognize a gadget whose time has come. After Deak Parsons, the weapons scientist who armed the Little Boy atomic bomb in flight to Hiroshima, visited China Lake and met with McLean, Captain Parsons's agency, the Navy Bureau of Ordnance, granted the Sidewinder project $3.5 million to develop it as a fleet weapon. BuOrd also saw fit to transfer authority over the weapon's development from Washington to China Lake, allowing McLean and his fellow gadgeteers to gain full control of their project.

In the summer of 1956, two hundred Sidewinders were tested at sea by the first two Navy squadrons earmarked to receive the missile: the USS *Randolph*'s Attack Squadron 46, which flew the F9F Cougar, and Fighter Squadron 211, flying FJ Furys in the Pacific, from the USS *Bonhomme Richard*. The new missile's lethality could not be denied. The results, demonstrating a single-shot kill probability greater than 60 percent, so pleased Admiral Burke that squadrons operating from all of America's fifteen attack carriers were soon equipped with Sidewinders. The Navy eventually purchased thirty-five hundred of the first-generation version. By late 1957, nineteen Navy and seven Marine squadrons were diversely equipped with jets carrying the new missile. Many more were sold on the export market. The British, Swedes, and Norwegians were enthusiastic purchasers, and demand soared after the Taiwanese proved themselves so adept as "chauffeurs," delivering Sidewinders to their Russian-trained Chinese counterparts over the Taiwan Strait. The missile edge in aerial warfare had come to stay.

The Sidewinder's success compensated for the fact that the naval aviation community had not been able to embrace a standard air superiority fighter since the F6F Hellcat was adopted in 1943. The F2H Banshee, FJ-1 Fury, F3H Demon, F7U Cutlass, F10F Jaguar—all suffered from various technical and handling problems, none possessing the power or versatility to merit fleetwide adoption. The trend toward reduced pure aerodynamic performance, a loadout of missiles, and reliance upon radar systems operated by a second aviator known as a RIO, or radar-intercept officer, who would wage aerial combat beyond visual range with his head down, looking at a radar screen, seemed to peak with the Douglas F6D Missileer. A multiengine, missile-flinging "fleet defense fighter" that more resembled a light bomber or patrol plane than a fighter, it was terminated in the development stage before any were delivered to the fleet.

Pilots who flew jets powered by a single engine developed a special relationship with the aircraft. According to a veteran naval aviator, "In a car, when your engine quits, you roll to the side of the road, curse a bit, and get out and walk. In a small light airplane, when the propeller stops propelling, you pick a good hayfield and glide to a rough, but rarely fatal, return to terra firma. In any multiengine plane, the chances of losing all the power at the same time are minuscule (unless of course you run out of gas, which is your own damn fault anyway). In the single-engine fighter, when the engine quits, you are immediately in very serious trouble. You either get the fire lit off again—now!—or you have to get out, using a Rube Goldberg ejection seat and a parachute. There is no such thing as a nonfatal crash landing in high-performance jet fighters. They glide like proverbial bricks, and their light aluminum noses are lousy crash barriers."

The aviator went on: "Like a pro quarterback with a game knee, if [a pilot] starts thinking about his engine's reliability, he'll favor it. In so doing, he'll give up an advantage to his enemy, and he'll lose. So fighter pilots, particularly the single-engine types, really worship the engine that never quits, that grumbles ever so slightly when badly abused, that gives immediate responses to power demands, and that always brings him home no matter how worn, tired, or shot up it may be."

The next single-engine jet fighter after the F9F Panther that really satisfied its operators on that critical score was the Vought F8U Crusader. Against the grain of modernity, the aircraft retained a 20 mm cannon as its primary armament and was fitted to carry the Sidewinder as well, and would use it profitably. Long and sleek, with short, swept wings, and distinguished by the gape-mouthed air intake in its nose, the Crusader came into service in mid-1958, having prevailed in a Navy design competition. Powered by a single Pratt & Whitney J57 turbojet, it had the ability to climb straight up and exceed a thousand miles per hour in level flight.

However, early in 1958, Arleigh Burke let it be known that he favored development of another design contest winner, the McDonnell Douglas F4H Phantom, as the successor to the F3H Demon in the role of the Navy's principal general-purpose fighter. Underpowered and awkward to fly, the Demon was unpopular with naval aviators. A test pilot said it "looked ugly, flew badly, and was a menace anywhere near a carrier deck."

The final evolution of the Crusader was the F8U-3 Crusader III, a redesign that bore little resemblance to its predecessor. With blazing speed, easily capable of Mach 2 flight, the single-seat fighter put a heavy burden on the pilot to fly while managing the radar illumination necessary to using Sparrow missiles. The aircraft that emerged as its rival, the McDonnell Douglas F4H-1, had a dedicated radar-intercept officer in a rear seat and was also capable of performing attack missions with a large payload of air-to-ground munitions.

Planning the fiscal 1959 budget, the House Armed Services Committee forced the Navy's hand, and the Navy chose the F4H-1. With the pilot spared the distraction of operating his sensors and weapon systems, he was free simply to fly the plane. By virtue of being free to concentrate on his radar, the RIO, it was estimated, would be able to detect bogies at 50 percent greater ranges. With further improvements, the F4H would evolve into the F-4 Phantom II, powered by a pair of powerful J79 engines, capable of Mach 2 speed, armed with a quiver of four Sparrow and four Sidewinder missiles, and able to carry 18,000 pounds (8,100 kilograms) of bombs. The plane first flew in May 1958 and began carrier suitability trials the following year. McDonnell-Douglas would produce it in great numbers for the Navy and the Air Force, and once again, with its arrival, and with the advent of the A4D, later A-4 Skyhawk light bomber—small, lightweight, and capable of carrying an improbably large bomb load, as a complementary aircraft for the strike squadrons—stability returned to the composition of American carrier air wings.

THE NAVY'S EFFORTS to deploy nuclear weapons at sea in the early fifties confronted a series of challenges, of both physics and politics. The Air Force had insisted on exclusive ownership of "strategic" missions—heavy attack capability against hostile state industry and infrastructure. For years that service's multiengine bombers were the only vehicles capable of delivering five-ton atomic weapons. As the AEC continued to innovate, the development of smaller warheads opened up further possibilities. Chagrined at the Navy's inability to take down the Yalu River bridges in Korea, Arthur Radford, Commander of the U.S. Pacific Fleet, ordered priority development of a Navy "heavy attack" capability.

The services seized on the German innovation of the V-1 "buzz bomb," the world's first cruise missile. Nazi Germany's terror campaign launched against England from missile sites in northern France in 1944 inspired the Navy to explore development of a program of remote-controlled "assault drones." Though the ambition to fly bomb-laden F6F Hellcats into ground targets by remote guidance would fail in Korea, the technology of TV camera remote control survived to inspire an evolution. Before World War II was over, the Navy and Army air forces had built nearly fourteen hundred near replicas of Germany's V-1. The Republic-Ford JB-2 (Jet Bomb) missile, later adopted by the Navy as the LTV-N-2 Loon cruise missile, was to be unleashed during the invasion of Japan from the decks of small escort carriers and amphibious landing ships.

After the war, further development of sea-based missilery revealed that the best platform for a naval cruise missile was a submarine. Even just partially submerged, it offered a more stable platform for a launch than any surface ship could. The converted World War II fleet submarines *Cusk* and *Carbonero* had been test-firing pulsejet-propelled Loon surface-to-surface missiles since 1948. The requirement that the firing submarine operate with two other subs that provided radar tracking and radio missile guidance made for an operationally brittle system. Compounding its impracticality was the underlying inaccuracy of the submarine-launched assault missile (SLAM) system. Fired from sixty miles offshore, the Loon was shown to have just a 40 percent chance of landing within a mile of its target, insufficient to destroy hardened military or small tactical targets. Better results were too much to hope for from a directed weapon with no terminal guidance. The future of the Navy's SLAM program would evolve from the adoption of an altogether new strategic weapon, the Regulus missile.

More a pilotless aircraft than a guided missile—also known as a "jet-propelled assault drone"—Regulus was well suited to carry a miniaturized atomic warhead. In June 1949, Admiral Dan Gallery, the assistant

CNO for guided missiles, asked the Navy Department's AEC division for a fission warhead suitable for Regulus. On July 19, Congress authorized an expenditure of $3 billion to expand the Atomic Energy Commission's capacity to build nuclear weapons, opening a new gaseous diffusion plant in the Ohio River Valley to separate fissionable U-235. The purpose of the initiative was to develop a new "family" of atomic weapons suitable for use by a variety of air and naval delivery systems— like the *Forrestal*. When Navy Secretary Charles M. Thomas presided at the ship's launching on December 11, he called her the "country's most versatile and most dispersable weapon in our nuclear arsenal." The top U.S. naval commander in the Mediterranean, Admiral Robert B. Carney, called her "the unstoppable power of a great free society."

To arm the new missile, the weapons wizards at Los Alamos produced a one-and-a-half-ton warhead known as the W-8 or "Elsie." Regulus would use radar guidance to deliver it to within cratering radius of its target, remote detonated by a pilot flying a guidance aircraft. In February 1955 the cruiser USS *Los Angeles* took Regulus to sea in its scout plane hangar, but the SLAM's future was in submarines.

The new system promised to cure the defects of existing modes of atomic strike. The AD Skyraider was too slow, vulnerable to the merest piston-driven Yak. The F2H Banshee and F9F Cougar were decent fighter-bombers but performed poorly fully laden with a heavy nuclear payload. The AJ-1 Savage was difficult to operate from carriers. But a Regulus missile hauling a high-yield Elsie warhead could deliver an atomic blow at the speed of an Air Force F-86 fighter. Two cooperating guidance submarines, activating an electronic grid system, would guide the missile into a vertical dive from thirty-five thousand feet, to detonate at a preset altitude. The need for a retinue of guidance boats made it a daylight-only fair-weather system.

In March 1953, the submarine USS *Tunny* (SSG-282), with a pair of Regulus I nuclear cruise missiles stowed in her oversized topside hangar, became the first sub to deploy on a nuclear deterrence mission. While the Regulus system advanced the fleet's capability in the heavy-attack mission, and the first carrier-capable jet-powered strategic bomber, the Douglas A-3 Skywarrior, was to begin equipping Heavy

Attack Wings based at North Island, San Diego, Whidbey Island, Washington, and Jacksonville, Florida. In December 1957, the Navy's larger ambition was to field a proper ballistic missile—a program called Polaris.

Arleigh Burke had been an early backer of Hyman G. Rickover as he took on the Navy's engineering establishment while pushing for the fastest possible development and adoption of nuclear propulsion, but the chief's most important personnel decision may have been to place Rear Admiral William F. "Red" Raborn in charge of OPNAV's Office of Special Projects, which upon its founding in 1955 was given cognizance over the Polaris submarine-launched ballistic missile project.

The primacy of Polaris within the Navy and the CNO ensured that Raborn and his crew would have whatever they needed—be it money, matériel, or people. Aiming to deliver the system on time and under budget, Burke tried to keep the willful and meddling Rickover from having any direct involvement with Polaris. The Naval Reactors boss seemed likely to assert his clout over the important and prestigious new submarine-based weapon, for Rickover always had a lot to say about how his nuclear-propelled vessels were tinkered with and employed.

Raborn reported directly to Arleigh Burke and Secretary of the Navy Charles Thomas. Raborn was directed to have the new system ready with "interim capability" by early 1963 and full capability by early 1965. The first-generation Polaris A1 missile was supposed to have enough specific impulse—thrust over time per unit of weight—to carry a lightweight (six-hundred-pound), high-yield (half- to one-megaton) nuclear warhead about fourteen hundred miles. If the inertial navigation system could pinpoint the location of the firing submarine to within a three-mile radius, a high level of missile accuracy could be achieved: a "circular error probable" (CEP)—the mean radius of a circle whose boundary is expected to include the landing points of 50 percent of the shots—of a little more than a mile.

In November of that year, Secretary of Defense Charles E. Wilson directed the Navy to partner with the Army in developing the Jupiter intermediate-range ballistic missile for naval use. Wilson wanted Jupiter deployed on surface ships by 1960, and possibly in submarines by 1965. What unnerved naval officers most about the idea was the missile's means of propulsion: liquid fuel. The requirement to store, handle, and fuel the missile at sea prior to launch opened up diverse disastrous contingencies aboard ship. The smallest mishap in pouring the easily combustible fuel mixture of liquid oxygen and kerosene on a pitching deck could destroy a ship. Burke and his colleagues saw potential for a submarine-launched ballistic missile driven by solid propellant. The trick would be to find a formula that produced enough specific impulse to carry aloft from underwater a warhead of a reasonable size. On November 15, 1955, the Navy established its Special Projects Office (SPO) to lead the effort to develop the Polaris system. Rear Admiral William "Red" Raborn was named its director.

Born in Decatur, Texas, in 1905, Raborn attended the U.S. Naval Academy, graduating in 1928. Having directed the Gunnery Training Section at the Bureau of Aeronautics during World War II, he subsequently served in the Pacific on aircraft carriers. He was the executive officer of the carrier USS *Hancock* when her deck was hit by a kamikaze. He later had command of the escort carrier *Bairoko* and fast fleet carrier *Bennington,* where he was praised for his performance during a disastrous fire that killed ninety-one of his shipmates. He had a reputation as a technologist, a thinker, a tinkerer, and an enthusiast. "Colorfully Texan in his speech," according to *The New York Times,* he was unsurpassed for his human touch, understanding what was needed to motivate a team.

Burke was all in on supporting the plan for a submarine-launched ballistic missile revolution. It was a fundamental part of the New Look, which was defined by technological progress and evolving flexible offensive nuclear capabilities. He was willing to give up a planned second nuclear-powered aircraft carrier in the 1958 shipbuilding plan to secure more submarines. The first, the USS *Enterprise* (CVN-65), was to begin construction at Newport News in 1958. Burke deleted a second *Enterprise*-class flattop in return for an additional Polaris submarine plus an atomic-powered attack submarine in the budget.

Raborn was the Navy's foremost expert on rocketry, a field that crossed the boundary between the disciplines of aviation and ordnance. Burke thought Raborn's status as a naval aviator would insulate the Polaris program from bureaucratic attack by the carrier aviation partisans, who were eager to have their own capability in atomic strike warfare. With Raborn at the helm, Polaris was on the horizon.

25

TROUBLE IN THE SUEZ

As Mao continued his expansion into Indochina, the United States and Taiwan agreed to the Sino-American Mutual Defense Treaty, in response to the Chinese bombardment of Quemoy, also known as Kinmen. Ratified by the Senate in February 1954, it did not guarantee protection for Quemoy or the other Nationalist islands in the Strait close to the mainland.

In his inaugural address, Eisenhower had said, "We must be ready to dare all for our country. For history does not long entrust the care of freedom to the weak or the timid. We must acquire proficiency in defense and display stamina in purpose." Yet fiscal caution and prudence would turn out to be a fundamental part of Eisenhower's approach to "waging peace" during the Cold War.

Economic slowdown late in 1953, the result of the transition from the Korean War and its heavy military spending, produced a recession in 1954. The following year saw a boom, with unemployment falling from 5.6 percent to 4.4 percent, and disposable personal income rose 3.8 percent annually through the midfifties. Eisenhower feared not only that large deficit spending would push the country toward socialism, but that easily available credit would increase prices and wages, bringing about inflation and a devaluation of the dollar. With the world financial system based on the gold-backed U.S. currency, system stability depended on its soundness. As the calendar turned to 1956, questions were raised for the first time in the postwar era about the United States' ability to sustain its position as the economic leader of the world.

Eisenhower had reduced Truman's last budget for fiscal 1954 from $78.6 billion to $64.4 billion for fiscal 1955, in part by realizing savings following the end of the Korean War. He now based his reelection campaign on promises to shore up the nation's foundational economic strength by reducing the federal debt and balancing the budget, to the extent of taking an active part in setting the Pentagon's budget. Intending to hold defense spending for fiscal 1958 at $38 billion, with authorizations for future spending capped to $38.5 billion, the president demanded that the Navy slow its ambitions to build nuclear-powered aircraft carriers of the *Enterprise* class to one every other year instead of one every year. As of June 1956, Burke presided over a 670,000-man Navy, among 2.8 million men under arms in all services, with 404 major combatant ships and 14 CVAs (aircraft carriers). The principal task of all those assets remained the not inconsequential matter of containing the Soviet Union—the fundamental U.S. foreign policy aim dating back to George F. Kennan and James Forrestal. Of all the places in the world that Eisenhower meant to practice containment with some urgency, the Middle East and the Mediterranean were near the top of the list. The risk of a world conflict starting there over the problems of oil and/or Israel had been Forrestal's nightmare scenario.

Enduring the rigors of his reelection campaign in 1956, having suffered a heart attack and a debilitating bout of chronic ileitis (an inflammation of the small intestine), the West's leading cold warrior received another sizable shock: The State Department informed him in September that the Russians, acting through the government of Czechoslovakia, had sold Egypt as much as $200 billion worth of arms, including hundreds of armored vehicles, artillery pieces, and two hundred aircraft, among them a squadron of MiG-15 jet fighters.

It appeared that the Soviets were bent on securing a new client state that had a dominant position in the eastern Mediterranean, valuable bases and ports, and the ability to command one of the most valuable waterways in the world, the Suez Canal. This news was followed by a report that the Soviets had offered to finance an enormous public works project in Egypt, the Aswan High Dam, which would capture the waters of the Nile River for irrigation of new cotton-growing farmland and high-volume hydroelectric generation to promote industrialization and an improved standard of living.

In response, Eisenhower dispatched Secretary of State Dulles at once to Geneva to meet with Egyptian president Abdel Gamal Nasser and the British foreign secretary, Harold Macmillan. Nasser's willingness to explore a deal with the West seemed to present the Atlantic powers with an opportunity to block the Soviet encroachment into the eastern Mediterranean.

As for Egypt, Nasser's ambitions were not attached to the superpower rivalry on its own terms. His goal was to check, and possibly destroy, Israel by forming a pan-Arabic league, which he would lead by virtue of his high standing after parleying shrewdly with the two superpowers. Dulles and Macmillan proposed to work with the World Bank to finance construction of the dam in return for Egypt's help in striking a peace settlement with Israel, whose commandos had been clashing with Egyptian guerrillas—known as fedayeen—in Gaza. Nasser fancied Egypt a neutral nation in the Cold War. He also encouraged neutralism on the part of nations such as India and Yugoslavia. In May 1956, when he conferred diplomatic recognition upon Communist China, Washington was outraged.

On July 26, 1956, Egypt fired the first broadside in a developing regional brushfire war that, not unlike the one recently concluded in Korea, had the potential to escalate into a superpower conflict. A week after Washington, irritated by what it viewed as Egyptian duplicity in acquiring weapons from the Soviets, rescinded its offer to finance the dam project, Nasser, in humiliation, retaliated by seizing or "nationalizing" the joint British-French-run company that had owned and operated the Suez Canal since its construction in 1869, offering his estimation of its market value as compensation. The Eisenhower team appeared satisfied and arrived at a legalistic view of what Egypt had done, viewing its taking of the canal as a case of eminent domain, little different from a rural county's seizing ranch frontage to build a new superhighway, lawful so long as a fair price was paid.

Great Britain and France, however, were outraged. Britain was not about to tolerate Egypt's brash move. In 1955, nearly fifteen thousand ships had passed through the canal, of which roughly one-third were British oil tankers. Two-thirds of Britain's crude oil imports traversed the canal. France had long been suspicious of Nasser for his machinations against their influence in the region, most notably in Algeria, where a determined insurgency was under way.

Though Eisenhower warned the new prime minister, Anthony Eden, against taking military action, Eden insisted on immediate military operations to retake the canal. Winston Churchill, too, saw a need to be decisive. Referring to Nasser, he said, "We cannot have that malicious swine sitting across our communications."

Equally adamant that Nasser's move presented a strategic threat was the State of Israel. Prime Minister David Ben-Gurion was looking for an opportunity to cut the Egyptian president down to size by using the great strength of the Israel Defense Force. Conferring secretly with French prime minister Guy Mollet and Eden, who viewed Nasser as a blustering, dangerous "Hitler on the Nile," Ben-Gurion intended to turn loose Lieutenant General Moshe Dayan's assault forces as part of an understanding with the two Western powers.

In the first week of August, the light carrier HMS *Theseus* departed Portsmouth embarking the Sixteenth Independent Parachute Brigade. General Sir Charles Keightley, commander in chief of British Land Forces Middle East, was tapped as Supreme Allied commander; Vice Admiral Pierre d'Escadre, the aptly named ("of the squadron") commander in chief of the French Mediterranean Fleet, was appointed his deputy.

Ike dispatched Secretary of State Dulles to London on August 15 to join a twenty-two-nation conference whose mission was to find a peaceful settlement. A U.S. proposal to put operation of the Suez Canal under a public international authority, while also recognizing Egypt's sovereign rights over the land containing the facility, was accepted by the conference with slight amendment. But Egypt did not accept the proposal, so it could not be put into effect.

Dulles and Eisenhower still thought war had been averted, and most Americans seemed to agree. According to a September 28 Gallup poll, 55 percent opposed the deployment of U.S. armed forces to the Middle East if war started, while 46 percent believed that the conflict over Suez constituted the most serious current threat to the United States.

THAT SAME MONTH, on the twenty-fifth, Admiral Burke flew to Woods Hole, Massachusetts, to join an entourage of Pentagon brass that included Rear Admiral Pete Galantin, the director of submarine/antisubmarine warfare, Rear Admiral F. B. Warder, and Burke's aide, Thomas R. Weschler. The National Academy of Sciences and the Committee on Undersea Warfare, chaired by the president of Pennsylvania State University, Dr. Eric Walker, cosponsored a summer symposium on the USSR's submarine capability and potential antisubmarine concepts to meet it. Another prominent speaker at the conference, which became known as Project Nobska, after the nearby lighthouse, was the head of the Woods Hole Oceanographic Institution, Dr. Columbus O'Donnell Iselin. His presentation on "The implications of advanced design on undersea warfare" assessed the potential threat of Soviet nuclear-powered ballistic missile submarines, which were assumed to be not far behind the advanced American effort. The United States, Iselin and others urged, needed to make greater use of the submarine in antisubmarine missions.

In September, Walker's committee presented their conclusions to Admiral Burke and most of his top staff. "To the dismay of carrier-strike-warfare zealots," wrote Admiral Galantin, a leading submariner, "the committee made a very good case the submarines could provide the cheapest, most effective means of naval strategic nuclear weapons delivery. It went on to recommend that the Navy appraise its capacity to carry out its primary mission: sea control—meaning a greater emphasis on anti-submarine warfare."

The tactical innovations that arose from Project Nobska were highly classified and were the province of Submarine Development Group

Two in New London. That outfit's chief of staff, Philip Beshany, believed the advanced new attack submarine known as the 594 class, after the hull number of its lead ship, USS *Permit,* then under construction at Mare Island Naval Shipyard in Vallejo, California, had great potential as an antisubmarine weapon. To kill a submarine, one had best be operating in its own medium—underwater. The development group would pioneer the use of advanced trainers capable of simulating highly structured and controlled submarine warfare exercises, using computers to collect data and analyze it.

MEANWHILE, IN THE Middle East, a mounting Israeli military mobilization in the Sinai had been sniffed out by a U-2 surveillance aircraft. After British diplomats told Dulles that they knew nothing of it, America's chief diplomat detected chicanery afoot, calling the poker-faced British demurrals "a form of ignorance that is almost a sign of a guilty conscience." Heavy message traffic between Paris and Tel Aviv suggested French collusion in the Israeli planning, though Eisenhower suspected Israel was planning to attack another neighbor, Jordan, not Egypt.

On October 29, Israeli paratroopers and mechanized forces entered Egypt's Sinai Peninsula in the strength of six brigades, swiftly effecting a victory and occupation, advancing to the banks of the canal. French and British paratroopers arrived there a few days later, supported by aircraft from Royal Navy carriers HMS *Eagle, Bulwark, Ocean,* and *Albion* as well as bombers based on Malta and Cyprus. An amphibious force was on the attack too, bringing major elements of two infantry divisions, each with a regiment of forty-eight Centurion main battle tanks. Major French naval combatants were the light carriers *Arromanches* and *La Fayette* embarking Corsairs and Avengers, and the storied World War II battleship *Jean Bart,* with a fifteen-inch main battery.

As events on the ground became more kinetic, Eisenhower was relieved to learn from U-2 flights that no Soviet fighter aircraft were in Syria. The flights also revealed a French-Israeli conspiracy to undermine previous agreements against shipping excessive quantities of arms

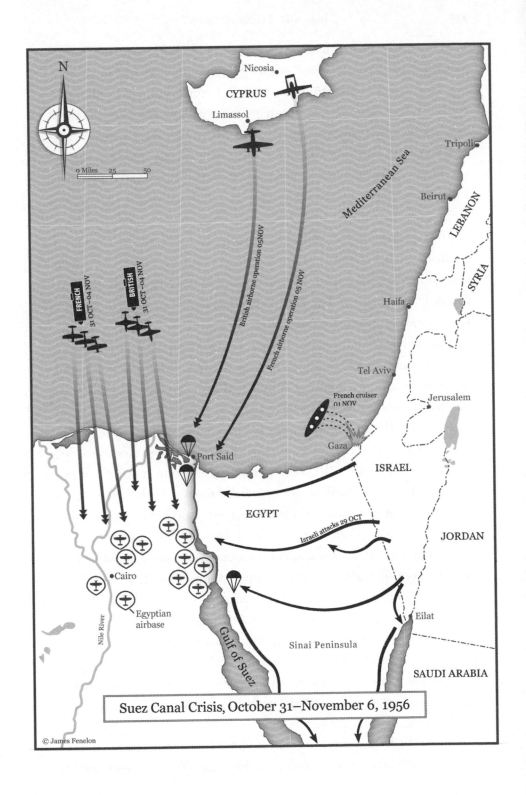

N

CYPRUS
Nicosia
Limassol

Mediterranean Sea

Tripoli
Beirut
LEBANON
SYRIA
Haifa
Tel Aviv
Jerusalem

0 Miles 25 50

FRENCH
31 OCT – 04 NOV

BRITISH
31 OCT – 04 NOV

British airborne operation 05NOV

French airborne operation 05 NOV

French cruiser
01 NOV

Gaza

Port Said

ISRAEL

EGYPT

Israeli attacks 29 OCT

JORDAN

Cairo

Egyptian
airbase

Eilat

Nile River

Gulf of Suez

Sinai Peninsula

SAUDI ARABIA

Suez Canal Crisis, October 31–November 6, 1956

© James Fenelon

to the Middle East. Israeli airfields boasted a far larger number of French-made Dassault Mystère jet fighter-bombers than Eisenhower expected to find. Meanwhile, the National Security Agency's SIGINT collectors had vacuumed up unusually heavy radio traffic between Britain and France. Transmissions between Paris and Tel Aviv were heavy in the last two weeks of October as well. Ike saw that if the Soviets responded to three nations ganging up on Egypt by sending in its own forces to secure or seize Middle Eastern oil, the United States would face a grave threat.

On October 28, the State Department had conveyed to Admiral Radford its belief that hostilities were imminent. Radford in turn wanted to "put the entire world on notice that we are ready to move instantly if necessary." The U.S. Sixth Fleet was at the forefront of the Pentagon's plans. As chairman of the Joint Chiefs, Radford promptly augmented the U.S. presence in the eastern Mediterranean, directing the commander of U.S. Naval Forces Europe, Eastern Atlantic and Mediterranean, Vice Admiral Walter F. Boone, to move his headquarters from London to sea, to the command ship USS *Pocono,* then at Iskenderun, Turkey, by November 2. He ordered a Navy hunter-killer group consisting of the antisubmarine carrier *Antietam,* six destroyers, two submarines, and a fleet oiler to be diverted from training and report to the Sixth Fleet. Plans were canceled to send Sixth Fleet units to join a multinational naval exercise code-named Beehive.

A company of Marines was airlifted from Norfolk to bolster base security at the Naval Station at Port Lyautey, Morocco. Two Army regimental combat teams, a Marine battalion, and a wing of Air Force heavy-lift cargo planes were also dispatched to the Med. As the Middle Sea's seaways grew crowded, Admiral Arleigh Burke signaled Vice Admiral Charles R. "Cat" Brown, commander of the Sixth Fleet: "SITUATION TENSE; PREPARE FOR IMMINENT HOSTILITIES." Brown returned an appropriate query: "AM PREPARED FOR IMMINENT HOSTILITIES. WHO'S THE ENEMY?" Burke responded, "KEEP CLEAR OF FOREIGN OP AREAS, BUT DON'T TAKE ANY GUFF FROM ANYBODY."

And indeed, the submarine USS *Hardhead* got a testy reception. Proceeding submerged near elements of the British force—which totaled two hundred ships, including five aircraft carriers—she was detected by one of the Royal Navy destroyers, which moved in and made preparations to attack. As it did so, the submarine surfaced hastily and hoisted a large American flag before sailing on the surface down through the midst of the Royal Navy convoy. The British flagship signaled, "WHY DON'T YOU COME JOIN US?" The reply from the *Hardhead* was "NO THANKS. WE'RE HOLDING YOUR COAT THIS TIME." And so the Americans did. Their real mission was to mass enough presence to deter the Soviets from making an appearance, which could have been destabilizing. As the British and French landings proceeded, Admiral Mountbatten restricted bombardment duty to destroyers, concerned about massive damage that would be inflicted upon important canal infrastructure by battleship main batteries.

Meanwhile, Admiral Brown carried out Burke's order with brio. When Admiral Robin Durnford-Slater's striking force found itself within signaling distance of its American counterpart, a Royal Navy admiral flashed Brown, asking him to vacate the operating area off Cyprus, adding sharply, "YOU ARE INTERFERING WITH MY MISSION." Brown responded, "I ALSO HAVE A MISSION" and refused to move his fleet. His command carried out that mission with dispatch, completing the evacuation of US nationals from Egypt and Israel by November 3, but the arrival of so many ships in the area complicated life for all of them and put operational security at risk.

The U.S. warships appeared to be shadowing the British force on a parallel course. The American flagship, the heavy cruiser USS *Salem*, challenged a British carrier: "WHAT SHIP? WHITHER BOUND?"

The reply came back: "HMS OCEAN."

The *Salem*'s follow-up—"WHAT FLEET?"—received no response.

On the evening of November 1, at a campaign rally in Philadelphia, Eisenhower addressed the tensions in the Mediterranean by letting fly a salvo of antitribal idealism, declaring, "We cannot and will not condone armed aggression—no matter who the attacker, and no matter who the victim. We cannot—in the world, any more than in our own nation—subscribe to one law for the weak, another law for the strong; one law of those opposing us, another for those allied with us."

Such intramural tensions compelled Eisenhower to deploy the Sixth Fleet carrier tracking force to the region. Arleigh Burke ordered it to operate off the Egyptian coast and to be prepared for any contingency. The Sixth Fleet was the means to Eisenhower's end goal: to keep the Soviets from "seizing the mantle of world leadership through a false but convincing exhibition of concern for smaller nations." He wrote to Dulles on November 1, "The Soviets need only to propose severe and immediate punishment of these three [Britain, France, and Israel] to have the whole of two continents on their side."

Concerned about the possibility of Soviet mischief elsewhere, Eisenhower approved orders in early November that augmented forces attached to the DEW Line, increased ocean reconnaissance and the number of antisubmarine groups, placed heavy troop carrier wings on a twelve-hour alert, and prepared additional carrier task forces to deploy to the Middle East.

With the allied forces in the Med facing complicated circumstances, Soviet premier Nikita Bulganin saw opportunity, but not in the Middle East. His chance lay closer to home. Facing unrest within the Eastern bloc, with violent protests by students under way in Budapest, and with reformers in Warsaw agitating to undo Poland's exploitative economic relationship with Moscow, he calculated that the Western powers were distracted by the turmoil around the Suez. In October 1956, he ordered Red Army tanks and mechanized infantry into the Hungarian capital. In a bid to maintain firmer control over its Eastern European buffer zone, perhaps Moscow's greatest geopolitical asset, Bulganin installed a new, pro-Soviet government in Budapest under Imre Nagy, a Communist official who had made his name as a Hungarian nationalist after World War II, when as interior minister he deported hundreds of thousands of German-Hungarians. In his new role as a cog within the Soviet bloc, he promptly outdid himself as a maverick and provocateur. Stunning the world, he announced the end of one-party Communist rule in Hungary and the restoration of pluralistic democracy. Further, he said, Hungary would be quitting the Warsaw Pact.

On November 4, Soviet tanks rolled into Budapest to crush, once and for all, the national uprising. Vicious street fighting broke out, but the Soviets' preponderance of heavy forces ensured a swift victory. At 5:20 A.M., Nagy announced the invasion to the nation in a grim thirty-five-second broadcast, declaring: "Our troops are fighting. The government is in place." Within hours, though, Nagy sought asylum at the Yugoslavian embassy in Budapest. He was captured shortly thereafter, and two years later was executed.

The Soviet action stunned many people in the West. Khrushchev had pledged a retreat from the harsh, ruthless Stalinist policies of the past, but the violence in Budapest suggested otherwise. An estimated twenty-five hundred Hungarians died and two hundred thousand more fled as refugees. Sporadic armed resistance, strikes, and mass arrests continued for months thereafter, causing substantial economic disruption. Inaction on the part of the United States angered and frustrated many Hungarians. But Eisenhower had a well-tuned understanding of how much military force was needed for a given job, and he instantly saw this situation as beyond America's sphere of control or influence. Secretary of State Dulles emphasized that the United States supported the "liberation" of "captive peoples" in Communist nations. Yet as Soviet tanks bore down on the protesters, the United States did nothing beyond issuing public statements of sympathy for their plight.

Ike's inaction placed him in a difficult position vis-à-vis the French-British-Israeli tripartite adventurism in the Sinai. The United States risked being seen, embarrassingly, as condemning Soviet aggression in Hungary while managing a Western invasion of Egypt by its friends.

On November 5, the Soviet Union sent diplomatic notes to Britain, France, and Israel threatening to crush the aggressors and restore peace in the Middle East through the use of force. Eisenhower responded, "If those fellows start something, we may have to hit 'em and, if necessary, with everything in the bucket."

Keen to bring about a cease-fire, on November 6, Election Day, Eisenhower unleashed an impassioned campaign of personal diplomacy aimed mostly at Whitehall. But it was old-fashioned power politics that enabled him to get the job done. He mobilized world opinion against England and France through the UN Security Council—an embarrassing project that placed him in alignment with his Soviet counterparts against his lifelong friends. Ike knew his best play was to exploit Britain's fiscal weakness, which was driving Prime Minister Eden's notably deteriorating domestic political situation. Britain was running out of financial reserves. Refusing to repatriate dollars that Britain had supplied to the International Monetary Fund, Eisenhower muscled Great Britain into accepting a cease-fire, threatening to cause a run on the British pound or drive its value to zero if Eden didn't require his withdrawing commanders to step lively. France had no choice but to go along, and the two nations ended their military operations that night at midnight and effected their withdrawal the first week of December, whereupon the International Monetary Fund disbursed $1.3 billion to the British Exchequer.

As Soviet intentions remained unclear, Admiral Burke beefed up the Sixth Fleet augmentation, ordering the new supercarrier *Forrestal* and the older attack carrier *Franklin D. Roosevelt,* together with a heavy cruiser and three divisions of destroyers, to depart Norfolk for the Azores, where they would stand by. Superpower tensions remained high until November 15, when United Nations forces were brought into Egypt to provide a buffer between the Egyptians and the departing invaders. From that point on, the threat of Soviet intervention faded.

Tension defused, Radford instructed Burke to deactivate the various task forces that had been formed to augment the Sixth Fleet. On December 13, Admiral Boone returned to London from his flagship USS *Pocono*. There were pieces to pick up within the Atlantic Alliance, and it would be done at all levels.

As fraught, messy, and imperfectly handled as the Suez crisis had been, America could claim some degree of victory. "Never in the postwar era," Henry Cabot Lodge reported to Ike from the United Nations, "was American prestige higher than in the aftermath of Suez. Small nations could scarcely believe the United States would support Egypt, a Third World country, in a fight against two of America's oldest allies, nor that it would come to the aid of a Muslim state resisting Israeli aggression. Never has there been such a tremendous acclaim for the president's policy. It has been absolutely spectacular." Eisenhower capped off his successful fall season with a landslide victory over Adlai Stevenson, winning reelection by carrying forty-one states to Stevenson's seven.

ON JANUARY 5, 1957, members of the U.S. Senate and House of Representatives returned to Washington from Christmas recess to receive President Eisenhower for a major speech on foreign policy. He explained to them that the end of the colonial era opened promising new vistas for emerging nations but also created instability that international Communism would try to exploit. "Russia's rulers have long sought to dominate the Middle East," he said. "The U.S. must frustrate their plans." He asked Congress to approve a program of economic and military aid to friendly Middle Eastern nations, and to permit the employment of U.S. armed forces to secure and protect the territorial integrity and political independence of nations requesting such aid against overt armed aggression by any nation controlled by international Communism. The Eisenhower Doctrine was in place. Though it would have been no guide to action in the recent case of the Suez, this authority was duly granted, and Eisenhower planned for his agenda to move forward on the momentum of his victories.

Commonly it is said that "massive retaliation" was the principal military strategy of the Eisenhower administration. But that term describes no strategy at all. It is merely a feature of a properly constituted nuclear deterrent force. The principal strategy of the Eisenhower administration was the Eisenhower Doctrine. To be sure, there was little original in it. Eisenhower's doctrine clearly derived from Truman's, and from containment theory going back to George Kennan. However, it did have more proactive potential than its predecessors did, insofar as it empowered foreign governments under siege to activate American intervention, summoning powerful and potentially escalatory outside support.

The nature of U.S. national strategy in the 1950s is better expressed by a series of maps produced and annotated by Vice Admiral Forrest Sherman's staff when he was CNO and collected under the title "U.S. Lifelines: Procurement of Essential Materials." With input from four government agencies, the maps illustrate the routes of trade that delivered by sea several types of raw materials considered essential to American industry, national economy, and way of life in the late forties. Antimony ore, chrome ore, tin ore, vanadium ore, manila and sisal fibers, lead, manganese, zinc, tungsten, bauxite, cobalt, copper, tin, rubber, crude oil, sugar, pepper, and even coffee (rated as an "essential" material for its comprehensive impact on morale during the fleet's morning and midwatches) were all imported by sea, using long maritime trade routes that reflected America's reliance on foreign sources of important raw materials.

But as important as major sea routes of communication always were to the United States, the advent of the Soviet atomic bomb focused Air Force interest on the problem of national air defense. On September 1, 1954, the Joint Chiefs of Staff had established the Continental Air Defense Command (CONAD), designating Ent Air Force Base in Colorado as the headquarters of the U.S. Air Force Air Defense Command, augmented by representatives of the other services.

The Navy modified thirty-four of the several hundred World War II–built destroyer escorts (DEs) to serve as radar picket ships for these air defense barriers, redesignating them as destroyer escort radar picket ships, or DERs. They received an aluminum deckhouse, two tripod masts for the AN/SPS-28 air-search radar, and a tactical air control and navigation (TACAN) pod; the AN/SPS-8 height-finding radar also was installed. They provided additional radar coverage, as well as navigational checkpoints and search and rescue (SAR) assistance for aircraft that had to ditch in the ocean.

In the air, the Navy used Lockheed WV-2 Warning Star radar picket aircraft to support the mission of the DEW Line. The four-engine planes, derived from the company's Super Constellation commercial airliner, had the AN/APS-20 air-search and AN/APS-45 height-finding radars and contained combat information centers. The normal flight crew numbered twenty-seven, and defense line flights lasted about twelve hours. The Navy purchased 152 of these aircraft. In order to provide centralized direction to the Navy effort, Commander Naval Forces Continental Air Defense (COMNAVFORCONAD) was estab-

lished in September 1954, at Ent Air Force Base. The first COMNAV-
FORCONAD had a staff of about forty-five personnel to coordinate
the assignment and scheduling of Navy forces assigned to the air defense mission: radar picket ships, airborne early warning aircraft and
airships, and fighter aircraft. Whether in the air or afloat, it was grind-
ing duty for airmen and sailors assigned to it.

The Navy also placed jet fighters under Air Force control for continental air defense. All-Weather Fighter Squadron Three, VF(AW)-3,
based at Naval Air Station North Island in San Diego, was placed
under Air Force operational control, the only Navy squadron to be
placed permanently under such control for air defense. The squadron
twice won Air Defense Command's best-unit award. VF(AW)-3 primarily protected the seaward approaches to Southern California, but
from 1961 to 1963 it sent a detachment of its swept-wing F4D Skyrays
to Key West to augment air defenses in southern Florida. Navy carrier-
based jet fighters operating out of their home air stations ashore were
available to augment continental air defense forces in an emergency. By
1957, an average of twelve hundred Navy fighters were at the disposal
of COMNAVFORCONAD for this mission.

As the Inshore and Contiguous Barriers were becoming operational,
the need for a third radar barrier farther out to sea as an extension of
the DEW Line became apparent. The Atlantic Barrier became operational in 1956 and the Pacific Barrier in 1958.

IN EARLY 1957, pleas came from the Pacific Fleet to let them see the
"wonder ship" *Nautilus* and test their tactics against her. Admiral
Burke was in favor of the idea; Rickover was strongly opposed. Rear
Admiral Pete Galantin, head of the CNO's submarine warfare branch,
had the task of justifying the proposed Pacific deployment when Rickover's office called. At once the boss came on the phone. "He never
wasted breath in idle chatter, never beat around the bush," Galantin
recalled. After his usual curt hello, Rickover said, "Galantin, I hear
you're trying to send *Nautilus* to the Pacific. I never heard such a stupid
thing! I want to see you!" The branch chief reported to Rickover's clut-

tered office in the main Navy building on Constitution Avenue. "I faced the frail, deceptively mild-appearing titan of nuclear power technology. The conversation started calmly enough," Galantin wrote, but "as always in those days Rick soon raised his voice to express conviction that the operators didn't know what they were doing, were interfering with his careful plans. . . . After interjecting some comments that were ineffectual in stemming his wrath, I said, 'Well, Admiral, there's only one reason I know for that ship not to go to the Pacific, and that is if you tell me she's not reliable.' "

The remark hit Rickover right where he lived. "His bright, clear, blue eyes seemed to shoot sparks, and his face flushed. Shaking his finger at me, he shrilled, 'Galantin, the art of greatness is to keep the unexpected from happening!' I came away from our meeting believing that Rick was going to fight to maintain his complete control over *Nautilus's* operations. . . . As it turned out, I had said the one thing that would tie his hands. I had identified him with his product and cast suspicion on what he cherished above all—excellence of technological performance." Rickover assented to the employment of the *Nautilus* as an exercise-range target, simply to defend his competence. His competence was more than borne out against the Pacific Fleet's sonar jockeys. They never laid a glove on her.

The unique capabilities of the first "true submarine" recommended her for diverse assignments. Concerned by intelligence reporting that the Soviets were on pace to build one hundred submarines annually in the coming years, adding to an undersea fleet that might already number 450 boats, against 125 American, Arleigh Burke in the fall of 1956 announced that nuclear-powered subs were to be given an antisubmarine-warfare role. Given the caginess displayed by the Vladivostok-based Northern Fleet, which had managed never to reveal the capabilities of its subs during the Korean War, when Task Force 77 was left completely unchallenged, the slope of the learning curve facing the United States in antisubmarine warfare remained unknown. And yet in any war with the Soviets, proficiency in sea control would be at the heart of the matter. A bright spot, though, was the relative certainty that superiority in marine engineering and machine-tooling to fine tolerances gave the United States an advantage in underwater acoustics.

From the time he relieved Captain Wilkinson of command of the USS *Nautilus* on June 18, 1957, in Seattle, Captain William R. Anderson had dreamed of carrying off a feat with the sub that would take her notoriety to a new level. Wilkinson and his fellow *Nautilus* "plankowners"—the first crew of a ship or boat after her commissioning—had given the debut atomic-powered submarine a level of popularity "greater than that of a hit Broadway show," according to Anderson. "I could not merely sustain the laurels that had been showered on her so far. She needed to try something that would take her to a new level." An Arctic transit would be it. The extreme north remained a mystery to submariners. "We didn't know the depth of the water," Arleigh Burke noted. "We didn't know how deep ice went down from the icebergs or whether it was even. We didn't know about currents in the Arctic or winds, and didn't know what the thickness of the ice was. We know practically nothing about the Arctic. It was one of the last areas of the world that had not been explored."

His idea was an audacious one. He would explore the seaways beneath the Arctic ice cap, although whether its waters were even navigable was an open question. What was known was that the Russians "had long considered [the Arctic] to be their own private domain," Anderson wrote. Exploring it would add to the Navy's capability to fulfill both offensive and defensive strategic missions.

Anderson had just ten days to take his chances under the ice. The *Nautilus* was due to participate in a six-nation NATO naval exercise code-named Operation Strikeback in mid-September. The British, among others, were keen to test the value of an atomic submarine.

BUT OF ALL the ways America sought to deter a surprise atomic missile attack by the Soviets, none was deemed more pressing than the Polaris missile, the world's first submarine-launched ballistic missile

(SLBM). Polaris would have pride of place among the technological innovations that defined Admiral Burke's technology-pushing tenure as CNO during the age of the New Look.

On its face, the launch of a missile from underwater seemed an unimaginably difficult feat. In actuality, naval engineers considered it far simpler than doing the reverse: dropping a flying missile out of the air and expecting it to perform predictably after entering a denser medium—seawater—at high speed. The Navy had been doing that for thirty-five years, dropping aerial torpedoes. The fluid dynamics of going the other way were considerably easier. "Why can't we shoot a missile to the surface from a slow, steady platform, pierce the interface vertically in a second, and be on our way?" leading submariners asked. They were ever alive to the perils of the roiling, unstable interface between sea and air that was the ocean surface. The advantages of a stable underwater launch platform were concealment and an all-weather capability.

Red Raborn invested the full energies of his evangelistic Baptist upbringing in the campaign to develop the sea-based ballistic missile system. In soliciting contractors' bids, Raborn was less interested in getting low prices than in finding contractors with the competence, commitment, and capability to perform at a high level. Lockheed got the nod to serve as the project's principal missile contractor, building a dedicated plant in Sunnyvale, California. Westinghouse handled the submerged launcher, and MIT's Instrumentation Laboratory signed on to design the missile guidance system, while General Electric subcontracted to produce the gyroscopes and accelerometers. Aerojet General took on the missile's propulsion system.

Cultivating a team spirit in his military and industrial consortium, Raborn concerned himself with the involvement of employees' families as contributing members of the Polaris team. On frequent visiting days at the Special Projects offices, wives and children were given to understand that Polaris would open a new capability in national defense, that it was for their individual protection. As families bought in to the mission, morale improved even as demands grew to work long hours and weekends. Absenteeism was low. Military personnel serving in Polaris offices were required to wear crisp uniforms. Author Robert J. Watson wrote, "It was a military operation, a campaign."

The master blueprint for the Polaris "campaign" was displayed graphically on a detailed flow chart depicting each individual engineering process required to make the system operational. The so-called Program Evaluation Review Technique (PERT) illustrated the most time-critical project tasks by displaying the sequence of tasks in the schedule that had to be completed by a certain date. Each task was assigned three different probabilistic time estimates: optimistic, expected, and pessimistic. Through the network of time arrows ran one "critical path," the sequence of tasks that would take the longest to complete. This marked the shortest possible time for the completion of the whole missile. A delay in any task on the critical path delayed the whole project. As actual progress went along, the critical path shifted. Every Monday morning, Raborn gathered his managers for each subsystem to review their progress and push them to perform as they had never thought possible. The manager of a subsystem that sat on the critical path could count on receiving an intensive grilling. "He cajoled us," said Jack W. Dunlap, a member of the civilian steering committee. "He scolded us, and he whopped us once in a while. It was his ability to get people to go all out clear down to the people in the plants. He was a flag officer with a touch for evangelism at all levels."

Like Rickover, Raborn was a driver and a passionate worker—the difference being that everyone in the Navy seemed to adore Red Raborn. His secret weapon in the Special Projects Office was his technical director, Captain Levering Smith. Not only the Navy's foremost expert on rockets, he was, said Admiral Pete Galantin, "the indispensable man. His personal absolute integrity and honesty were the foundation of his scientific and engineering excellence." Raborn rated Smith as "the finest scientist in uniform," the naval officer most capable of coping with the manifold uncertainties of the rapidly evolving rocket technology. Aside from the complexities of the missile itself, there would be a host of complex subsidiary systems, many of which would require development or outright invention. It would be Smith's job to direct and coordinate a massive assault on any and all technologic barriers that revealed themselves.

In addition to the peerless Levering Smith, Raborn held another trump card in dealing with the Pentagon—a "magic piece of paper": a memo from the CNO, Admiral Burke, affirming that Raborn "was to have absolute top priority on anything he wants to do" and that everyone in the Navy was to be responsive to his requests. If they found that they could not be, they were to report to Burke, and he would take it upon himself to say no if he felt the denial was proper. This unprecedented talisman got Raborn whatever he needed from the Navy's frequently rivalrous bureaus, though Burke preferred to build willing support within the Pentagon rather than compulsory (and thus potentially grudging) support. In this, his and Raborn's personal credibility and persuasive gifts carried the day. The economics of the SLBM program were useful too.

At a conference in the secretary of defense's office in 1955, Raborn displayed a slide indicating that basing ballistic missiles on submarines would be $50 million a year less expensive than Army schemes using the liquid-fueled Jupiter on surface ships. "Well, Admiral, you showed me a lot of sexy slides this morning," Secretary of Defense Charlie Wilson said. "But I'll tell you, that last slide showing the saving, that was the sexiest one of all."

Raborn made sure to keep his Polaris campaign "road show" updated and current, and to keep his emotional pitch about the moral need for such a program in national defense tuned to an appropriately compelling fervor. "Where he was unique," Carleton Shugg, president of Electric Boat, recalled, "was in person-to-person contact with a smaller group." He employed just enough flag-waving and just enough corn pone. Whenever the opportunity offered, Raborn briefed his audience's staff prior to the main event. The preview prepped office opinion to be sympathetic and forewarned him of any resistance. He spent time cultivating the Treasury Department, where Secretary George Humphrey was sold hard and bought in, and with important members of Congress. Raborn's supreme and decisive opportunity came in the form of an invitation to Ike's Cabinet Room to brief the president and the entire Joint Chiefs of Staff on his progress.

As the northern exploits of the *Nautilus* would come to reveal the Arctic as an avenue of travel and also of attack, the Eisenhower administration appreciated ever more keenly the nation's vulnerability to Soviet bombers using polar air routes. Moscow's knockoff B-29s had demonstrated the range to reach northern U.S. cities by traveling over the North Pole, making the Polaris project as a nuclear deterrent an even more pressing priority.

26

"*NAUTILUS* 90 NORTH"

CAPTAIN WILLIAM ANDERSON HAD GOTTEN WIND THAT THE
cadre of submariners at Atlantic Fleet headquarters in Norfolk opposed his idea to take the atomic-propelled *Nautilus* to the North Pole.
As he was preparing to fly to San Francisco, then to Hawaii, for the
change-of-command ceremony that would place him in command of
the revolutionary vessel, he decided to stop over at the Pentagon. But
his notion that it would be fruitful to pay his respects to Admiral
Rickover—and perhaps secure the influential man's blessing for a polar
transit—seemed to go up in smoke as soon as he entered the office of
the Naval Reactors chief. Without pleasantries, Rickover met Anderson, who knew enough to get straight to the point. He told Rickover of
his ambition, whereupon the admiral jutted out his jaw, and, eyes blazing, spat, "Anderson, you're going to take that ship up there and get
into trouble and you're going to wreck this program!"

According to Anderson, "Astonishment is too mild a word for my
reaction to his belligerent words and tone."

Flummoxed, he fumbled to find a response. Mindful that he needed
to choose his words with care, Anderson said, "Admiral, I appreciate
your concern. You know me. You know that I'm a step-at-a-time guy
and I don't intend to put that ship or crew in danger. This mission has
been planned not as a stunt but as a test. We are intending only a brief,
Cold War trip to a place the Soviets consider to be their private back-

yard. We have good reason for going there." Anderson drew the CNO's prized agenda into the equation, explaining that with Polaris subs coming, it would be "crucial that we gather data and develop expertise about operating in the Arctic." The *Nautilus* was the perfect vehicle to carry out such a pivotally important under-ice test, he said. Rickover eased back against his desk, seeming to absorb what Anderson was saying, then thrust out his right hand. "Anderson, call me when you need me." Anderson thanked him and turned to leave, fancying that he had passed some sort of test of his conviction and commitment to the historic mission.

ON AUGUST 19, 1957, the *Nautilus* got under way and departed New London. Transiting Block Island Sound, she made a rendezvous with the diesel-powered submarine USS *Trigger* off Greenland, which was to accompany her atomic-powered counterpart under the ice before the *Nautilus* turned east toward England to join Operation Strikeback, a NATO exercise, and then a follow-up special exercise with the Royal Navy. Anderson, realizing that he had these ten free days before he was due in England, decided to use this window to probe as far north as he could manage beneath the Arctic ice. He found its boundary off Spitsbergen, Norway, and proceeded north, diving beneath it.

Varying in size from several miles in diameter to only a few yards, individual ice floes are always moving under the influence of wind and currents. They pile up, break apart, and constantly change their size and shape. As the ice drifts in open water, it presents a significant hazard to navigation. In other words, the polar ice pack is an extremely dangerous dynamic environment.

Although the *Nautilus* was equipped with special gear for navigating under ice—an SQS-4 scanning sonar, and an array of upward-beaming Fathometers that could sense the bottom of the ice cap above—they were not calibrated to produce accurate returns at the high submerged speeds the *Nautilus* maintained. The ice cap was thicker and the keels and pressure ridges descending from them were deeper than they appeared on the *Nautilus*'s Fathometers. Pushing north toward the Pole, Anderson experienced a profound sense of pushing a frontier. It could induce claustrophobia. "Essentially we were entering an unexplored cave two thousand miles deep," he wrote. "With no charts to go by, I was gathering what foreknowledge of routes, depths, ice conditions and clearances I could, through mile after mile of ice floes." The underside of the ice was notoriously uneven.

From the air one could see that the ice pack was broken by plenty of openings in which to potentially surface. There were open-water pools known as "leads" and areas of partially frozen or very thin, easily breakable ice known by the Russian word "polynya." As his team in the control room took readings with the Fathometers, Anderson peered through the periscope, which he craned at an upward angle. He realized he was experiencing a unique form of tunnel vision. He wanted to surface and look around. The submarine was nearing the limit of its first under-ice foray.

The summer sunlight filtering through the ice overhead made it unnecessary to use the floodlight mounted topside, Anderson found. The underside of the ice floes, so diverse in their size and the extent of their reach into the depths, appeared through the periscope to be "scudding overhead like gray clouds." At length the operator of one of the overhead sonars reported a large opening in the ice. This polynya, the soundings showed, was some four hundred by fourteen hundred yards in size. Anderson decided to rehearse a surfacing tactic known as a vertical ascent. Rather than rise slowly, in a level horizontal orientation, the sub would emerge like a porpoise, breaching the surface nose first, as if threading a needle. Anderson raised the periscope to check the sonar readings, and everything seemed in order. He felt the *Nautilus* rise toward the opening, angling upward, then was startled to find his view through the periscope showing him an onrushing wall of solid ice.

The deck lurched beneath his feet and there was a sickening crunch as the submarine piled into an ice layer eight to ten feet thick. His periscope optics went black. As a shudder swept through the *Nautilus,* "It would not have surprised me at all," Anderson wrote, "if a torrent of ice-cold seawater rained down through a massive rent in our sail—if the ship had heeled over, its superstructure breached, and she headed for the bottom of the sea, taking all of us with her."

"Flood negative!" Anderson shouted, filling the sub's buoyancy control tank to take her down again. He ordered a course that took the submarine steaming back to the edge of the ice pack, where he would rendezvous with the *Trigger*. Making contact with the other sub using the underwater telephone, he traveled 150 miles south and emerged in open ocean. Inspecting the damage, he was relieved to find that the submarine's injuries were superficial. A pair of broken periscopes, a deep dent, and a tear in the sail, which flooded the bridge gyro repeater stand. Anderson took the *Nautilus* down to 250 feet to test it out once the damage had been assessed, his primary concern being his ability to participate in Operation Strikeback a few days later.

Eager to search out a submarine tender to effect repairs, Anderson instead found his own crackerjack crew up to the task of repairing the vessel afloat. Two of his crew, both trained and proficient steel welders, went topside in the midst of a gale to straighten and weld fast the wrecked and leaky periscopes and repair a deep tear in the fairing that connected them to the sail. "It was the most amazing repair job at sea I had ever witnessed," Anderson wrote. The *Nautilus* reached port in Scotland two days ahead of schedule, made rendezvous with a submarine tender, and got her periscopes replaced in time for the exercises with NATO and the Royal Navy.

The manner in which the world's first nuclear submarine ran rings around the allied naval forces was kept strictly under wraps. Though noisy, the *Nautilus* was so fast that destroyers scanning with active sonar had trouble keeping their sonar beams fixed on her. With limitless underwater endurance, making submerged speeds of twenty knots or more, and an ability to take refuge below seven hundred feet, the *Nautilus* was nearly beyond the reach of modern antisubmarine warfare systems. A year later, the reporter Jack Anderson broke the story of how the *Nautilus* "theoretically sank the entire British Navy three times over while hiding beneath an aircraft carrier."

Impressed, the British would soon build their own nuclear sub,

HMS *Dreadnought,* furnishing it with a reactor required to be obtained from the United States under a bilateral agreement. A true revolution in submarine warfare was at hand.

When William Anderson next visited the Pentagon, early in November 1957, he was the toast of the Office of the Chief of Naval Operations. A quorum of OPNAV's staff turned out to hear him tell of his voyage beneath the Arctic ice and his performance in Operation Strikeback. It demonstrated that U.S. atomic-powered submarines would have ready access to these under-ice reaches that the Soviets saw as their private domain. From the fringes of the ice pack just east of Spitsbergen, Anderson noted, it was only 420 miles to Murmansk, 1,200 to Leningrad, and 1,440 to Moscow.

Such strategic vulnerability was very much a point of Pentagon and defense agency interest after the Soviets launched a satellite payload into space on October 4, 1957. Moscow's success in propelling the eighty-three-kilogram metallic sphere known as Sputnik into low Earth orbit from a spaceport in southern Kazakhstan unsettled U.S. military planners and panicked an American public that had taken U.S. technical superiority over the Soviet Union as a national birthright. Senator Lyndon Johnson spoke for many when he said, "What American wants to go to bed by the light of a Communist moon?" Robert J. Coontz, an instructor at the United States Naval Academy, said, "The main feeling that I had at the Academy was, 'Oh my God, they got the jump on us. Where did we go wrong?' or 'Damn the money-squeezing politicians who won't give us what we need and expect us to make bricks without straw.'"

Running submerged for most of October, Anderson and his shipmates were unaware of the national psychodrama of Sputnik's passage over the free world. But in its persistent beeping the Eisenhower administration heard a call to action. In a bid to match the Soviet achievement, the Air Force rushed forward with a highly publicized launch of a Vanguard rocket two months later in Florida. It ended in disaster at the Cape Canaveral launchpad, where the tall spacecraft rose a few feet atop a base of exhaust flames, then fell back to the pad in a huge explosion. Amplifying the humiliation was the fact that the Pentagon had allowed the launch to be carried on live national television.

Across the United States there was a feeling that things were going wrong. Anderson felt sorry for Eisenhower, whose good legacy seemed to be at risk, from low Earth orbit to Little Rock, Arkansas, where he had sent federal troops to escort African American students into a traditionally white school after Governor Orval Faubus blocked them from entering in defiance of the landmark *Brown v. Board of Education* Supreme Court decision desegregating U.S. public schools. "Hell, they were even blaming him for Elvis Presley being drafted into the Army the year before," Anderson wrote. The president was eager for the United States to hold a military posture that the Russians respected.

At a meeting of the National Security Council in late October, Ike wore a grave expression. G. Edward Larson, an assistant to presidential adviser Harold Stassen, said, "If we lose repeatedly to the Russians as we have lost with their satellite, the accumulated damage would be tremendous. We should accordingly plan to accomplish the next great breakthroughs first. Do we have any such plans?"

After briefing the staff at OPNAV, Anderson was in the bustling Pentagon Mall, trying to hail a cab to Union Station, where an overnight coach would return him to New London, when he saw a familiar face. Captain Peter Aurand, Eisenhower's naval aide, greeted Anderson boisterously and offered to give him a ride to the train station in his limousine. They were passing the Lincoln Memorial when Aurand invited him to postpone his trip home, stay over in the capital, and come to the White House the next morning. Ike saw that Anderson and his amazing submarine might well offer an answer to the challenge posed by Sputnik.

After Aurand greeted Anderson and the two settled down in the West Wing, the presidential aide asked the submariner, "Do you think you could take the *Nautilus* completely around the world submerged?" Clearly, he was fishing for a prospective feat to bring back to the president. Anderson, underwhelmed at the prospect of open-ocean circumnavigation, said that such a feat was simply a matter of devoting enough time and nuclear fuel to it. "There is a more challenging transit to be made," he said, "an ocean-to-ocean voyage under the ice, crossing the entire Arctic Ocean via the North Pole, transiting from the Pacific to the Atlantic under ice." The idea was bold and enthralling, an underwater Northwest Passage in the opposite direction—call it the Southeast Passage. Aurand's face lit up as he turned to a large map on the wall and studied its converging lines of longitude at 90 degrees north latitude.

"Captain, let me work on this," Aurand said. Happy to leave on that high note, Anderson begged off a meeting with the president and left the White House to catch his train for New London.

And so, two days after returning to New London, Anderson received a call from Admiral L. R. "Dan" Daspit, the Navy's director of undersea warfare. He told Anderson there was interest at the White House in using the *Nautilus* to seek the undersea Northwest Passage in reverse. Eisenhower "bit on the idea like a fresh piece of fish," as Aurand would put it. When support was voiced by Arleigh Burke, who had recently been reappointed for a second two-year term as CNO (on the way to an unprecedented three), "two very large stars had come into alignment," Anderson wrote. Summoned back to the capital, the skipper briefed the mission to the president and was given approval on condition of maintaining the strictest secrecy. Eisenhower had been angered when details of the *Nautilus*'s first under-ice foray in September 1957 had leaked to the press from the Navy Department. This time he planned to orchestrate a maximal public relations windfall if Anderson was successful.

Back in New London, Anderson confided the news of the classified mission to three of his senior officers, his exec, navigator, and chief engineer. A few days later, as the submarine was leaving New London bound for the Panama Canal en route to Seattle, Anderson disembarked and flew to Fairbanks, Alaska, then to Nome, where, posing as a civilian scientist, he hired a bush pilot to take him and Dr. Waldo K. Lyon, an expert on sea ice who had been assigned to augment the *Nautilus*'s crew, up in a Cessna 180 for a reconnaissance flight over the Bering Strait and along the Alaskan coast as far north as Meyers Chuck. Anderson and Dr. Lyon found the strait daunting, choked by a great deal of sea ice, some of it drifting as large floating spikes—ice floes that had collided, then risen up, causing their lower edges, Anderson knew, to reach deep toward the ocean floor. While these held peril for his crew, he was encouraged to find several stretches of open water along the route he had plotted. The flight ended with some drama when the Cessna ran critically short of fuel. Refused permission to land near an Air Force radar station, the pilot settled for touching down by an Inuit village that kept a store of fuel for bush pilots working in the area.

On his return to the *Nautilus,* Anderson received a surprise visitor, Rear Admiral Hyman Rickover. As the two submariners settled into Anderson's stateroom to discuss the mission, the captain realized he had never briefed the boss on the upcoming voyage. The conversation was cordial, however, and at the end of it, Rickover did something unexpected. He reached into his pocket, produced a small piece of paper, and handed it to Anderson. It read, "If necessary to reduce primary system leakage, it is satisfactory to the Bureau of Ships to reduce pressure from 1600 psi to 1400 psi. Signed, H. G. Rickover." What the note meant was that if the atomic reactor suffered a leak in its coolant cycle, Anderson was authorized to turn down the power, slowing his reactor below the minimum power settings prescribed by Rickover's office. Having received written authorization to use his own judgment and depart from procedure, Anderson gained confidence in the capability of his submarine. What was more, Rickover's giving him this operational flexibility inspired Anderson. It meant there was leeway in the reactor system to permit a safe reduction. It might even mean that the exacting, notoriously demanding admiral trusted him.

Another surprise visitor greeted Anderson in Seattle. A Navy psychiatrist, Dr. Jack Kinsey, was studying the stresses that submarine sailors experience on long submerged cruises. "When a crew does not know whether it is in the Indian Ocean or under an ice floe at the North Pole without consulting the log, when there is no day or night, and the same eccentricities annoy day after day, naval staff officers wonder how long nerves can stand the strain," observed a science journalist in *The New York Times*. Dr. Kinsey thought he might find out. Anderson considered the good doctor's presence useful cover for the sub's mission.

While the *Nautilus* remained in port in Seattle, Anderson waited anxiously for approval from Washington for the polar transit. It finally came, but as the S2W atomic reactor was powering up, there was a failure in the main turbine system. The sub had been idle too long, inviting such a material casualty, Anderson thought. He believed in what he called "the dictum of the aviators": To keep a plane in good shape, keep it flying. So too with submarines. He was grateful only that Rickover had left by the time the failure happened. Anderson's engineers, however, made short work of the turbine problem, and the *Nautilus* was plying the waters of Puget Sound shortly after midnight on June 9, 1958, bound for Portland, England, via the North Pole.

The first order of business was operational security: Sailors scrambled topside to slather gray paint over the sub's identifying hull number, 571, displayed in white numerals on the bow and sail. The much greater threat to their success, however, lay immediately ahead: the challenge to submarine seamanship posed by the ice-choked shallows of the Bering Strait. "Probably the most hazardous body of water in the world," Anderson called it. His executive officer, Commander Frank Adams, led a series of lectures to the crew, assisted by Dr. Lyon, on under-ice navigation, breaking down the innumerable details of standing special watches and carrying out the order to collect comprehensive scientific data. During their transit across Puget Sound, one of the crew suffered a sudden cerebral hemorrhage and died instantly. Anderson took the *Nautilus* to Port Townsend to bring the body of thirty-two-year-old Torpedoman First Class Theodore J. Szarzynski to Bremerton Naval Hospital. He also queried the commander of the Thirteenth Naval District whether the mission should be canceled in view of the fatality. Such a thing was out of the question, Anderson was informed.

The *Nautilus* took in her lines and soon was heading to sea again. "A nuclear-powered submarine," according to Anderson, "is . . . the most comfortable means of sea travel known to man. At our cruising depth there is absolutely no motion; the ship is as steady and level as the ordinary living room. Even when the roughest storm imaginable is raging overhead, at a depth of 250 feet and below, the water is as calm as a millpond." Though the bathythermograph registered the outside water temperature at a chilly 39 degrees Fahrenheit after the *Nautilus* left Japan's current system, the sub's air-conditioning system maintained the interior at a comfortable 72 degrees Fahrenheit with low humidity, while keeping the air well scrubbed of CO_2. Shortly after leaving Puget Sound, the crew advanced all clocks eight hours to conform to Greenwich Mean Time—requiring double duty of the sub's cooks, who were required to prepare a hundred-man breakfast right on the heels of dinner.

ON THE FOURTH day, approaching the Aleutian Islands, Anderson found the water deepening considerably and, concerned about the effects of colder water on the sub's fittings, used the opportunity to check for leaks. After diving to the sub's strictly classified maximum depth of well below seven hundred feet, all compartments were reported watertight. The *Nautilus* passed deep between two islands in the Aleutian chain before approaching her navigational Waterloo in the Bering Strait. Anderson felt severely restricted and sandwiched by the sudden shallowness of the seaway.

Recent heavy storms, which were undetectable at depth, had tossed the sea ice. Anderson was alarmed to find the surface 60 percent covered by blocks of ice whose undersides rolled past overhead just twenty-five feet above the submarine's sail. After midnight on June 15, passing west of St. Lawrence Island, the *Nautilus* was forced to dive deep to avoid a block of ice that reached thirty feet below the surface. "Had we not had enough water beneath us to go deeper and sneak under it, we would have had to take horizontal evasive action. It was precious little room for ship control." Anderson glanced at Waldo Lyon, who stood nearby to offer advice, and was confident that the startled look on the scientist's face mirrored his own.

Blocks of ice that had been cast loose from the shore during the recent storms tended to be larger and deeper in draft than other ice floes.

Spooked by the deep-thrusting ice, Anderson reversed course and tried the east side of St. Lawrence Island. Although the Alaskan coastline was known to cut loose unpredictable configurations of massive ice floes, some with "keels" reaching forty-five feet deep or more, Waldo Lyon was more familiar with these waters than he was with those on the Siberian side. Anderson took a periscope fix on the island, admiring the calm, sunny, windless day. That night on the first watch, eight to midnight, the master gyrocompass, used to determine true magnetic north, quit working. Turning north up the east side of St. Lawrence Island, Anderson was disconcerted by the shallowness of the water above the sail, which was barely submerged. Shortly after 0500, the ship's master compass also failed. As his watch officers were dealing with this loss of orientation, Anderson spotted an unidentified surface contact dead ahead on the horizon. His first impression through the periscope was that it was a snorkeling Soviet submarine. *What the hell is he doing up here?* he thought, before a closer look revealed it was just a big log that had floated out of the mouth of the nearby Yukon River, its protruding roots resembling a submarine's snorkel. The log ended up landing a stiff blow to the *Nautilus*'s periscope but inflicted no damage.

As the *Nautilus* approached the Bering Strait, the gateway to the Arctic, and entered the Chukchi Sea, Anderson finally went to his stateroom to rest. He had not been asleep long when his conning officer awakened him to report that the *Nautilus* had just passed beneath an ice keel forty-seven feet deep. Anderson ordered, "Take us down to 140 feet," which left the sub just twenty feet above the sea floor—no room for error. It was then that he realized they were under a gigantic mass of ice more than a mile wide with no easy way to get out from under it. A chill ran up and down his spine. As Anderson ordered the helm to reverse course, he mouthed a prayer that the recording pen that was tracing the findings of the upward-beaming Fathometer would show the downward-pointing ice keel that threatened his vessel receding from the submarine. He flinched as if to retract his head between his shoulders, visualizing his submarine as a small boy squirming his way under a large fence.

The officers of the watch all exhaled in relief when the sub cleared the obstacle, finally passing below it with a clearance of just twenty-five feet. After another hour or so of steaming, there, right ahead, stood a still more formidable obstacle, a veritable wall of solid ice standing athwart the intended path of the *Nautilus* into the Arctic Basin. As best Anderson could tell from his instruments, this monster had a keel that reached as far as eighty feet below the surface. The sub passed beneath this towering obstacle with as little as five feet to spare, Anderson twisting all the body English he could manage into the close-run passage. He was sure the submarine's sail had dragged through a thick field of slush on the underside of the frozen rampart. Feeling a heavy responsibility for his ship and 115 men, he finally concluded, to his regret, that he had underestimated the polar ice. A retreat south was in order, given that the waters grew shallower immediately ahead and only Neptune knew what kind of ice was in store for them in these tight underwater caves. "We just didn't have a good solid picture of what was ahead of us," recalled chief sonarman Al Charette.

Turning south for Pearl Harbor, Anderson broke the bad news to the crew over the intercom, then began looking for a place to surface to send a radio message to Admiral Burke at the Pentagon about permission's status. Composing his dispatch, Anderson expressed optimism that an attempt made later in summer, after the Arctic ice had melted somewhat, would likely be successful.

At length Burke replied, "I CONCUR ENTIRELY WITH YOUR PRUDENT ACTION IN WITHDRAWING FROM THE ICE PACK. IT IS OBVIOUS THAT YOU HAVE MADE A MAXIMUM EFFORT. I TENTATIVELY CONCUR WITH YOUR RECOMMENDATION TO LAY OVER AT PEARL HARBOR UNTIL CONDITIONS IMPROVE."

As he turned south, Anderson swore his crew not just to secrecy but to complete amnesia about the abortive polar transit. Morale was considerably bolstered by Burke's affirming response, as well as the prospect of having nearly three weeks in Hawaii as a result of the change in plans, enjoying the hospitality of Commander, Submarine Force, Pacific, Rear Admiral Elton W. "Joe" Grenfell and his boss, the commander in chief of the Pacific Fleet, Admiral Herbert G. Hopwood, both of whom, upon the submarine's arrival at Pearl Harbor's entrance, appeared in a small boat that came alongside and stepped aboard to pay their respects.

Not long afterward, it might have been possible for the casual observer to mistake the *Nautilus* for a nuclear-powered floating floral arrangement. Following the admirals came other well-wishers in boats. They swarmed close aboard to bombard her with salvos of orchids, plumeria, bird of paradise, and hibiscus, one of them capping it off by draping across her bow a thirty-foot lei. Fireboats and harbor tugs broke out their hoses and sent up big arcs of seawater, the mists of which refracted festively in the morning sun.

When he checked in at headquarters, Captain Anderson discovered the Navy had prepared for him a busy schedule of briefings to give to an array of audiences, from the White House to New London to Norfolk. He agreed to do all of it, his only request in return, duly granted, being to take along on his plane a few dozen of his crew.

Hawaii was welcome liberty for those who stayed behind. The Royal Hawaiian Hotel, the famous Pink Palace, continued its long tradition of catering to naval personnel, as did all the other island hot spots. That summer, three thousand civilians were given guided tours of the submarine. An even luckier three hundred went to sea on trials near the end of the three-week layover.

As July ripened and warmed, Anderson and Dr. Lyon agreed it was a good time to try again. They figured the icy seas north of the Aleutians were sure to have thawed and opened up. On the twenty-third, the *Nautilus* got under way and set course north. The submerged run from Pearl to the Aleutians was complete on July 26. Hawaii's blue swells gave way to cold gray whitecaps. By the time the rugged coastline of Siberia came into view, Anderson calculated that they had made the 2,901-mile passage in six days, four hours, nine minutes—an average speed of 19.6 knots, a new underwater record.

Finding the Chukchi Strait now clear of ice, Anderson rang up full speed and the reactor pushed the submarine swiftly through the shoal waters that had caused so much trouble on the last trip. Still, the Siberian currents carried a familiar and ominous chill. When they crossed the twenty-five-fathom curve, Anderson slowed to ten knots. Surfacing to repair a couple of wonky ice detectors, Anderson noticed heavy ice in the west. It was dirty shore ice, stacked forty feet high in formations that had "rafted" or broken off from land and drifted out to sea. It looked black. And dangerous. Anderson figured such a massive frozen obelisk would project as deep as 120 feet below the surface. "I had no desire to sandwich *Nautilus* between this black ice and the bottom," he wrote. "We had had enough of that on the first trip." He remembered too well the urge, so powerful on the previous foray, to duck his head and hunch his shoulders as they avoided the massive ice floes and their deeply plunging keels.

Changing course to the east, toward open water, Anderson used his active sonar to locate the descending slope that marked the beginning of the deepwater basin off Point Barrow, Alaska, that led to the Arctic Basin. Surfacing again to freshen the air and repair more of the acoustic ice detectors, Anderson juked east on the surface toward a heavy fog bank. When the air search radar detected an unidentified plane, he took her down again. At that point, the passive sonar, which he used to listen for the sounds of distant ship engines or screws, returned an exotic sound: a chorus of yelps from a school of walruses that had surrounded the submarine. As these mammals did not behave as if they were Soviet-aligned, operational security was ensured. On August 1, locating the subsurface valley off Point Barrow that led to the Arctic Basin, the *Nautilus* dived into the deepening seas. The North Pole was eleven hundred miles distant. Nothing stood in its way as the sub accelerated past twenty knots.

The next day, continuing north beneath the ice layer, they crossed 84 degrees north latitude. Anderson noticed the master gyrocompass was losing its north-seeking ability. Holding a Great Circle course, he suggested that his navigator use the auxiliary gyroscope to fix their position using dead reckoning with help from the inertial navigation computer. The latter device, invented by North American Aviation to guide missiles to their targets, collected inputs from accelerometers and gyroscopes to calculate the vessel's position without reference to external things such as stars, satellites, land formations, or magnetic poles.

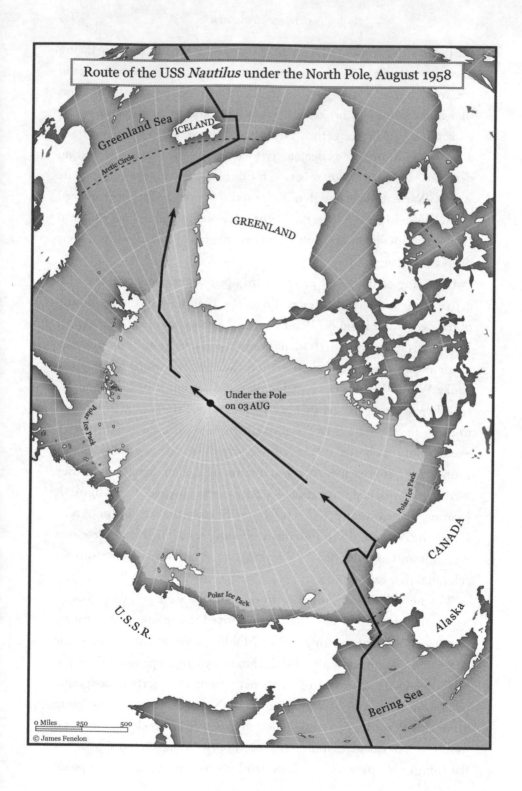

Route of the USS *Nautilus* under the North Pole, August 1958

Greenland Sea

ICELAND

Arctic Circle

GREENLAND

Under the Pole
on 03 AUG

Polar Ice Pack

Polar Ice Pack

Polar Ice Pack

CANADA

U.S.S.R.

Alaska

Bering Sea

0 Miles   250   500

© James Fenelon

Anderson's sonarmen took occasional soundings on the bottom, which was of little help because there were no charts for these unknown waters.

Dr. Lyon was hunched over his sonar gear hour upon hour, watching the recording pens trace the contours of the underside of the ice overhead. It varied from eight to eighty feet in thickness, and some of the pressure ridges, forced downward by the collision of floes, reached down to 100 or even 125 feet. The downward-pointing Fathometer spiked and dropped several times, showing mountainous promontories on the sea floor. "A mixture of suspense, anticipation, and hope was discernible throughout the ship. Few could sleep," Anderson recalled.

A wag had suggested that once they reached their objective, they should throw the rudder hard over and turn twenty-five tight circles around the North Pole, making the *Nautilus* the first ship in history to circle the earth nonstop more than two dozen times. As soon as the navigator, Lieutenant Shep Jenks, informed the captain that they were within half a mile of the Pole, according to the electronic ship's log, Anderson picked up the intercom: "All hands, this is the Captain speaking. In a few moments *Nautilus* will realize a goal long a dream of mankind—the attainment by ship of the North Geographic Pole. With continued Godspeed, in less than two days we will record an even more significant historic first: the completion of a rapid-transit polar voyage from the Pacific to the Atlantic Ocean. The distance to the Pole is now precisely four-tenths of a mile. As we approach, let us pause in silence dedicated with our thanks for the blessings that have been ours during this remarkable voyage—our prayers for lasting world peace, and in solemn tribute to those who have preceded us, whether in victory or defeat."

Anderson thought reverently of Peary, Cook, Byrd, Amundsen, and the others who had braved this long-unnavigable frontier before him.

The ship's jukebox was turned off and a hush fell over the ship, broken only by the pinging of sonar transmissions gauging the distance to the bottom—more than 13,400 feet at the Pole—and to the ice overhead, and feeling out the unknown waters in their path. Anderson looked at his electronic log again and realized a long-anticipated moment had arrived. He toggled the intercom again. "Eight, seven, six, five, four, three, two, one, mark! August 3, 1958, time, 2315–11:15 P.M. Eastern Daylight Saving Time. For the United States and the United States Navy, the North Pole!" Cheers erupted from the enlisted crew's mess.

He refrained from throwing the rudder hard over and circling the world twenty-five times. The historic ocean-to-ocean passage was no time for stunts, and it would not be complete until they arrived in England. Steering for the gateway to the North Atlantic, passing between Greenland and Spitsbergen, Norway, Anderson surfaced, and his communications jockeys tuned in Navy Radio Japan. He transmitted a terse but telling message addressed to Admiral Burke in Washington: "*Nautilus* 90 North."

As the *Nautilus* transited the Denmark Strait en route to Portland, Maine, Burke sent a helicopter to fetch Anderson in Reykjavík. The press was astir and there were gaggles to attend. Before dawn, an H-19 Chickasaw appeared and whisked the soon-to-be-famous skipper back to the United States.

Meeting him, Eisenhower was warm, elated, and congratulatory. As flashbulbs popped, the president presented Anderson with the Legion of Merit and the Presidential Unit Citation. Navy Secretary Thomas Gates was on hand to explain that this PUC was the first one ever awarded to a ship and its company in peacetime. First Lady Mamie Eisenhower, who had christened the submarine in New London, was pleased to receive Anderson's gift of the ship's clock, stopped at the moment the *Nautilus* reached the North Pole. The warmth of the day seemed to chill a bit when reporters began asking where Hyman Rickover was. He had not been invited. Once Rickover's admirers and supporters in Congress got wind of the insult, what *The Boston Globe* called an "embarrassing rhubarb" ensued that the man who had personally seen to it that there would *be* a USS *Nautilus* was not sharing the well-deserved limelight. When the *Nautilus* went to New York City for a ticker tape parade in a heavy rain amid worldwide publicity and acclaim, the White House made sure Rickover was there as the president's personal representative.

* ★ *

AFTER APPEARING WITH his submarine, Anderson flew back to Portland for a high-spirited reception with Ambassador John Hay Whitney. Numerous foreign leaders expressed their appreciation of the *Nautilus*'s Arctic feat. "Please accept my sincere and heartfelt congratulations on the achievement of the American pioneer spirit," the West German chancellor, Konrad Adenauer, wrote to Eisenhower. "It is fine and good that a great country of liberty should give so brilliantly the proof of inventiveness and courage," wrote France's Charles de Gaulle. Amintore Fanfani, the president of Italy's Council of Ministers, wrote, "With the bold undertaking of the *Nautilus,* which takes its place in the glorious tradition of the greatest voyages of all time, the American Navy has opened a new path for mankind. The fact that it has been opened by free and democratic America constitutes a guarantee that it will be dedicated to the progress of humanity and the peaceful bringing together of the peoples of the world. Allow me, Mr. President, to express the most cordial congratulations of the Italian government and the Italian people, who have been particularly associated in the course of history with great conquests of the sea."

27

FORWARD FLEETS LIKE FIREFIGHTERS

WHILE THE *NAUTILUS* WAS STEAMING NORTH, BIDDING TO BOOST Dwight D. Eisenhower's prestige, the small Middle Eastern country of Lebanon was putting him to the test. With Lebanese Muslims rioting out of fear that the delicate balance between Christianity and Islam in the pluralist government was in peril, President Camille Chamoun requested military assistance from the United States. Secretary of State Dulles brought the request to the White House. With intelligence sources indicating that the Lebanese rebels were being supplied with arms from Syria, and official radio broadcasts from Moscow, Cairo, and Damascus openly encouraging insurrection, Eisenhower did not need convincing that coordinated Communist mischief was once again afoot. The Lebanese president lamented to his State Department liaison about the incapacity of the West to deal with the danger of Communist subversion, adding that the Communists had been perfecting their techniques since 1948 and that the West, in his view, had not done anything about it.

The request from a government under attack in such circumstances was a clear trigger to the Eisenhower Doctrine. Adding to the regional tensions and President Chamoun's desperation, on July 14, leftist officers in the Iraqi army assassinated their king and prime minister. American assistance took the form of a contingency plan code-named

Operation Blue Bat, designed to assist a friendly government confront-ing a rebellion.

Vice Admiral James L. Holloway, Jr., who had just relieved Admiral Walter F. Boone as CINCNELM (commander in chief, U.S. Naval Forces Europe, Eastern Atlantic and Mediterranean), was in Washing-ton presiding over a promotion board when his executive assistant rushed in with a message from Admiral Burke: "HOIST YOUR FLAG IN LEBANON. ACTIVATE BLUE BAT PLAN, BUT WITHOUT BRITISH PARTICIPA-TION." The order effectively tapped Holloway as the action officer of the Eisenhower Doctrine. The plan was to occupy and secure the Bei-rut airport with the two Marine battalions assigned to the Sixth Fleet, and to bring in a third from Cherry Point, North Carolina. Rear Admi-ral Cat Brown, the Sixth Fleet commander, in his flagship the heavy cruiser *Des Moines* in Villefranche, France, received in turn the terse order "LAND THE LANDING FORCE." He sent an order to Task Force 61, his amphibious unit, to carry out the landings the following day.

Brown also issued a flurry of orders, summoning his carriers to-gether once again. He had three aircraft carrier battle groups at his dis-posal. The brand-new *Saratoga,* a *Forrestal*-class supercarrier, was at Cannes, the *Essex* at Athens, and the *Wasp* at Naples. This powerful naval air force would be on hand to support the Marines as they secured the airport and then moved out to take control of Beirut's harbor. With-out active hostilities under way, it did not seem a daunting objective for fourteen thousand well-trained U.S. troops. But then Khrushchev raised the ante. The Soviet premier made it known that the Red Army would carry out maneuvers in the Trans-Caucasus and Turkmenistan, districts of the Soviet Union that bordered Turkey and Iran, both friendly to the United States. Moscow further demanded the with-drawal of the Marines and announced that it had the right to act "to halt a dangerous situation near our border."

On July 12, 1958, when President Chamoun had requested a forty-eight-hour response, naval forces provided the only option to help him. The Air Force would begin ferrying supersonic F-100 Super Sabre fighter-bombers from the U.S. East Coast to Adana, Turkey, relying on aerial refueling. Army troops in Germany required similar loading up for airborne transit to Turkey. The Sixth Fleet's forces, on hand already in theater, piled in directly from the sea.

Having enjoyed diverse duty in World War II, including service in a destroyer on Atlantic convoy duty and also in history's last battleship-versus-battleship engagement, the battle of Surigao Strait, fought off the Philippines in October 1944, Vice Admiral James Holloway could lay claim to having seen just about everything. But even he could not have foreseen the need to go ashore and serve as a field-grade officer directing the movement of ground forces in Beirut. When Muslim factions in the Lebanese army used tanks to block a Marine battalion from proceeding from the Beirut airport to the harbor on July 16, Holloway flew to Crete to join his flagship, USS *Taconic*. A second battalion had gone ashore to displace the first one, which was to move down and take control of the docks. Holloway showered, shaved, and was enjoying his first cup of coffee when word came that the Lebanese Muslims had set up the armored roadblock on the highway outside the city. He diverted en route and flew directly to Beirut, making a temporary flagship of a handy destroyer.

Holloway alerted the embassy about the problem, and the U.S. ambassador to Lebanon, Rob McClintock, soon arrived at the scene with the top general of the Lebanese army by his side, President Chamoun's chosen successor, Emir Fuad Chehab. Taping his four-star flag to the front fender of McClintock's Cadillac embassy car, Holloway jumped in with the ambassador and the emir, and the driver sped them to the site of the trouble. Television news cameras had discovered the standoff and were clustered all around. The admiral jumped out of the car and pushed through the thicket of cameras. "We generally didn't want to start a bloody war if it could be avoided," he later commented. However—just in case—the *Saratoga* had all her Douglas A3D Skywarriors loaded out and manned for the delivery of atomic weapons. The *Essex* kept a pair of new A4D-2 Skyhawks, assigned to Attack Squadron 83, the "Rampagers," spotted at the catapults on "ready-five" alert—ready to fly at five minutes' warning—two armed with the aircraft rockets, and two more with three-hundred-kiloton nuclear weapons on their centerline pylons. A Marine armed with an automatic weapon stood guard over each aircraft and its bomb.

En route to the disturbance ashore, Holloway turned to Chehab and said, "We're going to march now, General, so get the orders changed. We've got to go through. We've got orders from the president of [the] United States." Chehab argued that they considered the American presence "a reflection on [their military honor]." No matter; Holloway was determined to see the Marines proceed to their objective. He and Chehab got out of the car at Watermelon Circle and confronted the Lebanese soldiers at the roadblock. "It was a very touchy situation," Holloway said. Chehab told the rebels what was what, and Holloway led the column through the formation of Lebanese tanks—"their barrels even then down our throat," Holloway recalled. Swagger stick in hand, the American admiral then began waving the Marines through the gate to the harbor waterfront. A fighter sweep composed of F9F Cougars from the *Essex* shook Lebanon's beaches late that afternoon and underlined American intentions and capabilities.

The next day, to retain initiative and momentum, Holloway ordered the commander of Task Force 61 to land another Marine battalion on the beaches north of Beirut and to emplace artillery in the hills overlooking the road to Damascus. That gave U.S. forces effective control of the Syrian capital, reducing fears of outside military intervention. The Marines avoided running patrols overtly so as not to provoke hostilities.

Within seventy-two hours after the Marines went to shore, Soviet premier Khrushchev announced from the Kremlin that he "viewed this American adventuring with alarm, and that the Soviet Union was very capable of turning the Sixth Fleet's aircraft carriers into flaming coffins for the American sailors." The lurid rhetoric about the destruction of carriers seemed calculated to hit the U.S. Navy where it lived.

Holloway had established enough backing to act boldly in response. Air Force General Nathan Farragut Twining had said to him, "I'm going to give you anything you want. We're not going to do like the British and the French did at Suez, going in with too little and too late." The fleet remained on station, unchallenged, movements and operations unimpeded. The Marine battalions protected the Lebanese president until the rebellion could be dispersed and its leaders arrested.

The incident was an important midterm test of the Eisenhower Doctrine. If Nasserite Communists could sweep in and displace a government, the doctrine would have had little practical application or relevance in world affairs.

FULGENCIO BATISTA, THE corrupt gangster-dictator of Cuba, would have done well to follow the example of the Lebanese president. After repulsing Fidel Castro's revolutionary forces in 1953, he imposed an oppressive security crackdown that served mostly to swell the ranks of the Communist insurgency. Confronted with the growing rebellion supported by outside Communist entities, he ought to have invoked the Eisenhower Doctrine and requested direct military support from the United States. Between 1953 and 1958, the United States had already given him $9.8 million in aid, much of it used for training his officers in the United States. The string attached was a restriction that Batista not use the granted assets, without the express approval of Washington, for internal purposes such as fighting an insurgency. In March 1958, the State Department determined that Batista was violating that agreement. Without consulting the Joint Chiefs of Staff, it suspended military assistance to Cuba. Admiral Burke, wanting to keep Cuba in the American orbit, believed the suspension was inconsistent with U.S. foreign policy and recommended that the arms shipments continue.

On New Year's Day 1959, under pressure from the hills and dales around the major cities in Cuba, Batista was forced to flee Cuba, leaving the United States with an America-denouncing Communist firebrand less than two hundred miles off the coast of Florida. Although a March 1960 National Intelligence Estimate shortly raised "serious questions as to the degree to which Cuba may now be or may become subject to international Communist control," Arleigh Burke knew a rat when he smelled one, and he acted within the Joint Chiefs to develop options to intervene to restore a friendly government.

★ ★ ★

BETTER NAVAL RELATIONS with foreign powers were a top priority
for Arleigh Burke during his tenure as CNO. An opportunity came to
his attention when he was speaking with Admiral Friedrich Oskar
Ruge, West Germany's chief of naval operations, who mentioned that
the Bundesmarine's Baltic Sea presence was a rather cobbled-together
force of minesweepers, patrol craft, and land-based patrol aircraft.
Ruge let it be known on a visit to Washington that he might like some
assistance. Burke thought about it for a moment, then said to him, "I'll
tell you what I'll do. I'll give you my old squadron, DESRON 23." The
much-decorated destroyer unit from World War II was bound for
scrapping. Burke told him the eight Fletchers had "taken a hell of a
beating during the war"—only seven of the eight had survived it. "But
we'll help you train your crews, and if you'll take good care of the ships,
I'll give them to you." Ruge agreed, but decided in the end that he
didn't want the whole squadron. The Germans ended up taking three
ships—the *Dyson, Claxton,* and *Charles Ausburne.* Spain and Greece
each took one as well.

The *Charles Ausburne,* with eleven battle stars, was handed over to
the Germans on April 12, 1960, to be commissioned as *Zerstörer 6*
(NATO hull number D-180). She was finally placed under command
of a former U-boat captain, Otto von Bülow, who had been decorated
with the Knight's Cross of the Iron Cross with Oak Leaves.

Burke recalled how on the day of the transfer, "She was at the dock
with U.S. flags flying, a beautiful ship, and they played the U.S. national anthem, hauled the flag down, our crew marched off. Admiral
Ruge and I were on a platform right opposite the ship on the dock. As
soon as the last of our men left the ship, the captain stood at the ladder
to wait for the German captain. The German captain was in a building
perhaps a hundred yards from the ladder so he had a little time to walk.
He walked down first, his executive officer following, and then each
division came down. . . . I wanted this to be a good German occasion, so
I arranged for the U.S. Navy band to play 'Lili Marlene,' a popular
wartime German love song, largely forbidden from public performance

since 1945." Admiral Ruge broke into tears. "The skipper, too," Burke
noticed, "had a hard time with his composure as he came aboard."

FORBIDDEN NATIONALISM WAS very much an issue for the Chinese as
well.

Communist China continued to test Washington's will by staging
attacks on the Quemoy islands. On August 23, 1958, Communist Chinese artillery batteries massed on the mainland opened a ferocious barrage. As the explosive tolling of shell detonations reached fifty thousand,
rocking Quemoy, the office of the Chief of Naval Operations issued a
paper stating that while initial operations to defend Quemoy might
have to be conventional for political reasons, atomic strikes against
China would eventually be necessary if the Chinese assault did not
cease. Once again the nuclear option was in play.

"It is probable," the Joint Chiefs informed CINCPAC, Admiral
Harry D. Felt, "that initially only conventional weapons will be authorized, but prepare to use atomic weapons. Prepare, if the use of atomic
weapons is authorized, to extend bombing of ChiCom targets deeper
into China as required." A squadron of fifteen Guam-based Air Force
B-47 Stratojet bombers, which had no conventional capability, was
placed at the ready for Taiwan's defense.

General Twining presented, and President Eisenhower approved, a
message directing CINCPAC to (1) reinforce U.S. air defenses on Taiwan at his discretion and prepare to assume responsibility for Taiwanese air defenses, using U.S. forces if necessary, and (2) prepare to escort
and protect Nationalist supply ships going to reinforce the islands and
to augment the Seventh Fleet as practicable. The attack carrier USS
Midway and other naval units were sent to the western Pacific from
Pearl Harbor. On August 24, Rear Admiral Wallace M. Beakley, the
commander of the Seventh Fleet, recognizing the potential for escalation in the conflict, ordered Vice Admiral Roland Smoot, the commander of the Taiwan Defense Command, who had a sterling combat
record as a World War II destroyerman, to coordinate U.S. and Nationalist forces to defend the Offshore Islands. The Chinese bombard-

ment was severe, and though non-naval in nature, its purpose was to impose a blockade—"creeping interdiction," as the U.S. embassy in Beijing called it. Though Admiral Smoot assigned three destroyers to patrol twelve miles off Quemoy and ordered the USS *Hancock* to prepare to launch combat air patrols over the strait and to be ready to strike Communist forces if so ordered, Red Chinese PT boats evaded American patrols that night to sink one Nationalist LST and damage another.

Additionally, the Seventh Fleet ordered the carrier *Lexington* and the antisubmarine carrier USS *Princeton* to make best speed to operate near Taiwan and also sortied all available minesweepers to augment Smoot's blocking force. As the convoys to the Offshore Islands continued to arrive, the Nationalist position gained strength. Washington began to fear that it was being goaded into a greater military commitment than it might be comfortable with. On September 11, Eisenhower announced that the island of Quemoy would not be allowed to fall. Apparently anticipating that hostilities in the Taiwan Strait would escalate into a broader conflict over a longer period, the president ordered the carrier *Essex* and four destroyers to depart the Mediterranean and make a long transoceanic transit to reinforce the Seventh Fleet.

On September 8, Soviet premier Khrushchev sent a letter to Eisenhower warning that an attack on China would be regarded in Moscow as an attack on the Soviet Union. Moreover, Moscow said, the Communists' fight against the Nationalists was an internal Chinese affair. In talks between the parties conducted in Warsaw in mid-September, the Americans pressed for a cease-fire and the Communists demanded they withdraw their forces from the area. Within a few weeks, the Chinese agreed to a one-week cease-fire if the United States stopped escorting the Nationalist convoys. After the expiration of the cease-fire, Chinese forces resumed occasional shelling but not with the intensity that might portend an intent to impose a blockade. While Chinese propaganda played down the crisis, state radio broadcasts demanded that the Nationalist garrison surrender—it was cut off and isolated, the propaganda declared. Of course, the mission of the U.S. naval force there was to give evidence that it was not.

As the propaganda war heated up, Smoot's forces again began to escort Nationalist convoys into the islands. Chinese artillery fired on the convoys whenever they came within range. On several occasions, Taiwanese F-86F Sabres flying combat air patrol over the islands found themselves confronted by Communist MiGs, and dogfights ensued. The Taiwanese pilots had their way in these fights, their advantage accruing from their use of the new AIM-9B Sidewinder air-to-air missile. Under a covert effort known as Operation Black Magic, the United States had provided a few dozen of the infrared-sensing heat seekers to Taiwanese forces, as well as some Marine Corps advisers who helped to fit their aircraft to carry the new weapon. The MiG had always enjoyed an altitude advantage over the Sabre, and Communist Chinese MiGs routinely cruised over the Nationalist Sabres, engaging when they had a favorable position. The Sidewinder took away that advantage.

In the first combat action, taking place on September 24, 1958, Taiwanese Sabres ambushed a flight of Chinese MiG-17s, using Sidewinders to destroy five of them. It was the first successful use of air-to-air missiles in combat. One of the Communist jets returned to base with an unexploded missile stuck in its fuselage. The Soviets promptly exploited this priceless technological windfall, reverse-engineering from it their own heat-seeking air-to-air weapon, the Vympel K-13.

Dulles, acting under President Eisenhower's instructions, decided against regularizing U.S. air operations in the Taiwan Strait and reached agreement with Taipei that U.S. and Nationalist combat aircraft would not overfly mainland China either, thereby ruling out air attacks on ChiCom shore batteries.

Rear Admiral Paul P. Blackburn, Jr., Commander Taiwan Patrol Force (subordinate to Smoot's command), was also in command of Fleet Air Wing One and Task Force 72. Blackburn wanted badly to fix the locations of the Communist Chinese radars that directed the artillery fire. Naval reconnaissance aircraft based on Taiwan had used their advanced ELINT (electronic intelligence) capability to produce an up-to-the-minute map of enemy radar sites—a "radar order of battle" for the area. Smoot's photo interpreters used the data to pinpoint the locations of the radar installations.

The destroyers of the Taiwan Neutrality Patrol, as naval surface components of Admiral Smoot's command, occasionally relied on their own devices and seamanship in carrying out the mission of collecting intelligence. "The less adventurous skippers," one veteran of the patrol said, "simply drove up and down on a straight course that could be predicted days in advance and they achieved nothing in intelligence gathering. However, Jim Montgomery had a different approach. The captain of the *De Haven* would steam at high speed directly for the Chinese coast with all his radars 'lit' and broadcasting chatter on every radio frequency his communications shack could dial up. As soon as we hit the edge of Chinese territorial water, an array of fire-control radar would lock on us. We would record their bearing and pulse repetition rate and then hightail it out of there back out over the horizon. We would then move up or down the coast a way and do the same fast approach directly for the Chinese coast. Again the fire-control radars would lock on and we would record the bearing and PRR [pulse repetition frequency] before turning eastward. With this data we could cross the bearings and match the PRR and pinpoint the location of the shore-defense radars and batteries. It produced significant data."

Secretary Dulles, continuingly faithful to his president's wish to avoid a bloody escalation, now sought a diplomatic solution to the crisis. He prevailed upon the Joint Chiefs to leave the Chinese coastal weapons alone, thinking there might be a role for the United Nations to settle the crisis. The British and French, he thought, might be persuaded to introduce a resolution in the Security Council calling for a UN-supervised cease-fire and demilitarization of the Offshore Islands. Admiral Burke, who as CNO sat on the Joint Chiefs of Staff, as all the service chiefs did, was opposed to this idea. He argued that Beijing and Taipei would reject such an agreement out of hand, and moreover that it would strain U.S. relations with Taipei and possibly also strengthen Beijing's case that it should take over Nationalist China's seat in the United Nations.

At the highest level in Washington there was a lack of consensus about the value of the small, remote islands or the necessity of spending millions of dollars, and possibly many lives, in defending them.

"My own feeling," said Admiral Robert Carney, Burke's predecessor as chief of naval operations, "was that we shouldn't give up one square inch of territory that the free world owned for any purpose whatsoever." And yet according to Carney, earlier in the Eisenhower administration, Defense Secretary Charles E. Wilson had "absolutely electrified all of us in a Security Council meeting one day" arguing that the United States had no stronger case for holding Quemoy than the Russians would have had for holding Staten Island. "He didn't see why we didn't get out," Carney said. "It came as a complete surprise to [JCS chairman] Radford and to the rest of us."

In Hawaii, Admiral Felt saw an impetus to action arising from nonmilitary dynamics. "From a pure military point of view," he said, "[the islands] are not worth the risk of getting involved in a war even though it might be possible to keep it limited. However, I agree with the view that these islands are symbolic in the eyes of neutral and weak friendly Asian nations. This part of the world is waiting to see whether the US will retreat in the face of armed aggression against one of its allies or whether she will take positive action to hold small pieces of territory which are being disputed by use of armed force. In this case, I believe that the psychological factors outweigh the pure military ones."

As Smoot wrote to the commander in chief of U.S. Pacific Command, Admiral Felix Stump, on August 4, "Paramount politico-military implication is positive affirmation of U.S. support which Chinese officials honestly feel is lukewarm."

"The ChiComs are probing," Admiral Felt informed the Joint Chiefs. "They are trying to provoke the US into taking actions which can be condemned in the world press and the UN. I believe they can be discouraged with action short of a full-scale war."

Mao's regime had made notable progress in recasting traditional Chinese culture and society in the Communist mold. As a May 1958 National Intelligence Estimate observed, Mao had followed Stalin's model for organizing the domestic economy: "It has collectivized almost all the peasants and has nearly eliminated private ownership in industry and commerce." But the regime's stringent curtailment of consumption and the constant pressures to conform and to work ever-longer hours had provoked resistance among the peasant class. Only by large infusions of Soviet capital, credit, goods, and services had China been able to show an eye-popping average annual rate of growth of industrial output of about 16 percent. Even so, China's industrial output at the end of 1957 was small compared to that of Japan or the United Kingdom.

In the end, China was forced to abandon its latest effort to solve its Chiang Kai-shek problem by forcing him and his loyal forces off the islands. Beijing conceded by its behavior that it had been outclassed by the Seventh Fleet and by Taiwan's missile-armed jets.

Eisenhower, Smoot informed Stump via telegram on August 4—though it is not clear how he would have been in a position to know—"attaches gravest significance to Krushchev [sic] Mao Tse-tung conference in Beijing. Considers conference dominated by Soviet Minister of Defense. Is convinced Chinese Communists are prepared and have the capability to attack Taiwan. That they will do so with all-out conclusive effect. They are willing to take risk of retaliation and that now is most timely and propitious time.

"Action required which he most urgently emphasized," Smoot informed his superior at Pearl Harbor, "was positive demonstration of U.S. recognition of the seriousness of the situation and to this end urges the most rapid action on acquiring Sidewinder speedup of F-86 program as show of force by Seventh Fleet in the area."

The United States was armed and ready. However, on October 6, Beijing radio announced that Communist forces were suspending the bombardment of the Offshore Islands, ostensibly in order to spare the lives of Chinese inhabiting them. Admiral Beakley in turn ceased escorting convoys into Quemoy and reduced the frequency of destroyer patrols in the Taiwan Strait. As had just happened off Lebanon, a robust American naval presence in a forward area seemed to have forestalled a wider war.

AFTER THE INDOCHINA problem tested the application of containment in Asia, and Chinese aggression against Taiwan probed America's willingness to remain engaged on the far side of the Pacific, the Americans tried to set up a security alliance known as the Southeast Asia Treaty Organization, or SEATO, in 1955. It attempted to bind the United States, Great Britain, France, Australia, New Zealand, the Philippines, Pakistan, Thailand, and Japan into a regional security alliance. But the alliance had no teeth. Its covenants imposed no requirement of mutual military action on the part of the other members. And few had major military forces to contribute in any event. SEATO will be remembered, in the words of British diplomat Anthony Eden during its time, as "a fig leaf for the nakedness of American policy" and "a zoo of paper tigers."

After its failure to subdue Quemoy, China was compelled to realize, once and for all, that its ambition to conquer both the Offshore Islands and Taiwan itself, in the face of such committed U.S. support, was a considerable flight of fancy.

28

SIOP

THE NAVY'S ACQUISITION OF A STRATEGIC MISSILE COMPONENT following the development of Polaris provided an impetus to overhaul the national strategic war plan. Prior to the ballistic missile, each service had its own war plan. CINCPAC and CINCLANT were empowered to pick their own targets, with nuclear weapons at their disposal. "There was absolutely no coordination in the atomic weapons area," said Rear Admiral Kent Liston Lee, who had learned his way around such devices while serving as an A4D Skyhawk squadron commander who had transferred to the Air Force's Strategic Air Command headquarters in Omaha from the Office of Naval Research in 1957.

The old atomic war plan was workable as long as one service controlled the great majority of atomic warheads, as SAC did until 1958. With the advent of Polaris, however, the order of battle was to change, and single-service control of diverse land- and sea-based weaponry threatened to become complex. Eisenhower directed that the services prepare to work together under a joint command. "Everybody's weapons will be in one plan," the president ordered. The Strategic Air Command continued to dominate the new Joint Strategic Target Planning staff, so Arleigh Burke, wanting a credible Navy voice there, sent Admiral Lee to Omaha to be his man.

Lee had not been crazy about working at the Naval Research Laboratory, the billet he had held prior to heading to Omaha. It was a paper-pushing job, administering contracts to academic scientists and technicians doing work for the Navy and making sure they were paid. But the chill winds of Omaha, Nebraska, tested many a man's soul. It was sometimes said that the only difference between Omaha and the North Pole was all the barbed wire. And perhaps the fact that the crews of atomic-propelled submarines were not hell-bent to get there.

Strategic Air Command's intelligence squadron, a crew of hawk-eyed photo interpreters, analyzed imagery from satellites and the U-2 flights to pick out Soviet assets that deserved to be pretargeted with a nuclear warhead. "[The target has] to be within range of the weapon, whether it's an A4D from an aircraft carrier or a Polaris missile, and its destruction within the capabilities of the weapon," Admiral Lee said. Each system was assigned a launch time, a flight route, and a time over target. A running record was kept of all the variables so there wasn't a twentyfold overkill on one target and none on another. "You build up to a point where you have a damage expectancy of, say, better than ninety percent on each one of the important targets," Lee continued. The whole plan was to feed the information into a computer that was programmed to resolve conflicts, both route conflicts and target conflicts. Once all that was done and the retargeting and rescheduling were input, it was all printed out. Each principal commander got a copy of the printout, and he then had to schedule his forces accordingly. "That was the national war plan," Lee said. "That was what we had to follow." Known as the Single Integrated Operational Plan, or more commonly SIOP, it was almost completely independent of the Joint Chiefs of Staff, except that they were expected to rubber-stamp it whenever the commander of SAC, General Thomas Power, thought to show it to them from time to time.

SAC's top priority for destruction, the Soviet bloc's airpower, was a large system of targets, or Designated Ground Zeros (DGZs), that included more than eleven hundred airfields, plus missile bases and their defenses, government and military control centers, storage sites for nuclear weapons and petroleum, refineries, and aviation and atomic research and industrial centers. A separate list was of urban-industrial areas identified for "systematic destruction." SAC listed in excess of twelve hundred cities in the Soviet bloc, from East Germany to China. Moscow and Leningrad were priority one and two respectively. Moscow included 179 DGZs, while Leningrad had 145, including "population" targets. In both cities, SAC identified airpower installations, such as Soviet Air Force command centers, which it would have devastated with thermonuclear weapons early in an atomic exchange.

If the United States had strategic warning of a Soviet attack, it would preemptively strike with a full force of 3,500 weapons against an "optimum mix" of 1,050 DGZs, including military bases, air defenses, and 151 urban-industrial areas. Having sought an "optimum mix" war plan that hit important military and urban-industrial targets, SAC's planners gave priority to the Air Power target system in terms of numbers of DGZs. Strikes on civilian population centers were out of bounds per se. While Air Force leaders were willing to accept mass civilian casualties as collateral to the destruction of military targets, as was the case during the Korean War, they ruled out intentional attacks on civilians, as they violated international legal norms of the day. These rules were summarized in the Hague Rules of Air Warfare, written in 1923 but not ratified by the United States and broadly violated by all combatants in World War II. SAC planned to use lower-yield atomic bombs against targets in Eastern Europe for political reasons, though airfields near Warsaw and Budapest would be struck without such restraint. "When I was out there [in Omaha] the first time in 1960, we might have [had] eight thousand weapons to target. It's probably plus or minus ten percent," Admiral Lee commented.

In the mid-1950s, the Navy acquired the 5,200-acre ammunition depot in Charleston, South Carolina, christening it the Naval Weapons Station Annex and using it for the storage of all types of submarine-based ordnance, including Polaris missiles.

The gradual deployment of the Polaris missile submarine force began bringing Polaris A1s into SIOP in batches of sixteen. As more and more Navy-owned atomic warheads came online, Omaha took notice. "Down in the basement where the Strategic Air Command's targeters went about the grim work of designing Doomsday's blueprint, crews were shaking their heads in disbelief. They couldn't believe it," said Rear Admiral Gerald E. Miller, who served as deputy director of the Joint Strategic Target Planning Group in the early seventies. "Here comes another five hundred weapons. Where are we going to target them? We were on the flat part of the damage curves. We couldn't get any more damage against the hard targets, and for the soft targets, it didn't take but about a thousand weapons to knock out the entire urban-industrial base of the enemy."

Eisenhower's and Burke's ambitious construction program to produce forty-one Polaris-capable strategic-missile submarines, also known as SSBNs or "boomers," was called the "41 for Freedom" program. The boomers, fundamentally different from the torpedo-armed "attack" submarines, or SSNs, whose mission was destroying other naval craft, were the heart of an invulnerable nuclear retaliatory force that was large enough and thus survivable enough to deter all thought in Moscow of attempting a "decapitating" first strike. The U.S. Navy's SSBN program began with the conversion of the attack submarine USS *Scorpion*. She was cut in half at the General Dynamics Electric Boat Shipyard in Groton, Connecticut; a module containing sixteen vertical Polaris missile tubes was inserted amidships, and the segments were rewelded together as perfectly as possible. Also at Electric Boat, the first boomer, USS *George Washington*, was commissioned on December 30, 1959.

A number of conventional submarines performed oceanographic survey work. In the spring of 1960, the submarine USS *Archerfish* was specially equipped to participate in Operation Sea Scan, a scientific study of marine weather conditions, water composition, ocean depths, temperature ranges, and gravitational fields. Famed for the great exploit in November 1944 of sinking the Japanese aircraft carrier *Shinano*, the largest warship ever sunk by a submarine, the *Archerfish* entered the Philadelphia Naval Shipyard in January to be outfitted for this unusual new mission. During this time, she was redesignated an "auxiliary submarine," AGSS-311. Embarking a team of civilian scientists and recruiting a crew of unmarried men under skipper Kenneth Woods, she commenced the first phase of Operation Sea Scan on May 18, visiting the Caribbean, where she recorded the deepest spot in the Atlantic, the

Milwaukee Deep in the Puerto Rico Trench, 27,480 feet below the surface. Tracing grid lines across open ocean was slow, painstaking work. Crossing the Atlantic to Thule, Greenland, then Portsmouth, England, she went on to call at Hammerfest and Bergen, Norway; Faslane, Scotland; Belfast, Northern Ireland; and Halifax, Nova Scotia, only returning to New London on December 3. Small repairs and refitting complete, she began a cruise to the Pacific in January 1961, spending most of the next three years collecting oceanographic data for the office of hydrography. Measuring gravitational forces with sensitive gravity meters was important for the submarine-launched ballistic missile program. With such data in hand for the principal patrol areas, the boomers could fire their Polaris missiles that much more accurately.

PROCEEDING DOWN THE East Coast to Charleston, the newly minted SSBNs took on board sixteen Polaris missiles each. The weapons were carefully inserted into the vertical missile tubes, and after the crews had checked the circuitry for the navigation and fire-control systems, each boomer was prepared to undertake a new type of deployment: the strategic deterrence patrol. It involved steaming out to a predesignated sector of ocean roughly the size of Texas. Once it was reached, only the captain and the navigator knew exactly where the boomer was.

En route to the classified "patrol box," prudent submarine skippers carried out a series of violent hydrobatic maneuvers commonly referred to as "angles and dangles." These maneuvers involved diving at a steeply downward angle at full speed and then jerking back up sharply toward the surface. Sudden changes in depth and course changes, snap-rolling at maximum speed by as much as thirty-five degrees, gave a workout to the bow planesmen and diving officers, but the principal purpose of the exercise was to determine whether the boat had been well rigged, with loose items secured against the risk of falling to the steel deck and thereby betraying the submarine's location by sending a sharp acoustic signal into the water. The last thing a boomer skipper could afford was to be detected by the enemy. Evoking the fears stirred up by Sputnik, Rickover described Polaris submarines as "underwater satellites." He considered their invulnerability a principal asset, re-marking, "The enemy would be in the position of trying to find a black cat on a vast and empty plain on a moonless and starless night."

Executing the "41 for Freedom" program, the shipyards at Groton and Newport News carried out a furious construction program of atomic-powered fast attack and ballistic missile submarines beginning in 1959. Secretary Wilson's office named the new ships in tribute to great figures in American history, suggesting revolution and even civil war. The USS *George Washington* was followed by the *Patrick Henry, Theodore Roosevelt, Robert E. Lee,* and *Abraham Lincoln*. The next five boomers were the first to be built from the start as SSBNs. The five ships of the *Ethan Allen* class—including *Sam Houston, Thomas A. Edison, John Marshall,* and *Thomas Jefferson*—carried the improved two-stage Polaris A2 missile, with a range of 2,500 nautical miles. The improved *Lafayette*-class boomers, which Electric Boat, Mare Island, Portsmouth, and Newport News would build through the early sixties, were armed with the triple-warhead-carrying Polaris A3, also with a 2,500-nautical-mile range. The extension of range was significant stra-tegically, as it imposed a larger burden upon the Soviet Union to defend wider and wider expanses of sea with their antisubmarine forces.

With a robust sea-based nuclear deterrent in prospect, Eisenhower was less moved by the Air Force's entreaties to overbuild the land-based intercontinental ballistic missile force. The Regulus missile patrols con-tinued as well. With that program nearing its end date, on January 4, 1960, the guided-missile submarine *Halibut* was commissioned at Mare Island Naval Shipyard near San Francisco. Carrying three nuclear-tipped Regulus II cruise missiles in her large hangar, she joined the ro-tation for a uniquely dangerous type of strategic patrol, cruising on the surface off the Kamchatka peninsula at night, running lights on, trying to blend in with Soviet commercial fishing traffic idling as they awaited another day of dragging their nets. A few months later, the *Growler* and the *Grayback* became the first subs built from the keel up to carry Regu-lus II missiles. But the arrival of Polaris meant the exit of Regulus.

On November 1, 1952, "Ivy Mike" explodes in the world's first detonation of a hydrogen fusion weapon. The unprecedented 10.4-megaton blast destroyed the island of Elugelab.

During his much-publicized visit to South Korea, President-elect Dwight D. Eisenhower speaks with Admiral Arthur Radford, Commander in Chief Pacific, on December 13, 1952.

Rear Admiral Hyman G. Rickover, pioneer of nuclear naval propulsion, which led to the development of a nuclear Navy.

Admiral James L. Holloway, Jr., who served as Chief of Naval Personnel, 1953–57.

USS *Nautilus* launch ceremony at the Electric Boat Company, Groton, Connecticut, on January 21, 1954. *Nautilus* was the world's first nuclear-powered submarine.

USS *Tunny* off Point Mugu on August 26, 1954, with a Regulus I guided missile positioned to launch. The Regulus as a submarine-based weapon grew from the earlier LTV-N-2 Loon tests.

Dr. William B. McLean, head of the AIM-9 Sidewinder development team.

A pilot stands beside the new AIM-9B Sidewinder air-to-air missile for scale in 1956. The first trials took place in 1954.

America's first supercarrier, USS *Forrestal,* the day after launching at
Newport News, Virginia, on December 11, 1954.

During shakedown operations, the new *Forrestal* catapults an FJ-3 Fury
on March 12, 1956. The Fury was a Navy-modified version of the F-86 Sabre,
which saw much success against the Mig-15 in Korea. A second FJ-3 and
an F2H-3 Banshee await launching from *Forrestal*'s bow catapults.

USS *Forrestal* awaits refueling in the Mediterranean Sea on April 29, 1957,
following an alleged coup attempt in Jordan earlier that month. *Forrestal*'s flight deck
a year into her active service career reflects the wide array of carrier aircraft in use
at the time, as well as showing the new angled deck configuration.

President Dwight Eisenhower (left) and his Chief of Naval Operations,
Admiral Arleigh Burke, during a presidential visit to
USS *Saratoga* on June 6, 1957.

U.S. Marines disembark an LCVP from USS *Chilton* on Red Beach,
Beirut, Lebanon, July 16, 1958. Operation Blue Bat marked
the first invocation of the Eisenhower Doctrine.

Commander William Anderson on the USS *Nautilus* bridge in preparation to pass beneath the ice cap at the North Pole, August 3, 1958.

Commander William Anderson (right) and senior scientist Dr. Waldo Lyon measure the thickness of the ice above the *Nautilus,* August 3, 1958.

The first Polaris missile fired beneath the surface from nuclear submarine USS *George Washington*, July 23, 1960.

Rear Admiral William F. Raborn, Jr., Navy Department Special Projects Officer (center), expresses relief following the successful Polaris missile launch from USS *George Washington* on July 23, 1960.

29

To Build a Better Battleship

IT WAS THE END, TOO, OF THE ERA OF THE TRADITIONAL BATTLE-ship. The Navy's penchant for tinkering was never on display more fully than in the various schemes dreamed up by the Ship Characteristics Board (SCB) in the 1940s and fifties to modify and rearm battleships in exotic new configurations for service in the missile age.

The renovation of the old battleship *Mississippi* as an experimental auxiliary guided-missile ship (EAG) in April 1948 came to an end eight years later. She was decommissioned in September 1956, sold to Bethlehem Steel, and towed away to be broken up for scrap metal. The last of the faster and stouter *Iowa*s were decommissioned in early 1958, with the *Wisconsin* being the final one of the four to go into mothballs in the reserve.

Construction of what was to become the Soviet navy's lone battlecruiser, *Stalingrad,* with a twelve-inch main battery, had been canceled after Stalin's death. That left Moscow with no capital ships, no bluewater navy, and no suitably heavy opponents for U.S. battleships to wargame-shoot at. The four *Iowa*-class fast battleships had in fact been recommissioned for duty in Korea. But the day was past when U.S. warships needed a sixteen-inch main battery capable of busting through thirty feet of concrete or seventeen inches of face-hardened armor. The battleship's best use in the missile age seemed not to have evolved much since 1945: providing air defense to carrier task forces and giving fire support to amphibious operations with their large and diverse gun batteries.

Just as guided missiles had changed naval aviation, they brought transformation to the realm of the surface combatant as well. In early 1956, an SCB study envisioned an *Iowa*-class "guided missile battleship," or BBG, fitted with two Polaris ballistic missile launchers with a capacity for sixteen of the nuclear weapons. She would also have four RIM-8 Talos surface-to-air missile launchers with eighty missiles per launcher, plus a dozen RIM-24 Tartar SAM launchers with 504 missiles. So the preserved *Iowa*s were temporarily coveted as candidates for rehabilitation as missile ships. A July 1956 estimate projected completing such a ship by July 1961, but the high cost of the conversion, approaching $200 million each, finally led the Navy to end it. Variations on the BBG configuration included "an air defense ship / fleet oiler"—an *Iowa* fuel carrier armed with two Taloses, two Tartars, and four Regulus IIs. It was a formidable main battery for a tanker. Then there was the *Iowa*-class "commando ship," furnished with spacious quarters for troops, and six LCM-6 landing craft and ten helicopters to take them where the action was. As of April 1956, BBG conversions were included in the tentative fiscal year 1958 shipbuilding program, but they were abandoned late in 1956.

The failure of any of the battleship conversions to thrive led the Navy to explore converting cruisers into missile ships. The large cruiser (or battlecruiser) *Hawaii,* redesignated after World War II as an experimental ship for guided missiles, was one of the early candidates for conversion—in her case to fire V-2 missiles. Operation Sandy—the awkward 1947 exercise that saw the USS *Midway* launch a V-2 from her flight deck—put a damper on the fleet's enthusiasm to use the relic German weapon at sea. Some senior admirals considered such an experiment not worthwhile unless the missiles carried nuclear warheads. The Bureau of Ordnance wanted space for twenty-five V-2s on the *Hawaii*—hazardous installations, to be sure, as each launcher needed a liquid oxygen tank located near it to provide fuel for the missiles.

For reasons of cost at a time when spending had to focus on producing war-ready resources, the program to convert the *Hawaii* was terminated in planning for fiscal 1952, after which missile cruiser conversion work focused on smaller vessels: the World War II *Baltimore* class. And thus were born the U.S. Navy's first two guided-missile cruisers, the *Boston* and the *Canberra,* designated CAG-1 and CAG-2 respectively. Their configuration preserved the signature armament of these ships, their two forward triple eight-inch turrets. The after turret was replaced with a pair of double Mark 10 Terrier surface-to-air missile launchers served by a missile magazine holding seventy-two missiles. The cascade of new radar trackers and guidance-beam antennas spilling down from her mainmast required four 1,500-kilowatt turbogenerators to boost her electrical generation capacity.

The *Cleveland*-class light cruisers offered still more cost-effective options. For $42 million, the Navy could have a real SAM thrower, a fast Talos-armed task force escort with a magazine capacity of 114 shots. Converted *Cleveland*s, displacing 10,000 tons fully loaded, kept their two forward triple six-inch batteries, adding one twin Terrier launcher aft plus a helicopter pad by removal of the after two main-battery turrets. The *Galveston* became the first of the guided-missile light cruisers, or CLGs, commissioned May 28, 1958, followed by the *Little Rock* a year later. These were the first ships to carry the Talos missile. In September 1960, the *Oklahoma City* was the third of six *Cleveland*s so converted, the *Little Rock* and *Oklahoma City* featuring an enlarged and rebuilt superstructure as flagships to comfortably accommodate an admiral and his staff.

Meanwhile, back in Hyman Rickover's world, the first nuclear-powered surface combatant, the USS *Long Beach,* was being completed at the Fore River Shipyard in Quincy, Massachusetts. Launched on July 14, 1959, she had two C1W nuclear reactors, producing eighty thousand shaft horsepower, driving her 721-foot-long hull at thirty knots to wherever her missile systems might be needed. Another novelty of the *Long Beach* was her boxlike superstructure, which contained an advanced radar system known as SCANFAR. The heart of it was a phased-array air-search radar system known as the AN/SPS-32, innovative in the way it steered its beam of radio waves electronically rather than by the physical movement of a rotating antenna. Phased-array radars, with their ability to change the direction of a radar beam faster than could a moving antenna, were designed to track or even guide missiles in supersonic flight toward a target.

The system made the *Long Beach* powerful indeed. She could target up to four aircraft at once out to three hundred nautical miles and up to altitudes of a hundred thousand feet. Her sonar system could detect submarines out to ten thousand yards, or nearly six statute miles, and her new ASROC antisubmarine rocket launcher could prosecute them with rocket-assisted homing torpedoes, tipped with other conventional or nuclear warheads, at that range as well. Arleigh Burke's navy reflected the view of the Eisenhower administration that atomic weapons were simply weapons of another name, gadgets in a tool kit that could be used as commanders saw fit to accomplish an objective in a military operational setting.

The advent of guided-missile systems and phased-array radar marked the beginning of the final evolution of the cruiser warship type, begun in 1943, as a versatile defender of carrier task forces against air attack. By the late fifties, battleships were relics of the reserve fleet. The strike and tactical power-projection function of the fleet were vested in carrier aviation and submarines.

Although the SCB would continue its study of converting battleships to missile ships into 1960, the pivot point had arrived. The abandonment of the BBG conversion experiments left the way open for a new type of primary fleet asset to emerge. Although the queenly aircraft carrier, now represented by the *Forrestal* class, continued to warm many hearts, the ballistic missile submarine would soon lay claim to being the Navy's new capital ship.

30

FROM THE DEEP TO TARGET

ON JULY 20, 1960, IN AN EMPTY PATCH OF OCEAN ABOUT THIRTY miles off Cocoa Beach at Cape Canaveral, Florida, a great bubble of air broached the surface and produced roiling turbulence.

The ballistic missile submarine USS *George Washington,* about sixty feet below, had opened and flooded one of her Polaris missile tubes. A young lieutenant named Bernard Botula, the boomer's fire-control officer, pressed a button on his control panel. Compressed air rushed into the missile tube, one of sixteen installed vertically in two rows of eight in the center of the submarine's hull. The *George Washington*'s 381-foot-long hull bounced. A giant steel cap covering the top of the tube swung open and a column of compressed air propelled the twenty-eight-foot-long, $1.5 million weapon through fifty feet of water. As the missile broke through the surface and climbed, sailors on board the USS *Observation Island*—an experimental auxiliary that was the first surface ship outfitted with a fully functional fleet ballistic missile firing system—gasped. But then, after a timing device ignited the first stage solid-fuel engine, the missile rose into the sky, righting itself with bursts from its jetavators—miniature jets that functioned as rudders for course correction—and spreading a white smoke plume. Just under a minute later, when it had gained about fifteen miles of altitude, the first stage fell away and the second stage ignited and burned for another minute. At this point, some seventy miles up, the dummy warhead separated from the second stage, soaring toward its target on the Atlantic Missile Test Range eleven hundred miles away at a speed topping fourteen thousand miles per hour. An inertial guidance system sensed the slightest deviation in that preset course.

Commander James B. Osborn sent a message to CNO Arleigh Burke, who was present with other top brass on the *Observation Island,* and to the White House: "POLARIS—FROM OUT OF THE DEEP TO TARGET. PERFECT."

Journalists struggled to find admirals willing to make bold pronouncements following a dramatic demonstration. The Polaris program's chief salesman, Admiral Red Raborn, was the exception, saying that the first successful test of the system was "the most significant happening in weaponry since the day when the airplane first flew. I believe," he said, "that it will be just as important as the airplane as to the defense of our country."

National politics, however, had taken a turn. Eisenhower's steady stewardship of multiple international crises did not benefit his designated successor, Vice President Richard M. Nixon. Nixon's rival for the White House was a dynamic young World War II naval hero, John F. Kennedy, Jr., scion of the influential Boston family, who had a sense of the day's social tremors. On October 19, 1960, Dr. Martin Luther King, Jr., was arrested in Atlanta for leading a civil rights protest. Supporting King looked to cost Kennedy votes in the South. Defying several campaign advisers, he called Coretta Scott King on October 26 to offer help in securing her husband's release. Kennedy was subsequently endorsed by Martin Luther King, Sr., father of the civil rights leader. Shrewdly, Kennedy chose a powerful Texan, Senator Lyndon Baines Johnson, as his running mate. The African American vote went heavily for Kennedy across the nation, providing the margin of victory in several states.

On November 15, 1960, the *George Washington,* skippered by Commander Osborn and with a crew of about a hundred, departed Charleston newly loaded with ballistic missiles, headed to Dam Neck, Virginia, for training in the Fleet Ballistic Missile fire-control system, then set course for the North Atlantic to carry out her first strategic deterrence patrol, over a vast designated expanse of ocean. Cruising slowly beneath the seas between the Arctic ice pack and the north coast of the Soviet Union, "tracing long racetrack ovals, and the occasional lazy eight, just to keep the helmsman interested," a submarine could remain in the friendly waters off Greenland and lob missiles into Moscow and Leningrad within fifteen minutes. Or hit Moscow from the Arabian Sea. Or Vladivostok from the environs of distant Wake Island. Red Raborn's people were working "hard push" schedules to increase the missile's range: researching fuels with better specific impulse, lighter metals for use in engines, and miniaturizing everything, the more room to allow for the warhead. The State Department, meanwhile, was in negotiations with Great Britain to base SSBNs (nuclear-powered ballistic missile submarines) at Holy Loch, Scotland, in 1961. Some thought it remarkable that the United States had developed all this capability, from preliminary design to deployment, in just five years. Red Raborn could be credited for that much.

AIRPLANES FLYING FROM aircraft carriers dropping conventional bombs had not been able to stop the Chinese army from coming across a river in Korea in 1950. In the following years, various schemes to fulfill the "heavy bombardment" mission had risen and fallen, prompted by the Navy's chagrin over this galling fact. While Polaris was never touted as having a tactical application, submarine development in New London had produced an attack submarine with revolutionary hull form. The submarine USS *Albacore*'s hydrodynamically efficient "teardrop" hull, built with unusual features such as a fixed cruciform tail arrangement that put the control surfaces forward of the propeller, was adopted in the swift new *Skipjack*-class nuclear-powered attack submarine, which was capable of underwater speeds as high as twenty-nine knots.

As the 1950s drew to a close, the aircraft carrier had survived a revolution in weaponry that was supposed to have sent it down the road of the catapult and the longbow. Four of the new *Forrestal*-class supercarriers were in commission: the *Forrestal, Saratoga, Ranger,* and *Independence;* the first nuclear-powered carrier, *Enterprise,* and the *Kitty Hawk,* the lead ship of a powerful new class, were under construction. The cruisers escorting them were numerous and powerful, firing antiaircraft missiles with a one-hundred-mile range.

But it was Polaris that changed public attitudes and strategic thinking in the Navy Department. Newspaper photos of great fourteen-ton missiles sprouting from the sea and taking flight atop a gout of smoke and a pillar of flame captured the imagination and signified the U.S. Navy's new worldwide reach. Where naval forces had prevailed over land forces, they had generally done so by virtue of mobility and stealth. So too now, except that the maritime forces had closed the gap in terms of sheer firepower as well. On the strength of a decade's progress in technology, the service that had fought a battle for survival and then tried in vain to stop Chinese soldiers from using bridges to cross a river had now acquired a revolutionary capability in power projection.

Far from Bikini and those days of sharp questioning in congressional hearing rooms, securely hidden in their secret harbors where the sun forbears to shine, the U.S. Navy's new capital ships, made effective by skilled nuclear-trained engineers and technicians and equipped with megaton main batteries, could shiver the foundation of the earth.

Acknowledgments

From Jim

Having completed and published a book narrating the story of the Pacific War up to the point of two atomic bombs exploding over Japan and the emperor reluctantly surrendering to America and consenting to occupation by U.S. forces, I discovered that I did not have it in me to go back in time and produce another campaign or battle narrative. Instead, I felt called to carry events forward. Doing so took me into much new territory. Accordingly, I have been mightily fortunate in having so many friends and associates who've been generous with their knowledge of the complex and eventful years of the early Cold War and naval developments therein.

Heading the list of those who shared their abundant knowledge with me is David Rosenberg of the Institute for Defense Analyses. For scarcely a question I've asked Dave in the past four years has he failed to return a trove of PDFs of valuable specialized scholarship, some of it written by himself but all of it, it seemed, cataloged in his capacious analogue encyclopedia of a mind. Few people I know can match the breadth and depth of his knowledge on a full range of subjects pertaining to U.S. naval history.

Matching David's generosity and kindness have been my friends and colleagues at the Naval Historical Foundation, including board chairman Admiral William (Fox) Fallon, executive director Sonny Masso, and Dave Winkler.

The many excellent publishing professionals of the Ballantine Bantam Dell Publishing Group within Penguin Random House have been my faithful and diligent publishers, sponsors, and advocates for twenty years and four books now. I will be forever indebted to executive editor Tracy Devine for starting me on this path in 2000, and now to executive editor Susanna Porter for picking up so readily and ably where Tracy left off. Thank you, Kara Welsh, Emily Hartley, Michael Harney, and Benjamin Dreyer; Virginia Norey for her design; Sydney Shiffman, Pamela Alders, Andy Lefkowitz; Carlos Beltran for the beautiful book jacket and Emily DeHuff, my excellent and meticulous copy editor. I note that Bantam Books was established in the fraught year when the narrative of this book begins, that hinge of history, 1945. I am proud to have their famous rooster on the spines of all my volumes.

Thanks, too, to John Bruning, Jim Bryant, Sam Cox, Darrell Gary, Mohammad Issa, Wilson Nasi, Vince O'Hara, Dan Pedersen, Enrique Prado, Craig Reed, Peter Swartz, Sam Tangredi, Steve Younger, and Karl Zingheim for their help.

During a particularly challenging time, my family has benefited from the kindness and support of many friends. Thank you, Julie and Buddie Ballard, Sandy Bayne, Cynthia and Avery Bengtson, Dawn and Dusty Black, Randy Boston, Christine and Brian Caudle, Tasha and Robert Cline, David Crenshaw, David and Sherry Dalgleish, Amy and Randy Erben, Cari and Monte Ezell, Jeff Foster, Lisa, Lou, and Cornell Fuka, Becky and Kerry Getter, Laura and Bob Grim, Kathi and John Haralson, Hospice Austin, Diana and Billy Johnson, Anne Keene, Alex Kershaw, Roy Kircher, Dana and Jeff Kocurek, Jennifer Kuczaj, Marcus Luttrell, Morgan Luttrell, Beth and Chris McKay, Lisa and James Mikus, Thresa and Mike Nasi, Erick Nchanji, Michael Newton, Sheila and Chris Newton, Shelly and Erol Ozdil, Bill and Diana Patterson, Melinda and Marc Patterson, Donna Phillips, Cathy and Joe Garcia-Prats, Liz and Ted Price, Nancy Prideaux, Ashley and David Putman, Helen Rella, Francis Rietti, Cecily and Tom Rodman, Marty Ross, Ann Sherrow, Stephen Stauss, Allison Suttle, Lisa and Paul Terrill, Natalie and Curtis Thigpen, Stacey and Brad Thompson, Amy and Mark Updegrove, Terri and Chris Von Dohlen, Chris Vyhnal, Adam Ward, Cissy and Mark Warner, Lucy and Phil Weber, and Adam Weiss. The trouble with a list like this is that you invariably make omissions, for which, if I did, I apologize. My only intent here is to express our deep appreciation to each and every member of Team Hornfischer. You know who you are, and we do too.

My wife, Sharon, holds up the home front. She stands by me with consummate care, thus making everything else possible. Our children, David James, Grace Ann, and Henry Hutchins, have been a joy to share this life with; my fervent prayer is that they find and embrace their own passions. I thank them for supporting mine.

From Sharon

Lucky is the person who gets to live a life with a true passion for their work. And lucky is the person who gets to live with that person. My husband was in the right career, he was passionate about writing and passionate about his work in publishing. As I look back on our life together, it seems foreordained that Jim and I were to land in central Texas.

Yes, I am a native Texan, but I believe greater forces were at play. We were open to living anywhere, really. Jim applied for a job at the Naval Institute Press, in Annapolis, Maryland, but he didn't hear back until we had already moved to Austin. Jim was destined to live and work where his full potential as a writer and historian of the battles of the Pacific War could be nurtured and supported. When we moved to Texas, we were unaware that the hometown of Admiral Chester W. Nimitz, Commander of the Pacific Fleet during World War II, and the Nimitz Museum were just a few miles down the road in Fredericksburg. The Nimitz became a frequently visited place for Jim and me in the early 1990s as we discovered this jewel in our own backyard. The Nimitz Museum CEO, Rear Admiral Charles D. Grojean, and the irreplaceable Helen McDonald were among the first to support Jim's interest and passion for research on the Pacific theater.

At the Nimitz, Jim was able to meet key players in this world, veterans who had served during this period, allowing Jim to obtain primary sources via oral histories and interviews with these patriots. Jim met renowned historians like Rich Frank, who became a close friend, and colleagues like John Wukovits, who became a friend and future literary client, authoring many amazing military histories of his own. The Nimitz supported these rich relationships of the like-minded, allowing shared intellectual concepts which enriched and deepened their knowledge, which they in turn shared collegially with one another and the world through their speaking events and publications.

Jim was invited to be a guest speaker at the Nimitz Museum's annual symposium each September, where he further enriched his knowledge. Additionally, we began to be invited to ship reunions, where we spent many working vacations through the years. As our children arrived, they too were included in the reunions, which were perfect for a family man with a passion for his work. We could work, play, and introduce our children to many of our nation's superheroes, the veterans of World War II. This was extra-special to me, as my late father, Lieutenant Colonel Robert Wyatt Simmons, a pilot in that war, passed away before he could meet Jim or our children. Jim and I both felt humbled and honored to be on the invitation list to hear these veterans tell their stories.

The Nimitz Museum, under the current leadership of president and CEO General Mike Hagee, USMC (Ret.), has continued to support Jim and his body of work. Jim was, and I continue to be, honored to call Mike a friend. Jim has donated his archives to the already amazing catalog of material housed at the Nimitz for future generations of researchers, students, and historians to continue to study and learn the strategies and history of the Pacific theater. May this museum continue to flourish as it supports future generations' interest in history.

A big and heartfelt thank-you also to Frank Weimann, literary agent and founder of the Literary Group, for taking a chance on Jim, back when Frank was a bright-eyed twentysomething looking to make the move from editor to literary agent. We have always been glad of this initial opportunity, and the freedom to explore the literary world outside New York City by supporting Jim's Austin branch of the Literary Group.

I am grateful that the Naval Institute Press did not offer Jim a job in a timely fashion. And even more appreciative for their friendship through the years, and very proud of their recently published graphic novel adaptation of Jim's first book, *The Last Stand of the Tin Can Sailors*, which came out in October 2021.

I thank the Department of the Navy for honoring Jim with their Distinguished Public Service Award. It took the moving of a few mountains to arrange for this beautiful and stirring award presentation to take place in our home on short notice, just weeks before Jim's death. This event was made possible under the extraordinary leadership of Rear Admiral Ted LeClair, USN, and Captain Jim Lockard, USN, who served as our boots-on-the-ground logistics team while also coordinating and leading a seamless in-person and Zoom event with less than four days' planning. Thank you, Morgan Luttrell, for the strong and heartfelt words you spoke at the ceremony. Your unscripted banter with Jim gave him his last best laugh and put a smile in all our hearts.

I thank Rear Admiral Samuel Cox, USN (Ret.), Vice Admiral Peter H. Daly, USN (Ret.), Admiral William J. Fallon, Rear Admiral Edward "Sonny" Masso, and a host of others for nominating and awarding my husband with this recognition. Receiving this award filled Jim with immense gratitude for the recognition that his life's work was appreciated and mattered. I, along with the rest of Jim's family, thank you.

I also thank the Naval Historical Foundation for bestowing on Jim the Distinguished Service Award for his achievements on behalf of naval history. Jim was honored to be a member of the board of this esteemed organization. Becoming acquainted with staff and fellow board members Admiral William J. Fallon, Rear Admiral Edward "Sonny" Masso, and Dr. Dave Winkler, Commander, USNR (Ret.) was a particularly high honor for Jim.

I was tasked with the job of completing some final details for this book and found myself fortunate and grateful for the expert design skills of James Fenelon, who generously rendered the maps for this book. I also owe a huge thank-you to Brent Jones, who developed the photo sections and captions, and then contributed invaluable help and expertise in the final editing stage. Their time, skill, knowledge, and support were instrumental in bringing Jim's words and vision to the page. I am very appreciative of their help and comforted by their selfless showing of friendship honoring Jim's memory.

An extra thank-you to Susanna Porter and Sydney Shiffman at Penguin Random House / Bantam Books for their professionalism and patience as they shepherded this novice through the editorial process. I am indebted to you for your marvelous work in bringing to fruition this Cold War volume that completes the legacy of Jim's writing life.

Bibliography

In the final stages of his illness, the author was unable to prepare the endnotes for this book. However, with the help of Sharon Hornfischer, his extensive bibliography has been compiled.

Books and Articles

Alexander, James Edwin. *Inchon to Wonsan: From the Deck of a Destroyer in the Korean War*. Annapolis: U.S. Naval Institute Press, 1996.

Amme, Carl H. "The Soviet Navy in the Mediterranean Sea." *Naval War College Review* 21, no. 10 (June 1969), pp. 154–59.

Arnold, Henry H. *Global Mission*. New York: Harper, 1949.

Barlow, Jeffrey G. *From Hot War to Cold: The U.S. Navy and National Security Affairs, 1945–1955*. Stanford: Stanford University Press, 2009.

Bruning, John R. *Crimson Sky: The Air Battle for Korea*. Dulles, Va.: Brassey's, 1999.

Burrows, William E. *By Any Means Necessary: America's Secret Air War in the Cold War*. New York: Farrar, Straus and Giroux, 2001.

Cagle, Malcolm. *The Naval Aviation Guide*. 2nd ed. Annapolis: U.S. Naval Institute Press, 1969.

Clark, Eugene Franklin. *The Secrets of Inchon: An Untold Story of the Most Daring Covert Mission of the Korean War*. New York: G. P. Putnam's Sons, 2002.

Clark, J. J., with Clark G. Reynolds. *Carrier Admiral*. New York: David McKay, 1967.

Cleaver, Thomas McKelvey. *MiG Alley: The U.S. Air Force in Korea, 1950–1953*. New York: Osprey, 2019.

Condit, Kenneth W. *The Joint Chiefs of Staff and National Policy, 1947–1949*. Vol. 2 of *History of the Joint Chiefs of Staff*. Washington, D.C.: Office of Joint History, Office of the Chairman of the Joint Chiefs of Staff, 1996.

Cowley, Robert, ed. *The Cold War: A Military History*. New York: Random House, 2006.

Crane, Conrad C. *American Airpower Strategy in Korea: 1950–1953*. Lawrence: University Press of Kansas, 2000.

Cranwell, John Philips. "Sea Power and the Atomic Bomb." *U.S. Naval Institute Proceedings,* Oct. 1946. usni.org/magazines/proceedings/1946/october/sea-power-and-atomic-bomb.

Cumings, Bruce. *The Korean War: A History.* New York: Modern Library, 2010.

Donovan, Robert J. *Tumultuous Years: The Presidency of Harry S. Truman, 1949–1953.* New York: W. W. Norton, 1982.

Dorwart, Jeffrey M. *Eberstadt and Forrestal: A National Security Partnership, 1909–1949.* College Station: Texas A&M University Press, 1991.

Drea, Edward J., et al. *History of the Unified Command Plan, 1946–2012.* Washington, D.C.: Joint History Office, 2013. jcs.mil/Portals/36/Documents/History/Institutional/Command_Plan.pdf.

Eccles, Henry E. "The Russian Maritime Threat: An Approach to the Problem." *Naval War College Review* 21, no. 10 (June 1969), pp. 4–14.

Farrar-Hockley, Anthony. *The British Part in the Korean War.* Vol. 1, *A Distant Obligation.* London: Her Majesty's Stationery Office, 1990.

———. *The British Part in the Korean War.* Vol. 2, *An Honourable Discharge.* London: Her Majesty's Stationery Office, 1995.

Ferrell, Robert H. *Off the Record: The Private Papers of Harry S. Truman.* New York: Harper and Row, 1980.

Finn, Peter, and Petra Couvée. *The Zhivago Affair: The Kremlin, the CIA, and the Battle over a Forbidden Book.* New York: Pantheon, 2014.

Firebaugh, Millard S., ed. *Naval Engineering and American Sea Power.* Dubuque, Iowa: Kendall/Hunt Publishing, 2000.

Fontaine, André. *History of the Cold War: From the Korean War to the Present.* New York: Pantheon, 1969.

Friedman, Norman. *Aircraft Carriers: An Illustrated Design History.* Annapolis: U.S. Naval Institute Press, 1983.

———. *U.S. Battleships: An Illustrated Design History.* Annapolis: U.S. Naval Institute Press, 1985.

Fursenko, Aleksandr, and Timothy Naftali. *Khrushchev's Cold War: The Inside Story of an American Adversary.* New York: W. W. Norton, 2006.

Gaddis, John Lewis. *George F. Kennan: An American Life.* New York: Penguin Press, 2011.

Gaddis, John, ed. *Strategies of Containment: A Critical Appraisal of American National Security Policy During the Cold War.* New York: Oxford Center for Oral History Press, 1982.

Galantin, I. J. *Submarine Admiral: From Battlewagons to Ballistic Missiles*. Champaign: Center for Oral History of Illinois Press, 1996.

Gallery, Daniel V. *Eight Bells, and All's Well*. New York: W. W. Norton, 1965.

Garrett, William B. "The U.S. Navy's Role in the 1956 Suez Crisis." *Naval War College Review* 23, no. 3 (March 1970), pp. 66–78.

Gellman, Barton. *Contending with Kennan: Toward a Philosophy of American Power*. Westport, Conn.: Praeger, 1985.

Gorshkov, S. G. *The Sea Power of the State*. Annapolis: U.S. Naval Institute Press, 1976.

Graebner, Norman A., ed. *The National Security: Its Theory and Practice, 1945–1960*. 1st ed. New York: Oxford University Press, 1986.

Grassey, Thomas B. "Retrospective: The Midway Class." *U.S. Naval Institute Proceedings*, May 1986. usni.org/magazines/proceedings/1986/may/retrospective-midway-class.

Gray, Colin S. *The Leverage of Sea Power: The Strategic Advantage of Navies in War*. New York: Free Press, 1992.

Hall, Cargill, and Clayton D. Laurie. *Early Cold War Overflights, 1950–1956: Symposium Proceedings*. Vol. 2. Washington, D.C.: National Reconnaissance Office, 2003.

Haslam, Jonathan. *Russia's Cold War: From the October Revolution to the Fall of the Wall*. New Haven: Yale University Press, 2011.

Hattendorf, John B., ed. *Mahan on Naval Strategy*. Annapolis: Naval Institute Press, 2015.

Henry, Ken, and Don Keith. *Gallant Lady: A Biography of the USS* Archerfish. New York: Forge Books, 2004.

Herrmann, Paul. *Conquest by Man*. Translated by Michael Bullock. New York: Harper and Bros., 1954.

Hessler, William H. "A Geopolitics for America (Prize Essay, 1944)." *U.S. Naval Institute Proceedings*, March 1944. usni.org/magazines/proceedings/1944/march/geopolitics-america-prize-essay-1944.

Hewlett, Richard G., and Francis Duncan. *Nuclear Navy, 1946–1962*. Chicago: University of Chicago Press, 1974.

Hinton, Harold B. "Denfeld Was Heir to Service Fight." *New York Times*, Oct. 28, 1949, p. 3.

Holloway, James L., III. *Aircraft Carriers at War: Personal Retrospective of Korea, Vietnam, and the Soviet Confrontation*. Annapolis: U.S. Naval Institute Press, 2007.

Hook, Sidney. "The Faiths of Whittaker Chambers." *New York Times Book Review*, May 25, 1952.

Hoopes, Townsend, and Douglas Brinkley. *Driven Patriot: The Life and Times of James Forrestal*. New York: Alfred A. Knopf, 1992.

Hoover, J. Edgar. *Masters of Deceit: The Story of Communism in America and How to Fight It*. New York: Henry Holt, 1958.

Howarth, Stephen. *To Shining Sea: A History of the United States Navy, 1775–1991*. New York: Random House, 1991.

Howe, Jonathan Trumbull. *Multicrises: Sea Power and Global Politics in the Missile Age*. Cambridge, Mass.: MIT Press, 1971.

Hughes, Wayne P., Jr., and Robert P. Girrier. *Fleet Tactics and Naval Operations*. 3rd ed. Annapolis: Naval Institute Press, 2018.

Hurley, Alfred F., and Robert C. Ehrhart, eds. *Air Power and Warfare: Proceedings of the 8th Military History Symposium, U.S. Air Force Academy, 18–20 October 1978*. Washington, D.C.: Office of Air Force History, Headquarters USAF, and United States Air Force Academy, 1979. media.defense.gov/2010/Sep /22/2001330054/-1/-1/0/AFD-100922-028.pdf.

James, D. Clayton, with Anne Sharp Wells. *Refighting the Last War: Command and Crisis in Korea, 1950–1953*. New York: Free Press, 1993.

Jurika, Stephen, Jr. *From Pearl Harbor to Vietnam: The Memoirs of Admiral Arthur W. Radford*. Stanford: Hoover Institution Press, 1980.

Khlevniuk, Oleg. *Stalin: New Biography of a Dictator*. New Haven: Yale University Press, 2015.

Khrushchev, Nikita. *Khrushchev Remembers*. Translated and edited by Strobe Talbott. New York: Little, Brown, 1970.

———. *Khrushchev Remembers: The Last Testament*. Translated and edited by Strobe Talbott. New York: Little, Brown, 1974.

Kingseed, Cole C. *Eisenhower and the Suez Crisis of 1956*. Baton Rouge: Louisiana State University Center for Oral History Press, 1995.

Knight, Jonathan. "American Statecraft and the 1946 Black Sea Straits Controversy." *Political Science Quarterly*, vol. 90, no. 3, 1975, pp. 451–75. jstor.org /stable/2148296.

Kohnen, David, ed. *21st Century Knox: Influence, Sea Power, and History for the Modern Era*. Annapolis: Naval Institute Press, 2016.

Kramarenko, Sergei. *Air Combat over the Eastern Front and Korea*. South Yorkshire, UK: Pen and Sword, 2008.

Krock, Arthur. *Memoirs: Sixty Years on the Firing Line*. New York: Funk and Wagnalls, 1968.

Leffler, Melvyn P. *A Preponderance of Power: National Security, the Truman Administration, and the Cold War*. Stanford: Stanford University Press, 1992.

Lehman, John. *On Seas of Glory: Heroic Men, Great Ships, and Epic Battles of the American Navy.* New York: Touchstone, 2001.

Leviero, Anthony. "Midway Fires V-2 Underway at Sea." *New York Times,* Sept. 9, 1947, p. 4.

Li, Xiaobing. *China's Battle for Korea: The 1951 Spring Offensive.* Bloomington: Indiana University Press, 2014.

Mahan, Alfred Thayer. "The United States Looking Outward." *Atlantic,* December 1890. theatlantic.com/magazine/archive/1890/12/the-united -states-looking-outward/306348/.

Makos, Adam. *Devotion: An Epic Story of Heroism, Friendship, and Sacrifice.* New York: Ballantine, 2015.

Malone, Thomas F., Edward D. Goldberg, and Walter H. Munk. "Roger Randall Dougan Revelle." *New York Times,* editorial, Nov. 20, 1945.

Maloney, Sean M. *Securing Command of the Sea: NATO Naval Planning, 1948–1954.* Annapolis: U.S. Naval Institute Press, 1995.

Marolda, Edward J., ed. *The U.S. Navy in the Korean War.* Annapolis: U.S. Naval Institute Press, 2007.

MccGwire, Michael. "Changing Naval Operations and Military Intervention." *Naval War College Review* 30, no. 2 (Spring 1977), pp. 3–25.

McClenahan, William M., Jr., and William H. Becker. *Eisenhower and the Cold War Economy.* Baltimore: Johns Hopkins University Press, 2011.

McCullough, David. *Truman.* New York: Simon and Schuster, 1992.

McFarland, Keith D., and David L. Roll. *Louis Johnson and the Arming of America.* Bloomington: Indiana University Press, 2005.

Miller, Jerry. *Nuclear Weapons and Aircraft Carriers.* Washington, D.C.: Smithsonian Institution Scholarly Press, 2001.

———. *Nuclear Weapons and Aircraft Carriers: How the Bomb Saved Naval Aviation, 1945–1975.* Annapolis: U.S. Naval Institute Press, 2001.

Miller, William O. "The United Nations and Oceania: New Dimensions in the Cold War Refrain." *Naval War College Review* 22, no. 6 (June 1969), pp. 45–59.

Millis, Walter, ed. *The Forrestal Diaries.* New York: Viking, 1951.

Moore, J. E. *The Impact of Polaris: The Origins of Britain's Seaborne Nuclear Deterrent.* Huddersfield, UK: Richard Netherwood, 1999.

Muir, Malcolm. *Black Shoes and Blue Water: Surface Warfare in the United States Navy, 1945–1975.* Honolulu: University Press of the Pacific, 2005.

Mydans, Carl, and Shelley Mydans. *The Violent Peace: A Report on Wars in the Postwar World.* New York: Atheneum, 1968.

Nimitz, Chester W. "Your Navy as Peace Insurance." *National Geographic,* June 1946, p. 681.

———. "The Future Employment of Naval Forces." *Marine Corps Gazette,* March 1948, p. 36. In Westermeyer, ed., *Legacy of American Naval Power,* p. 131.

O'Rourke, G. G., with E. T. Wooldridge. *Night Fighters over Korea.* Annapolis: U.S. Naval Institute Press, 1998.

Peraino, Kevin. *A Force So Swift: Mao, Truman, and the Birth of Modern China, 1949.* New York: Crown, 2017.

Polmar, Norman. *Guide to the Soviet Navy.* 4th ed. Annapolis: U.S. Naval Institute Press, 1986.

———. *Ships and Aircraft of the U.S. Fleet.* 14th ed. Annapolis: U.S. Naval Institute Press, 1987.

———. *Aircraft Carriers: A History of Carrier Aviation and Its Influence on World Events, Vol. II: 1946–2006.* Lincoln, Neb.: Potomac Books, 2008.

———, Thomas A. Brooks, and George Fedoroff. *Admiral Gorshkov: The Man Who Challenged the U.S. Navy.* Annapolis: U.S. Naval Institute Press, 2019.

Potter, E. B. *Nimitz.* Annapolis: U.S. Naval Institute Press, 1976.

Powaski, Ronald E. *The Cold War: The United States and the Soviet Union, 1917–1991.* New York: Oxford University Press, 1998.

Power, Thomas S. *Design for Survival: A General's Urgent Report to the American People.* New York: Coward-McCann, 1964.

Prados, John. *The Sky Would Fall: Operation Vulture, the Secret U.S. Bombing Mission to Vietnam, 1954.* New York: Oxford University Press, 1983.

Rearden, Steven L. *History of the Office of the Secretary of Defense.* Vol. 1: *The Formative Years, 1947–1950.* 1st ed. Washington, D.C.: Office of the Secretary, Historical Office, 1984.

Rose, Lisle A. *Power at Sea.* Vol. 1, *The Age of Navalism, 1880–1918.* Columbia: University of Missouri Press, 2006.

———. *Power at Sea.* Vol. 2, *The Breaking Storm, 1919–1945.* Columbia: University of Missouri Press, 2006.

———. *Power at Sea.* Vol. 3, *A Violent Peace, 1946–2006.* Columbia: University of Missouri Press, 2006.

Rosenberg, David Alan. *American Postwar Air Doctrine and Organization: The Navy Experience.* Military History Symposium, U.S. Air Force Academy, Oct. 1978, p. 245.

———. "American Atomic Strategy and the Hydrogen Bomb Decision." *Journal of American History,* June 1979, p. 62.

———. "The Origins of Overkill: Nuclear Weapons and American Strategy, 1945–1960." *International Security* 7, no. 4 (Spring 1983).

————. "Being 'Red': The Challenge of Taking the Soviet Side in War Games at the Naval War College." *Naval War College Review* 41, no. 1 (Winter 1988), pp. 88–93.

————, and W. B. Moore. "Smoking Radiating Ruin at the End of Two Hours: Documents on American Plans for Nuclear War with the Soviet Union, 1954–55." *International Security* 6, no. 3 (Winter 1981–1982). jstor.org/stable /2538605.

Ruge, Friedrich. *The Soviets as Naval Opponents 1941–1945.* Annapolis: U.S. Naval Institute Press, 1979.

Shalett, Sidney. "Navy Tells Plans for the Atom Age: To Keep 7 Fleets." *New York Times,* Jan. 14, 1946, p. 1.

Slouka, Mark. *Nobody's Son: A Memoir.* New York: W. W. Norton, 2016.

Speller, Ian. *Understanding Naval Warfare.* London: Routledge, 2014.

Spurr, Russell. *Enter the Dragon: China's Undeclared War Against the U.S. in Korea, 1950–1951.* New York: Morrow, 2010.

"Stabilizer Balked Midway V-2 Test." *New York Times,* Sept. 11, 1947, p. 5. nytimes.com/1947/09/11/archives/stabilizer-balked-midway-v2-test .html.

Stimson, Henry L., and McGeorge Bundy. *On Active Service in Peace and War.* New York: Harper and Brothers, 1947.

Swan, Patrick A. *Alger Hiss, Whittaker Chambers, and the Schism in the American Soul.* Wilmington, Del.: Intercollegiate Studies Institute, 2003.

Swanson, Michael. *The War State: The Origins of the Military-Industrial Complex and the Power Elite, 1945–1963.* CreateSpace, 2013.

Swartz, Peter M. *Sea Changes: U.S. Navy Deployment Strategy, 1775–2002.* Sponsor Review, Center for Strategic Studies, July 2002.

Tepsurkiev, Yuriy, and Leonid Krylov. *Soviet MiG-15 Aces of the Korean War.* London: Osprey, 2008.

Thompson, Warren E. *Naval Aviation in the Korean War: Aircraft, Ships, and Men.* South Yorkshire, UK: Pen and Sword, 2012.

Toland, John. *In Mortal Combat: Korea, 1950–1953.* New York: Morrow, 1991.

Truman, Harry S. *Memoirs by Harry S. Truman.* Vol. 1, *Year of Decision.* New York: Doubleday, 1955.

————. *Memoirs by Harry S. Truman.* Vol. 2, *Years of Trial and Hope.* New York: Doubleday, 1956.

Vego, Milan. "The Role of the Attack Submarines in Soviet Naval Theory." *Naval War College Review* 36, no. 6 (Nov.–Dec. 1983), pp. 48–64.

Waggoner, Walter H. "Truman Orders Reserves Strengthened and Trained." *New York Times,* Oct. 18, 1948.

Weeks, Albert Loren. *Myths of the Cold War: Amending Historiographic Distortions.* Lanham, Md.: Lexington Books, 2014.

Weigley, Russell F. *The American Way of War: A History of United States Military Strategy and Policy.* New York: Macmillan, 1973.

Weir, Gary E. *An Ocean in Common: American Naval Officers, Scientists, and the Ocean Environment.* College Station: Texas A&M University Press, 2001.

Weisgall, Jonathan M. *Operation Crossroads: The Atomic Tests at Bikini Atoll.* Annapolis: U.S. Naval Institute Press, 1994.

Westermeyer, Paul W., ed. *The Legacy of American Naval Power: Reinvigorating Maritime Strategic Thought; An Anthology.* Quantico, Va.: Marine Corps University Press, 2019.

Oral Histories

Anderson, Dillon. Columbia Center for Oral History, 1972.

Anderson, George. Columbia Center for Oral History, 1967.

Ballentine, John Jennings. Columbia Center for Oral History, 1964.

Burke, Arleigh. U.S. Naval Institute, 1979.

Carney, Robert C. Columbia Center for Oral History, 1964.

Condon, John P. Columbia Center for Oral History, 1973.

Conolly, Richard L. Columbia Center for Oral History, 1959.

Dennison, Robert Lee. Oral history, U.S. Naval Institute, Aug. 1975.

Durbrow, Elbridge May. Oral history interview by Richard D. McKinzie, Truman Library, 1973.

Fechteler, William Morrow. Columbia Center for Oral History, 1962.

Franke, William B. Columbia Center for Oral History, 1973.

Holloway, James L., Jr. Columbia Center for Oral History, 1963.

Megee, Vernon E. Columbia Center for Oral History, 1967, 1968.

Nimitz, Chester W. Columbia Center for Oral History, 1967.

Stewart, Joseph L. Columbia Center for Oral History, 1972.

Stump, Felix B. Columbia Center for Oral History, 1964.

Official Documents

CINCPAC, Bikini Scientific Resurvey, Press Summary no. 12, July 1947.
    CINCPAC, Bikini Scientific Resurvey, Press Summary, July 26, 1947.

Congressional Record, "Proceedings and Debates of the 81st Congress," First Session, 1949. Washington, D.C.: National Academy of Sciences, 1998.

Defense Nuclear Agency, *Operation Crossroads 1946: United States Atmospheric Nuclear Weapons Tests,* Department of Defense, Nuclear Test Personnel Review, Washington, D.C.

De Florez, Luis. Testimony. New York: Senate Military Affairs Committee, Dec. 10, 1946. NHHC 1-108.

Department of the Navy, General Board. "National Security and Navy Contributions Thereto for the Next Ten Years," quoted in Rosenberg, *American Postwar Air Doctrine and Organization,* pp. 256–57.

Department of the Navy. *Operational Experience of Fast Battleships: World War II, Korea, Vietnam.* Washington, D.C.: Naval Historical Center, 1989.

Farrell, Thomas Major General, to Major General L. R. Groves, December 3, 1945. Records of Office of the Chief of Engineers of the Commanding General: Manhattan Project [RG 77], Operation Crossroads, December 1945–September 1946, box 4, folder 8.

Foreign Relations of the United States, 1946, Vol. 6, *Eastern Europe and the Soviet Union,* eds. Rogers P. Churchill and William Slany (Washington, D.C.: U.S. Government Printing Office, 1969), Document 473, history.state.gov /historicaldocuments/frus1946v06/d473.

Foreign Relations of the United States, 1946, Vol. 6, *Eastern Europe and the Soviet Union,* eds. Rogers P. Churchill and William Slany (Washington, D.C.: U.S. Government Printing Office, 1969), Document 474, history.state.gov /historicaldocuments/frus1946v06/d474.

Foreign Relations of the United States, 1946, Vol. 6, *Eastern Europe and the Soviet Union,* "The Chargé in the Soviet Union (Kennan) to the Secretary of State" (Washington, D.C.: U.S. Government Printing Office, 1969), Document 475, pp. 698–709, history.state.gov/historicaldocuments/frus1946v06 /d475.

Foreign Relations of the United States, 1948, Vol. 3, *Western Europe,* eds. David H. Stauffer, Ralph R. Goodwin, Marvin W. Kranz, Howard M. Smyth, Frederick Aandahl, and Charles S. Sampson (Washington, D.C.: U.S. Government Printing Office, 1969), Document 36, history.state.gov/historicaldocuments /frus1948v03.

Forrestal, James V. Remarks to Senate Foreign Relations Committee, Jan. 15, 1946, 8 NHHC-1, 12.

———. Remarks to the President's Air Policy Commission, Dec. 3, 1947, NARA 1, 36.

———. Remarks to the Women's National Press Club Luncheon, Feb. 4, 1948, NARA 1, 41.

———. Testimony to House Armed Services Committee, Feb. 16, 1949, NARA 1, 48.

Halsey, William F. Statement to the Senate Military Affairs Committee, Dec. 6, 1945, 5 NHHC 4-824.

———. Speech, "The Navy and Our National Security," Waldorf-Astoria Hotel, New York, Dec. 14, 1945, NHHC 4-827–30.

———. Speech, New York State Bar Association, Jan. 26, 1946, 4 NHHC 4-836.

Hensel, Struve. Letter to *The New York Times*, Nov. 27, 1945, NHHC 2-447.

Joint Chiefs of Staff, Evaluation Board. *The Evaluation of the Atomic Bomb as a Military Weapon: The Final Report of the Joint Chiefs of Staff Evaluation Board for Operation Crossroads*, National Security Archive Document 33, June 30, 1947.

Lockwood, Charles A. *Down to the Sea in Subs*. In Charles A. Lockwood, oral history, Columbia Center for Oral History, Oral History Research Office, 1965.

Lulejian & Associates, *History of the Strategic Arms Competition, 1945–1972* (study for the deputy CNO for plans and policy), "U.S. Aircraft Carriers in the Strategic Role, Part I: Naval Strategy in a Period of Change: Interservice Rivalry, Strategic Interaction, and the Development of a Nuclear Attack Capability, 1945–1951," 1975.

Mills, E. W. "Bureau of Ships Nuclear Power Program," National Research Council, Undersea Warfare Symposium, Apr. 6, 1948. Columbia Center for Oral History Research Office.

Newson, Henry W. Joint Staff Planners, Joint Chiefs of Staff, "Tests of the Effects of Atomic Explosives," Dec. 22, 1945.

Nimitz, Chester W. Letter to James V. Forrestal, 1 NHHC 4-1015.

———. Senate testimony, Dec. 6, 1945.

———. Speech to the Army Industrial College, Jan. 7, 1946, NHHC 4-870.

———. Speech to the National Geographic Society, Jan. 25, 1946, 6 NHHC 4-879.

Papers of James V. Forrestal, "History of Operation Crossroads," Chapter 21, Part II, Archives Branch, Naval History and Heritage Command, Washington, D.C., 1934–1951.

———, "The Hazards of Merger," Archives Branch, Naval History and Heritage Command, 3–750, Washington, D.C., 1934–1951.

———, "The Unification Dispute," Archives Branch, Naval History and Heritage Command, Washington, D.C., 1934–1951.

———, April 2, 1949, and April 3, 1949, Exhibit 3, Medical National Naval Medical Center, Bethesda, Maryland, "Board of Investigation Convened at the U.S. Naval Hospital, National Naval Medical Center, Bethesda, Maryland, on 23 May 1949 to Investigate and Report Upon the Circumstances Attending the Death of Mr. James V. Forrestal" (Willcutts Board), May 31, 1949.

Parsons, W. S. Memorandum to Rear Adm. W. H. P. Blandy, Dec. 3, 1945.

Schnabel, James F., and Robert J. Watson. *The Joint Chiefs of Staff and National Policy, 1945–1947: The Korean War.* Vol. 3 of *History of the Joint Chiefs of Staff.* Wilmington, Del.: Michael Glazier, 1979.

Spruance, Raymond A. Letter to Senate Naval Affairs Committee, re S. 2044, July 10, 1946, NHHC 4-891.

Stalin, Joseph. "Speech to Voters, Stalin Electoral District, Moscow," Feb. 9, 1946, History and Public Policy Program Digital Archive, Gospolitizdat, Moscow, 1946. digitalarchive.wilsoncenter.org/document/116179; soviethistory.msu.edu/1947-2/cold-war/cold-war-texts/stalin-election -speech/.

Stimson, Henry. Letter to James V. Forrestal, May 26, 1945. Forrestal Papers, NHHC 1-249.

Taylor, Maxwell D. Address to the 83rd graduating class of Submarine School, New London, Dec. 20, 1946.

USS *Midway,* Cruise Book, 1947–1948.

White House. "Twentieth Report to Congress on Lend-Lease Operations, period ending June 30, 1945," Aug. 30, 1945.

Image Credits

Insert 1, page 1, top: United States Navy, National Archives 80-G-701293

Insert 1, page 1, bottom: Naval History and Heritage Command, NHF-137-M.01

Insert 1, page 2, top: United States Navy, National Archives 80-G-701624

Insert 1, page 2, bottom left: United States Navy, National Archives 80-G-302295

Insert 1, page 2, bottom right: Library of Congress

Insert 1, page 3, top left: United States Navy, National Archives 80-G-421847

Insert 1, page 3, top right: United States Navy, Naval History and Heritage Command NH 74329

Insert 1, page 3, bottom: United States Navy, National Archives 80-G-702511

Insert 1, page 4, top: Library of Congress

Insert 1, page 4, bottom: Library of Congress

Insert 1, page 5, top left: United States Navy, National Archives 80-G-438923

Insert 1, page 5, top right: United States Navy

Insert 1, page 5, bottom: Abbie Rowe photo, National Archives ID 200168

Insert 1, page 6, top: United States Navy, Naval History and Heritage Command NH 49826

Insert 1, page 6, center: United States Navy, November 1947 Naval Aviation News

Insert 1, page 6, bottom: United States Navy, Naval History and Heritage Command NH 93832

Insert 1, page 7, top: United States Air Force

Insert 1, page 7, center: United States Navy, National Archives 80-G-707176

Insert 1, page 7, bottom: United States Navy, National Archives 80-G-408056

Insert 1, page 8, top: United States Navy, Naval History and Heritage Command NH 95925

Insert 1, page 8, bottom: Naval History and Heritage Command, NH 92056

Insert 2, page 1, top: United States Navy, National Archives 80-G-428152

Insert 2, page 1, bottom left: United States Navy, National Archives 80-G-430048

Insert 2, page 1, bottom right: United States Navy, Naval History and Heritage Command NH 92741

Insert 2, page 2, top left: United States Army

Insert 2, page 2, top right: United States Army

Insert 2, page 2, bottom: United States Marine Corps, Naval History and Heritage Command NH 42351

Insert 2, page 3, top: United States Marine Corps, Naval History and Heritage Command NH 96876

Insert 2, page 3, bottom: United States Navy, National Archives 80-G-421944

Insert 2, page 4, top left: United States Navy, National Archives 80-G-422491

Insert 2, page 4, top right: United States Marine Corps

Insert 2, page 4, bottom: Truman Library

Insert 2, page 5, top: Truman Library

Insert 2, page 5, bottom: United States Navy, National Archives 80-G-420928

Insert 2, page 6, top: United States Navy, National Archives 80-G-421049

Insert 2, page 6, bottom: United States Navy, National Archives 80-G-422112

Insert 2, page 7, top left: United States Navy, Naval History and Heritage Command USN 1146845

Insert 2, page 7, top right: United States Navy, Naval History and Heritage Command NH 97091

Insert 2, page 7, bottom: United States Navy, National Archives 80-G-428267

Insert 2, page 8, top: United States Navy, National Archives 80-G-477573

Insert 2, page 8, bottom: US Department of Energy

Insert 3, page 1, top: National Nuclear Security Administration

Insert 3, page 1, bottom: United States Navy, National Archives 80-G-629194

Insert 3, page 2, top left: United States Navy, Naval History and Heritage Command NH 99117

Insert 3, page 2, top right: United States Naval Institute

Insert 3, page 2, bottom: Naval History and Heritage Command, UA 475.05.02

Insert 3, page 3, top left: United States Navy, Naval History and Heritage Command NH 72679

Insert 3, page 3, top right: Author's collection

Insert 3, page 3, bottom: United States Navy, November 1956 Naval Aviation News

Insert 3, page 4, top: United States Navy, Naval History and Heritage Command NH 54122

Insert 3, page 4, bottom: United States Navy, National Archives 80-G-687790

Insert 3, page 5: United States Navy, National Archives 80-G-K-22688

Insert 3, page 6, top: United States Navy, National Archives K-22610

Insert 3, page 6, bottom: United States Navy, National Archives 1036879
Insert 3, page 7, top: United States Navy, National Archives 1037145
Insert 3, page 7, bottom: United States Navy, National Archives 1037825
Insert 3, page 8, top: United States Navy, National Archives K-25571
Insert 3, page 8, bottom: United States Navy, National Archives 1048931

Index

Britain (*cont.*)
  financial situation of,
    at time of Suez
    crisis, 352
  Korean War, 203,
    204, 206, 207, 220,
    224, 243, 244, 248,
    249, 251, 286
  nuclear submarine,
    365–366
  opinion about war
    with Soviets, 90
  Palestine and, 82, 84
  talks with Nasser and
    Dulles, 343
  unification of Army
    and Navy in, 20–21
  U.S. in
    Mediterranean
    and, 81, 82, 83,
    134, 310–311
  war plans with U.S.
    against Soviets,
    128–131
Broiler/Doublequick
  plan, 128
Brown, Charles R.
  "Cat," 348, 349,
  381
Brown, Eldon W., 210
Brown, Jesse L.,
  275–276
Brown, John H., 204
*Brown v. Board of
  Education,* 367
Brutus, Henry C., 156
"bug catchers,"
  178–179
Bulganin, Nikita, 350
Burke, Farleigh A.
  as advocate of
    nuclear weapons
    for Navy, 180–181

  appointed Chief of
    Naval Operations,
    327
  atomic submarines
    and, 338, 339
  atomic weapon's
    delivery by
    submarines, 396
  background, 326–327
  burning of Mitscher's
    papers, 87
  characteristics, 327
  compulsory military
    service and, 328
  Cuba and, 384
  Demon fighter jet
    and, 334
  Eisenhower and, 311,
    316–317, 328
  on importance of
    antisubmarine
    warfare, 132
  on importance of
    Navy to American
    forces overseas,
    316
  improved naval
    relations with
    foreign powers as
    goal of, 385–386
  Israeli, British, and
    French attack on
    Egypt and, 348,
    352
  Korean War,
    278–279, 287
  as Mitscher's chief of
    staff, 83, 85
  on Mitscher's
    death, 87
  on Mitscher's
    health, 87
  Nautilus and, 368, 373

  Navy's strength, 342
  Operation Chromite
    landing at Inchon,
    241–242
  Raborn and, 360
  rebuilding armies of
    Europe, 141
  relations with chiefs
    of NATO nations'
    naval forces, 312
  on shortage of
    experienced pilots,
    aircrew, and
    aviation-rated
    sailors, 21
  Soviet submarine
    threat and,
    345–346
  Taiwan and, 389
  technological
    innovations, 328,
    358
  Truman at
    Norfolk, 49
Burns, James H., 191
Byrnes, James
  approach to Soviet
    Union, 32, 40
  governance of
    occupied Germany
    negotiations,
    78–79
  loyalty to agreements
    made at Teheran
    and Yalta, 79
  occupation of Japan
    by Soviet
    Union, 32
  at Paris Peace
    Conference, 87, 88
  shortage of
    experienced pilots,
    aircrew, and

About the Author

James D. Hornfischer was a writer, literary agent, and book editor. He was the *New York Times* bestselling author of *Neptune's Inferno, The Last Stand of the Tin Can Sailors, Ship of Ghosts,* and *The Fleet at Flood Tide,* all widely acclaimed accounts of the U.S. Navy in the Pacific during World War II. His books have received numerous awards, including the Naval Historical Foundation Distinguished Service Award, the Samuel Eliot Morison Award for Naval Literature, and The Department of the Navy Distinguished Public Service Award. James D. Hornfischer died in 2021.